D1521454

THE GLOBAL
JIHAD MOVEMENT

THE GLOBAL
JIHAD MOVEMENT

Rohan Gunaratna and Aviv Oreg

Rowman & Littlefield
Lanham • Boulder • New York • London

Published by Rowman & Littlefield
A wholly owned subsidary of The Rowman & Littlefield Publishing Group, Inc.
4501 Forbes Boulevard, Suite 200, Lanham, Maryland 20706
www.rowman.com

Unit A, Whitacre Mews, 26–34 Stannary Street, London SE11 4AB

British Library Cataloguing in Publication Information Available

Library of Congress Cataloging-in-Publication Data

Gunaratna, Rohan, 1961–
  The global Jihad movement : a handbook / Rohan Gunaratna and Aviv Oreg.
    pages cm
  Includes bibliographical references and index.
  ISBN 978-1-4422-4541-9 (cloth : alk. paper)—ISBN 978-1-4422-4542-6
(electronic)
  1. Jihad. 2. Terrorism. I. Oreg, Aviv, 1963– II. Title.
  BP182.G86 2015
  363.325—dc23   2014045468

∞™ The paper used in this publication meets the minimum requirements of
American National Standard for Information Sciences—Permanence of Paper
for Printed Library Materials, ANSI/NISO Z39.48-1992.

Printed in the United States of America

Contents

Acknowledgments

We first met a decade ago in the Middle East, where it all originated. Our initial discussion focused on the need for a reference book about the Global Jihad Movement. International, regional, and local organizations, members, supporters, and sympathizers are part of this global phenomenon of Global Jihad. We both agreed that it is time to name them, to differentiate between them, and to describe their overall organization and operational performance. Their mutual and multilateral relations inside and outside the "jihadi framework" needed documentation too. The different jihadi groups are referred to by the media, the general public, and even by experts from the academia or intelligence services as one "al-Qaeda." This affected the ability of governments and their partners to effectively counter this growing global phenomenon.

The outcome of this initial conversation and many ensuing conversations is this reference book that can easily name "who's who in the Global Jihad." Today, the Global Jihad phenomenon comprises millions of activists around the globe and they are ideologically supported by tens of millions of supporters and sympathizers. Although they are categorized as "political Islam," they belong to the Muslim Brotherhood, the Deoband school of thought, and Tabligh Jama'at, just to name a few. The vast majority of Muslims around the world reject the Salafi and the Salafi Jihadi approach of the constituents of the Global Jihad Movement. They perform different moderate and completely nonviolent interpretations of the Islamic holy book—the Quran. Furthermore—Muslims all over the world are the prime victims of the violent activities of the different elements of the Global Jihad Movement.

We believe that one of the pillars to counter "Global Jihad" is for the world to join hands in the struggle. When the jihad is global, the efforts to counter it should be global. Thus, the outcome of the book represents a multinational combined effort of analysts from different parts of the world, to understand the past and future directions of the Global Jihad phenomenon and its operational derivative threat.

For creating a conducive environment for research, I, Rohan Gunaratna, would like to express my appreciation to Ambassador Barry Desker who served as the dean of the S. Rajaratnam School of International Studies (RSIS) during the period of researching and writing this book. I would also acknowledge the dedicated staff of the International Centre for Political Violence and Terrorism Research in Singapore for producing the research that is a part of this book. I would like to express my gratitude to mentors Prof. Bruce Hoffman, Prof. Gerard Chaliand, and Brigadier General Russ Howard for their guidance over the years. I would also like to thank my family for their steadfast support.

I, Aviv Oreg, would like to thank my good friends and distinguished professional colleagues Mr. Yoram Schweitzer from the Israeli Institute for National Security Studies (INSS) and Ron Sandee from the U.S.-based NEFA Foundation. Being the former officer in charge of the desk that covered international terrorism inside the Israeli Department of Military Intelligence, Yoram holds years of experience and a wealth of knowledge. As a veteran of Dutch military intelligence, Ron acquired hundreds of thousands of "Global Jihad" hours both in the battlefield and as a senior analyst in the back office. For the last fifteen years Yoram, Ron, and I have been following the evolution of the jihadi phenomenon, sharing views and information, looking for original documents, and brainstorming over them trying to understand the strategic directions of the jihadi camp, and the operational threat of Global Jihad elements. The outcome of this collaboration and cooperation enabled this book and their contributions are priceless. I would like to thank all those that I love the most who inspired me throughout the long process of writing. To my loving family—my wife Monica and my children Rotem, Roni, and Inbar; for my parents Ava and Mude, as well as my brothers Yuval, Elad, and their families. I also give thanks to all my friends from Rishon, New York, Siena, and elsewhere.

We like to thank Ling Jun Toong, Rebecca C. Lunnon, and Colonel Douglas Woodall who edited this book. We would also like to thank our reviewers for their invaluable suggestions. To Marie-Claire Antoine and her staff at Rowman & Littlefield, our deep appreciation. We would like to dedicate this book to our parents.

Foreword

Rohan Gunaratna and Aviv Oreg have written an excellent book about the genesis, the development, and the possible prospect of Islamist terrorism. It shows, step by step, how, from the early eighties, the Global Jihad Movement has been organized. It brings new insights on the role played during the decade of struggle by Abdullah Azzam, Osama bin Laden, Ayman al-Zawahiri, Abu Musab al-Zarqawi, and Abu Bakr al-Baghdadi. During these years, and until his assassination in 1989, Azzam was more important than Osama bin Laden. Today, Ayman al-Zawahiri and Abu Bakr al-Baghdadi have emerged as the central figures. The authors also trace the emergence of the Salafi and, later on, the Salafi-Jihadi ideology, which today is so important in the Iraq and Syrian civil wars.

The developments in the Iraqi-Syrian and Afghanistan-Pakistan theaters remind us not to underestimate the phenomenon of Islamism. We should not judge its capacity to threaten and destroy by examining what they have been able to achieve in the West after 9/11. It is true that the terrorist successes in the West after 9/11 are relatively modest: Madrid (2004) and London (2005) caused some 250 deaths; and there were a few successful attacks in France (eight deaths in 2011), in the United Kingdom (two deaths in 2012), and in Boston, Massachusetts (three deaths in 2013). Many attempts have failed due to large police mobilization. Terrorism is a very costly nuisance rather than an existential threat that requires a permanent mobilization of important resources, both human and material. Against a movement calling for Armageddon, the security measures in the West proved effective until the emergence of the Islamic State of Iraq and Syria (ISIS). Will ISIS—after the declaration of the so-called Islamic Caliphate—prove to be a greater danger than al-Qaeda?

The greatest achievement of al-Qaeda has been al-Qaedism, an ideology. Despite the fact that al-Qaedism reflects only the aspirations of a small minority within Islam, the ideology has nevertheless spread. Today, al-Qaedism is a network. Al-Qaeda in Af/Pak, the core organization that declared war against the West, has suffered important losses. Osama bin Laden was killed in June 2011, but the movement is alive under Ayman al Zawahiri. A franchise of al-Qaeda, ISIS, is at conflict with Jabhat al-Nusra, the al-Qaeda franchise in Syria. Today, they represent a high-order threat among the threat groups.

Gunaratna and Oreg describe with great care the different franchises of the network that today extends from west Africa to the Philippines.

Al-Qaeda in the Arabian Peninsula (AQAP) based in Yemen, a country with a weak state, is by far today al-Qaeda's most dangerous branch. Led by Nassir al-Wuhayshi, some of its militants are from Saudi Arabia, where they were heavily repressed a few years ago. They control some areas of the country and are considered dangerous enough to force the United States to close its embassy in Sanaa.

Al-Qaeda in the Islamic Maghreb (AQIM) has been largely boosted by the collapse of Muhammad Qadhafi's regime.

In fact, the Security Council of the United Nations approved an intervention to protect the population of Benghazi, not to get rid of the dictator. The collateral damage caused by the fall of the regime assisted the various movements in Sahel. It brought the French to launch an intervention of their special troops to stop the advance of the jihadists south of the river Niger.

Ultimately, with an unstable regime in Libya and a shaky situation in several countries (Mali, Niger) the Anglo-French intervention looks like a tactical victory, but a strategic mistake.

Boko Haram (BH), active for a decade in northeast Nigeria, has become, in recent years, more active and dangerous and might become more than a local threat.

Jemaah Islamiyah of Southeast Asia (JI), an Indonesian-led political movement, has been the cradle of jihadism in the region. After JI bombed Bali in 2002, the group was successfully repressed. Nonetheless, Indonesian jihadists created splinter groups with roots and support among segments of Indonesian society. JI's associate in the Philippines, the Abu Sayyaf Group (ASG) survived despite the U.S. Special Forces' successful involvement in the very south of the Philippines.

Shabaab al-Mujahidin is not as strong as it once was, though this movement recently trained anywhere between 1,000 to 1,500 foreign jihadists and is in contact with AQAP.

In 2006, the United States made the mistake of using Ethiopian troops as proxy to weaken the Shabaab. This strengthened the movement the following two years. Sending troops from a Christian state to reduce jihadists was a counterproductive move, especially considering that the two countries had been rivals for centuries and had fought a war in the 1970s over territorial claims by the Somali state. To draw a more familiar parallel, it would be like sending Russian troops to crush a Polish insurrection. Today, Kenyan troops are mainly used as proxy, prompting the Shabaab deadly attack in Nairobi in September 2013.

All the jihadist groups are recorded in the book with their genealogy. Those active in Pakistan and Afghanistan are Afghan and Pakistani Taliban, Lashkar-e-Toyba (LeT), Jaish-e-Mohamed (JeM), the Islamic Movement of Uzbekistan (IMU), Islamic Jihad Union (IJU), and the Turkistan Islamic Party (TIP). In addition to Asia, the book covers organizations active in the Middle East, Africa, and the Caucasus.

The Global Jihad Movement: A Handbook by Rohan Gunaratna and Aviv Oreg should be considered by scholars and practitioners as the most complete and perceptive book on violent and radical Muslim movements. One may disagree on some minor points like the explanation of the failure of Basayev while trying to launch a jihad in Dagestan.

The two main targets of al-Qaeda in the future are going to be not only the West, especially the United States, but also the Middle East, both Arab states and Israel. The Syrian civil war looks, for the time being, to be a mobilizing epicenter for jihadists willing as radical Sunnis to crush Shias. This is not only directed against Syrian Alawis, but also against the Baghdad regime and Hezbollah in Lebanon. We are actually witnessing an offensive led by Saudi Arabia and other Gulf countries with the help of Turkey and Jordan to weaken Iran and its allies in the Middle East.

This seems to be a large part of today's agenda of al-Qaeda, ISIS, and other jihadist organisations despite the fact that "crusaders" (with the United States at their head) and "Jews" (as coined by Osama bin Laden) will remain major targets.

Like al-Qaeda, ISIS is developing an ideological and operational global footprint. With the U.S.-led international coalition commencing operations against ISIS in September 2014, existing and emerging groups and cells worldwide are turning to ISIS. Both al-Qaeda and ISIS are multinational terrorist and insurgent groups capable of providing leadership. Will ISIS replace al-Qaeda as the core of the Global Jihad Movement? This work, covering three decades of violence and radicalism by Muslim movements, deserves to become a classic.

Gerard Chaliand
Center for Conflict and Peace Studies
Kabul, Afghanistan

Preface

> God willing, the end of America is imminent. Its end is not dependent on the survival of this (or that) Abdallah. Regardless if Osama is killed or survived the awakening has started, praise be to god. This was the point of these operations.
>
> —al-Qaeda leader Osama bin Laden,
> *Al Jazeera*, 27 December 2001

As the then pioneering vanguard of the Global Jihad Movement, al-Qaeda spearheaded the Islamic awakening to ignite Muslims' zeal. Having mobilized Muslim youth worldwide to fight the anti-Soviet multinational Afghan jihad campaign (1979–1989), Osama bin Laden founded al-Qaeda. By executing al-Qaeda's most iconic attack against America's most iconic landmarks, the coordinated simultaneous attacks on 11 September 2001, al-Qaeda inspired and instigated threat groups worldwide to lead the Islamic revival. Although al-Qaeda's role as the jihad's operational vanguard ended, it remained in the background as a training and a propaganda organization.

A new generation of threat groups such as the Islamic State of Iraq and Sham (ISIS), al-Nusra, the Taliban, al-Shabaab, Boko Haram, al-Qaeda in the Islamic Maghreb, al-Qaeda in the Arabian Peninsula, and Jamaah Ansharut Tauhid emerged after the

9/11 attacks. Although its mission to lead the fight has been completely accomplished, al-Qaeda had successfully passed the torch of Islamic revival to be held by others—some organized groups, others disorganized individuals. Some groups such as ISIS are challenging al-Qaeda for leadership. By declaring an Islamic Caliphate, ISIS aspires to lead the entire Islamic *Ummah* to the final victory over the Jews and Crusaders and implementation of Sharia law over the Muslim lands.

A new global threat landscape is emerging. Old actors such as al-Qaeda are struggling to survive. New players such as the Islamic State of Iraq and Syria (ISIS) and its splinter Jabhat al-Nusra (JAN) are competing for supremacy in the Global Jihad arena. At the heart of the dramatic developments in the Middle East is the establishment of an Islamic Caliphate, the imposition of Islamic canon law, the growing infighting between players for power, and legitimacy in the Global Jihad Movement.

The competitors of ISIS include the Islamic Movement of the Taliban. Afghan Taliban leader Mullah Muhammad Ismael in December 2012 said, "I don't find it farfetched to envision the day when we see the Americans running away in defeat from Afghanistan with their heads down, just like the Russians before them, and that is not difficult for Allah."[1] It is not only the developments in Iraq and Syria, but the developments in Pakistan and Afghanistan that are contributing to the heavily charged global landscape of threat. With prospects of the U.S.-led coalition withdrawing from Afghanistan, both Afghan and Pakistani Taliban, al-Qaeda al-Jihad, and a dozen like-minded groups located on the Afghanistan-Pakistan border are slowly returning to Afghanistan to re-create pre-9/11 sanctuaries. With the U.S.-led coalition withdrawal, the Afghan security forces will fight back with limited success. The insider threat stemming from Taliban infiltration of Afghan army and police is affecting Western capacity building.

Al-Qaeda diminished in size, but its influence shaped the ideology and practice of its associated groups. About 20,000–30,000 fighters from two dozen threat groups are located on the Pakistan-Afghanistan border, mostly in North Waziristan. They include the Afghan Taliban, the Haqqani network, Hezbi-Islami, Pakistan Taliban, al-Qaeda al-Jihad, Islamic Movement of Uzbekistan , Islamic Jihad Union, and the Turkistan Islamic Party. In addition to operating in Pakistan and Afghanistan, some conduct lethal and nonlethal operations overseas. Their media networks politicize, radicalize, and mobilize Muslims, especially youth, to participate or support their campaigns. The blowback from the U.S.-led coalition's withdrawal will empower and embolden insurgents, terrorists, and extremist groups worldwide.

The Context

Afghanistan is the most important cradle and theater. Re-creating sanctuaries is the most important priority for the Global Jihadist Movement. Reminiscent of the Soviet Union's withdrawal in February 1989, the jihadists and Islamists are already celebrating the Obama administration's decision to withdraw. Calling it Islam's victory over the West, they hail it as a strategic defeat of the United States. While most of them will focus on reestablishing a Taliban-like state, others bloodied by conflict will return home to establish Islamic states in their home countries or in neighboring or distant conflict zones. With a number of threat groups and state interests competing to advance their interests, Afghanistan will likely look like today's Syria in the coming years.

In Afghanistan, entities, surrogates, and proxies of Pakistan, the United States, France, India, Russia, China, Saudi Arabia, Iran, Uzbekistan, Tajikistan, and other state players will intervene overtly and covertly. With no boots on the ground, militarized counterterrorism—U.S. drone warfare and Special Forces—will be insufficient to push back the Taliban's avowed return. While Pakistan will control developments in Afghanistan's Pashtun areas, Tehran will influence developments in Herat and the surrounding areas bordering Iran. The regional War Lords and Transnational Criminal Organizations (TCOs) will compete to retain and expand their influence.

The developments elsewhere in the Middle East and Africa will compound the emergence of this new threat in south Asia.

Although al-Qaeda al-Jihad is based near the Afghanistan-Pakistan border, its influences reach threat groups in North Africa, the Levant, and the Arabian Peninsula. Groups operating outside the region, notably from the Middle East, are likely to return to Afghanistan for primary and peripheral training and operational roles. Although Western democracies perceive the Arab Spring as a victory, Middle Eastern threat groups received a boost from the Arab Spring. Arab Spring, contrary to expectations, created a permissive environment for both democratic politics and violent extremism. The West, by arming Libyan and now Syrian fighters, destabilized the Maghreb and Sahel and the Levant and beyond. Muslims from the West, Caucasus, and Southeast Asia are traveling to establish an Islamic state in Syria. The developments have already affected Jordan, a pillar of stability, and may eventually destabilize the Gulf. International neglect of Tuaregs from Libya moving to Mali led to the creation of a new African hot spot in the Sahel after Somalia and Nigeria. Exploiting the new environment, Salafi Jihadism and the ideology of al-Qaeda is spreading rapidly in Africa. The ideological and operational relationship between the Middle East and Asia is growing.

Israel's retaliation to constant rocket attacks by Hamas in Gaza in November 2012 increased global Muslims' resentment and anger against the West. While most Muslims celebrated the United Nations General Assembly granting Palestinians non-member observer status, the jihadists found no importance in it. As they are committed to an armed revolution, they questioned why people were celebrating. In discussions monitored by SITE on the Ansar al-Mujahideen and Shumukh al-Islam forums on 29 November 2012, jihadists argued that peaceful solutions are impossible, and that only through jihad will Palestinians achieve statehood. These viewpoints are characteristic of al-Qaeda al-Jihad, and are spreading throughout the Middle East. The Salafi Jihadi ideology politicized and radicalized a segment of the population, especially the youth. If the recently established "Arab Spring governments" fail to meet the public's expectations, violence against the new rulers may become the order of the day.

Africa is developing as a new epicenter of terrorism. Al-Qaeda in the Islamic Maghreb (AQIM) expanded from North Africa to the Sahel. AQIM shared its expertise with Boko Haram (BH) in Nigeria. In November 2012, Abu Bakr Shekau, its leader, expressed BH's solidarity with associates of al-Qaeda al-Jihad in Afghanistan, Iraq, North Africa, Somalia, and Yemen. After Qadhafi's fall, northern Mali emerged as a training ground and a battlefield. Malians are supported by European Muslims, especially French, North Africans-Algerians, Moroccans, and Libyans. Al Shabab lost ground, but its ideology has spread to bordering areas of Uganda, Kenya, and Tanzania. Like al-Shabaab, BH is likely to join al-Qaeda al-Jihad in 2014. Unless stability is restored in Africa, al-Qaeda Movement's footprint will grow. The threat from chemical, biological, radiological, and nuclear terrorism (CBRN) is on the rise. The emerging threat of terrorism confronting the world will likely not be confined to conventional terrorism. About 80 percent of the attacks use small arms and bombs. However, recent developments in Syria, Iran, and North Korea, and their links to or terrorist access to their arsenal, increase the likelihood of a biological outbreak. In the spectrum of unconventional agents, anthrax and smallpox are favored by threat groups. With terrorists recruiting from a cross section of society, a dozen scientists and technicians became vulnerable to supporting or staffing terrorist weapons acquisition and manufacturing programs. Both securing government storage and research facilities as well as periodic screening of scientific and support staff are paramount to prevent proliferation. In the event of an outbreak, accidental or deliberate, first responders should be vaccinated and immunized.

Likely Future Developments

The global threat landscape is likely to change dramatically. Functionally and regionally, the developments in Afghanistan, Syria, and Iraq will be the most influential. The Salafi Jihadists and a segment of Islamists consider Afghanistan "the mother of all battles." If the jihadists reconstitute Afghanistan for a second time, it will affect not only Western security, but also Asia's rise. Driven by success, returning fighters will reignite conflicts in Kashmir, Xinjiang, Uzbekistan, Mindanao, Arakan, Pattani, tribal Pakistan, and other Muslim lands.

In the backdrop of Obama's pivot to Asia, battle-hardened fighters will threaten Asia. Seasoned to fight Western armies in Afghanistan, they will contest Asian armies, law enforcement, and intelligence services. Asian armies, twenty years behind Western militaries, will experience a new threat from IEDs, suicide attacks, etc. Like in Afghanistan, the returning fighters may bleed standing armies in existing and new zones of conflict. Committed to a generation-long fight, the strength of foreign veterans is their patience and resilience. They will serve as fighters, ideologues, combat trainers, financiers, and in other roles.

New Capabilities

Since 11 September 2001, governments developed wide-ranging capabilities to fight insurgency and terrorism. Most governments use lethal and nonlethal methods to fight terrorism and insurgency. They use intelligence to detect attacks during planning and preparation, and law enforcement to investigate and charge terrorists at home. Some countries used military support to combat terrorism and insurgency abroad. Lethal and nonlethal operations by governments are the most effective. However, these approaches are not the most efficient. They can buy time for governments to fight operational terrorism, but cannot stem the tide of ideological extremism, the precursor of terrorism.

Contemporary terrorist groups are adept at harnessing modern communications platforms to reach out to their supporters and sympathizers. Unlike Cold War terrorists, post–Cold War terrorists engage not only their coethnic and coreligionists at home, but also their diaspora and migrant communities abroad. To prevent the extremists from politicizing, radicalizing, and mobilizing vulnerable communities and reinforcing terrorist rank-and-file beliefs, governments should build partnerships with community organizations. Working together, they should create platforms both to counter ideology and promote moderation.

Working with a range of partners, governments need to develop nonlethal capabilities to manage existing and emerging threats. Terrorism, a vicious by-product of ideological extremism, is mitigated by developing a comprehensive strategy of hard and soft power. The criminal justice and prisons systems in most countries are designed for deterrence and punishment, not prevention and rehabilitation. In the tool kit of the modern counterterrorism practitioner, rehabilitation and community engagement are emerging as indispensable tools. For rehabilitation and community engagement to be successful, it has to be multi-faceted and a long-term public-private sector partnership should be developed and led by creative and innovative leaders. More than operational counterterrorism, developed since Munich in 1972, the contemporary use of rehabilitation and community engagement initiatives are recent in conception and development.

The Future

Al-Qaeda, the core of the global terrorist movement, suffered massive degradation and resulted in the death of Osama bin Laden. However, their associates and the new leader, Dr Ayman al-Zawahiri, present a very real danger. Despite a smaller U.S. footprint after the formal withdrawal in 2014, the United States will still remain the tier-one target of both al-Qaeda al-Jihad and the movement. Some associates such as al-Qaeda in the Arabian Peninsula (AQAP) present a comparable, if not greater, threat to the United States. Yemen, where AQAP is based, remains unstable. Pakistan Taliban, as demonstrated in the Times Square attempt, developed anti-Western orientations. Several new groups influenced by Salafi Jihadism such as al-Nusra Front have emerged in Syria, Egypt, and Libya. In place of one single al-Qaeda, a multiplicity of anti-U.S. suicide-capable groups have emerged during the last years. Like ordinary and organized crime, extremism and terrorism will remain long-term threats to the world. Some actions by state and nonstate actors aimed at countering the growing extremist and terrorist threat had unintended consequences. The trailer "Innocence of the Muslims" released by a private U.S. citizen, U.S. government overt and covert support for the Arab Spring, and announcing the U.S. military pullout from Afghanistan increased the threat of ideological extremism and its vicious by-product—terrorism. Of all threats, the most significant will emerge from the U.S. lack of political will to sustain U.S.-led coalition presence. The failure to build a credible Afghanistan military, law enforcement, and intelligence capabilities before U.S. withdrawal will create an environment of high threat reminiscent of pre-9/11. A global strategy is needed more than ever before to better manage the existing and emerging security challenges in Africa, the Middle East, and south Asia.

Book Design

The starting point to address a proper strategy is to understand the threat. This book contains six chapters, each capturing the essence of the specific threat elements comprising the Global Jihad.

Chapter 2 deals with ideology focusing on the emergence of the Salafi and the Salafi Jihadi ideologies. The Salafi and Salafi Jihad ideologies are still the most important factor behind the operational performance of Global Jihadi elements. Ideological conflicts are discussed between Abdullah Azzam's "jihad arena" and Ayman al-Zawahiri's "internal jihad." Osama bin Laden's decision to adopt a new approach—the "Global Jihad" ideology—in the second half of the 1990s is discussed extensively. These notions have always been and still are the most important factors effecting and shaping the terrorist performance of the different jihadi elements operating worldwide.

The chapters that follow zoom in on the elements comprising the Global Jihad Movement. Chapter 3 discusses al-Qaeda and its formal infrastructure, hierarchy, and echelon. We start with the influential personalities that have been leading the organization since its inception in 1988. Although the al-Qaeda infrastructure was severely degraded by the United States and

Pakistani counterterrorism operations since 9/11, al-Qaeda survived. While the core reconstituted as a training and propaganda vanguard, its family members regrouped and maintain operational capabilities in Asia, Africa, and the Middle East.

Chapter 4 addresses the affiliate groups of al-Qaeda. This chapter focuses on those groups that already crossed the Rubicon. Into their targeting policies, the affiliates adopted al-Qaeda's Global Jihad strategy by incorporating Western targets in their vicinity. Although they present a potential global threat, most of the jihadi-affiliated groups today focus their operational activities internally. During the early years that followed the 11 September attacks, the activities of Jamoah Islamiyah, Abu Sayyaf Group, Islamic Jihad Union, and Lashkar-e-Toyba were more elusive and were based solely on personal relations. Since 2005, the spectrum of Global Jihad groups witnessed groups formally merging with al-Qaeda, completely adopting its strategy and targeting policy thus creating several al-Qaedas worldwide. By 2014, al-Qaeda in the Arabian Peninsula (AQAP), al-Qaeda in the Islamic Maghreb (AQIM), Shabaab al-Mujahidin al-Somali, and Jabhat al-Nusra officially merged with al-Qaeda. Until its rejection by al-Qaeda in 2013, the Islamic State (IS) was very much a part of the al-Qaeda family. IS has its genesis in al-Qaeda in Iraq (AQI) that evolved into the Islamic State of Iraq (ISI) and the Islamic State of al-Sham (ISIS). Al-Qaeda officially announced its rejection of ISIS/IS and ceased all ties with the organization following the brutal methods practiced by the group in its campaign in both Syria and Iraq.[2] Today the best resourced threat group, IS presents an unprecedented threat to the Middle East and beyond.

Chapter 5 discusses the jihad arenas. Throughout the Muslim world, multiple jihad arenas emerged during the last three decades. They drew jihadi fighters from Islamic communities around the world. Fighters came from communities to train and fight against external invaders, creating an alumni that continues to promote the jihadi struggle. Even after fighting in the specific "jihad arena" ended, they continued to pose a threat. We frequently find "Afghan graduates," "Iraq veterans," and Syrian alumni involved in off-the-battlefield operations. In this chapter, we deal with the "classical" jihad arenas of Afghanistan, Iraq, and Chechnya and the evolving new jihad arenas of Egypt ruled Sinai Peninsula, Libya, and Syria. The new arenas emerged as a direct consequence of the so-called Arab Spring, characterized by demonstrations and riots throughout the Middle East at the beginning of 2011. New jihad arenas serve as magnets for jihadis from all over the world and continue to emerge in Somalia, Yemen, and recently in Mali and probably in the northern part of Nigeria.

In chapter 6, we discuss the foot soldiers, the inspired individuals of the Global Jihad Movement. The overwhelmingly vast majority of the plots conducted by jihadi elements on Western soil since 9/11 were executed by homegrown individuals and cells. We analyze the process of radicalization that these individuals are going through from the preradicalization stages, where they conduct regular and normative lifestyle patterns, until the final jihadi stage in which they conduct jihadi activity, some instances culminating in suicide attacks. In the name of Islam, the attackers and supporters perceive it as martyrdom, the epitome of jihad.

Notes

1. *Al-Samoud* Magazine, 79th Issue, Afghan Taliban, 7 December 2012.

2. http://snamalislam.com/vb/. Accessed 18 June 2014.

1

Introduction

The Global Jihad Movement is a collection of organizations, regional and local cells, and sometimes individuals. These entities profess the radical ideology of jihad or holy war, a departure from mainstream Islam. After rejecting traditional Islamic teaching, they operate in different regions around the world under the banner of militant jihad. The dominant force of the Global Jihad Movement is "The al-Qaeda organization" or "al-Qaeda." Referred to as al-Qaeda central or al-Qaeda classic, al-Qaeda forms the core of the Global Jihad Movement whose ideology inspires other participants in the movement. "Al-Qaeda" is a term that is not interchangeable with the Global Jihad Movement. Throughout its existence, the Global Jihad Movement enjoyed symbiotic bilateral and multilateral relations among its entities vis-à-vis the al-Qaeda organization. During the early years of al-Qaeda, the early 1990s, al-Qaeda provided support and logistics for different organizations of the Global Jihad Movement. They operate in their specific regional confrontation zones against local "infidel" and "apostate" regimes. Within the last decade and a half, al-Qaeda invested tremendous efforts to harness these global jihad entities to adopt the new policy it has been promoting since the late 1990s, to engage in a war against U.S.-led Western powers. The operational and logistical collaboration between al-Qaeda and other elements is important for understanding the current threat of terrorism.

The Structure and Characteristics of Terrorist Organizations

Like any organization, terrorism is based on a model that integrates the individual, the group, and the society. Terrorists should not be examined separately from social and political contexts, nor the nature of the hierarchy in which they operate.[1]

Terrorism is a rational political choice. Terrorist groups have a consistent set of values, beliefs, and images of the external environment. A group with a consistent set of values, goals and ideals, and the means to those goals are essentially a collective coherent set, or an organization.[2]

Other characteristics make terrorist organizations similar to other organizations as follows:

1. Terrorist groups have a defined structure and protocol to make collective decisions.
2. Functionally differentiated roles exist for members of the organization.
3. There are recognized leaders in positions of formal authority.
4. The organization pursues collective goals, and claims collective responsibility for its actions.[3]

Leadership and Its Role

Leadership is crucial to terrorist organizations. Leaders eliminate inefficiency in the terrorist organization's structure and activities. They play a crucial role in establishing the group's goals and disseminating its ideology.[4] This role is also present in networked entities without clear structures. The leader of a terrorist organization also plans and oversees the operations of the group. These leadership functions indicate that terrorist organizations that aim for efficiency and large-scale attacks require a coherent command and control structure.

When carrying out operations, the leader of a terrorist organization monitors and audits the midlevel operatives involved in operations. Second, the leader provides operatives with incentive-based compensation. Next, the leader engages in punishment strategies in the event of shirking by members.[5] Through these roles, the leader ensures communication, auditing, task assignment, and enforces punishment for noncompliance with the organization's operations.

While the leader's role and presence cause vulnerabilities for the terrorist organization, it also enables terror organizations to have communication structures, and this ensures efficiency during operations.

Leadership is important, as it ensures that necessary measures are employed to keep the organization together and functional. A terrorist organization provides its members with opportunities for action, a sense of belonging, social status, and material rewards. The organization's leadership is crucial in fulfilling these needs and maintaining the group's well-being. It also ensures organizational integrity, which is necessary to achieve its goals. Organizational integrity is thus often viewed above and beyond the group's ideology or goals. While organizational goals are mutable and dependent on external dynamics and counterterrorism efforts, integrity and structure are vital for the group to exist and operate.[6] Failure to maintain organizational integrity leads to dissention and to decline.[7]

Command Cadre and Network Structures

Contemporary terrorism discourse deals mainly with two types of terrorist group structures as follows: a command cadre (hierarchical) structure and a network structure. The command cadre structure is similar to that of an army, where the leadership provides midlevel operatives and members with material as well as nonmaterial (ideological) incentives.[8] A network, on the other hand, is composed of a set of actors (or nodes) connected through ties. Networks are self-organizing and self-enrolling.[9]

Network organizations are resilient against disruption. Terrorists regard them as advantageous because the Internet facilitates the creation of terrorist cells without the need for individuals to meet in person. Communication between nodes in planning actual operations is minimal, making it harder for law enforcement personnel to dismantle.

However, such forms of "leaderless terrorism" are unsuitable for carrying out complex tasks that require communication, cooperation, and professional training.[10] Network organizations are incapable of carrying out complex attacks such as the 11 September 2001 attacks in New York and Washington, DC.[11]

The command cadre structure enables groups to carry out big, complex strikes that require coordination and centralized professional training. "This structure is characterized by clear lines of authority, functional specialization, and centralized decision making. There are separate departments for particular tasks, and training takes place for operatives and managers at all levels."[12] In a command cadre structure, complex tasks are broken down into specific jobs to ensure the efficient planning and execution of complex attacks.[13] Terrorist groups with this organizational structure usually operate in weak or failed states. As the War on Terror progresses, active groups will move to regions of failed governance to operate in a command cadre structure.[14]

For terrorist groups, there exists a trade-off between efficiency and resilience. Efficiency, which requires communication and connectedness, makes the group more vulnerable to counterterrorism efforts.[15] For a group like the al-Qaeda organization, the ability to carry out large-scale, efficient attacks remains important. Therefore, a command cadre structure continues to be an organizing principle for the organization.

Decline of Terrorist Organizations and Organizational Structure

The systems theory of organization explains that terrorist organizations receive exogenous as well as constituent support.[16]

Exogenous support refers to support from sources other than its constituent base. These sources form the group's identity and their input manifests as acts of political violence and terrorism. This conversion of input into output comprises the throughput of a terrorist organization. The throughput enhances the organization's identity, because a successful operation will increase the group's cohesion and legitimacy. This in turn increases the exogenous support and constituent support (as legitimacy for the group will increase in the eyes of constituent members). Cyclically, this increase will improve and influence the group's throughput process.[17]

Such a structure and feedback cycle occurs when a group functions as a hierarchical organization where exogenous support, constituent members, and the leadership occupy certain roles and functions. Every successful action (or attack) carried out by such a group strengthens its base and makes future attacks more effective.[18]

Counterterrorism strategies dismantle an organization or hinder its actions by attacking the weaknesses in its structure. These weaknesses include points of communication between exogenous support, constituent members, leadership, and group input. The ultimate target of counterterrorism strategies is this infrastructure.

Organizations such as al-Qaeda realize the importance of this command cadre, hierarchical structure, and the efficient feedback loop that it creates. While the structure makes the organization susceptible to interception and dismantling by law enforcement officials, it also generates the terrorist group's efficiency and facilitates growth.[19]

A terrorist organization provides its members with "primitive" societal needs.[20] If the organization is unable to fulfill those needs, it either changes its focus or ceases to exist. In the event of decline, an organization such as al-Qaeda reverts back to its hierarchical structure to establish an efficient feedback loop, in order to convince its constituents and exogenous support base of the organization's legitimacy. In the face of decline, terrorist groups demonstrate and ensure organizational integrity over everything else. As we will discuss later, the al-Qaeda organization has lost four "chiefs of staff," four chiefs of the special (external) forces unit, and at least half a dozen senior regional field commanders ("generals") over the last thirteen years. It was, however, still able to regroup and mobilize suitable replacements from within. Subsequently, it has been able to continue its operational activity and maintain its status as the sole directive of jihadi terrorism thus preserving its status as biggest terrorist threat to Western forces in the current jihad arenas (tribal Pakistan, Iraq, Somalia) and the international arena as a whole.

Historical Development: Global Jihad Movement and the al-Qaeda Organization

The Global Jihad Movement represents the main terrorist threat to the United States and its allies. As will be elaborated in chapter 2 addressing ideology, the movement is based on the ideology of "Salafiya Jihadiya," a misinterpretation of the holy book of Islam, the Qur'an, and the sayings of the Prophet Muhammad, the Hadith. The Salafiya Jihadiya ideology evolved in the second half of the twentieth century. It is an extremist offshoot of the Salafi ideology that developed in the Muslim world during the first half of the twentieth century. The Salafi ideology calls for a total return to the lifestyle of the early days of Islam.[21] It calls for the implementation of Sharia law (Islamic religious law) across the Muslim world, to serve as a prelude to its implementation across the globe. Those who subscribe to the Salafi ideology regard it as the only way to overcome the superiority of the West, which, in their view, has shaped Middle Eastern politics for the last two centuries. The Salafi ideology was established in Egypt towards the end of the 1920s, with the establishment of the Muslim Brotherhood.[22] The influence of the Muslim Brotherhood's ideology on the Global Jihad Movement remains relevant today. During its early development, the different Salafi movements kept a low profile and used preaching, propaganda ("Dawa and Tabligh"), and social activity as their modus operandi, publicly opposing any use of violence.[23] Salafi ideology seeks the support of the people before imposing Sharia.

As an extremist offshoot of the Salafi ideology, Salafiya Jihadiya calls for the use of extensive activism to implement Salafi ideology across Muslim and non-Muslim lands. This activism includes the use of violence and total jihad (holy war) against those who do not share their religious-political beliefs. Their enemies include Christians, Jews, Hindus, and all Muslims who are not "Salafis."[24] The Salafiya Jihadiya first emerged in Egypt during the 1960s, and was led by the Egyptian educationist Sayyid Al-Qutb.[25] The ideology soon spread and gained support worldwide.

The Blowback

The genesis of the Global Jihad Movement can be traced back to the 1980s. The operational entity of the Salafiya Jihadiya ideology emerged in Afghanistan during the instability period of the 1980s. Afghanistan experienced instability since the mid-1970s, as a result of violent power struggles between local communists and the Islamists. The internal dispute became a regional war following the Soviet Union's invasion of Afghanistan in December 1979. This created a surge of romanticism within the greater Muslim world that perceived the conflict as a religious war between the modern crusaders, the Communist Soviets, and Muslims. Muslim volunteers from all over the world went to Afghanistan to participate in the evolving "jihad." Non-Afghan Islamic religious leaders who were in Afghanistan were responsible for receiving the volunteers upon arrival and assigning them to different Afghan Mujahidin groups.

Dr. Abdullah Azzam, a Palestinian religious cleric, originally from Silat al-Hartia, a small Palestinian village in the Jenin area, was one of the first Arabs to organize the Muslim volunteers.[26] Azzam was the spiritual mentor and ideologue of the Global Jihad Movement, and he established the Maktab al-Khidamat (MaK) or the Afghan Service Bureau in 1984.[27] Located in the Pakistan-Afghan border city of Peshawar, MaK dealt with the growing stream of Muslim volunteers coming to participate in the war against the Soviets. The MaK accommodated the new arrivals in several guesthouses in Peshawar, and following several days of formal paperwork, the MaK allocated and distributed the volunteers across different Afghan fighting groups.[28] There, they received basic training and were sent to the Afghan front to fight the Red Army.[29]

Among those volunteers arriving at Peshawar was Osama bin Laden, who came from Saudi Arabia in 1984.[30] Even though bin Laden came to Afghanistan as a wealthy man, he wanted to take part in the war as a foot soldier and a local commander in the field.[31] Initially, Azzam and bin Laden cooperated, and bin Laden heavily financed MaK activity.[32] However, as the war with the Soviets was ending, a dispute between bin Laden and Azzam over MaK resources and strategic direction emerged.[33] Bin Laden subsequently broke away from MaK and formed the al-Qaeda organization in Peshawar, Pakistan, on 11 August 1988.[34] Although Azzam ideologically conceived of al-Qaeda al-Sulbah (The Solid Base), bin Laden emerged as its undisputed founder and remained its leader until his death on 1 May 2011.[35]

Since bin Laden had been on the front lines and controlled MaK finances, the bulk of its members preferred to join him. Nevertheless, Abdullah Azzam was still considered a threat to some members in the circles around bin Laden. In November 1989, Azzam was assassinated in Peshawar.[36]

Global Jihad Trajectory

At the end of the Afghan war, the global landscape was dominated by four different trends as follows:

A. Internal Jihad (Jihad from Within): The success in Afghanistan excited the Muslim world. Numerous radical organizations and entities were established throughout the Muslim world, supported and led by veteran jihadists returning to their homelands from Afghanistan. These organizations carried out terrorist attacks in their homelands with the aim of toppling local secular regimes and establishing a so-called Islamic Caliphate. Enthusiastic about their success in Afghanistan, these veterans believed victory in their homeland was only a matter of commitment, which they possessed, and time. All nations with Muslim populations in the Middle East, central Asia, the Indian subcontinent, and Southeast Asia experienced the effects of internal jihad. Serious challenges to the local secular regimes were presented by Mujahidin and terrorist groups that came together in Egypt, Algeria, Pakistan, and to a lesser degree in Jordan, Saudi Arabia, Yemen, Tunisia, Libya, Tajikistan, Uzbekistan, Indonesia, the Mindanao region of the Philippines, and many other countries.[37]

B. Searching for New Jihad Arenas: According to Salafiya, a jihad arena is a region in the world where Muslims fight non-Muslims. In this view, it is the obligation of every Muslim in the world to take part in the fighting.[38] Following the end of the Afghan war in 1989, new jihad arenas were designated in different parts of the world, where Muslims fought non-Muslims. Global Jihad fighters traveled to fight alongside local Muslims in Tajikistan, Bosnia, Chechnya, Kashmir, Mindanao (Philippines), Sulawesi and the Maluku Islands (Indonesia), Somalia, and Afghanistan.[39]

C. Infrastructure Buildup: This was the main activity of the newly established al-Qaeda organization under bin Laden. Bin Laden wanted to provide the necessary logistical backup in order to support fighters in the states undergoing internal jihad and those fighting alongside their Muslim brothers in "jihad arenas." In 1989, bin Laden returned to his Saudi homeland with the reputation of having fought in the Afghan war.[40] Later that year, Hassan al-Turabi's Islamist Sudanese regime invited bin Laden and his al-Qaeda followers to Sudan.[41] In Sudan, bin Laden was able to establish a base and construct a vast complex of training camps for newly recruited jihad fighters.[42]

These new recruits received early and advanced training in bin Laden camps in the Sudan and went on to fight in their homelands or in "jihad arenas."[43] By the end of 1995, following the attempted assassination of Egyptian president Hosni Mubarak in Addis Ababa, the capital of Ethiopia, the Sudanese regime faced severe international pressure to expel bin Laden and his forces from Sudan.[44] As a consequence, bin Laden was expelled from Sudan in May 1996.[45] He returned to Afghanistan where he allied himself with the victorious Taliban, which had violently taken control over the country in 1996. In Afghanistan, al-Qaeda established a larger network of training camps for Mujahidin throughout the country.[46] Numerous jihad fighters from different parts of the world operating with different organizations received training in al-Qaeda's camps in Afghanistan.

D. External Jihad: In the early years following the war in Afghanistan, al-Qaeda was occupied with assisting the "internal jihad" and the fighting in "jihad arenas." At this point, al-Qaeda decided to abandon external jihad. Only a small group of a few dozen Afghan veterans, who were a part of the "Ittihad al-Islami al-Afghani" (Abd al-Rasool Sayyaf Group) main training camp in Sadah, with no connection to the al-Qaeda organization, decided to move their activities into the international arena and conduct external jihad against the West on Western soil.[47] By late 1995, this group was disbanded by the U.S. Central Intelligence Agency (CIA) and the Federal Bureau of Investigation (FBI). Its dominant leaders (Ramzi Yousef, Wali Amin Shah, and Abd al-Karim Murad) were arrested.[48] The other members of the group were put on the "Most Wanted" list, with rewards of millions of dollars for their arrest.[49] The group's senior fugitive, Khalid Sheikh Mohamed (KSM), tried to interest bin Laden in external jihad in early 1996 and suggested a terrorist attack scenario that resembled the 9/11 attacks, but these ideas were rejected by bin Laden.[50]

The final shift from internal to external jihad occurred between late 1997 and early 1998. Bin Laden decided to focus the majority of his efforts on external jihad. Bin Laden believed that external jihad would force the West, primarily the United States, to withdraw its military forces from the Middle East, and as a result allow Islamic elements to take over the secular regimes. In February 1998, bin Laden announced the establishment of the World Islamic Front for Jihad against the Jews and the Crusaders, a cover for al-Qaeda's aim to pursue operations outside Afghan borders. Although external jihad was declared against all Western targets, American targets were given the highest priority.[51] Six months later, al-Qaeda executed its first external attack on the U.S. embassies in Nairobi, Kenya, and Dar es Salaam,

Tanzania, causing 225 fatalities and approximately 5,000 casualties, most of them locals.[52] In October 2000, al-Qaeda attempted a second[53] attack against the U.S. Navy, successfully striking the USS *Cole* in the Gulf of Aden, killing seventeen U.S. Marines and nearly sinking the ship.[54]

On 11 September 2001, al-Qaeda executed its most devastating attack so far, targeting American symbols of power in New York and Washington, DC. In response to the attack, a U.S.-led coalition force intervened in Afghanistan on 7 October 2001, and quickly gained control over the territory. As a consequence, the profile of Global Jihad terrorism in the international arena changed significantly.

Notes

1. Martha Crenshaw, "The Psychology of Terrorism: An Agenda for the 21st Century," *Political Psychology* Vol. 21, No. 2 (June 2000), pp. 405–20.

2. Crenshaw, "The Causes of Terrorism," *Comparative Politics* Vol. 13, No. 4 (July 1981), pp. 379–99.

3. Crenshaw, "An Organizational Approach to the Analysis of Political Terrorism," *Orbis* Vol. 29, No.3 (Fall 1985), p. 466.

4. Rohan Gunaratna and Aviv Oreg, "Al Qaeda's Organizational Structure and Its Evolution," *Studies in Conflict & Terrorism* Vol. 33, No. 12 (2010), p. 1044.

5. Jacob N. Shapiro, "Terrorist Organizations' Vulnerabilities and Inefficiencies," *Terrorism Financing and State Responses: A Comparative Perspective*, eds. Jean K. Giraldo and Harold A. Trinkunas, Stanford: Stanford University Press, 2007, p. 59.

6. Crenshaw, 1985.

7. Charles H. Levine, "Organizational Decline and Cutback Management," *Public Administration Review* Vol. 38, No. 4 (1978), pp. 316–25.

8. Jessica Stern, *Terror in the Name of God: Why Religious Militants Kill*, New York: Harper Collins, 2003, p. 167.

9. Gunaratna and Oreg, p. 1045.

10. Stern and Amit Modi, "Producing Terror: Organizational Dynamics of Survival," *Countering the Financing of Terrorism*, Thomas J. Biersteker and Sue E. Eckert, eds., New York: Routledge, 2008, pp.

27–28. "Leaderless terrorism" refers to groups and individuals that conduct terrorist activity in the name of Islamic radicalism based on their own resources, capabilities, and initiative with no external support. They are part of the Global Jihad Movement.

11. Ibid.

12. Ibid.

13. Candace Jones, William S. Hesterly, and Stephen P. Borgatti, "A General Theory of Network Governance: Exchange Conditions and Social Mechanisms," *The Academy of Management Review*, Vol. 22 (October 1997), No. 4, p. 923.

14. James D. Fearon and David D. Laitin, "Ethnicity, Insurgency, and Civil War," *American Political Science Review*, Vol. 97 (February 2003), No. 1, p. 75–90.

15. John B. Alterman, Martha Crenshaw, Teresita Schaffer, and Paul Wilkinson, "How Terrorism Ends," United States Institute of Peace Special Report, 25 May 1999, p. 3.

16. Crenshaw, Martha, "Theories of Terrorism: Instrumental and Organizational Approaches," *The Journal of Strategic Studies* 10.4 (1987): 13–31.

17. Todd H. DeGhetto, "Precipitating the Decline of Terrorist Groups: A System's Analysis," Diss., Naval Postgraduate School, California, United States of America, 1994.

18. Ibid.

19. Ibid.

20. Gunaratna and Oreg, p. 1046.

21. The word "Salaf" in Arabic means predecessors or ancestors, and refers to the Companions of the Prophet Muhammad, the early Muslims who followed him and the scholars of the first three centuries of Islam.

22. Yaakov Shimoney and Evyatar Levin, *The Political Lexicon of the 20th Century*, Jerusalem: Bet Ha'hoza'a Ha'yerushalmi, 1971, pp. 18–19.

23. Gunaratna and Oreg, p. 1047.

24. According to our assessment, supporters of the Salafi ideology across the Muslim world do not exceed 5 percent. Salafi Jihadists are about 5 percent of the total Salafi adherents. If we transfer these percentages into numbers, about 50 million Muslims believe that Sharia law should be implemented worldwide, and up to one million Muslims are ready to use militant jihad to achieve this goal.

25. S. J. Van Hulst, *Violent Jihad in the Netherlands: Current Trends in the Islamist Terrorist Threat*, The Hague: General Intelligence and Security Service Communications Department, March 2006, p. 21.

26. Thomas Hegghamer, "Abdullah Azzam 'Imam of Jihad," *Al Qaeda in Its Own Words*, Gilles Kepel and Jean-Pierre Milelli, eds., Cambridge: Harvard University Press, 2008, p. 82.

27. Ibid, p. 93–94.

28. Lawrence Wright, "Paradise Lost," *The Looming Tower: Al-Qaeda and the Road to 9/11*, New York: Knopf, 2006, p. 117.

29. For example, see the Indonesian *"Pondok Ngruki"* graduates (that later became the base for the Southeast Asian JI) that were allocated to Abd al-Rasool Sayyaf's group and trained and fought there. See Sidney Jones, "Jemaah Islamiyah in South East Asia: Damaged but Still Dangerous," *International Crisis Group (ICG) Asia Report*, No. 63, 26 August 2003, p. 3.

30. Bin Laden's father was a Yemeni citizen who migrated to Saudi Arabia in the early 1930s. In Saudi Arabia, he established himself as a businessman and made close connections with local Saudi sheikhs from the royal family. Using his connections, he became the owner of the largest construction company in Saudi Arabia at the time. The family preserved Islamic traditions but held a pro-Western approach and provided family members with Western education at leading educational institutions. They also spent summer vacations in select resorts in the European Continent. Bin Laden's father was killed in a plane accident in 1967, leaving a large inheritance. Each of his more than fifty children (from several women) received millions of U.S. dollars. See Wright, pp. 76–96.

31. Daniel Benjamin and Steven Simon, *The Age of Sacred Terror*, New York: Random House, 2003, p. 101.

32. Yonah Alexander and Michael S. Swetnam, *Usama Bin Laden's al-Qaida: Profile of a Terrorist Network*, New York: Transnational Publisher Inc., 2001, p. 1.

33. Azzam wanted to end jihad in Afghanistan first but bin Laden, urged by Egyptian hard-liners, decided to use the momentum of jihad following its success in Afghanistan.

34. Founding documents of al-Qaeda recovered from Bosnia, *ICPVTR Database*, Singapore, January 2008; Pervez Musharraf, *In the Line of Fire*, London: Simon and Schuster, 2006, p. 219; Peter L. Bergen, *The Osama bin Laden I Know: An Oral History of al Qaeda's Leader*, New York: Free Press, 2006, p. 80.

35. Abdullah Azzam, "Al-Qaeda al-Sulbah," *Al-Jihad (Afghanistan)*, No. 41, April 1988, pp. 46–49.

36. Hegghamer, p. 95.

37. The National Commission on Terrorist Attacks Upon the United States, *The 9/11 Commission Report: Final Report of the National Commis-*

sion on Terrorist Attacks Upon the United States (9/11 Report), New York: Norton, 2004, p. 58, web (hereafter referred to as The 9/11 Report).

38. For example, see Abu Hamza al-Masri's reference to the Bosnian "Jihad arena" in Evan F. Kohlmann, "The Afghan-Bosnian Mujahideen Network in Europe," Swedish National Defence College, Center for Assymetric Threat Studies, April 2006.

39. Following the war in Afghanistan, the Mujahidin groups began an internal struggle for supremacy over Afghanistan. Since the mid-1990s, the violent struggle over Afghanistan was conducted by the Taliban against a coalition of other forces forming the "Northern Front." Global Jihad fighters who allied with the Taliban considered Afghanistan a jihad arena for fighting against the Northern Front. For example, see "Prepared Statement of John Walker Lindh to the Court," United States District Court, Eastern District of Virginia, Alexandria, VA, 4 October 2002, http://news.findlaw.com/cnn/docs/terrorism/lindh100402statment.html, accessed 15 June 2012.

40. "Profile: Osama bin Laden," Council on Foreign Relations, September 2007, http://www.cfr.org/terrorist-leaders/profile-osama-bin-laden/p9951, accessed 15 June 2012; CNN Wire Staff, "Timeline: Osama bin Laden, Over the Years," CNN, 2 May 2011.

41. Bergen, p. 124.

42. "Al-Qaeda" in Arabic literally means "the base." For example, see Anisseh Van Engeland and Rachael M. Rudolph, From Terrorism to Politics, Hampshire, England: Ashgate Publishing, Ltd., 2008, p. 172.

43. The 9/11 Report, p. 60.

44. Pressure was initiated by the Arab states of the Middle East and North Africa (Egypt, Jordan, and Algeria) that suffered from the logistical support bin Laden provided to their own local Muslim radicals.

45. See Barton Gellman, "U.S. Was Foiled Multiple Times in Efforts To Capture Bin Laden or Have Him Killed," The Washington Post ,3 October 2001.

46. The 9/11 Report, p. 62.

47. For details on the Abd al-Rasool Sayyaf Group's main training camp in Sadah, see Gunaratna and Oreg, p. 1049. The activity of this group in the international arena in the first half of the 1990s was professional. They were responsible for the deadliest attacks and the most ambitious plans of the period: the first attempt to collapse the World Trade Center in New York using a car bomb in the parking lot of the towers. This attack on 26 February 1993 killed six people and wounded about 1,000 others. See "FBI 100: First Strike: Global Terror in America," Fbi.gov, 26 February 2008, www.fbi.gov/page2/feb08/

tradebom_022608.html, accessed 15 June 2012. The "Bojinca plot" was an ambitious attempt to crash eleven American commercial jets into the Pacific Ocean in a day. *The 9/11 Report,* pp. 146–50.

48. Yousef was arrested in January 1995. See Laurie Mylroie, "The World Trade Center Bomb: Who Is Ramzi Yousef? And Why It Matters," *U.S. News and World Report,* Vol. 118, No. 7 (February 1995), pp. 50–54. Shah was arrested in 1995. See Steven Emerson, "Inside the Osama bin Laden Investigation," *Journal of Counterterrorism and Security International* (Fall 1998), p. 17. Murad was arrested in 1995. See "Pilot Is Given Life Term for Bombing Plots," *New York Times,* 16 May 1998.

49. Among those leaders who became fugitives were Hambali, an Indonesian citizen, who later became the military chief of JI, and Khalid Sheikh Mohamed (KSM), who joined al-Qaeda in late 1998 and became the mastermind of the 9/11 attacks. See "Hambali," *Rotten Library Biographies,* http://www.rotten.com/library/bio/crime/terrorists/hambali/, accessed 15 June 2012.

50. Despite the fact that they worked separately at this stage in different entities, they knew each other from Afghanistan (the "melting pot"). *The 9/11 Report,* pp. 148–49.

51. Bergen, pp. 195–97.

52. *The 9/11 Report,* pp. 115–16.

53. The first attempt was executed in January 2000 against the USS *Sullivan* but failed.

54. The first attempt in January 2000 failed as the dingy full of explosives sank on its way to hit the USS *Sullivan. The 9/11 Report,* pp. 181, 190–91.

2

The Ideological Imperative

General Background and Historical Development

Al-Qaeda or Global Jihad ideology is not uniform. Even though these ideologies originated from the same roots, religious figures within the movement emphasized different interpretations and approaches. The Global Jihad Movement that emerged during the 1980s in Afghanistan was composed of diverging religious beliefs and attitudes, causing internal tension over the implementation of ideology, targeting policy, and operational agenda. Historical perspectives of the evolution of Sunni radicalism presented here will contextualize the Global Jihad ideology.

Al-Qaeda or Global Jihad ideology refers to a radical ideology within Sunni Islam. The first split in Islam took place over Prophet Muhammad's successor. The Sunnis viewed the right candidate as Abu Bakr, the first caliph, while Shias viewed the right candidate as Ali. The conflict intensified into a violent clash between the supporters of Ali (Sia'at Ali-Shi'a) and the supporters of the Ummayyad clan (Sunni).[1]

Within Sunni Islam, there are four dominant schools of thought (*Mad'hab*):

- **Hanafi**—Named after Abu Hanifa Naaman Bin Sabit (699–767).[2] The Hanafi school of thought allows for a modern interpretation of the Quran and Hadith (the Prophet's tradition), subject to the discretion of the ruler of the day.[3] The Hanafi school of thought is the most common and spread throughout the largest part of the Muslim world, stretching from Turkey and the Balkans in the west through central Asia to south Asia and the Indian subcontinent. The Hanafi school of thought is a moderate and progressive ideology even if exceptions are possible, such as the Taliban Movement, which is a Hanafi group.

- **Maliki**—Named after Malik Bin Anas (715–795).[4] Malik based his rules on local tradition and heritage in North Africa.[5] The Maliki school of thought is common in North Africa and the African continent and is more conservative and traditional than the Hanafi and Shafi'i schools.[6]

- **Shafi'i**—Named after Mohamed Bin Idris al-Shafi'i (769–820). Al-Shafi'i was the most important Islamic thinker. He restricted all rational interpretation of Islam and discretion of Islamic rule, and was the first thinker to systematize the methodology of *Ijtihad*.[7] He stipulated that the Suna (the tradition of Prophet Muhammad) is the only religious reference that may be used to correct and adapt the Quran. The Shafi'i school of thought is the second most common *Mad'hab* among the four schools and is practiced throughout east Russia, east Africa, and Southeast Asia.[8] The Shafi'i school is also more traditional than the Hanafi school.

- **Hanbali**—Named after Ahmad Bin Hanbal (780–855).[9] The Hanbali school regards each sentence and verse of the Quran and the Hadith literally. Hanbal was much more rigid in his interpretations than his mentor al-Shafai. Hanbalis are against any judicial manipulation that undermines the literal command and meaning of the written word in the Quran and Hadith. Hanbalis and neo-Hanbalis such as the cleric Taqi al-Din Ahmad Ibn Taymiyyah (1263–1328) are the most conservative and hard line within all *Mad'hab*.[10] Hanbalism provides the philosophical basis for Wahhabism, which is the sole school of thought in Sunni Saudi Arabia and the primary reference for its laws.[11]

The four schools of thoughts differ in their interpretation of the Quranic term "jihad," or holy war. While the Shafi'i, Maliki, and Hanafi schools extend the interpretation of jihad to other aspects of life (behavior, belief, etc.), the Hanbali school limits jihad to war and the waging of holy war only.[12]

Salafiya is a school of thought that emerged from the Hanbali school during the twentieth century. *Salaf* in Arabic means ancestors and refers to the Sahaba, Prophet Muhammad's loyal companions. In the Islamic tradition, the Salaf lived a pure life that is a role model for all Islamic communities. Salafis aspire to imitate this lifestyle by living according to only the literal meaning of the Quran and the Hadith.[13] The Muslim Brotherhood (MB) and Hizb il-Tahrir (HUT) are currently well-known political movements that follow the Salafi approach. The MB started in Egypt in 1928 by Hassan al-Banna.[14] The movement calls for rapprochement, both personal as well as community based, and for the reintroduction of the Quran and Sharia as state law.

The focus of the MB's *Dawa* (preaching of Islam) changed over time. During the Egyptian monarchy era (until 1952), the MB focused its propaganda on the notion of national independence and parliamentary procedure. During the Najib and Nasir regime (the postrevolution republic era of Egypt, since July 1952), the MB emphasized social justice and its brand of Islamic socialism, which opposed the Nasir regime's Marxist and non-Arab socialism. By this period, the MB adopted a nonarmed approach to political change, yet from 1970 to 1980 the neo-MB, which emerged during the 1960s, focused on its concept of the Islamic State and Islamic government, which were in some cases followed by calls for violent revolution.[15]

Al-Banna saw the legitimate political and religious order as vital, even after the death of Prophet Muhammad. For al-Banna, Islam could only exist when there was an Islamic political leader. Al-Banna did not call for the restoration of the Islamic Caliphate, which was removed after the collapse of the Ottoman Empire, but for the restoration of the spirit of Prophet Muhammad's four genuine inheritors (al-Khulafa al-Rashidun). Al-Banna emphasized the implementation of MB ideology at the local level in Islamic states, before their eventual convergence to reestablish the caliphate. According to al-Banna, the adoption of Sharia as the law of the state solidifies the legitimacy of any regime. This belief originated from the neo-Hanbalist writings of Ibn Taymiyyah. Even though the MB slogan was that the Quran is the one and only constitution, al-Banna believed in some of the more important concepts of those that supported state constitutions, such as keeping the freedom of the individual; the concept of consultation (Shura); accountability of the ruler to the people, and the separation of authorities.[16] Al-Banna viewed these concepts as derived from the Quran and believed that the parliamentary system should continue without other political parties.[17] After the 1952 revolution of the "Free Officers," led by Nasir and Najib, the MB crafted a proposal for an Islamic constitution in Egypt, which was published in December 1952. This moderate protocol contains only basic concepts of al-Banna's ideology, and lacks specific details regarding political parties, elections, or civilian laws. It recommends keeping all new proposed laws "within Islamic boundaries," so as not to contradict "Islam."[18] The MB supported the "Free Officers" and proposed to have a parliamentarian regime ("Regime d'assemblee").[19] In Hassan al-Banna and the Egyptian MB's view was that only an Islamic state of Egypt represented a completely independent Egyptian nation-state.

Al-Banna promoted jihad only against colonization (fighting against non-Islamic forces in Muslim lands invaded by these forces, turning these invaded regions into "jihad arenas") and not against Muslim rulers (internal jihad).[20] The military branch (Katiba) of the MB, also known as the "first level brothers," traveled to Palestine to fight against the Jews in 1948, and to fight against British troops deployed along the Suez Canal in 1956.[21] Thus, al-Banna was not a "terrorist" operating against the internal Egyptian political order.[22]

Nevertheless al-Banna and the MB's ideology of political Islam paved the way for a more radical and violent approach during the 1960s, with the emergence of Salafiya Jihadiya.[23] The main ideologue of this new movement was Egyptian Sayyid Qutb, a senior leader from the MB, who during the 1960s rose against the MB's passiveness and called for violent activism—

using jihad to purify Islamic society, restore Islamic dignity, and reclaim the Islamic golden era.[24]

A direct ideological line links Hassan al-Banna, the founder of the Muslim Brotherhood during the Egyptian monarchy era, and Sayyid Qutb, the ideologue of Salafiya Jihadiya, during the republic days of Gamal Abd al-Nasir. In both periods, the political and social approach of the MB was the dominant factor within these radical Islamic circles.[25] In contrast to al-Banna's idea of struggle in jihad arenas against external occupying non-Islamic forces, Sayyid Qutb developed the concept of jihad against Muslims and Islamic rulers in Islamic countries (internal jihad).[26] Qutb's ideas paved the way for radicals to rationalize jihad against *infidel* Islamic rulers.[27]

During the early stages of his public writings, Qutb believed that a ruler did not derive religious authority in virtue, but that election by Muslim people is necessary, and that his authority derived from the way he implemented the Sharia. Qutb's approach evolved with his introduction of *Hakimiya*—the exclusive authority of God (Allah).[28] This notion derived from the Pakistani religious scholar and founder of the religious-political party Jamaat-e-Islami (JI) Syed Maddoudi, who preached that *Hukm* (God's exclusive authority) extends to all aspects of life, including the political, religious, and judicial. Qutb argued that every Muslim must engage in *Thawra* (revolution) against anyone who usurped Allah's authority.[29]

Qutb believed that Nasir and Nasirism were the best examples of tyrannical, anti-Islamic regimes. Qutb's writings do not explicitly call for the use of political violence and terror in order to topple Nasir's regime, but the Qutbis (Qutb's supporters) possessed radical and violent interpretations of his writings.[30] Qutb advised his followers that the second phase of *Jahilia* (pre-Islamic, pagan ignorance) existed for the last two centuries, particularly in Islamic states, and that only a new and Islamic government would bring back true Islam and reclaim Islam's position in the world. He believed that such a movement should begin in Egypt. Following his execution by the Nasir regime in 1966, Qutb's reading of the volatile terms *Jahilia*, *Hakimiya*, and *Takfir* inspired violent interpretations and applications. In

"Al Farida Al Ghaiba," an article by Abd al-Salam Faraj, one of Qutb's followers, Faraj argues that "the contemporary leaders of the Muslims are infidels (*Kufr*) (and) . . . Infidels must be killed." The first priority of jihad is "the revolt against current regimes of those who are faithless and the reconstruction of Islamic order instead."[31] Faraj called for acts of armed rebellion against Nasir.

Given that the followers of Qutb's *Hakimiya* aspire to establish an Islamic state, *Hakimiya* has become the antithesis of secularism, nationalism, and democracy.[32] Despite old Sunni-Shiite rivalries, the Qutbis viewed Iran's Islamic Revolution as the model of how to establish an Islamic state.[33]

In his book *Cavaliers* (sometimes translated as *Knights*) *under the Banner of the Prophet*, Dr. Ayman al-Zawahiri, the current chief of al-Qaeda, refers to the significant role of Qutb's ideology in shaping the Salafiya Jihadiya Movement in Egypt.[34] According to al-Zawahiri, the neo-Salafi Jihad Movement, strongly influenced by Qutb, began its violent activity against the Egyptian government during the second half of the 1960s. Although the Islamic movement, represented by the MB, was already operating against the "enemies" of Islam much earlier, its operational activities were not aimed at the local regime, but directed against external enemies. The MB did not only accept the legitimacy of the Egyptian ruler (the king), but also supported his regime. Qutb, on the other hand, emphasized the importance of *Wahda* (uniqueness) and *Hakimiya* (exclusive sovereignty) in Islam, and insisted that the conflict between Islam and its enemies was an ideological one concerning the identity of a ruler. According to Qutb, this conflict exists between the path and tradition of Allah and common law, which consists of man-made, materialistic principles designed to mediate between the Creator and his creatures. Qutb's ideology regards the internal enemy as more dangerous than the external enemy. During the second half of the 1960s, Qutbis broke away from the MB's targeting policy and began attacking the Egyptian government (internal jihad). They insisted that the regime was hostile to Islam, deviated from Allah's path, and refused to be subordinate to Sharia. This new target served as a diversion to focus on the internal enemy for the first time. Until then, all MB's military activities were against external threats.[35]

Qutbis' influence grew significantly despite Qutb's execution by the Nasir regime. Al-Zawahiri argues that Qutb's doctrine played a crucial role in persuading young Muslims to
engage in internal jihad.[36] Qutb's call for complete submission
and devotion to Allah's oneness and his path was, and still is,
the spark for the Islamic Revolution. The religious devotion of
this revolution grows every day.

Qutb's execution focused public attention on his activities
and writings.[37] According to al-Zawahiri, "Qutb became the
role model of honesty, justice, and truth. He told the truth in
the face of the tyrant and paid for it with his life."[38] His refusal
to seek amnesty from Nasir greatly enhanced his image. The
Nasir regime believed that the Islamic movement disappeared
after Qutb's execution, after the arrests of thousands of Islamists
throughout Egypt during the 1960s. The purge was successful
only temporarily, reducing the activity of new Salafis. According to al-Zawahiri, the popularity of Qutb's ideas grew rapidly
and his call to uphold Allah's uniqueness and oneness was
enthusiastically accepted all over Egypt. For al-Zawahiri, this
reflected the establishment of the modern jihad movement in
Egypt.[39]

The death of Abd al-Nasir and the arrival of his successor
Anwar Sadat was a turning point for the Egyptian Islamic Movement. During Sadat's regime, the global hegemony shifted from
the Soviet Union to the United States. Sadat abolished many of
Nasir's restrictions. One of his first moves was to introduce freedom of speech to the population and, inadvertently among it,
the Islamic movement. As a result, the influence of the Islamists
on the Egyptian people grew, heralding an era of prosperity for
the Islamists. It was during this period that the young members
of the Islamic movement determined that the internal enemy
was as dangerous as the external enemy.[40] During the second
half of the 1970s, jihadism and fundamentalism dominated the
student unions of southern Egyptian universities, which rejected
all attempts by the MB to annex the new jihadists under their
banner, which stimulated a much more moderate approach vis-
à-vis the Egyptian government. One jihadist from a southern
university during that period was Sheikh Omar Abd al-Rahman

(The "Blind Sheikh"), who gained popularity within the new Salafi Jihadist circles and became their religious role model and mentor.[41]

In 1974, there was an attempt by the Salafi Jihadists to conduct a coup d'état against the Egyptian government using equipment stored inside the military polytechnic unit base, and in 1977, Yahiya Hashim led guerrilla activity against Egyptian government troops in the al-Minya Mountains. For al-Zawahiri, this reflected an ideological shift toward fighting the internal enemy instead of the external forces in jihad arenas.[42]

The Egyptian regime attempted to defeat the neo-Islamic movement, which quickly gained momentum, by enlisting U.S. cooperation to transform the local confrontation into a global one. According to al-Zawahiri, the United States acknowledged that the Egyptian regime could not contain Islamic movements in Egypt. Moreover, his perception was that the spirit of jihad would destabilize the Middle East and threaten U.S. positions in the region. Al-Zawahiri argued that given Egypt's influence within the Muslim world, the United States was concerned that the new trends of Islamic fundamentalism would lead to the establishment of an Islamic Caliphate in Egypt, a unifying force for the Islamic world to mobilize jihad against the West.[43]

Ideological Collision in Afghanistan: Azzam vs. Zawahiri

Abdullah Azzam, the spiritual mentor and ideologue of the Global Jihad Movement, adhered more closely to the MB's approach than to Qutb's approach in terms of the ideological location for jihad (jihad arenas vs. internal jihad). However, aspects of Azzam's jihadist doctrine belong to an extreme branch of Qutb's modern radical Islamic ideology. Azzam praised the use of the sword as the sole solution to Muslims' problems. He also promoted martyrdom (death for Allah). Azzam rejected all dialogue with the enemy, and argued that securing Muslim interests by using violent means occur as follows: jihad—by the rifle alone; no dialogue; no negotiation; no international peace conferences.[44]

For Azzam, implementation of Global Jihad comprised the following two dimensions: militant jihad and *Dawa* (as the propagation of militant jihad). Azzam stated that the combination of militant jihad and *Dawa* was necessary in order to secure victory for the Global Jihad. He stressed that both forms of jihad needed synchronization.

According to Azzam, there are four stages of militant jihad as follows:

1. **Hijra** (Migration)—Azzam states that every Muslim that does not live in *Dar al-Islam* (land of Islam) must migrate from *Dar al-Kufr/Dar al-Harb* (land of infidels/land of war) to *Dar al-Islam*, in the spirit of the Prophet Muhammad's *Hijra* from Mecca to Medina in AD 622. Azzam called for Muslims living in the West to immigrate back to Muslim and Arab countries. He also encouraged Muslims to perform *Hijra* for Allah—immigration to war zones to assist fellow Muslims in fighting the Western enemy. *Hijra* is the first step of militant jihad.

2. **I'dad** (Preparation)—For Azzam, *I'dad* is a religious obligation. This stage is composed of the following two kinds of preparation: psychological preparation, by studying the Quran and the holy tradition and imitating the lifestyle of early Muslims; and physical preparation, by undergoing military training (through simulations and in combat skills and the use of weapons, etc.). Training camps established for the purpose of *I'dad* should occur as follows:

   1. **Ribat** (Deployment to border zones)—This deployment can last for long periods of time until combat begins. Azzam emphasized the importance of this stage; some who go through *Hijra* and *I'dad* are not patient enough to remain through *Ribat*, and subsequently leave the border zone.

   2. **Qital** (Fighting)—The journey toward militant jihad peaks at this fourth stage. *Qital* in order to establish an

Islamic state features prominently in Azzam's philosophy.[45]

Azzam also set out the stages for the propagation of militant jihad. He used the term *Dawa* to refer to this:

1. **The call for Allah (God)**—An individual must lead his group of believers to study the Quran and the Hadith. Through steady indoctrination, these believers form "al-Qaeda al-Sulbah" (the solid base) of the Islamic community that will combat *Jahilia*.[46]

2. **The cold war**—This phase involves waging psychological warfare against the *Jahilia* community. During this period, individuals do not engage using military means. They attack their enemy's reputation by accusing him of corruption and immorality. They aim to alienate the enemy from his followers by undermining his credibility.

3. **Jihad or the "holy war"**—During this phase, individuals synchronize *Dawa* with the combat stage plan of jihad and use military means and skills to fight the enemy.

4. **The final victory**—During this stage, everyone—warriors and propagandists—will fight together under the banner of Islam.[47]

An active member of the Muslim Brotherhood, Azzam, like his mentor al-Banna, enthusiastically supported and promoted jihad in jihad arenas.[48] In 1984, Azzam issued an important religious ruling referring to jihad and the use of jihad. Basing this ruling on verses from the Quran and traditions from the Hadith regarding the famous Quranic concept of "the jihad against infidels," Azzam made a distinction between two kinds of jihad as follows:

1. **Offensive Jihad**—in cases where Muslims are the initiators of jihad against a non-Muslim enemy and on *Dar al-Harb*, jihad is not the collective duty of all Muslims, but of the group that initiated it. The group is responsible for filling the ranks of Islamic troops along the border in

order to deter the enemy, and for infiltrating the enemy's territory once or twice a year.

2. **Defensive Jihad**—When infidels are the initiators of a conflict and penetrate *Dar al-Islam*, it is the duty of all battle qualified Muslims, wherever they may be, to perform jihad.[49] According to Azzam, jihad is a personal obligation for all Muslims, even when infidels conquered *Dar al-Islam* previously. For example, every Muslim is obliged to wage jihad in order to liberate Andalusia (modern-day Spain, which was under Islamic rule during the golden era of Islam up until the fifteenth century).[50]

In his publications, Azzam did not limit his focus to Afghanistan, but discussed other jihad arenas as well, especially Palestine. Other jihad arenas include India, the Philippines, Kashmir, Chad, Eritrea, the former Yugoslav republic, Bulgaria, Uganda, Cyprus, and Lebanon.[51]

Throughout his preaching and publications, Azzam emphasized that Palestine's liberation was, is, and will always be the first priority of the Muslim world, and that Afghanistan should be regarded only as a preparation phase for the real challenge of liberating Palestine.[52] He stated:

Our presence in Afghanistan now, which is a fulfillment of the duty of Jihad and worship of fighting, does not mean that we have forgotten Palestine. Palestine is our beating heart and it has a higher priority than Afghanistan in our minds and hearts, and in our feelings and ideology. It is the blessed land that the Lord of Glory has mentioned in his honorable book four times, and it is the cradle of Islam, the first of the two Kiblah and the third holy place.[53] It is the point of departure from which our prophet, may Allah bless him and grant him salvation, had set out on his midnight journey to the seven heavens. Truly, if we were denied from carrying out Jihad in Palestine on account of limitations and border guards, and truly if we were prevented from pursuing the worship of fighting in the land of the Al-Aqsa Mosque for a limited period of time—it does not mean that our minds have abandoned the thoughts about Palestine. We shall not sit idly and rest until we shall return to Jihad in

Palestine. Our persons are in Afghanistan, and it was decreed for us by Allah, but our spirits hover above Jerusalem. Our bodies are in Kabul and it is imposed upon us, but our hearts are linked with the blessed lands that were soiled by the lowest of Allah's creatures in our world. We have promised ourselves that we will not retreat and will not be shaken from this divine path that connects Kabul and Jerusalem, and by the permission of Allah we are advancing, no matter how large the distance, how long the time and how long the road.[54]

In the abstract of Azzam's "Memories from Palestine," he expressed his personal desire to liberate Palestine and the al-Aqsa Mosque while creating a linkage between the Palestinian and the Afghan fronts:

I am a Palestinian and if I have to find a way to enter Palestine and Al Aqsa mosque I would prefer fighting over there. . . . The bloody case of Kabul is the story of wounded Palestine . . . the blood of Hindu-Kush is floating over Gaza. . . . The cry of the widows in Helmand Belah and Heart (districts in Afghanistan) are echoed in Nablus, Hebron and Jerusalem. It is a united case; the case of a wounded Islam under the attacking boots of the entire world. . . . We shall not rest till we get back to the Jihad in Palestine. . . . Indeed we were forced out of the Jihad in Palestine due to the current circumstances and (Israel's) border control but it does not mean we have stopped thinking about Palestine. . . . Palestine is to precede Afghanistan but after we had been handcuffed and the borders were closed and barracked we refused to continue living like that and immigrated to the land of Jihad in Afghanistan.[55]

In December 1988 in Oklahoma City, at a conference celebrating the first year of the Palestinian uprising, Azzam delivered a speech in which he declared:

The sons of Palestine this is your chance to train with all kinds of weapons in Afghanistan. Do not miss that chance. . . . Oh God provide victory for Moslem(s) fighting in Afghanistan, Palestine, Philippines, Eritrea, Somalia, Lebanon, Chad, Burma and anywhere in the world.[56]

Although the Israeli-Palestinian conflict zone was initially Azzam's preferred jihad arena, he began to favor Afghanistan as a jihad arena at the beginning of the Afghan war between the Soviet Union and Afghan Mujahidin.[57]

Azzam referred to the question, "Why Afghanistan first and not Palestine?" and provided the following reasons for his shifting priorities:

1. The Afghan war offered a window of opportunity to raise the flag of Islam, fight under the banner of Islam, and eventually establish an Islamic state in Afghanistan. This would be unlike the flag raised in Palestine, which was the flag of secularism and Islamic nationalism.
2. The Afghan war was large-scale combat in Afghanistan between crusaders and Muslims—the biggest war zone in the world since World War II.
3. Jihad in Afghanistan was led by clerics and Qaricepts, genuine leaders of the Islamic movement; while in Palestine, the flag of jihad was raised by a mixed leadership composed of nationalists, communists, and secularists; alongside true Islamic figures.[58]
4. The success of the Afghan war was dependent on the Mujahidin, whereas Palestinians relied solely on international (operational and logistical) support from the Soviet Union and the Eastern Bloc.
5. Accessibility to Afghanistan was almost completely free across poorly protected borders, while accessibility to Palestine was difficult due to the security measures Israel built along its borders.
6. The Afghan people are unique in their stubbornness and resistance.[59]

Azzam designated the jihad in Afghanistan as the spark of global fighting in jihad arenas, and an operational base for the renewed Islamic Caliphate. Azzam wanted to transform Afghanistan's local jihad against the Soviet invader into a global jihad.[60] According to Azzam, Palestine was the next arena of jihad after Afghanistan.[61] In a speech held in February 1989 in

Islamabad, Azzam declared the future priorities of the global Islamic movement:

> We will win over our enemy and will establish an Islamic state on a small piece of land such as Afghanistan. Afghanistan will extend, Jihad will annex more land and Islam shall fight in new locations such as the Jews in Palestine and will establish an Islamic state in Palestine [. . .] so we will have an Islamic state in Palestine and in Afghanistan and in other locations and eventually all these Islamic states will merge into one unified Islamic caliphate.[62]

In contrast to Azzam's ideology of jihad against a non-Islamic external enemy, a new ideological approach emerged within the ranks of the jihadi movement in Afghanistan. This approach argued that internal jihad was more important than fighting the external enemy in jihad arenas. This new approach, promoted by the Egyptian Qutbis, was led by al-Zawahiri in the 1980s to fight the Soviets.[63] Unlike Azzam, they considered the jihad in Afghanistan as a platform for internal jihad, a necessary prelude to the real battle of Islam against the Islamic infidel regimes in Muslim states. The supporters of this approach drew an analogy between the hypocrites of the early days of Islam—those who publicly supported the Prophet and his companions, but opposed them behind his back—and the current rulers of the Muslim world and Arab states.[64] This approach presents a distinction between good and bad in the Islamic world:

> (Oh Moslem) . . . to which of the two parties do you belong? On whose side do you stand? Do you belong in the party of America, Israel, France, Russia and their allies among the apostate rulers of our countries, their assistants, their soldiers, their journalists, their judges, and their clerics who spread confusion, pledge allegiance to them, and call them the care takers of the Muslims' affairs? Or, do you belong in the party of the monotheistic, Salafi Mujahideen? With whom do you side? Are you on the side of the secularism, its artificial laws, the American hegemony, the Israeli supremacy, the apparatus of oppression, the sexually oriented media, the hypocrite clerics, and those who confuse matters in order to serve the tyrants?

Or do you side with the monotheists, the people of the Jihad, the steadfast, the patient, those who were killed, the prisoners of war, the wounded, the widows, and the children who lost their parents in the battle to serve God? . . . O Muslim, pick a side and a party to fight for and under its flag. Would you sell your religion, become an apostate, and fight under the flag of its enemies? Or, do you support your Islam and fight under the flag of the Quran? Thus fight the Devil's allies as the devil's plots are weak.[65]

Al-Zawahiri declared that local Islamic rulers should be the first priority target of the jihadi movement:

Muslims are required to fight against rulers who do not govern using the laws of God and exchange those laws with the scum of manmade laws. They are required to fight against people who aid and support rulers in forsaking the laws of God. According to the Quran and the traditions of the Prophet, such rulers, their aides, and their supporters are infidels. It is permitted for a Muslim to assassinate any of these people if he can. This proves that the priority in killing infidels is given to infidel leaders who fight against Islam, against those who call for Islam, or against those who conduct jihad for the sake of Islam.[66]

Azzam made contact with Afghan Mujahidin groups as early as 1981.[67] In 1984, Azzam established the Maktab al-Khidamat (MaK), which was dedicated to placing Arab volunteers either with relief organizations serving Afghan refugees, or with Afghan factions fighting on the front line against the Soviets.[68] Azzam's first jihad-related fatwa, "Defending Muslim Land" in 1984, solidified the notion of defensive jihad. He claimed that at that time, Afghanistan and Palestine should be the focus of Muslim activities.[69]

In 1984, bin Laden, the young son of a rich Saudi owner of the largest construction work enterprise in the Middle East, who inherited millions of dollars after his father's death, joined the MaK. In the early stages, his ideologies coincided with Azzam's.[70] As the war proceeded, bin Laden, influenced by Egyptian jihadi radicals led by al-Zawahiri, supported Qutb's approach of freeing the Muslim world from within, by waging jihad against the Muslim rulers of Islamic nations (internal jihad) and violently implementing Sharia over the land.[71] An ideological gap developed between Azzam and bin Laden. The debate between Azzam and bin Laden was fundamentally a theological one, but also involved the next location of jihad after the Afghan war. Azzam's concept of jihad was to free Muslim land now ruled by non-Muslim regimes, such as Palestine and central Asian states of Kazakhstan, Uzbekistan, Turkmenistan, and Kyrgyzstan.[72] Azzam claimed that the best move was to continue with jihad even after the liberation of Afghanistan: "(After Afghanistan) we will wage Jihad in the Islamic republics of the former USSR and Palestine and Jerusalem."[73]

In *Knights under the Banner of the Prophet*, al-Zawahiri condemns Azzam's ideology as antiquated, as he feels it favors conflicts with external enemies and assumes concordance between the Islamic movement and the national regimes of Muslim countries. Zawahiri dismissed this approach as obsolete and asserted that the new Salafi Jihadi philosophy targeting the internal enemy ("infidel" Arab regimes) was based on solid, traditional foundations and better historical experience.[74]

Zawahiri claimed that the main reason for his first arrival to Afghanistan in the summer of 1980 was because Afghanistan was an important jihad arena that could rather serve as the base for jihad in Egypt and the Arab world and not necessarily for the sake of liberating Afghanistan from the Soviet occupiers.[75] Al-Zawahiri added that finding a safe haven for jihad in Egypt preoccupied him, especially in light of persecution by the Egyptian security apparatuses and the topographical characteristics of the Egyptian terrain that made it easy to control.[76]

Al-Zawahiri discussed the Afghan arena, and why it was the preferred place for jihad. Some of these points coincide with Azzam's reasons for favoring Afghanistan, although they reached different conclusions as follows:

1. The jihad movement needed an arena that would serve as an incubator, and provide political, organizational, and operational training.

2. Young Muslims in Afghanistan fought in the true spirit of Islam in order to liberate Islamic lands, while fighting in other locations was conducted with mixed ideologies, which included nationalism, pan-Arabism, secularism, and even communism. The best example for this was Palestine. Zawahiri claimed that these mixed ideologies, which dominate the Muslim world, blurred the boundaries between loyalists and enemies in the eyes of young Muslims. Doubts were raised about the true nature of the enemy:

Was it an external enemy that occupied Islamic land?

Was it an internal enemy that used violence against Muslims to prevent the establishment of Sharia?

Was it an internal enemy that spread immorality and profligacy under the false slogans of progress, freedom, nationalism, and liberation—all of which led Muslim countries into an abyss of internal destruction?

Was it a surrender to external forces—which is the current situation in most of the Islamic nations within the framework of the global new order?

In Afghanistan, everything was clear: Muslim youths were fighting under the banner of Islam against an external, aggressive infidel.

3. Afghanistan was a practical example of jihad against an Islamic ruler who went against Islam and signed a pact with the enemies of Islam. The Najiballah regime in Afghanistan was the best example of a ruler who practiced Islamic prayers, fasts, and the *Haj* (pilgrimage), while at the same time practiced Islamic law incorrectly and harshly punished Muslims who participated in jihad.

4. The defeat of the Soviet troops in Afghanistan and the collapse of the Soviet Union destroyed the illusion of a superpower's infallibility. It was an important lesson for the Muslim youth in their battle against the United States.

   a. The Afghan arena served as a melting pot and allowed jihadists from all over the world to meet and interact.

   b. The most important reason for pursuing Afghanistan as a jihad arena was because the presence of the young

Arabic and Islamic Mujahidin in Afghanistan transformed the Afghan conflict from a local-regional issue
into a global Islamic one in which the whole Islamic
Ummah (nation) could participate.[77]

In the final chapter of his book, al-Zawahiri refers to the future of the Islamic movement, its historical achievements and lessons, and the goals of the jihadi movement in the first half of the
2000s. For al-Zawahiri, even though the targeting policy shifted as
al-Qaeda turned to the external enemy and started to attack
Western—primarily American—targets, the arenas of internal
jihad remained the primary battlefield.[78] Al-Zawahiri writes:

Giving up the goal of establishing an Islamic state in the heart
of the Islamic world is forbidden. The movement that raises
the banner of Jihad must base its doctrine on the foundation
of taking control over some land in the heart of the Muslim
world and establishing an Islamic state over this land in a way
that it could be defendable and could also effectively conduct
from within its border the war for the restoration of the Islamic
caliphate that is to be handled according to the way of the
prophet. Victory of the Islamic movement under the banner
of Jihad over the "global coalition" would be achieved only
if it would have a solid fundamentalist base in the heart of
the Muslim world. All our achievements and all that has been
accomplished throughout the years of The Islamic movement
will become useless in case we will not be able to establish the
Islamic caliphate in the heart of the Muslim world. The attacks
we were able to conduct so far against the enemies of Islam,
successful as they turned to be in causing the enemy disgrace-
ful defeats, did not promote the goal of establishing the Islamic
state in the heart of the Muslim world. These operations as big
as they turned to be, remain within the framework of annoying
operations that can be handled and contained by the enemy.
Establishment of the Islamic state would not be achieved easily but it should always be regarded as the ultimate inevitable
goal of the Islamic Ummah (Nation).[79]

As the war in Afghanistan was ending (concluding in February 1989), this theological debate between Azzam and al-

Zawahiri intensified, especially regarding the continuation of jihad after the war.[80] Azzam wanted to continue with al-Banna's ideology and use Afghanistan as a platform to fight in other jihad arenas (Palestine[81] and former USSR central Asian republics.)[82] Al-Zawahiri wanted to implement Qutb's ideology and use Afghanistan as a platform to wage internal jihad against the secular "infidel" rulers of Islamic states (firstly Egypt), topple their regimes, and implement Sharia as state law.

The theological disagreement between Azzam and the Egyptian Qutbis became a personal conflict between al-Zawahiri and Azzam as each tried to pull bin Laden, a source of funding, to his side.

In Peshawar, al-Zawahiri was not considered to be a Mujahid, but merely a recruiter for fighters against Egypt. Al-Zawahiri used the good relations between Azzam and Ahmad Shah Massoud to undermine Azzam's credibility.[83] Al-Zawahiri described Massoud as a French agent and used it to attack Azzam, who always claimed that Massoud was a good man.[84]

Al-Zawahiri accused Azzam of being an American and Saudi agent and a spy, and tried to turn bin Laden and other groups against him. Azzam told his son-in-law Abdullah Anas, "I do not know what certain people are doing in Peshawar," "they are trying to create Fitna [separation and civil war] between me and the volunteers."[85] Azzam named al-Zawahiri as one of these instigators.[86] In another episode, one of al-Zawahiri's closest friends, Abu Abd al-Rahaman al-Khadr (a.k.a. Abd al-Rahman al-Canadi), spread rumors in Peshawar of a misuse of humanitarian funds that were allocated to the Mujahidin, by Azzam who diverted those funds to the American embassy in Islamabad and to a Christian welfare charity. This speculation resulted in increased tension between al-Zawahiri's and Azzam's supporters, peaking in violent clashes between the two sides in Peshawar.[87]

Many Mujahidin that fought in Afghanistan believe that this personal conflict between Azzam and al-Zawahiri over bin Laden's political and financial support was the real reason for Azzam's assassination in Peshawar on 17 November 1989. Many believe that it was plotted by al-Zawahiri's Egyptian supporters.[88]

The gradual distance between bin Laden and Azzam began prior to the theological-based conflict between Azzam and al-Zawahiri. Bin Laden wanted to focus much more of his time and finances on operational activities and to take an active part in the war in Afghanistan. The distance between the two peaked in 1987 as bin Laden established an Arab combat unit operating outside the framework of the original Afghan forces,[89] in full contradiction to Azzam's tendencies. For the establishment of the new unit, bin Laden allied with Egyptian activists such as Abu Ubeida Banshiri and Mohamed Atef (Abu Hafs al-Masri), who would later become prominent al-Qaeda leaders, and established camp al-Massada near the village of Jaji on the front line of the combat zone with the Russians. Bin Laden transferred new recruits, who came to implement jihad in Afghanistan, directly to his new camp, where they received basic combat training and went on to fight the Soviets completely autonomously.[90] The warriors of al-Massada gained their operational glory during the famous "Jaji battle" in April 1987, as they were able to hold their base while fighting against superior numbers of Soviet troops for three weeks until repulsion of the Soviet offensive.

The Establishment of al-Qaeda—Synchronization of Ideologies

During 1987–1988, bin Laden took initial steps to establish a new organization to promote radical Islamic and jihadi notions in the world following the Afghan war, based on the operational cadre of al-Massada and to serve as the basis for a "Global Islamic Army."[91] During September 1988, bin Laden and his close allies held several discussions in his Peshawar residence, concluding with the establishment of al-Qaeda. The goals of the new organization were vague and unclear, stating that "Al Qaeda is an organized Islamic entity which its aim is to distribute the word of Allah and turn Islam into a victorious religion."[92] On 10 September 1988, the new organization formally began running activities, composed at that time of fifteen activists, nine of whom held administrative positions.[93] Ten days later, the number grew to thirty activists, all from al-Massada camp[94] and by the end of the year, the organization was composed of about 100 members.[95] During the early years, the political objective of al-Qaeda remained unclear and no specific goal or concrete agenda was set.[96] However, the infrastructure of al-Qaeda was clear and included a leader (bin Laden), a consulting body (Majles al-Shura) responsible for the routine daily activity of the organization through subjectual—military (led by Abu Ubeida Banshiri), religious (Abu Saad al-Sharif), media (Abu Mosab Royters), and administrative (Abu Fadl al-Makky and Abu Hamam al-Saudi)—committees.[97]

As mentioned, the ideology of the organization, its overall strategy, and the derived targeting policy were not coherent, and changed from time to time.

Al-Qaeda was initially involved in the internal Afghan civil war that developed after the Soviet troops left the country. This involvement gained antagonism and criticism from the circles of Arab volunteers in Afghanistan, especially among Azzam's supporters.[98] In 1991, Al-Qaeda moved its troops and activity to the Sudan as bin Laden realized that the combat against foreign invaders had ended, and that there was a need to deploy forces as close as possible to the heart of events in the Middle East.[99]

In Sudan, bin Laden applied his plan to pilot al-Qaeda as the "base" ("al-Qaeda" in Arabic literally means "the base") and provide logistical and operational support in operating training camps for elements fighting internal jihad[100] and those fighting in newly emerging jihad arenas[101] as well.[102] Al-Qaeda's performance created, perhaps even without any intention by bin Laden, synchronization between al-Zawahiri's internal jihad and Azzam's external jihad in jihad arenas, and included both within the framework of its activity.

Following international and regional pressures imposed on the Sudan to expel al-Qaeda, the organization left Khartoum and went back to Afghanistan, allied with the Afghan Taliban led by Mullah Muhammad Omar and the Taliban forces that were fighting the Northern Alliance, and eventually gained control over most parts of Afghanistan in 1996.[103] Under the patronage of the Taliban, al-Qaeda facilitated a vast training infrastructure composed of large training complexes throughout the state, providing training to tens of thousands of radical Islamists from various countries.

Crystallization of the "Third Ideology"—"Global Jihad" against the West

Analyzing bin Laden's public addresses during the 1990s suggests that the ideology to divert al-Qaeda into Global Jihad, targeting mainly the American-led West, was gradually developed by bin Laden throughout the decade. During the first half of the 1990s, bin Laden referred to the growing presence of American troops over the "Islamic land" within the ideology of the MB and Azzam as deployment of an external invader in Islamic land that must be fought and eventually expelled (jihad arena). According to bin Laden, the American presence, and especially its military deployment, in Saudi Arabia[104] since the first Gulf War (1990–1991),[105] as well as its deployment in Somalia within the framework of Operation Restore Hope (1993), transformed these two countries into jihad arenas, just like Afghanistan, so that jihad should be applied against it. For that objective, al-Qaeda deployed a vanguard force in Somalia composed of the more experienced and capable of its troops headed by Mohamed Atef and Saif al-Adil. They were sent to Somalia in order to train local troops in guerrilla fighting skills and to engage in the fight against the United States. This project, known within the organization as "Project Somalia," peaked with the interception of a U.S. helicopter, killing eighteen U.S. Marines, an incident that eventually stimulated the evacuation of American troops from Somalia.[106] On the other hand, al-Qaeda's activities in Saudi Arabia were much slower, more gradual, and less visible. During the early 1990s, bin Laden urged the Saudi people to conduct guerrilla activities against the U.S. presence in the "land of the holy two places."[107] According to bin Laden, these calls exhorted two major attacks against U.S. Army complexes in Riyadh (1995) and Khobar (1996), and resulted in the deaths of several American citizens. The noncompliance of the United States to bin Laden's call for the evacuation of American forces from Saudi land led bin Laden to publicly announce in September 1996 a "Global Jihad" against the United States.[108] Two months later, bin Laden elaborated on his announcement and the reasons behind it:

> We thought that the attacks in Riyadh and Khobar were strong enough signals for American reasonable decision makers to avoid a full scale war between the American forces and the Islamic Umma (overall community). But they failed in understanding these signals as interpreting them correctly should have prompted the evacuation of all American troops from the Arab Peninsula.[109]

In February 1998, bin Laden announced a fatwa (religious edict) on the establishment of the World Islamic Front for Jihad against the Jews and the Crusaders in which he declared his decision to divert the fight against Americans (and Jews) wherever they are. With this approach, bin Laden created a "third ideology," the Global Jihad against the U.S.-led West. This was different to both Azzam's "jihad arenas" as well as al-Zawahiri's "internal jihad." The new strategy required al-Qaeda to adopt conceptual changes and tactical adaptations and to reinforce infrastructural internal adaptation in order to synchronize other Islamic elements, organized and unorganized, in the struggle against the West.

As bin Laden realized that al-Qaeda itself could not defeat the West, he understood that al-Qaeda must serve as a vanguard, positioned at the front of a huge Islamic camp fighting the West. Today, this huge camp with al-Qaeda at the helm comprises dozens of affiliated Islamic terror and guerrilla groups operating all over the world as well as millions of unorganized "Islam"-inspired individuals. This expanded Global Jihad Movement consists of the following components:

A. The Al Qaeda Organization (Core al-Qaeda) and al-Qaeda's Logistical Networks: Up until 2011 the "al-Qaeda organization" mostly operated as an organized entity, with worldwide infrastructures and echelons. With clearly defined leadership, membership, and a support base, core al-Qaeda, also known as "al-Qaeda classic" or "al-Qaeda senior leadership," led by Ayman al Zawahiri, exists in the Federally Administered Tribal Areas (FATA) of Pakistan, along the Pak-Afghan border region.[110] As a resilient group, al-Qaeda adapted to the demography and topography of FATA—spread over a 1,520-mile border and comprising seven tribal agencies and six frontier regions (FR).[111]

The Global Jihad Movement, spearheaded by the al-Qaeda organization, uses a vast logistical network to support its worldwide activity. These networks are responsible for the recruitment of new activists and their safe transfer from training camps to jihad arenas.[112] These networks are mostly involved in logistical activity such as the transfer of jihadi volunteers to Iraq and Syria. In rare cases, they initiated operational activities and carried out their own terrorist attacks with the approval of al-Qaeda's leadership. The most famous example of an attack initiated and executed by such a network was the Casablanca attack in May 2003 against Western targets.[113]

B. Al-Qaeda's Affiliated Local Organizations: "Al-Qaeda-affiliated groups" refers to local organizations that were supported by bin Laden during the 1990s. Al-Qaeda mainly provided training for these organizations, supporting their struggle to bring down local regimes in their own countries (internal jihad). Due to difficulties that the al-Qaeda organization faced following the U.S.-led invasion of Afghanistan in October 2001, a few al-Qaeda-affiliated groups extended their targets to include Westerners within the vicinity of their operations.[114] This target expansion was often the consequence of the friendly relations between local groups' leaders and al-Qaeda seniors, which developed during the Afghan war.[115] Such organizations include Jemaah Islamiyah of Southeast Asia (JI), the Abu Sayyaf Group (ASG) of the Philippines,[116] Harakat al-Jihad al-Alami (HUJA),[117] and the Islamic Jihad

Union (IJU),[118] an Uzbek group that split from the Islamic Movement of Uzbekistan (IMU).[119] These groups have plotted and carried out attacks on international targets on behalf of the al-Qaeda organization and in accordance with its directives. This includes the JI operation in Bali in October 2002 and the ASG plot to blow up a truck filled with explosives in front of the U.S. embassy in Manila, the capital of the Philippines, in 2002.[120] Some operatives, with or without the knowledge of the leaders of the Pakistan-based Lashkar-e-Toyba (LeT), a Kashmir specific jihadi group who trained them, served as operational support and logistical aid for other al-Qaeda plots. These operatives include the "shoe bomber," British national Richard Reid, who attempted to crash American Airlines Flight 63 from Paris to Miami in December 2001, and the French national Willie Brigitte, who failed to attack Australia's only nuclear power plant in 2003.[121]

In recent years, al-Qaeda's connections and collaborations with local organizations have become more formal. Since the U.S.-led offensive in Iraq in 2003, the world witnessed the establishment of regional "al-Qaedas" initiated by the al-Qaeda organization's leadership that is based on local groups. The Algerian group, Global Salafist Group for Preaching and Combat (GSPC), became al-Qaeda in the Maghreb (AQIM).[122] Al-Qaeda in the Arabian Peninsula (AQAP) and al-Qaeda in Yemen (AQIY) were also established during this period, and eventually merged into one organization.[123] In Iraq, Tawhid Wal Jihad changed its name to al-Qaeda in Iraq (AQI) and became the sole element within the umbrella of the Islamic State of Iraq (ISI), an umbrella organization for different jihadi groups.[124] A formal merger took place between al-Qaeda and the Libyan Islamic Fighting Group (LIFG)'s senior leaders, who are located on the Afghanistan-Pakistan border.[125]

Al-Qaeda's targeting policy has influenced its associated groups. These groups diverted some of their operational efforts from domestic targets to international targets. Since these mergers, the new regional al-Qaeda groups attacked Western targets within the vicinity of their operations in accordance with al-Qa-eda's directives. Such activities include AQIY attacks on Korean tourists, Western embassies, U.S. missions and compounds, and oil facilities.[126] AQIM attacked UN facilities, kidnapped Western tourists, and threatened to attack western targets.[127] On 1 February 2008, AQIM attacked the Israeli embassy in Nouakchott, Mauritania.[128]

We expect more regional groups such as the Somali Shabaab al-Mujahidin to combine efforts with al-Qaeda and begin attacking international targets within the vicinity of their operations in the Horn of Africa. The first sign of such a trend was reflected in the formal merging of al-Shabaab into al-Qaeda ranks, which was announced in early 2012.[129]

Jihad Arena Offshoots: The term "jihad arena" refers to regions in the international arena characterized by religious confrontations between Muslims and non-Muslims. According to Sharia, it is the personal obligation of each Muslim to travel to these areas and fight alongside his brothers.[130] Afghanistan during the war with the former USSR, Bosnia during the Balkan war, Chechnya, Kashmir, Somalia, south Philippines, and parts of Southeast Asia have been major jihad arenas and have attracted numerous zealous international jihadi fighters. Iraq, the Federally Administered Tribal Areas (FATA) in Pakistan, and Chechnya are the three traditional jihad arenas today. These arenas attract many young and enthusiastic Muslims from all over the world to participate in local struggles against infidels. Each arena now possesses a large concentration of trained and experienced warriors seeking to export their operational activity to the international arena. A new jihad arena has emerged in Syria since the outbreak of the civil war in 2012.

"Local Initiatives" of al-Qaeda-Inspired Elements: These like-minded individuals carry out terror attacks in the name of Global Jihad based on their individual capabilities, resources, and initiatives. They take advantage of the ease of employing terror tactics in order to achieve maximum damage and publicity. They often do not possess strong ideological or religious motivations, but are driven by their socio-economic discontent and personal frustrations directed against their home countries.[131] The majority of these terror incidents occur in Western Europe, North America, and Australia. These individuals are alienated second- and third-generation Muslim immigrants who are unable to integrate into Western society, who channel their hatred into terrorist activity in the name of Global Jihad. These individuals tend to come from radicalized sections of Muslim communities across Europe, although there are Muslim converts who have also engaged in Global Jihad. Although most "local initiative" terrorists are not operationally effective, they remain a source of concern. Their activity includes unsophisticated acts of violence such as stabbing, using Molotov cocktails, arson (as in the Muslim riots in France), and solitary assassinations. On occasion, they are capable of large-scale attacks, due to the availability of raw materials such as fertilizers and the accessibility of information on explosives on the Internet. An example of this is the attack on the Madrid train system in March 2004.[132] The investigations into the attacks found no proof of external involvement by Al Qaeda or any other extremist element, suggesting that local, homegrown terrorists were responsible. The Egyptian authorities claim that the Sinai Peninsula attacks against Western hotels and local tourist attractions in October 2004, July 2005, and April 2006 were part of local homegrown initiatives. According to formal Egyptian declarations, these attacks by radical elements within the local Sinai Bedouin community, without any external connections, were similar to the attacks in Madrid. Motivation stemmed from feelings of deprivation and low socio-economic status, a feeling resonating across many Muslim communities in Europe.[133]

The exposure of homegrown terrorist cells in the United States during 2010 reemphasized the threat that these groups pose to the West. These cells are composed of U.S. citizens from poor socio-economic backgrounds, who converted to Islam. They follow the Salafi Jihadi interpretation of Islam, which led them to support and conduct terrorist operations and plots on behalf of the Global Jihad.[134]

In the coming chapters, we will examine these different components of the Global Jihad Movement in order to map the threat of radical Islamism. We will focus on the operational capabilities, logistical deployment, internal and external connections with other jihadi elements, and the operational activity conducted by the different elements, focusing on operational activities targeting the West.

Notes

1. Ali, the fourth caliph (ruler) that followed Prophet Muhammad, was married to the Prophet's daughter Fatima, and hence, according to his followers, his sons (Hassan and Hussain) should have succeeded him. However, the Muawia clans were able to gain leadership using force, peaking in the Karbala battle (AD 680), in which the supporters of Ali were massacred by the Muawia. The Karbala battle is considered the fracture point that created the split in Islam between the Shiite minority (the supporters of Ali) and the Sunni majority. Recent assessments suggest that the Shiite population comprises 10–13 percent of Muslims and is the dominant sect in Iran. A third of Iraq's and Lebanon's populations are Shiites. The rest of the Islamic world is primarily Sunni. See Tracy Miller, *Mapping the Global Muslim Population: A Report on the Size and Distribution of the World's Muslim Population*, Pew Research Centre, October 2009, p. 1.

2. Hunt Janin, *The Pursuit of Learning in the Islamic World, 610–2003*, Jefferson, NC: McFarland Publishing, 2003, p. 47.

3. Assaf Maliach and Shaul Shay, *From Kabul to Jerusalem: Al-Qaeda, Global Islamic Jihad and the Israeli-Palestinian Confrontation*, Tel Aviv: Matar, 2009, p. 82.

4. Phillip Khûri Hitti, *Capital Cities of Arab Islam*, Vol. 58. Minneapolis: University of Minnesota Press, 1973, p. 54.

5. Ibid, p. 83.

6. Abubakr Asadulla, *Islam v. West: Fact or Fiction? A Brief Historical, Political, Theological and Psychological Perspective*, Bloomington, Indiana: iUniverse, 2008, p. 30.

7. Independent or original interpretation of problems that are not covered by the genuine references of Islam, i.e., the Quran, Hadith, and Ijma'a. In the early years of Islam every cleric had the right to practice Ijtihad but after three centuries the "gates of Ijtihad" were closed and no scholar has since been qualified to practice Ijtihad. See http://www.britannica.com/EBchecked/topic/282550/ijtihad.

8. Maliach and Shay, "From Kabul to Jerusalem," pp. 82–83.

9. Roy Jackson, *Fifty Key Figures in Islam,* New York: Routledge, 2006, p. 44.

10. Ibid, p. 83.

11. Wahhabism is a radical reform movement that was initiated by Muhammad Ibn Abd al-Wahhab (1703–1792) of Najd almost 200 years ago to rid Islamic societies of cultural practices and interpretations that he considered contrary to Islam. These practices included praying to saints; making pilgrimages to tombs and special mosques; and using votive offerings and talismans. He also objected to certain religious festivals, including celebrations of the Prophet's birthday, Shia mourning ceremonies, and Sufi mysticism. Consequently, the Wahhabis forbade grave markers and tombs at burial sites and the building of any shrines that could become a locus of *shirk* (idolatry or associating beings or things with Allah). The movement followed the teaching of Ibn Taymiyyah (1263–1328), who although from a Hanbali school of thought, refused to be bound by any of the four Sunni schools of thought, and emphasized *Ijtihad* (best judgment of his own). Ustaz Haniff Mohammed, personal interview (Gunaratna), Singapore, May 2011.

12. Maliach and Shay, pp. 83–84.

13. Martin Van Bruinessen and Julia Day Howell, eds., *Sufism and the "Modern" in Islam* (I. B. Tauris & Co. Ltd., 2007).

14. Abdel Moneim Said Aly and Manfred W. Wenner, "Modern Islamic Reform Movements: The Muslim Brotherhood in Contemporary Egypt," *The Middle East Journal,* Vol. 36, No. 3, September 1982, pp. 336–61.

15. Oliviee Qare, "From Al Bana until Qutb," *Zmanim,* Vol. 32 (Fall 1989), Tel Aviv University, p. 48.

16. Mark Weston, *Prophets and Princes: Saudi Arabia from Muhammad to the Present,* New Jersey: John Wiley and Sons, 2008, p. 362. The MB's motto is: "God is our objective; the Quran is our constitution; the prophet is our leader; struggle is our way and death for the sake of god is our highest aspiration."

17. Qare, p. 49.

18. Ibid.

19. Ibid.

20. Ibid.

21. Ibid, p. 50.

22. Ibid, p. 51.

23. Yoram Schweitzer and Aviv Oreg, "Al-Qaeda's Odyssey to the Global Jihad." http://www.inss.org.il/uploadImages/systemFiles/memo134%20%284%29_rev10April2014.pdf.

24. Qutb's notion of jihad is radical and paved the way for his followers to use armed jihad to realize his ideas.

25. Qare, p. 48.

26. Ibid, p. 49.

27. *Takfir* literally means accusing a Muslim of being an infidel. See Quintan Wiktorowicz and John Kaltner, "Killing in the Name of Islam: Al-Qaeda's Justification for September 11," *Middle East Policy*, Vol. 10, No. 2 (Summer 2003), p. 79.

28. Qare, p. 50.

29. Ibid.

30. Ibid.

31. Abd al-Salam Faraj, "Al Farida Al Ghaiba," cited in Qare, p. 50.

32. Ibid, p. 52.

33. Ibid.

34. One of the most devoted supporters of the Salafia Jihadia ideology, Zawahiri established the Egyptian Islamic Jihad (EIJ) organization in 1985 in Afghanistan which has conducted numerous terrorist attacks against formal Egyptian regime entities inside and outside Egypt. In 1998, Zawahiri joined hands with bin Laden and became al-Qaeda's second-in-command. Following bin Laden's death, Zawahiri became the overall leader of al-Qaeda.

35. Ayman al-Zawahiri, "Knights under the Prophet's Banner," *Asharq al-Awsat* (London), 3 December 2001, Part. 2 of a series, Knights under the Prophet's Banner, 2–12 December 2001.

36. Ibid.

37. Sayed Khattab, *The Political Thought of Sayyid Qutb: The Theory of Jahiliyyah*. New York: Taylor and Francis, 2006, p. 2.

38. Al-Zawahiri, 2 December 2001, Pt. 1.

39. Al-Zawahiri, 3 December 2001, Pt. 2.

40. "Al-Sharq Al-Awsat Publishes Extracts from Al-Jihad Leader Al-Zawahiri's New Book." Accessed 20 January 2015. http://triceratops.brynmawr.edu/dspace/bitstream/handle/10066/4690/ZAW20011202.pdf?sequence=4.

41. Ibid.

42. Al-Zawahiri, 5 December 2001, Pt. 4.

43. Al-Zawahiri, 7 December 2001, Pt. 6.

44. Maliach and Shay, p. 103.

45. Ibid, pp. 109–15.

46. In this article by Azzam published in *Al Jihad* magazine in April 1986, he uses for the first time the term "Al Qaeda" (the base), which has become synonymous with global radical Islamic violence.

Jahiliyyah here refers to those who have yet to accept the Salafi interpretation of Islam. See Sayyid Qutb, *Milestones*, Indianapolis: American Trust Publication, 1993, pp. 5–6.

47. Maliach and Shay, pp. 116–18.

48. Ibid, p. 189.

49. Ibid, pp. 88–89.

50. Ibid, p. 99.

51. Ibid, p. 127.

52. Ibid, p. 128.

53. *Kiblah* literally refers to the direction to which Muslims turn to pray.

54. Abdullah Azzam, "Determination and Resolution," *Al Jihad*, September 1987.

55. Maliach and Shay, pp. 129–30.

56. Ibid, p. 72.

57. Azzam is Palestinian by origin from a small village near Jenin in the West Bank. See Olivier Roy and Antoine Sfeir, eds., *The Columbia World Dictionary of Islamism*, New York: Columbia University Press, 2007, p. 63.

58. "Qaricept" refers to someone who memorizes the Quran.

59. Maliach and Shay, pp. 126–27.

60. Ibid, p. 138.

61. Ibid, p. 68.

62. Ibid, p. 106.

63. Zawahiri first traveled to Afghanistan in 1980 as a volunteer physician. In 1981 he went back to Egypt and was arrested in the mass arrests by Egyptian authorities following the assassination of President Sadat. In prison Zawahiri became the vocal leader of the prisoners and upon his release in late 1984 he went back to Afghanistan.

64. "Characteristics of Jihad Magazine (English Translation)," Combating Terrorism Center at West Point, http://ctc.usma.edu/aq/pdf/AFGP-2002-600142-Trans-Meta.pdf, accessed 10 June 2012, p. 2.

65. Ibid, pp. 5–6.

66. Ibid, p.18.

67. Bergen, p. 27.

68. Harvey W. Kushner, *Encyclopaedia of Terrorism*, Thousand Oaks, CA: SAGE Publications (2003), pp. 24, 72.

69. Abdullah Azzam, "Defense of Muslim lands," cited in Bergen, p. 27.

70. Ann Rathbone and Charles K. Rowley, "Al Qaeda," *The Encyclopaedia of Public Choice: Volume 1*, Rowley and Friedrich Schneider, eds., New York: Springer, 2004, p. 6.

71. Bergen, p. 74.

72. Ibid.

73. Maliach and Shay, p. 43.

74. Al-Zawahiri, 3 December 2001, Pt. 2.

75. Ibid.

76. Ibid.

77. Ibid.

78. With the establishment of the World Islamic Front for Jihad Against the Jews and the Crusaders in February 1998, al-Qaeda turned the focus of its operational activity and targeting policy on a new enemy—the West, primarily the United States.

79. Al-Zawahiri, 12 December 2001, Pt. 11.

80. See Bill Keller, "Last Soviet Soldiers Leave Afghanistan," *New York Times*, 16 February 1989.

81. Mustafa Hamid, "The Airport 1990," Combating Terrorism Center at West Point, http://www.ctc.usma.edu/wp-content/up loads/2010/08/AFGP-2002-600090-Trans-Meta.pdf, p. 1; Hamid, "Mustafa Hamid's Analysis of Mujahidin Activities," Combating Terrorism Center at West Point, http://www.ctc.usma.edu/wp-content/uploads/2010/08/AFGP-2002-600088-Trans-Meta.pdf, p. 37.

82. Uzbekistan, Tajikistan, Kyrgyzstan, Turkmenistan, and Kazakhstan.

83. Ahmad Shah Massoud was one of the Afghan Mujahidin leaders and a close associate of Azzam's. See "Abdullah Anas" in Bergen, p. 69.

84. Ibid.

85. Ibid.

86. Lawrence Wright, "Paradise Lost," *The Looming Tower: Al-Qaeda and the Road to 9/11* (New York: Knopt, 2006), p. 143.

87. Ibid, p. 149.

88. Bergen, p. 95.

89. Bergen, p. 49.

90. "Tariq Osama" document 76 as was seized from Enaam Arnaout's computer.

91. "Tariq Osama" documents 91–94.

92. "Tariq Osama" documents 127 and 127a.

93. Ibid.

94. Ibid. See also Jamal al-Fadl's testimony in "United States of America v. Usama bin Laden/Day 2, 6 February 2001," *Wikipedia: The Free Encyclopedia*, Wikimedia Foundation, Inc., 29 November 2008, http://en.wikisource.org/wiki/United_States_of_America_v._Usama_bin_Laden/Day_2_6_February_2001, accessed 12 June 2012.

95. "Tariq Al Musadat" documents 86, 87, and 88.

96. "United States of America v. Usama bin Laden/Day 2, 6 February 2001," pp. 192–197.

97. Ibid., pp. 205–12.

98. For example, see letters written by Mustafa Hamid, a longtime supporter of Azzam, regarding bin Laden's decision to involve his "Arab forces" in the Afghan civil war especially in the battle over Jalalabad. See Hamid, "Mustafa Hamid's Analysis of Mujahidin Activities."

99. Al-Fadl's testimony in "United States of America v. Usama bin Laden/Day 2, 6 February 2001," p. 216.

100. The success in Afghanistan inflamed the hearts and minds of millions across the Arab and Islamic world. As a consequence, a number of radical Islamic terror groups were established in many countries to challenge the secular regimes there. Led by returning veterans from Afghanistan, these groups conducted attacks against local regimes as well as against the innocent population in order to destabilize the secular regimes' authority. All the states in the Middle East and the extended Islamic world experienced some level of instability during these years.

101. With the conclusion of the Afghan war, new jihad arenas were created all over the world, attracting Islamic volunteers. Bosnia, Chechnya, Tajikistan, Somalia, Kashmir, the Maluku Islands and Sulawesi (Indonesia), and Mindanao (Philippines) became jihad arenas during the 1990s.

102. *The 9/11 Report,* p. 60.

103. The Afghani Taliban is an Afghani militant group that was established after the war with the Soviets concluded and Russian troops withdrew from Afghanistan. Following the Russian withdrawal, Afghanistan went into a turmoil of civil war. In order to promote Pakistani interests within the unclear internal political postwar Afghan spectrum, Pakistan ISI (Intelligence) formed the Taliban to operate as a Pakistani arm in the Afghan civil war. The Afghani Taliban was composed of Afghan students (Taliban in Arabic literally means students) who studied in different madrassas (Islamic religious schools) that operated in the country. Enjoying Pakistani support, the Taliban became the most dominant militant player in the Afghan civil war and eventually took control of the country in 1996.

104. The physical presence of the men and especially women of the U.S. Army in the sacred land in which Prophet Muhammad was born and in which the two most holy places are located (Mecca and Medina) was, according to bin Ladin and his followers, the most humiliating element.

105. In 1990, Iraqi leader Saddam Hussein invaded Kuwait and created regional instability as many states in the region, especially Saudi Arabia, were threatened by this move. Bin Laden offered the Saudi leaders al-Qaeda's defense services, which consisted of fighters from al-Masada, for use against the Iraqi aggression, but the offer was rejected as Saudi leaders preferred to enlist U.S. help. They allowed the United States to build military complexes on Saudi soil, which remained active even after Iraq's defeat in the first Gulf War.

106. Clint Watts, Jacob Shapiro, and Vahid Brown, "Al-Qa'ida's (Mis)Adventures in the Horn of Africa," Combating Terrorism Center at West Point, http://www.ctc.usma.edu/wp-content/uploads/2010/06/Al-Qaidas-MisAdventures-in-the-Horn-of-Africa.pdf, pp. 34–36.

107. Bin Laden, the Afghan hero, at that time had significant influence over the Saudi population. His frequent calls and addresses against the American presence in Saudi Arabia raised concerns and antagonism within the inner circles of Saudi decision makers. Saudi leaders negotiated with him and were prepared to allow him to return to Saudi Arabia and regain his citizenship and status on the condition that he moderated his approach and calls against the United States. When bin Laden rejected this offer, the Saudis attempted to assassinate him while he was living in Sudan. See Bergen, pp. 134–35.

108. "Bin Laden Declares Jihad on Americans," London AL-ISLAH in Arabic, 2 September 1996.

109. "Bin Laden Interviewed on Jihad Against US," London AL-QUDS AL-'ARABI in Arabic, 27 November 1996, p. 5.

110. *FATA Development Authority* http://www.fatada.gov.pk.

111. The agencies are: Bajaur, Khyber, Kurram, Mohmand, Orakzai, and North and South Waziristan. The frontier regions include: FR Peshawar, FR Kohat, FR Tank, FR Banuu, FR Lakii, and FR Dera Ismail Khan. FATA is stretched over an area of 27,220 square kilometers. See "FATA Disaster Management Authority," *FATA Disaster Management Authority,* http://fdma.gov.pk/index.php?option=com_content&view=article&id=62&Itemid=18. FATA is cut off from the rest of the world, even from mainland Pakistan. It has been left behind in global progress, with limited access to development assistance. Even compared to other parts of Pakistan or Afghanistan, FATA has not received the same attention.

112. In recent years, these networks have been mostly involved in the transfer of activists into Iraq. See Philip Carter, "Al Qaeda and the Advent of Multinational Terrorism: Why 'Material Support'

Prosecutions Are Key in the War on Terrorism," *FindLaw*, 12 March 2003, http://writ.news.findlaw.com/student/20030312_carter.html, accessed 1 June 2012; Anthony Barnett, Jason Burke, and Zoe Smith, "Terror cells regroup—and Now Their Target Is Europe," *The Observer*, 11 January 2004, http://www.guardian.co.uk/world/2004/jan/11/alqaida.terrorism, accessed 1 June 2012.

113. For Mohamed Gerbouzi's role in the attack, see Elaine Sciolino, "Morocco Connection Is Emerging as Sleeper Threat in Terror War," *The New York Times*, 16 May 2004, http://www.nytimes.com/2004/05/16/world/morocco-connection-is-emerging-as-sleeper-threat-in-terror-war.html?pagewanted=all&src=pm, accessed 1 June 2012.

114. This has happened in some cases as a result of directions given by al-Qaeda and in other cases through their own initiative.

115. The Afghan arena was a melting pot for jihadists from around the world. They trained and fought together, and subsequently maintained relations following their return to their home countries. There, they established the so-called local groups to fight "infidel" local regimes.

116. See Nelly Sindayen, "Abu Sayyaf—Beyond the Kidnap Game," *Time Magazine Asia*, 18 November 2002, http://www.time.com/time/asia/covers/1101021125/abu_sayyaf.html (expired link).

117. The Itihad al-Islami al-Afghani's Sadah camp, led by the Afghan leader Abd al-Rasool Sayyaf, served as the melting pot for the Baluchi KSM, the Indonesian Radwan Ismail al-Din (better known as Hambali), the Philippine Abd al-Razeq Janjalani, and the Pakistani Hafiz al-Saeed. As KSM became the chief of al-Qaeda's Special Operations Unit, Hambali became the military chief of JI, Abd al-Razeq Janjalani founded and headed the Philippine group Abu Sayyaf (Sayyaf—in honor of Abd al-Rasool Sayyaf), and Hafez al-Saeed established and headed the Pakistani group Lashkar-e-Toyba (LeT). This allowed for the al-Qaeda Special Operations Unit to operationally cooperate with JI, ASG, HUJA, and LeT. See "Global Jihad Entities Cooperation—Where It All Began," *CeifiT* 14 December 2008, http://www.ceifit.com/?categoryId=41118&itemId=60829, accessed 1 June 2012.

118. "Suicide Bombers Hit Embassies in Uzbekistan," *ABC News*, 31 July 2004, http://www.abc.net.au/news/2004-07-31/suicide-bombers-hit-embassies-in-uzbekistan/2017866, accessed 1 June 2012.

119. Senior members in the newly established IJU were mostly influenced by al-Qaeda's senior leader Abu Layth al-Libi. See Giudo Steinberg, "Uzbekistan/Turkey: The Islamic Jihad Union," *Qantara.de*, republished in *Women Living under Muslim Laws*, http://www.wluml.org/english/newsfulltxt.shtml?cmd%5B157%5D=x-157-561617,

accessed 1 Mar 2012; Ronald Sandee, "The Islamic Jihad Union (IJU)," *The NEFA Foundation,* 14 October 2008, p. 3.

120. Gunaratna and Oreg, p. 1051.

121. "KSM's Transatlantic Shoe Bomb Plot," *The NEFA Foundation,* http://nefafoundation.org/miscellaneous/shoebombplot.pdf. For LeT involvement in a plot to blow up a nuclear facility in Australia, see "'Australia Terror Plotter' Jailed," *BBC News,* 15 March 2007, http://news.bbc.co.uk/2/hi/europe/6454373.stm, accessed 1 March 2012.

122. Lianne Kennedy Boudali, *The GSPC: Newest Franchise in al Qaeda's Global Jihad,* Combating Terrorism Center at West Point, April 2007, http://www.ctc.usma.edu/Kennedy-GSPC-041207.pdf.

123. Jane Novak, "Arabian Peninsula Al Qaeda Groups Merge," *The Long War,* March 2012.

Evan Kohlmann, "State of the Sunni Insurgency in Iraq: August 2007" at www.nefafoundation.org/miscellaneous/iraqreport0807.pdf.

Inal Ersan, "Zawahiri Says Libyan Group Joins Al Qaeda," *Reuters,* 3 November 2007, *Journal,* 26 January 2009, http://www.longwarjournal.org/archives/2009/01/arabian_peninsula_al.php, accessed 1 March 2012.

124. Evan Kohlman,, "State of the Sunni Insurgency in Iraq: August 2007" at www.nefafoundation.org/miscellaneous/iraqreport0807.pdf.

125. Inal Ersan, "Zawahiri Says Libyan Group Joins Al Qaeda," *Reuters,* 3 November 2007, http://www.reuters.com/article/2007/11/03/us-libya-qaeda-idUSL032828220071103, accessed 15 July 2012.

126. For the full list of AQIY engagement in attacking foreign targets, see *The NEFA Foundation,* http://www1.nefafoundation.org/documents-area-yemen.html.

127. For the full detailed engagement of AQIM in attacking Western targets, see *NEFA Foundation,* http://www.nefafoundation.org/documents-area-north-africa.html.

128. "AQIM: 'Statement On Attack on the Israeli Embassy in Nouakchott,'" *The NEFA Foundation,* 2 February 2008, http://www1.nefafoundation.org/miscellaneous/nefaaqim0208-2.pdf, accessed 15 July 2012.

129. "Al-Shabab 'Join Ranks' with al-Qaeda" *Al Jazeera,* 10 February 2012 at http://www.aljazeera.com/news/africa/2012/02/201221054649118317.html.

130. Gunaratna and Oreg, p. 1048.

131. See Danna Harman, "Radical Islam Finds Unlikely Heaven in Liberal Britain," *The Christian Science Monitor,* 5 August 2002, http://www.csmonitor.com/2002/0805/p01s03-wogi.html, accessed 15 June

2012. The homegrown individual's knowledge of jihad or Salafism is low. An analogy can be drawn between them and the 1970s and 1980s when most terrorist organizations—Japanese Red Army, the different Palestinian groups, the European Bader Meinhof, Red Brigades, ETA and the IRA, as well as the Latin groups of South and Central America (Carlos the Jackal's gang)—operating in the international arena possessed extreme leftist ideologies but the junior activists of these groups were not well read in the works of Marx and Trotsky.

132. The Madrid attack was carried out by low-level criminal Muslim activists who came together in one of the most important Madrid mosques (M-30). They were able to get standard explosives by dealing drugs and they learned how to set a charge through an Internet website. J. Jordán and R. Wesley, "The Madrid Attacks: Results of Investigations Two Years Later," *Terrorism Monitor,* Vol. 4, Issue 5, 9 March 2006, http://jamestown.org/terrorism/news/article.php?articleid=2369921 (expired link).

133. Joshua L. Gleis, "Trafficking and the Role of the Sinai Bedouin," *Terrorism Monitor,* Vol. 5, Issue 12, June 2007, http://jamestown.org/terrorism/news/article.php?articleid=2373485, pp. 9-12 (expired link).

134. For example, see "The L.A. Plot to Attack U.S. Military, Israeli Government, & Jewish Targets," *The NEFA Foundation,* June 2007 (updated January 2008), http://www.nefafoundation.org/miscellaneous/LA_Plot.pdf, p. 3.

3

Al-Qaeda

The Global Vanguard[1]

Al-Qaeda is the most prominent element in the Global Jihad Movement. In less than two decades, al-Qaeda, under Osama bin Laden's leadership, positioned itself as the pillar of radical Islam and as the operational center for the entire spectrum of radical Islamist movements. Since the end of the Afghan war, al-Qaeda has served as a meeting point for all Islamic radicals around the world and as the sole reference and inspiration for radical Islamic operational activity. In the eyes of the mass media and the public, al-Qaeda seems to be synonymous with all Islamist radicalism and Islamist terrorist activity across the globe.

Since the 9/11 attacks in New York and Washington, al-Qaeda controls most of the operational activity of Global Jihad in the international arena and seeks to integrate it with its political and operational policy. As al-Qaeda possesses full control over its own operational infrastructure, it also has significant control over the activity of its partners and its logistical affiliates. After al-Zarqawi's death, it gained further control of the Iraqi branch even if it seems this influence is rediminishing since mid-2013. Since its formal inception in 1988, al-Qaeda has used a hierarchical structure and an inbuilt organizational infrastructure to function operationally and logistically. This chapter presents the formal layout of al-Qaeda, represented by its main command apparatus, which supervises and directs several entities that are responsible for the ideological, logistical, and operational aspects of the organization's day-to-day activities. We identify the personalities who hold important positions within al-Qaeda's echelons from its inception to the present. The Global Jihad Movement has more characteristics of a network structure. In contrast, the al-Qaeda organization has always been, first and foremost, an infrastructural organization with formal echelons, subdepartmental divisions, and distribution of duties reflecting characteristics of a guerilla and terrorist organization.

Analysts have debated over the structure—even the existence—of the al-Qaeda organization. This affects how governments perceive al-Qaeda and respond to it.[2] This is especially so following the American-led offensive in Afghanistan in October 2001 as al-Qaeda suffered losses to its physical structure, including training camps and leadership, and was forced to relocate from a relatively stable environment in Afghanistan to a fluid existence in tribal Pakistan. In its new location, al-Qaeda has been forced to avoid law enforcement organizations and has had to regenerate and reequip itself continuously. This has given strength to the debate that al-Qaeda has declined as an organization, that its operational efficiency has decreased, and that the organization is no longer capable of carrying out large-scale attacks.[3] Some argue that the terrorist threat is now coming from other entities of the Global Jihad Movement—local Islamic groups, lone individuals, or small cells that though inspired by al-Qaeda evolve and work independently.[4]

This chapter argues that al-Qaeda has long existed as a formal organization with a solid structure, even though it has not always been based in a fixed or identifiable territory. We argue that al-Qaeda's infrastructure has enabled it to survive the U.S.-led "Global War on Terrorism" that followed al-Qaeda's 9/11 attacks in New York and Washington. We assert that only through this organizational layout was al-Qaeda able to regroup immediately, rehabilitate its chain of command and control by appointing suitable replacements, and thus continue its activity in the domestic (Afghanistan-Pakistan border zone) and international arenas.

Al-Qaeda exists first and foremost as a group possessing the characteristics of a guerrilla and terrorist organization. In recent years, it has inspired other entities to adopt its approach and has consolidated and propagated a central ideology. Counter to a recent trend among scholars and analysts to downplay al-Qaeda's role in the Global Jihad Movement, we continue to emphasize al-Qaeda as the dominant factor in the movement, as well as one of the main terrorist threats in the international arena.[5]

The Structure of Al-Qaeda

Scholars and analysts of Global Jihad have debated al-Qaeda's inner structure since the organization's inception. A central question is the extent to which al-Qaeda is limited to a functional role as an umbrella organization with loose ties between its internal branches, and as an inspirational source for other Islamist entities around the globe. As established in the introduction, although al-Qaeda-affiliated loose entities conduct prominent operational activities, al-Qaeda is still dominant as the center for all the operational activities of Global Jihad elements. Al-Qaeda is deeply involved in the operational activity of four out of the five most radical Islamic elements that are involved in terror attacks in the name of Global Jihad. The majority of the most devastating attacks internationally in recent years can be directly attributed to al-Qaeda.

To determine how al-Qaeda's operations will change over time, it is necessary to understand the internal structure and hierarchy of the organization since its establishment. This would be of particular interest to security and intelligence agencies that are concerned with operational countermeasures to dismantle al-Qaeda's organizational structure worldwide.

Al-Qaeda's internal structure and hierarchy was first exposed following the seizure of several documents in Afghanistan.[6] These documents have since been published in the Harmony database at West Point. It is not clear when, where, and by whom these documents were written. The cooperation between al-Qaeda and the Afghan Taliban, referred to in the text, dates these documents to a period after the return of al-Qaeda to Afghanistan from Sudan in 1996. These documents can be considered an al-Qaeda codex or protocol. The foundations for the hierarchy and organizational structure were laid down much earlier throughout a series of discussions by the senior leadership of al-Qaeda. Egyptian journalist Ahmad Mussa published a series of documents seized from Afghanistan in the Egyptian newspaper *Nahadat al-Misr.*[7] These documents de-

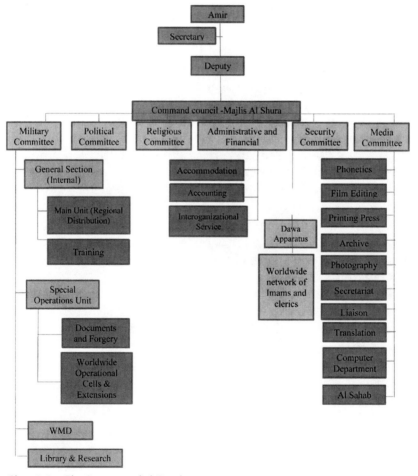

Chart 3.1. The Structure of al-Qaeda.

scribed al-Qaeda's early infrastructure, which then evolved into a fully fledged organizational structure. The information in the Harmony database at West Point and the documents published by Ahmad Mussa were supported and in some cases verified by the testimony of former al-Qaeda activist Jamal al-Fadl.[8] Based on these documents, the organizational structure and hierarchy of al-Qaeda is presented in the chart on the previous page.

The Amir

The Amir, or overall leader, holds direct responsibility over all of al-Qaeda's activities. The Amir represents both internal and external operations—inside and outside Afghanistan and since 2002 outside FATA. He possesses religious, operational, and logistical authority over al-Qaeda's activities. He is involved with operational, strategic, tactical, logistical, and organizational planning. The leader approves the annual work plan and budget, and is in charge of changing them according to new developments. He oversees the internal functions of the organization and is actively involved in the nominations, promotions, and manning of all senior positions in the organization.[9]

Bin Laden, the founder of al-Qaeda, was the organization's undisputed Amir throughout the years until he was killed by U.S. Special Forces on 1 May 2011. However, during the second half of the 2000s, there had been increasing indications of a decrease in bin Laden's dominance and position within the organization.[10] As a consequence, his deputy al-Zawahiri gained more authority within the organization and was selected to head the organization after bin Laden's death.[11] Nevertheless, until his death, bin Laden remained al-Qaeda's overall Amir.[12] After bin Laden's death Ayman al-Zawahiri became the overall Amir of al-Qaeda.

The Deputy

The deputy's characteristics should resemble those of the leader. His duties depend on what the leader entrusts to him.[13] Since the formation of the World Islamic Front for Jihad against the Jews and the Crusaders, a formal unification of several organizations dominated by al-Qaeda and to a lesser extent by the Egyptian Islamic Jihad (EIJ), Al Zawahiri served as deputy of al-Qaeda.[14] al-Zawahiri gained more authority, especially after the official merger between al-Qaeda and the EIJ and the establishment of Qaedat al-Jihad in June 2001.[15] In 2007–2008, Mustafa Abu Yazid a.k.a Sheikh Sai'd assumed responsibility for several utilities and tasks that were previously under the authority of al-Zawahiri, and was appointed as the overall leader in charge of Afghanistan.[16] This suggests that Yazid may have been the de facto deputy of al-Qaeda or "chief executive" of the organization. In May 2010, Yazid was killed in a U.S. drone strike in the North Waziristan Agency of FATA.[17] After bin Laden's death and the nomination of Ayman al-Zawahiri as the new leader of al-Qaeda, the burning question is who will be appointed as the new leader's deputy. The question is urgent especially since the United States and its allies also seek to remove Zawahiri.[18] Al-Qaeda veterans make up the leading candidates for the new deputy position, among whom Saif al-Adil is the most senior. He stayed in Iran in recent years and during 2010 returned to the organization's ranks in Pakistan.[19] Yet, after bin Laden's elimination on 1 May 2011 Saif and other leaders returned to Iran as a matter of precaution.[20]

The Secretary

The secretary is appointed by the Amir and is responsible for carrying out secretarial duties such as organizing the leader's appointments, external relations, and work schedule. The secretary accompanies the Amir wherever he goes.[21] It is not clear whether this position is currently occupied and by whom. It seems that Nassir al-Wuhayshi a.k.a Abu Bassir al-Yamani[22] was al-Qaeda's secretary during the 1990s.[23]

The Command Council

The Command Council (Majlis al-Shura) is the highest decision-making body of al-Qaeda. Nominated by the Amir, its members plan and supervise all aspects of the organization's activity. The Command Council consults the Amir throughout the decision-making process. It is considered the highest authority in the organization, excluding the leader and his deputy. The council consists of seven to ten members, chosen every second year by the leader, and assembles twice a month. The Command Council authorizes the organization's regulations and policies, work plan, and annual budget and elects the members of the organization's different committees.[24]

Even if the final decision is taken by the Amir, the Command Council fills a key role within the decision-making process of al-Qaeda, as well as in its day-to-day running. Only the most senior members of the organization can be part of it. The council is usually composed of committee leaders and only a select few sub-unit leaders. The following members had served as members of the Command Council at one stage or another:

Osama bin Laden served as the head of the Command Council.

Ayman al-Zawahiri served as a member of the Command Council.

Subhi Abd al-Aziz Abu Sita a.k.a. **Mohamed Atef** a.k.a. **Abu Hafs** was the former head of the Military Committee. He was from Egypt and was killed during the bombardment of Kandahar by U.S. forces in November 2001.[25]

Madani al-Tayyib a.k.a. **Abu Fadhel al-Makky** was the head of the Finance Committee of the organization. He is related to Osama bin Laden through marriage.[26] When al-Qaeda established headquarters in Sudan in the first half of the 1990s, he was involved with al-Qaeda's efforts to acquire nuclear capabilities.[27] Currently, he is most likely in Saudi custody.[28]

Muhammad Salah al-Din Abd al-Halim Zaydan a.k.a **Saif al-Adil** was the former head of the Security Committee of al-Qaeda. He replaced Atef as the head of the Military Committee after the latter's death.[29] He departed to Iran in 2003, most likely because of his criticism of Osama bin Laden's decisions regarding external operations.[30] Al-Adil was arrested by the Iranian authorities and has been under restraint or supervision by Iranian forces.[31] Early indications suggest al-Adil was released in early 2010 and went back to the Waziristan tribal region of Pakistan.[32] Recent reports suggest that by 2012 al-Adil was back in Iran.[33]

Suleiman Abu Gheith was the former al-Qaeda spokesman.[34] He departed to Iran in 2003 and was arrested by the Iranian authorities. Like al-Adil, early indications suggest that Abu Gheith was released from Iranian custody in 2010 and went back to the Waziristan tribal region of FATA in Pakistan.[35] During 2013 Gheith was arrested in Jordan and is currently held in US custody.[36]

Abdullah Ahmad Abdullah a.k.a. **Abu Mohamed al-Masri**[37] was a senior operational activist who supervised the attacks in Kenya and Tanzania in August 1998. He departed to Iran with other senior members of the organization in 2003 and was arrested by the Iranian authorities. Abu Mohamed al-Masri is still in Iranian custody.[38]

Mamdouh Mahmud Salim a.k.a. **Abu Hajer al-Iraqi**[39] was one of al-Qaeda's most senior figures during its early days. He is considered one of the founding fathers of the organization. Salim was arrested in Germany after the 1998 bombings in the Horn of Africa and is currently imprisoned in the United States.[40]

Nashwan Abdulrazaq Abdulbaqi a.k.a. **Abd al-Hadi al-Iraqi** was the former head of the general section (internal unit) of the Military Committee of al-Qaeda.[41] He was responsible for the military activity of the organization in the Afghanistan-Pakistan border zone.[42] Abd al-Hadi al-Iraqi was arrested in Turkey in 2006 and is in American custody.[43]

Mustafa al-Uzayti a.k.a. **Abu Faraj al-Libi** was probably the former head of the Military Committee, after Saif al-Adil's departure to Iran in 2003.[44] He was arrested in Mardan, Pakistan, by coalition forces in May 2005 and has been in U.S. custody since then.[45]

Mustafa Abu al-Yazid a.k.a. **Sheikh Sai'd al-Masri** is a senior al-Qaeda activist and the head of the Administrative and Financial Committee.[46] Yazid gained greater authority and probably holds some of the deputy's responsibilities. He became a kind of "chief executive (CEO)" of the committee. Yazid was killed by a U.S. drone attack in April 2010 in the Waziristan tribal region along the Afghanistan-Pakistan border.

Khalid Sheikh Mohamed (KSM) was the former head of al-Qaeda's Special Operations Unit, which was responsible for "external operations." He was the mastermind of the 9/11 attacks,[47] and was arrested in West Ridge, Rawalpindi, Pakistan on 28 February 2003.[48] He has been in American custody since then.

Khalid al-Shanqiti a.k.a. **Mahfouz Ould al-Walid** a.k.a **Abu Hafs al-Mauritani**, a senior al-Qaeda theologian, was the former head of the Religious Committee. He departed to Iran in 2003 with a group of senior al-Qaeda activists. al-Shanqiti was arrested by the Iranian authorities and in 2010 was among those released from Iranian custody and went back to Waziristan. Al-Shanqiti eventually left the region and went back to his home country of Mauritania.[49]

Khaled Habib was the former head of the general section (internal) of the Military Committee of al-Qaeda.[50] Appointed in the summer of 2005, Habib probably succeeded Abu Faraj al-Libi as the head of the overall Military Committee after Abu Faraj's arrest in May 2005.[51] Habib was killed in a U.S. drone attack in FATA in October 2008.[52]

Hamza Rabia, the former head of al-Qaeda's Special Operations Unit, was responsible for "external operations." Rabia succeeded KSM after the latter's arrest in February 2003.[53] Rabia was killed by a U.S. drone strike in FATA in December 2005.[54]

Abd al-Aziz al-Masri is probably Ali Sayyid Mohamed Mustafa al-Bakri, an al-Qaeda explosives and chemical expert.[55]

Abu al-Khair al-Masri a.k.a. **Abdullah Mohammed Rajab Abd al-Rahman** was the former leader of the Political Committee of al-Qaeda.[56] He departed to Iran and is currently in Iranian custody.

Abu Khalil al-Madani is one of the least known members of the Command Council. In July 2008, the al-Sahab Foundation, al-Qaeda's media wing, aired video footage titled "Commander Abu Al Hasan Jihad and Martyrdom," commemorating Abu Hassan who conducted a suicide attack in Afghanistan. al-Madani was among those who spoke about Abu Hassan and was referred to in the video as a member of the Command Council.[57] He remains at large.

Dr. Fadhel al-Masri was the most senior Egyptian al-Qaeda activist and belonged to the early formation of al-Qaeda. In recent years, he criticized al-Qaeda's methods, policy, and most of all, Ayman al-Zawahiri. Dr. Fadhel is currently in Egyptian custody.

Qaricept Qari al-Saeed al-Jazairy was a member of the Command Council. His exact role is unknown. He returned home to Algeria and assumed a leadership role in the Global Salafist Group for Preaching and Combat (GSPC), the forerunner of al-Qaeda in the Islamic Maghreb (AQIM).[58]

Jamal Ibrahim Ashtiwi al-Misrati a.k.a **Sheikh Atiyahallah** was an al-Qaeda senior operative of Libyan origin who joined the committee in 2008 and became the deputy to Sheikh Sai'd. Following Sai'd's death Atiyahallah replaced him and became the council's CEO. Atiyahallah was killed by a drone attack in Waziristan in August 2011.[59]

Abu Yahya al-Libi joined al-Qaeda in 2005 after escaping a U.S. prison in Bagram. Al-Libi was selected by Zawahiri to head the Religious Committee and was selected in 2010 as the deputy to Atiyahallah in the Command Council. Abu Yahya al-Libi was killed in a drone attack in the North Waziristan tribal region of Pakistan in May 2012.[60]

The Military Committee

The Military Committee is the body responsible for al-Qaeda's operational and military activity. This includes the mujahidin's military training as well as mental and physical preparation for combat. In addition, the Military Committee is responsible for the development of combat skills, technical military skills, and programs and procedures for the creation of a disciplined army based on readings of the Quran.[61] The leaders of the Military Committee, also known as al-Qaeda's "chiefs of staff," were:

- 1991–1996: **Ali Amin al-Rashidi** a.k.a. **Abu Ubeida Banshiri**, who was one of the founding fathers of al-Qaeda. Banshiri drowned in a ferry accident in Lake Victoria, Uganda, in 1996.[62]
- 1996–2001: **Mohamed Atef**, who was killed during a U.S. attack in Kandahar, Afghanistan.[63]
- 2001–2003: **Saif al-Adil**
- 2003–2005: **Abu Faraj al-Libi**
- 2006–2008: **Khaled Habib**

The Military Committee is composed of four sections:

1. The General Section
   i. The Main Unit
   ii. The Training Unit
2. The Special Operations Unit
   i. The Documentations Unit
3. The WMD Subunit
4. The Library and Research Section

1. **The General Section**—This unit is responsible for all aspects of the internal guerrilla war (inside Afghanistan and the Afghanistan-Pakistan border zone).[64] Until the coalition offensive in Afghanistan that followed the 9/11 attacks, all the activities of the general section were focused against the Afghan Northern Alliance. Since the beginning of the coalition offensive, the unit has been focused on fighting the coalition forces and the Pakistani army that is conducting military operations against al-Qaeda and its affiliated local terrorist organization in the Afghanistan-Pakistan border zone. The general section is composed of two different subunits:

    i. The Main Unit—This unit is responsible for the fighting itself and is subdivided according to the geographic sections of the battle zone.[65] Each regional section is commanded by a senior al-Qaeda operative who is responsible for all the military activities within his jurisdiction. Among these regional leaders were senior al-Qaeda figures such as Abu Layth al-Libi who was responsible for the Khost, Paktia, and Paktika Provinces of Pakistan.[66] He was killed in the spring of 2008.[67] Another regional commander, Abu Abdullah al-Muhajer[68] a.k.a. Muhsin Musa Matwali Atwa a.k.a. Abu Abd al-Rahman al-Muhajir, was involved in planning the attacks against U.S. embassies in east Africa in 1998.[69] Abu Ubeida al-Masri was in charge of Konar Province of Afghanistan until early 2006.[70] Al-Qaeda guerrilla operations in Afghanistan have always been conducted in collaboration with, and under the leadership of, the Afghan Taliban.[71]

    ii. The Training Unit—This smaller unit is responsible for the training of fighters and operates alongside the main unit.[72] This unit also operates in accordance with the geographical divisions of the battle zone. The leader of the training subcommittee was probably Abu Mohamed al-Masri until his departure to Iran in 2003.

    We do not have complete information regarding Al-Qaeda figures who served as head of the general section. It seems that Abd al-Hadi al-Iraqi held this position until 2005.[73] Abd al-Hadi al-Iraqi was replaced by Khaled Habib.[74] It is possible that during the fall of 2001 this position was held by Saif al-Adil.[75] The last leader of the main unit (internal) of the Military Committee was the Libyan Abdullah Sai'd,[76] who was killed in late 2009 in an American drone attack.[77]

2. **The Special Operations Unit**—This is a special and discrete apparatus that is responsible for external operations (outside Afghanistan and the Afghanistan-Pakistan border zone). The unit is in charge of the initiation of external operations and all aspects (operational and logistical) that

support these operations. The unit is responsible for the allocation of equipment and training as well as the identification of al-Qaeda members suitable for these kinds of operations.[78] Al-Qaeda's external operations are considered special operations. Under this rubric of special operations, al-Qaeda has dispatched operatives to establish sleeping cells (extensions) in target countries since late 1993. It seems that this unit is operating through different regional extensions around the world.[79] For example, Mohamed Odeh was sent to Kenya undercover as a businessman engaged in the fishing industry.[80] These extensions are probably subordinate to the major central command, which operates mostly from Pakistan's major cities.[81]

All the known al-Qaeda attacks in the international arena were planned and carried out by the Special Operations Unit through its worldwide extensions. Among those attacks are:

- The 11 September 2001 attacks in New York, Washington, and Pennsylvania.
- The truck bomb attack at a Jewish synagogue in Djerba, Tunisia in April 2002.[82]
- The attacks on two Jewish synagogues and the attacks on two British targets (HSBC bank's local headquarters and the British consulate) a week later in Istanbul, Turkey, in November 2003.
- The car bomb attack on an Israeli-owned hotel and the attack on an Israeli commercial flight using surface-to-air missiles in the Kenyan city of Mombasa in November 2002.
- The attack on a U.S. Marine base in Kuwait on 8 October 2002.[83]
- The attack on London's transportation system on 7 July 2005.[84]
- The attack on the Marriott Hotel in Islamabad in September 2008.[85]
- The attack on the Danish embassy in Pakistan in June 2008.[86]

In addition, al-Qaeda's Special Operations Unit planned numerous ambitious attempts to conduct "spectacular" attacks in the international arena. Below is a list of some of the most significant:

- An attempt to crash American Airlines Flight 63 from Paris to Miami, using explosives hidden in the shoes of a suicide passenger, Richard Reid, in December 2001.[87]
- An attempt to conduct a second wave of attacks—resembling the 9/11 attacks—against the United States' West Coast, Southeast Asia, and London's Heathrow Airport,[88] and the major oil terminal in Port Rashid, UAE, in the summer of 2002.[89]
- An attempt to carry out a radiological attack (a "dirty bomb") in the United States using an al-Qaeda member with U.S. citizenship, Jose Padilla, in early 2002.[90]
- An attempt to carry out simultaneous truck bomb attacks on seven Western targets in Singapore, including the American and Israeli embassies and the Australian and British high commissions. It was discovered in October 2001 and dismantled in January 2002.[91]
- The attempt to blow up seven or eight American and British commercial jets flying over the Atlantic in the summer of 2006.[92]
- A plot to attack New York's subway system by employing an Afghan immigrant, Najibullah Zazi, in 2009.[93]
- A plot to attack a New York City train system by employing an American-born Muslim convert, Bryan Vinas, in 2009.[94]
- An attempt to conduct a wave of attacks in northwest England in early 2010.[95]
- A plot to execute attacks in Norway using peroxide explosives in 2010.[96]

Al-Qaeda's Special Operations Unit was also involved with directing and financing attacks and attempted attacks conducted by other organizations, such as:

- The first Bali bombing in October 2002.
- The attack on the Marriott Hotel in Jakarta in August 2003.
- The attack on the Australian embassy in Jakarta in September 2004.

All the above mentioned attacks were carried out by the Jemaah Islamiyah (JI) of Southeast Asia.[97]

According to our assessment, the casing of a nuclear facility in Australia (2003) conducted by a Lashkar-e-Toyba (LeT) facilitator was part of an al-Qaeda Special Operations Unit plot.[98] The November 2008 attack in Mumbai could have been undertaken through cooperation between the LeT and the al-Qaeda Special Operations Unit.

Bin Laden's decision to implement external operations was made most likely in late 1997 to early 1998. It is possible that Abdullah Ahmad Abdullah a.k.a. Abu Mohamed al-Masri was the first head of this unit, given his deep involvement in the first al-Qaeda external operation that was launched in east Africa in August 1998.[99] At the end of 1998 or in early 1999, Khalid Sheikh Mohamed (KSM) was appointed as chief of the external unit and received the approval to plan the 9/11 attacks.[100] After KSM's arrest in February 2003, he was replaced by Hamza Rabia, who continued KSM's activity, which culminated in the London bombings on 7 July 2005. After Rabia was killed by U.S. forces in December 2005,[101] Abu Ubeida al-Masri became al-Qaeda chief of external operations.[102] In late 2007, Abu Ubeida al-Masri died of hepatitis[103] and was replaced by Abu Salah al-Somali. Abu Salah al-Somali, whose identity was elusive, probably operated under the name of Abu Hafez, and was killed in December 2009 by a U.S. drone attack in FATA.[104] Diverse reports suggest Adnan Shukrijuma a.k.a Jaffar al-Tayar (Pilot), a U.S. resident of Saudi origin and longtime al-Qaeda activist, has succeeded al-Somali. According to these reports, Shukrijuma, who is most likely a licensed pilot, is the current chief of al-Qaeda's Special Operations Unit.[105]

1. The Documentations Unit—This is a small unit operating within the Special Operations Unit and its members forge documents for al-Qaeda activists.[106]

The list of al-Qaeda activists that belonged at one time or another to the Special Operations Unit include:

- **Abdul Rahim Mohammed Abdullah al-Nashiri**, who was in charge of the al-Qaeda Special Operations Maritime Unit,[107] and was the head of the Arabian Peninsula extension. Nashiri was arrested in 2002 and is currently in U.S. custody.[108]

- **Rawfiq Mohammed Saleh Rashid bin Attash** a.k.a. **Khaled Bin Attash**,[109] who was a senior al-Qaeda activist and bin Laden's former bodyguard. He was the head of administration in the External Operations Unit.[110] He was deeply involved in the USS *Cole* attack in October 2000. Attash was arrested in Pakistan and handed over to U.S. forces.[111]

- **Mohamed Naim Noor Khan** a.k.a. **Abu Talha al-Pakistani**,[112] who was a computer expert and probably responsible for communication between the units' headquarters and the internationally deployed extensions.[113] Khan was arrested in 2004 and has been in custody since then.

- **Tariq Noor Mohamed** a.k.a. **Abu Talha al-Sudani**, one of al-Qaeda's founding fathers who was most likely the head of the east Africa extension.[114] Abu Talha al-Sudani was killed in Somalia by American forces in 2007.[115]

- **Dhiran Barot** a.k.a. **Abu Issa al-Hindi**, who was the former head of al-Qaeda's Special Operations extension in the United Kingdom.[116] Barot, who planned operations in the United States and the United Kingdom, was KSM's protégé.[117] Barot was arrested in 2004 by the British, and has been in British custody since then.

- **Ahmad Khalfan Ghaliani**,[118] an al-Qaeda activist from Tanzania, who was operationally involved in the attack against the American embassies in Kenya and Tanzania in August 1998. Ghaliani was arrested in Pakistan in August 2004 and was handed over to the U.S authorities.

- **Fahd Ali Msalem** a.k.a. **Usama al-Kini**, an al-Qaeda activist from Kenya who was operationally involved in the attack against the American embassy in Nairobi in August 1998.[119] He was probably the recent head of the Pakistani extension of al-Qaeda's Special Operations Unit. Al-Kini was in charge of the Marriott Hotel explosion in Islamabad in 2008 and was probably also in charge of the attack on the Danish embassy in Islamabad in that year.[120] Msalem was killed in a U.S. drone strike in 2009.[121]

- **Sheikh Ahmad Salim Sweidan,** another al-Qaeda activist from Kenya, who was operationally involved in the attack against the American embassy in Nairobi in August 1998.[122] Sweidan was killed along with Fahd Ali Msalem.[123]

- **Rashid Rauf,** who was probably the head of the British extension and might have succeeded Barot.[124] Rauf secured a prominent position within the external unit and was deeply involved with the unit's "Liquid plot" in 2006 as well as other plots to target the New York City train and subway systems and a communal plot to hit targets in northwest England in 2010.[125] His whereabouts are unknown.

- **Ali Abd al-Aziz Ali** a.k.a. **Amar al-Baluchi,** who is a relative of KSM and his right-hand man.[126] Al-Baluchi was arrested in Pakistan in 2003 and has been in U.S. custody since then.

- **Mustafa Ahmed Hawasawi**, who was a former member of al-Qaeda's media wing. He was the financial master of the 9/11 attacks and operated from the UAE through KSM's directives.[127] Hawasawi was arrested and is currently in U.S. custody.[128]

- **Sae'd Behaji**, who was another of KSM's assistants in the 9/11 plot.[129] He remains at large.

- **Esam Radwan al- Din** a.k.a. **Hambali**, who was the military chief of JI. He operated from Karachi through KSM's directives. Hambali was in charge of joint al-Qaeda–JI Southeast Asia operations.[130] Hambali was arrested in 2003 and has been in U.S. custody since then.

- **Amjad Farooqi**, who was a Pakistani member of the Special Operations Unit. He was probably the coordinator between al-Qaeda's Special Operations Unit and local Pakistani groups.[131] Farooqi was killed by the Pakistani forces in FATA on 26 September 2004.
- **Ramzi Binalshibh**, a Yemeni al-Qaeda activist, who was recruited in Germany.[132] He was part of the Hamburg cell from which al-Qaeda recruited three of the four pilots in the 9/11 attacks. He was senior assistant to KSM in the operational preparations for the 9/11 attacks. Binalshibh was arrested in 2002 in Karachi Pakistan and has been in U.S. custody since then.
2. **The WMD Subunit**—This is also called the Nuclear Weapons Section, and the tasks of this unit are unknown. It appears that this unit is responsible for all aspects of nonconventional warfare in the organization. Al-Qaeda launched several projects in order to develop nonconventional capabilities.[133] The head of this unit is most likely Abd al-Aziz al-Masri a.k.a. Ali Sayyid Mohamed Mustafa al-Bakri, an al-Qaeda explosives and chemical expert.[134]
3. **The Library and Research Section**: The duties and responsibilities of this section, which operates within the military wing of al-Qaeda, are unknown. There are no available details relating to the members of this unit.

The Political Committee

The Political Committee is responsible for spreading political awareness among working individuals and the erstwhile Islamic Emirate of Afghanistan, a reference to the Afghan Taliban regime. The committee liaises and interacts with jihad movements in general, preparing qualified political cadre for the organization's political activities conducted in accordance with Sharia law.[135] According to our assessment, Osama bin Laden and subsequently Abdullah Rajeb a.k.a. Abu Khair al-Masri might have been the successive chiefs of the Political Committee.[136] During 2014 the al-Qaeda representative that was sent to Syria in order to mediate between the jihadi groups engaged in the Syrian civil war, Sanafi al-Nasr, whose real name is Abdul Mohsin Abdullah Ibrahim Al Sharikh, led, according to U.S. official sources, al-Qaeda's "Victory Committee" (or Shura al-Nasr), which is responsible for developing and implementing al-Qaeda's strategy and policies which may suggest he is the current leader of al-Qaeda Political Committee.[137]

The Media Committee

The Media Committee, also known as the Information Committee, acts as a propaganda committee. It focuses on spreading jihadi ideology in the general Muslim population in cooperation with other affiliated groups in the Muslim world that possess similar ideologies (including the Taliban Movement). The committee contains a special computer department and several subunits, such as a unit in charge of editing movies, the secretariat, the printing press, foreign relations, the photography branch, the phonetics branch, the translation branch, and the archive branches.[138] One of the most important affiliations of this unit is the al-Sahab (meaning "The Cloud" in Arabic and sometimes written as "Assahab") Foundation for Islamic Media Publication, the media production house of al-Qaeda, used for the production of propaganda.[139]

The first head of the Media Committee was Abu Mosab Reuter.[140] This committee has always been an important committee, and senior members of al-Qaeda, logistical as well as operational activists, were members of the Media Committee at various points. For example, al-Qaeda's deputy Ayman al-Zawahiri was formerly the leader of the Media Committee, with KSM as his subordinate and the head of the al-Sahab Foundation.[141] KSM was later selected to be the head of the Media Committee, for some time in parallel to his role as chief of the Special Operations Unit.[142] One of the key facilitators of the 9/11 attacks, Mustafa Ahmad Hawasawi (the financial intermediary between the hijackers and KSM), was an active member of the Media Committee under KSM.[143] This committee remains important and it appears that senior members of the organization such as the American Adam Ghadahn and the German Bekkay Harasch belong to its ranks.[144] The current leader of the Information Committee is the Moroccan Muhammad Abayath a.k.a Abd al-Rahman al-Maghrebi.[145] Abayath is al-Zawahiri's son-in-law.[146]

The Administrative and Financial Committee

The Administrative and Financial Committee undertakes administrative services for al-Qaeda members and their families. The committee is responsible for creating the organization's financial policy and its implementation.[147] Mustafa Abu al-Yazid a.k.a. Sheikh Sai'd al-Masri was the head of this committee since the mid-1990s until his death in 2010.[148] A former bookkeeper from Alexandria, Sheikh Sai'd was a member of the Islamic Group of Egypt. He served as bin Laden's accountant in Sudan.[149] There are unverified reports that his predecessor was Abu Fadhl al-Makki.[150] Within the last few years, there have been numerous reports with regard to Sheikh Sai'd's position, suggesting that he had been promoted to "the overall in charge of Afghanistan."[151] Sheikh Sai'd seemed to have received several tasks and obligations of the deputy to the Amir. We believe that Sheikh Sai'd remained the head of the Administrative Committee in addition to his new responsibilities until he was killed by a U.S. drone attack in April 2010 and was replaced by Sheikh Atiya Abd al-Rahman, who was killed in August 2011 in the Pakistani tribal areas.[152]

The Administrative Committee is subdivided into three different subunits:

Accommodation Unit—responsible for welcoming guests at airports, providing accommodation in guesthouses, and religious studies for guests.[153]

Accounting Unit—responsible for the transfer of funds.[154]

Interorganizational Services Unit—responsible for providing the necessary services for the well-being of members and their families. These services include health care, the organization's store, education, auto repairs, and housing and utilities.[155]

The Security Committee

The Security Committee provides personal security services to senior leaders. It prevents information leaks and conducts counterespionage activities to prevent infiltration of the ranks of the organization. The Special Security Chamber is responsible for the supervision, classification, and collection of information regarding each person who wishes to join the organization.[156] One of the former leaders of the Security Committee was senior al-Qaeda leader Muhammad Salah al-Din Abd al-Halim Zaydan a.k.a Saif al-Adil, who in fact was the committee leader from day one.[157] A former colonel in the Egyptian army, al-Adil was known for identifying and neutralizing spies. The Security Committee seems to be responsible for recruiting new activists. It seems that al-Qaeda's Special Operations extensions operated alongside the Dawa apparatus responsible for preaching jihadi ideology and most likely recruiting new members. The Dawa apparatus is most likely subordinate to the Security Committee, in order to prevent infiltration by Western intelligence agencies.[158]

The Religious Committee

The Religious (Fatwa or Law) Committee reviews Islamic law and decides if particular courses of action conform to the law.[159] The former leader of the Religious committee was most likely Khaled al-Shanqiti a.k.a. Abu Hafs al-Mauritani, who was released in 2010 after a long detention in Iran and moved to the Waziristan tribal region of Pakistan,[160] and from there made his way back to his home country of Mauritania.[161] The recent head of the Fatwa (Religious) Committee was Abu Yahia al-Libi,[162] until his elimination by an American drone attack in June 2012.[163]

Mobilization

Al-Qaeda maintains its formal structure by providing flexibility within the strict hierarchical system, which allows for mobilization within its ranks. This has enabled the movement of members between different committees and units at short notice, which is necessary in the event of sudden arrests and eliminations. There is mobility between the Media Committee and the Special Operations Unit.

While inner mobilization within the Military Committee (for example, Abu Ubeida al-Masri used to be a regional field commander in the Afghanistan-Pakistan border area before he became the head of the Special Operations Unit) seems to be logical (operational positions), it is unlikely that there would be personnel movement between noncombatant positions such as the Media Committee and the Special Operations Unit. However, several senior al-Qaeda members, such as Mohammad Hawasawi and KSM, have moved from the Media Committee to the Special Operations Unit. This shows that there is significant similarity in the qualifications needed for participation in these two different committees. An understanding of Western mentality and behavior is a prerequisite for operating in the two committees because the majority of al-Qaeda operatives and members are from the Middle East.[164]

Hence, we recommend placing high supervision on present senior members of the Media Committee, such as Adam Ghadahn and Muhammad Abayath a.k.a Abd al-Rahman al-Maghrebi, who might become external operational planners in the near future.

Al-Qaeda Leadership in Iran

The U.S.-led coalition offensive in Afghanistan resulted in the creation of a small and very senior al-Qaeda leadership group in Iran seeking to establish a safe haven. Even though there is an ingrained rivalry between the Shiite majority in Iran and the predominantly Sunni al-Qaeda, the two groups have been able to tactically cooperate on a basic level. Following strong U.S. pressure on the Iranian regime, these senior al-Qaeda figures have been placed under low-level Iranian custody, which provides some level of supervision, while allowing some level of freedom for activity. Some of the most senior figures are now based in Iran, including former heads of al-Qaeda committees and members of the Command Council. Since al-Qaeda lost many senior members in recent years, its key priority is the release of the al-Qaeda leadership under custody in Iran.[165] Varied reports accumulated during 2010–2011 suggested a pact between al-Qaeda and Iran which includes the release of several of the detained al-Qaeda leaders, among them Saif al-Adil, Suleiman Abu Gheith,[166] and Khalid al-Shanqiti (Abu Hafs al-Mauritani).[167] Yet, several of those released leaders were probably sent back to Iran as a measure of security following the death of Osama bin Laden on 1 May 2011.[168]

At any rate the al-Qaeda members who were held in custody in Iran most likely include:

Saif al-Adil—the former head of the Military and Security Committees in Al Qaeda and a member of the Command Council.

Abu Hafs al-Mauritani—the former head of the Religious Committee and a member of the Command Council.

Abu al-Khair—probably the former head of the Political Committee and a member of the Command Council.

Abdullah Ahmad Abdullah—senior al-Qaeda operational activist; may have served as the head of the Special Operations Unit in 1998.[169]

Saad bin Laden—the son of Osama bin Laden.[170] Died in 2010.[171]

Suleiman Abu Gheith—al-Qaeda spokesman and member of the Command Council.[172]

Conclusion and Assessment

Al-Qaeda suffered major setbacks in recent years as a result of the U.S.-led coalition's offensive in Afghanistan. It survived and regenerated in the Pakistani tribal area along the Pak-Afghan border region known as FATA. The organization has been able to adapt and preserve most of its formal infrastructure. Al-Qaeda's important committees continue to operate under a command cadre (hierarchical) structure, which suits the organization's goals more than a network-based structure. According to our assessment, al-Qaeda's strict hierarchy and precise organizational structure has protected the organization from collapse. The nature of this structure enables it to fill positions quickly and rehabilitate its chain of command, hence sustaining its operational and logistical performance. Since the coalition's offensive in Afghanistan in October 2001, al-Qaeda has lost four chiefs of staff (heads of the Military Committee), four chiefs of the Special Operations Unit, and at least half a dozen senior regional field commanders ("generals"). Yet, it was still able to regroup and mobilize suitable replacements from within.

After the elimination of its legendary leader Osama bin Laden by U.S. Special Forces in May 2011, al-Zawahiri-led al-Qaeda has adopted a more directorate position within the entire Global Jihad Movement. Even though in recent years, and especially with regard to Iraq and Syria, the pronouncements expressed by Zawahiri seeks to exercise control if not influence the conduct of campaigns. Subsequently, al-Qaeda directly and indirectly has been able to continue its activity and maintain its status as one of the major terrorist threats to Western forces in the current jihad arenas (Afghanistan and Iraq) and the broader international arena.

Notes

1. A version of this chapter has been published previously as Rohan Gunaratna and Aviv Oreg, "Al Qaeda's Organizational Structure and Its Evolution," *Studies in Conflict & Terrorism* Vol. 33, No. 12 (2010), pp. 1043–78.

2. For the Bruce Hoffman and Marc Sageman debate, see Bruce Hoffman, "The Myth of Grass-roots Terrorism," *Foreign Affairs* May–June 2008, http://www.foreignaffairs.com/articles/63408/bruce hoffman/the-myth-of-grass-roots-terrorism, accessed 21 May 2012.

3. Ibid. While Sageman does not regard al-Qaeda as the most important player, Hoffman does.

4. Same as previous footnote comment.

5. Refer to Marc Sageman's work, which emphasizes more the role of remote terror networks over the organized, structured al-Qaeda within the Global Jihad terror performance. Marc Sageman, *Leaderless Jihad: Terror Networks in the Twenty-First Century*, Philadelphia: University of Pennsylvania Press, 2008; Sageman, *Understanding Terror Networks*, Philadelphia: University of Pennsylvania Press, 2004.

6. "Al Qaeda Goals and Structure," Combating Terrorism Center at West Point, NY: Harmony Project, USMA, 14 February 2006, http://www.ctc.usma.edu/aq/pdf/AFGP-2002-000078-Trans.pdf, accessed 27 February 2012;"Interior Organization," Combating Terrorism Center at West Point, NY: Harmony Project, USMA, 14 February 2006, http://www.ctc.usma.edu/aq/pdf/AFGP-2002-000080-Trans.pdf, accessed 27 February 2012.

7. Ahmad Mussa, "Cairo Papers Exclusive of 10 Episodes of Handwritten Al Qaeda Documents," *Nahadat Misr in Arabic*, 11 September 2004, p. 3.

8. *United States of America vs. Usama Bin Laden, et al.* 2001 WL 102338 (S.D.N.Y. 6 February 2001) (No. S [7] 98 CR 1023 LBS), http://www.elastic.org/~fche/mirrors/cryptome.org/usa-v-ubl-02.htm, pp. 292–93, accessed 29 February 2012.

9. "Interior Organization," Combating Terrorism Center at West Point.

10. Numerous unverified reports concerning bin Laden's medical situation suggest that he suffered from diabetes and severe kidney malfunction, for which he received dialysis treatment on a short-term basis. See for example Thomas W. Gillespie, John A. Agnew, Erika Mariano, Scott Mossler, Nolan Jones, Matt Braughton, Jose Gonzalez, "Finding Osama bin Laden: An Application of Biogeographic Theories and Satellite Imagery." *MIT International Review* (2009), p. 3.

Bin Laden also disappeared almost completely from the media. In the years prior to his death, he conducted several audio addresses and only one video address, compared to numerous video and audio appearances in the years before.

11. A letter sent by al-Zawahiri to Abu Musab al-Zarqawi in 2005 suggests that bin Laden was not very involved with the making of Al Qaeda policy and that al-Zawahiri's influence had increased as his supporters gained senior positions within the organization. In addition, the majority of al-Qaeda's public statements in those years (2004–2009) were made by al-Zawahiri. See Ayman al-Zawahiri, "Zawahiri's Letter to Zarqawi," Combating Terrorism Center at West Point, 11 October

2005, http://www.ctc.usma.edu/wp-content/uploads/2010/08/CTC-Zawahiri-Letter-10-05.pdf,, accessed 21 May 2012.

12. Ronald Sandee, "Al-Qaida and Europe: The Case of the German-Pakistani Aleem Nasir," *NEFA Foundation* (June 2009), http://www.nefafoundation.org/miscellaneous/FeaturedDocs/nefa_AleemNasir-Network0609.pdf, accessed 1 March 2012, p. 3.

13. "Interior Organization," Combating Terrorism Center at West Point.

14. Egyptian Islamic Jihad is an Egyptian terrorist organization that operated in Egypt through the 1980s and 1990s and joined forces with al-Qaeda in Afghanistan. Its leader throughout its existence was Ayman al-Zawahiri.

15. U.S. Department of State, Office of the Coordinator for Counterterrorism, *Country Reports on Terrorism 2004*, Washington, DC, April 2005, p. 107.

16. Sandee, "Al-Qaida and Europe . . . ," p. 4.

17. Declan Walsh, "Afghanistan Head of al-Qaida 'Killed in Pakistan Drone Strike,'" *The Guardian*, 1 June 2010, http://www.guardian.co.uk/world/2010/jun/01/al-qaida-afghanistan-killed-pakistan-drone, accessed 1 March 2012.

18. Aviv Oreg and Yoram Schweitzer, "The Death of Bin Laden and the Future of al-Qaeda," *INSS Insight*, No. 256, 15 May 2011, p. 3.

19. Ibid.

20. Report on al-Qaeda in Iran, Global Pathfinder 2 Database, International Centre for Political Violence and Terrorism Research, Singapore, 20 July 2012.

21. "Interior Organization," Combating Terrorism Center at West Point.

22. Abu Bassir al-Yamani is currently the head of al-Qaeda in the Arabian Peninsula (AQAP). See Abdul Hameed Bakier, "Al Qaeda Leaders in the Arabian Peninsula Speak Out," *Terrorism Focus*, Vol. 6 Issue 3 (28 January 2009), http://www.jamestown.org/single/?no_cache=1&tx_ttnews%5Btt_news%5D=34420, accessed 1 March 2012.

23. "Abu Basir al-Yemeni," *GlobalSecurity.org*, 1 November 2006, http://www.globalsecurity.org/security/profiles/abu_basir_al-yemeni.htm, accessed 1 March 2012; Jane Novak, "Arabian Peninsula Al Qaeda Groups Merge," *The Long War Journal*, 26 January 2009, http://www.longwarjournal.org/archives/2009/01/arabian_peninsula_al.php, accessed 1 March 2012; Jane Novak, "New al-Qaeda Leader in Yemen?" *Armies of Liberation*, 24 June 2007, http://armiesofliberation.

com/archives/2007/06/24/new-al-qaeda-leader-in-yemen/, accessed 1 March 2012.

24. "Interior Organization," Combating Terrorism Center at West Point.

25. "Mohammed Atef," *GlobalSecurity.org*, 1 November 2006, http://www.globalsecurity.org/security/profiles/mohammed_atef.htm, accessed 1 March 2012.

26. J. Millard Burr and Robert O. Collins, "Searching for Friends, Surrounded by Enemies," *Revolutionary Sudan: Hasan al-Turabi and the Islamist State, 1989–2000*, Leiden: Brill, 2003, p. 219.

27. *United States of America vs. Usama Bin Laden, et al.* 2001 WL 102338 (S.D.N.Y. 6 February 2001) (No. S(7) 98 CR 1023 LBS).

28. "Abu Fadhl al-Makkee," *GlobalSecurity.org*, 1 November 2006, http://www.globalsecurity.org/security/profiles/abu_fadhl_al-makkee.htm, accessed 1 March 2012.

29. Vahid Brown, "Sayf al-'Adl and al-Qa'ida's Historical Leadership," *Jihadica*, 18 May 2011, http://www.jihadica.com/sayf-al-adl-and-al-qaidas-historical-leadership/, accessed 21 May 2012.

30. "Al Adl Letter," Combating Terrorism Center at West Point, NY: Harmony Project, 2006, http://www.ctc.usma.edu/aq/pdf/Al%20Adl%20Letter_Translation.pdf, accessed 7 March 2012.

31. "Iran: Top Al Qaeda Leader Arrested," *Stratfor*, 28 May 2003.

32. Syed Saleem Shahzad, "How Iran and al-Qaeda Made a Deal," *Asia Times Online* 30 April 2010, http://www.atimes.com/atimes/South_Asia/LD30Df01.html, accessed 7 March 2012.

33. Report on al-Qaeda in Iran, Global Pathfinder 2 Database, International Centre for Political Violence and Terrorism Research, Singapore, 20 July 2012.

34. Even though there is no clear evidence of Abu Gheith's position within the Command Council, it seems that he had a significant role in the internal dispute between al-Qaeda senior leaders over the 9/11 attacks. Abu Gheith's ability to express his thoughts in objection to bin Laden's approach contributes to our understanding of Abu Gheith's role within the Command Council. The National Commission on Terrorist Attacks Upon the United States, *The 9/11 Commission Report: Final Report of the National Commission on Terrorist Attacks Upon the United States (9/11 Report)* New York: Norton, 2004, p. 251, web (hereafter referred to as *The 9/11 Report*).

35. Thomas Joscelyn, "Osama bin Laden's Spokesman Freed by Iran," *The Long War Journal*, 28 September 2010, http://www.longwar

journal.org/archives/2010/09/osama_bin_ladens_spo.php, accessed 7 March 2012.

36. Report on al-Qaeda in Iran, Global Pathfinder 2 Database, International Centre for Political Violence and Terrorism Research, Singapore, 20 July 2012.

37. *United States of America vs. Usama Bin Laden, et al.*, Indictment No. S(9) 98 Cr. 1023 (S.D.N.Y. 1999), http://cns.miis.edu/pubs/reports/pdfs/binladen/indict.pdf, accessed 7 March 2012, p. 7.

38. Report on al-Qaeda in Iran, Global Pathfinder 2 Database, International Centre for Political Violence and Terrorism Research, Singapore, 20 July 2012.

39. Ibid.

40. "Mamdouh Mahmud Salim," *GlobalSecurity.org*, 1 November 2006, http://www.globalsecurity.org/security/profiles/mamdouh_mahmud_salim.htm, accessed 8 March 2012.

41. Bill Roggio, "Senior Al Qaeda Operative Abd al-Hadi al-Iraqi captured," *The Longwar Journal*, 27 April 2007, http://www.longwar journal.org/archives/2007/04/senior_al_qaeda_oper.php, accessed 8 March 2012.

42. "United States of America v. Abdul Zahir," United States Department of Defense, January 2006, http://www.defenselink.mil/news/Jan2006/d20060120zahir.pdf, accessed 8 March 2012.

43. "Abdul Hadi al-Iraqi," *GlobalSecurity.org*, 28 April 2007, http://www.globalsecurity.org/security/profiles/abdul_hadi_al-iraqi.htm, accessed 8 March 2012.

44. See Amar al-Baluchi biography in Office of the Director of National Intelligence, United States Department of Defense, "Detainee Biographies," Washington, DC: Office of the Director of National Intelligence, 2006, http://www.odni.gov/announcements/content/DetaineeBiographies.pdf, p. 1, accessed 8 March 2012.

45. "Abu Faraj al-Libbi," *GlobalSecurity.org*, 11 July 2011, http://www.globalsecurity.org/military/world/para/al-libbi.htm, accessed 8 March 2012.

46. "Shaikh Saiid al-Masri," *GlobalSecurity.org*, 24 October 2006, http://www.globalsecurity.org/security/profiles/shaikh_saiid_al-masri.htm, accessed 8 March 2012.

47. Office for the Administrative Review of the Detention of Enemy Combatants (OARDEC), "Verbatim Transcript of Combatant Status Review Tribunal Hearing for ISN 10024 (Khaled Sheikh Mohamed)," United States Department of Defense, http://www.defenselink.mil/news/transcript_ISN10024.pdf, accessed 8 March 2012.

48. Colonel Khalid Hussein, ISI officer heading the team that arrested Khalid Sheikh Mohamed, personal interview, March 2003.

49. Thomas Joscelyn, "Senior al Qaeda Ideologue Leaves Iran for Mauritania," Long War Journal, 11 April 2012 at http://www.longwarjournal.org/archives/2012/04/senior_al_qaeda_ideo.php#ixzz25 aP8JSDI.

50. "US Attack Killed Al-Qaida Leader's Kin," *The China Daily*, 13 February 2006, http://www.chinadaily.com.cn/english/doc/2006-02/13/content_519567.htm, accessed 8 March 2012. Other activists who held the same position before were, as a result of their position, also members of the Command Council. According to our assessment, since Habib held a senior position in al-Qaeda, he was probably also a member of the council.

51. Habib's role as head of the overall Military Committee is indicated in an As Sahab Foundation (al-Qaeda's media wing) publication commemorating an al-Qaeda martyr in Afghanistan, in which Habib was referred to as the commander of military operations. See "Qaida Al-Jihad (As-Sahab): Commander Abu Al-Hasan Jihad And Martyrdom," 10 July 2008, http://theunjustmedia.com:80/clips/afgha/July08/abu/abu3.htm, accessed 8 March 2012.

52. Ronald Sandee, "Core Al-Qaida in 2008: A Review," *The NEFA Foundation*, 8 April 2009, http://www.nefafoundation.org/miscella neous/FeaturedDocs/nefa_AQin2008.pdf, p. 3, accessed 8 March 2012.

53. Sandee, "Al Qaida and Europe . . .," p. 4.

54. "Abu Hamza Rabia," *GlobalSecurity.org*, 11 July 2011, http://www.globalsecurity.org/military/world/para/hamza-rabia.htm, accessed 8 March 2012. According to our assessment, since Hamza Rabia held a senior position in al-Qaeda, he was probably also a member of the council.

55. "Abd al-Aziz al-Masri," *GlobalSecurity.org*, 9 November 2006, http://www.globalsecurity.org/security/profiles/abd_al-aziz_al-masri.htm, accessed 4 March 2012.

56. "Abu Khayr," *GlobalSecurity.org*, 1 November 2006, http://www.globalsecurity.org/security/profiles/abu_khayr.htm, accessed 6 March 2012.

57. "Qaida Al-Jihad (As-Sahab): Commander Abu Al-Hasan Jihad And Martyrdom," 10 July 2008 at http://theunjustmedia.com/clips/afgha/July08/abu/abu.htm.

58. Lawrence Wright, "Paradise Lost," *The Looming Tower: Al-Qaeda and the Road to 9/11*, New York: Knopf, 2006, p. 189.

In addition to the above-mentioned figures of al-Qaeda's leadership, Jamal Ahmed al-Fadl, a former senior al-Qaeda operative, mentioned in his testimony more names of activists that were members of the Command Council at one point or another. The current position and whereabouts of these activists are unknown. They are Abu Faraj al-Yamani, Abu Ayoub al-Iraqi, Khalifa al-Muskat al-Omany, Saif al-Libi, and Abu Burhan al-Iraqi. See *United States of America vs. Usama bin Laden, et al.*, 2001 WL 102338 (S.D.N.Y. 6 February 2001) (No. S(7) 98 CR 1023 LBS), p. 205.

59. Bill Roggio, "Al Qaeda Announces Death of Atiyah Abd al Rahman," at http://www.longwarjournal.org/archives/2011/12/al_qaeda_announces_d.php.

60. Bill Roggio "Abu Yahya al Libi Killed in Latest Drone Strike, U.S. Officials Say," at http://www.longwarjournal.org/archives/2012/06/abu_yahya_al_libi_ru.php.

61. "Al Qaeda Goals and Structure," Combating Terrorism Center at West Point.

62. "Abu Obadiah al-Banshiri," *GlobalSecurity.org*, 1 November 2006, http://www.globalsecurity.org/security/profiles/abu_ubaidah_al-banshiri.htm, accessed 8 March 2012.

63. "Mohammed Atef."

64. "Al Qaeda Goals and Structure," Combating Terrorism Center at West Point.

65. Ibid.

66. Craig Whitlock and Munir Ladaa, "Al-Qaeda's New Leadership," *The Washington Post*, 2006, http://www.washingtonpost.com/wp-srv/world/specials/terror/laith.html#profile, accessed 8 March 2012.

67. Claude Salhani, "Jihad Turning Point?" *The Washington Times*, 5 February 2008, http://www.washingtontimes.com/article/20080205/COMMENTARY/189195617/1012/commentary, republished in *FrontPageMag.Com*, 7 February 2008, http://www.frontpagemagazine.com/readArticle.aspx?ARTID=29823, accessed 8 March 2012.

68. Jamie Glazov, "Symposium: Al-Qaeda's Central Leadership," *Front Page* magazine at http://frontpagemagazine.com/readArticle.aspx?ARTID=31375 .

69. Henry Schuster, "One of FBI's 'Most Wanted Terrorists' Confirmed Dead," *CNN*, 24 October 2006, http://edition.cnn.com/2006/WORLD/asiapcf/10/24/alqaeda.operative/index.html, accessed 21 May 2012.

70. "Pakistan: 'Top Security Sources' Reveal Al-Qa'ida Links of Attacked Seminary," *WNC: The News,* 1 November 2006, http://dlib.eastview.com/browse/doc/10306515, accessed 5 March 2012; "Pakistan Court Drops British Airline Plot Terror Charge," *Agence France-Presse,* 13 December 2006. Abu Ubeida al-Masri was a regional commander in the Afghanistan-Pakistan border zone. He was probably the external operations chief since early 2006, most likely following the elimination of the former head of the unit, Hamza Rabia. See "Abu Obadiah al-Masri," *Global Security.org,* 3 November 2006, http://www.globalsecurity.org/security/profiles/abu_obaidah_al-masri.htm, accessed 5 March 2012.

71. "Mustafa Abu al-Yazid's Interview on al-Jazeera," *The NEFA Foundation,* 22 June 2009, http://www.nefafoundation.org/miscellaneous/FeaturedDocs/nefa_yazidqa0609.pdf, pp. 2–4, accessed 8 March 2012.

72. "Al Qaeda Goals and Structure," Combating Terrorism Center at West Point.

73. Detainee biography of Abd al-Hadi al-Iraqi, United States Department of Defense, 27 April 2007, accessed 22 February 2012. It is most likely that bin Laden wanted to redeploy al-Iraqi to his homeland arena, probably to promote al-Qaeda central leadership interests in Iraq and vis-à-vis the semiautonomous al-Zarqawi.

74. "Khalid Habib," *GlobalSecurity.org,* 1 Nov 2006, http://www.globalsecurity.org/security/profiles/khalid_habib.htm, accessed 8 March 2012; Sandee, "Core Al-Qaida in 2008: A Review," p. 8.

75. The fact that al-Adil was nominated as the chief of the Military Committee immediately after Mohamed Atef's death suggests he was a senior member within the Military Committee at that time, perhaps as the head of the general section.

76. Sheikh Abdullah Saeed, "Signs of Victory Are Looming Over Afghanistan," *Global Islamic Media Front Publication,* http://223.25.242.81/showthread.php?p=12062 (expired link); republished at *WorldAnalysis.net,* 12 May 2009, http://worldanalysis.net/modules/news/article.php?storyid=629, accessed 24 June 2012.

77. "Mustafa Abu al-Yazid: 'Infiltrating the American Fortresses,'" *The NEFA Foundation,* 31 December 2009, http://www.nefafoundation.org/miscellaneous/nefaAbul-Yazid0110.pdf, accessed 8 March 2012.

78. "Al Qaeda Goals and Structure," Combating Terrorism Center at West Point.

79. The basic foundations for this kind of external operation were laid out in a preliminary paper concerning al-Qaeda's future activity,

policy, and tactics. According to our assessment, this paper was presented for discussion very close to the end of the Afghan war. In the years that followed, CeifiT observed many of the characteristics laid down in this paper manifested in al-Qaeda's activities. One of these is the establishment of regional extensions. See Mussa, "Cairo papers," pp. 1–2.

80. *United States of America vs. Usama Bin Laden, et al.* (S.D.N.Y. 28 February 2001) (No. S(7) 98 CR 1023 LBS), http://cryptome.org/usa-v-ubl-12.htm, accessed 22 February 2012, p. 1652.

81. In order to conduct and control operational activity in the international arena, al-Qaeda's Special Operations Unit needed means of control and accessibility such as airport access, nearby travel agencies, stable communication lines, access to international banking facilities, and stable Internet access. Therefore, unlike other al-Qaeda bodies, which operated solely in Afghan territory or the Afghanistan/Pakistan border zone, the Special Operations Unit probably operated mostly from major Pakistani cities such as Karachi, Lahore, Islamabad, and Gujarat.

82. Matthew Levitt, "KSM in Custody," *National Review Online*, 5 March 2003, old.nationalreview.com/comment/comment-levitt030503.asp; republished in *The Washington Institute for Near East Policy*, http://washingtoninstitute.org/print.php?CID=467&template=C06, accessed 8 March 2012.

83. For the full list of al-Qaeda's Special Operations Unit attacks and plots during Khalid Sheikh Mohamed's time as chief of external operations, see OARDEC, "Verbatim Transcript of . . . ISN 10024 (Khaled Sheikh Mohamed)," at http://www.defense.gov/news/transcript_isn10024.pdf, pp 18–19.

84. The 7/7 attacks in London were conducted when Hamza Rabia was the head of this unit. Al Qaeda's leadership publicly claimed responsibility for the attack. Digger, "Al-Qaeda Claims London Train Bombing In Video," *Diggers Realm*, 1 September 2005, http://www.diggersrealm.com/mt/archives/001189.html, accessed 13 March 2012.

85. "Usama Al Kini Head of Al Qaeda in Pakistan Killed by US Military," *Times Online*, 9 January 2009, http://npsglobal.org/eng/index.php/news/29-non-state-actors/370-usama-al-kini-head-of-al-qaeda-in-pakistan-killed-by-us-military.html, accessed 15 February 2012.

86. "Geo News Exclusive Interview with Sheikh Saeed Al Qaeda Leader," *Geo Television Network*, http://www.geo.tv/program_archive/SheikhSaeedInterview_e.asp, accessed 15 February 2012.

87. "Richard Reid Pleads Guilty," *CNN*, 22 January 2003, http://edition.cnn.com/2002/LAW/10/04/reid.guilty.plea/index.html, accessed 15 February 2012.

88. Britta Sandberg and Holger Stark, "Terror Plot: How al-Qaida Planned to Bomb Heathrow," *Spiegel Online (International)* 26 Apr 2011, http://www.spiegel.de/international/europe/0,1518,758973,00.html, accessed 15 February 2012.

89. Department of Defense, Joint Task Force Guantanamo, *Detainee Assessment Brief ICO Guantanamo Detainee, ISN US9YM-001453DP (S)*, 8 July 2008, pp. 4, 6.

90. "Authorities Arrest Alleged Terrorist; 'Dirty Bomb': Officials Accuse Chicago Man of Plotting to Spread Radioactive Material," *The Telegraph Herald*, 11 June 2002, front section, p. A1; Brian Knowlton, "Padilla Is Convicted on All Counts in U.S. Terror Trial," *The New York Times*, 16 August 2007, http://www.nytimes.com/2007/08/16/world/americas/16iht-terror.5.7148986.html, accessed 15 February 2012.

91. Ministry of Foreign Affairs, Singapore, "MFA Press Statement on the Request for Addition of Jamaah Islamiyah to the List of Terrorists Maintained by the UN," 24 October 2002, http://app.mfa.gov.sg/internet/press/view_press_print.asp?post_id=714, accessed 29 February 2012 (See section "Association with Al-Qaeda").

92. "Top Al Qaeda Leader Abu Ubeida al-Masri Confirmed Dead in Pakistan," *FoxNews.com*, 9 April 2008, http://www.foxnews.com/story/0,2933,348668,00.html, accessed 10 March 2012.

93. Jerry Markon, "Al-Qaeda Leaders Said to Have Ordered Attack on New York Subway System," *The Washington Post*, 24 April 2010, http://www.washingtonpost.com/wp-dyn/content/article/2010/04/23/AR2010042302807.html, accessed 29 February 2012.

94. Nic Robertson and Paul Cruickshank, "Recruits Reveal al Qaeda's Sprawling Web," *CNN*, 31 July 2009, http://edition.cnn.com/2009/CRIME/07/30/robertson.al.qaeda.full/index.html, accessed 29 February 2012.

95. Duncan Gardham and Gordon Rayner, "Arrest of 'Easter Bombers' Led to International al-Qaeda Network," *The Telegraph*, 18 May 2010, http://www.telegraph.co.uk/news/uknews/terrorism-in-the-uk/7738026/Arrest-of-Easter-bombers-led-to-international-al-Qaeda-network.html, accessed 29 February 2012.

96. Thomas Hegghamer and Dominic Tierney, "Why Does Al-Qaeda Have a Problem With Norway?," *The Atlantic*, 13 July 2010,

http://www.theatlantic.com/international/archive/2010/07/why-does-al-qaeda-have-a-problem-with-norway/59649/, accessed 29 February 2012.

97. OARDEC, "Verbatim transcript of . . . ISN 10024 (Khaled Sheikh Mohamed)," at http://www.defense.gov/news/transcript_isn10024.pdf, p. 18.

98. Attorney-General's Department, "Lashkar-e-Toyba," *Australian National Security*, 8 November 2010, http://www.ema.gov.au/agd/WWW/nationalsecurity.nsf/Page/What_Governments_are_doing_Listing_of_Terrorism_Organisations_Lashkar-e-Tayyiba, accessed 21 February 2012.

99. "East Africa Embassy Bombers," *GlobalSecurity.org*, 1 November 2006, http://www.globalsecurity.org/security/profiles/east_africa_embassy_bombers.htm, accessed 21 February 2012.

100. *The 9/11 Report*, pp. 149–50.

101. Craig Whitlock and Kamran Khan, "Blast in Pakistan Kills Al Qaeda Commander; Figure Reportedly Hit by U.S. Missile Strike," *The Washington Post*, 4 December 2005, final ed., p. A.01.

102. Several reports suggest Abu Ubeida al-Masri was responsible for the air plot in the summer of 2006. See for example "Terror Analysis: Al-Qaeda's Special Operations Unit," *CeifiT* 10 April 2008, http://www.ceifit.com/?categoryId=27211&itemId=40843, accessed 10 March 2012.
Ubeida's former position within the organization was regional leader along the Afghan-Pakistan border of the general section (internal). "Abu Obadiah al-Masri."

103. Craig Whitlock and Karen De Young, "Senior Al-Qaeda Commander Believed to Be Dead," *The Washington Post*, 10 April 2008, p. 10.

104. It seems that Abu Salah al-Somali used the alias Abu Hafiz, who was referred to as the head of the Special Operations Unit. See "Special Report: Al-Qaeda—On the Brink of a New Wave of Attacks?" *CeifiT*, 6 September 2009, http://www.upsite.co.il/uploaded/files/62 6_8230c8bf67553cd90811a026c3d14bbf.pdf, accessed 21 February 2012; "Terror Analysis: Senior Al-Qaeda Figure Saleh al-Somali Killed in Pakistan," *CeifiT*, 12 December 2009, http://www.ceifit.com/?categor yId=25149&itemId=92319, accessed 21 February 2012.

105. For Shukrijumah's profile, see "Adnan El Shukrijuma: Suspected Al-Qaeda Operative," *GlobalSecurity.org*, 12 September 2007, http://www.globalsecurity.org/security/profiles/adnan_el_shukri jumah.htm, accessed 13 March 2012.; Lisa J. Huriash, "Mother denies FBI Allegation That Her Son Now Leads al Qaeda," *The Miami Herald*,

7 August 2010, http://www.miamiherald.com/2010/08/07/1765874_p2/mother-denies-fbi-allegation-that.html, accessed 13 March 2012.

106. This unit was mostly composed of African al-Qaeda activists. Office of the Director of National Intelligence, United States Department of Defense, p. 1.

107. During his hearing, KSM admitted he was the overall commander in charge of the Gibraltar Straits plot to attack British and American warships. In other reports this plot was attributed in different documents to "Al Qaeda chief of naval operation Abd Al Rahim Al Nashiri," http://www.defense.gov/news/transcript_isn10024.pdf, p. 18; Gary Jones, "Osama's Navy," *Mirror Online* 12 February 2004, http://www.mirror.co.uk/news/allnews/content_objectid=13941634_method=full_siteid=50143 _headline=-OSAMA-S-NAVY-name_page.html ; republished by swhitebull, "Osama's Navy," *StrategyPage.com,* 12 February 2004, http://www.strategypage.com/militaryforums/93-3789.aspx, accessed 30 March 2012. By integrating both references, one might conclude that Nashiri was al-Qaeda's naval wing chief, subordinated to the Special Operations Unit headed at that time by KSM.

108. See "Top al Qaeda Operative Arrested," *CNN,* 21 Nov 2002, http://articles.cnn.com/2002-11-21/us/alqaeda.capture_1_al-nashiri-ramzi-binalshibh-abu-zubaydah?_s=PM:US, accessed 9 March 2012; Office of the Director of National Intelligence, United States Department of Defense, p. 7.

109. Attash's involvement with al-Qaeda's external operations was demonstrated throughout his hearing. OARDEC, "Verbatim Transcript of Open Session Combatant Status Review Tribunal Hearing for ISN 10014," United States Department of Defense, http://www.defenselink.mil/news/transcript_ISN10014.pdf, accessed 1 March 2012, pp. 4–6.

Attash also attended the famous opening meeting of the 9/11 attacks held in Kuala Lumpur. *The 9/11 Report,* pp. 168, 209.

110. Ali H. Soufan and date of interview is 21 August 2008: see also Ali H. Soufan, *The Black Banners: The Inside Story of 9/11 and the War Against al-Qaeda.* New York: W. W. Norton & Company, 2011.

111. Lucile Malandain, "Evidence Against 9/11 Plotters Revealed," *AFP,* 9 April 2011.

112. Katherine Pfleger Shrader, "Raised Terror Alert Based on Pakistani Computer Engineer's Data," *USA Today,* 3 August 2004, http://www.usatoday.com/tech/news/2004-08-03-engineer-of-terror_x.htm, accessed 30 March 2012.

113. For Khan's involvement with the Special Operations Unit (headed at that time by KSM and later by Hamza Rabia) through his cooperation with KSM's plot to target American financial institutions, see Ehsan Ahrari, "Al-Qaeda and Cyber Terrorism," *Asia Times*, 18 August 2004, http://www.atimes.com/atimes/Front_Page/FH18Aa01.html, accessed 30 March 2012.

114. "Abu Talha al Sudani," *GlobalSecurity.org*, 8 January 2007, http://www.globalsecurity.org/security/profiles/abu_talha_al_sudani.htm, accessed 9 March 2012.

115. John Rollins, *Al Qaeda and Affiliates: Historical Perspective, Global Presence, and Implications for U.S. Policy*, Congressional Research Service: DIANE Publishing, 5 February 2010, p. 20.

116. "Dhiran Barot," *GlobalSecurity.org*, 7 November 2006, http://www.globalsecurity.org/security/profiles/dhiren_barot.htm, accessed 9 March 2012.

117. Ibid.

118. "Ahmed Khalfan Ghaliani," *GlobalSecurity.org*, 28 February 2007, http://www.globalsecurity.org/security/profiles/ahmed_khalfan_ghailani.htm, accessed 9 March 2012.

119. "Fahid Mohammed Ally Msalem," *GlobalSecurity.org*, 12 September 2007, http://www.globalsecurity.org/security/profiles/fahid_mohammed_ally_msalam.htm, accessed 9 March 2012.

120. Zahid Hussain, "Usama al-Kini, Head of al-Qaeda in Pakistan, Killed by US military," *Times Online*, 9 January 2009, http://www.timesonline.co.uk/tol/news/world/asia/article5479455.ece. accessed February 2009.

121. Ibid.

122. Ibid.

123. Ibid.

124. Rauf's senior role in the 2006 transatlantic aircraft plot might be the most prominent indicator of his involvement with al-Qaeda's Special External Operations Unit. See "Terror Plot: Internet Cafes Raided," *CNN International*, 13 August 2006, http://edition.cnn.com/2006/WORLD/europe/08/12/terror.plot/index.html, accessed 12 March 2012.

125. Robertson and Cruickshank, "Recruits Reveal . . ."; Gardham and Rayner, "Arrest of 'Easter Bombers' . . ."; Markon, "Al-Qaeda Leaders Said. . ."

126. See Amar al-Baluchi's role within the al-Qaeda Special Operations Unit (and mostly during preparations for the 9/11 attack) as the nephew of then chief of the unit, Khalid Sheikh Mohamed, detailed in his hearing. OARDEC, "Verbatim Transcript of Open Session

Combatant Status Review Tribunal Hearing for ISN 10018," United States Department of Defense, http://www.defenselink.mil/news/transcript_ISN10018.pdf, accessed 9 March 2012.

127. For Mustafa Ahmad Hawasawi's role within al-Qaeda's Special Operations Unit (and mostly during preparations for the 9/11 attack), see OARDEC, "Verbatim Transcript of Open Session Combatant Status Review Tribunal Hearing for ISN 10018."

128. Mimi Hall, Kevin Johnson, and Toni Locy, "Alleged 9/11 Financier Also Caught," *USA Today*, 3 March 2003, http://www.usato day.com/news/world/2003-03-03-mohammed-usat_x.htm, accessed 9 March 2012.

129. Emerson Vermaat, "Bin Laden's Terror Networks in Europe," *Mackenzie Institute Occasional Paper*, http://www.mackenzieinstitute. com/2002/2002_Bin_Ladens_Networks.html, accessed 9 March 2008.

Al-Qaeda operatives who lived in the West were of special value to the organization as they were familiar with Western mores. KSM had to invest much more effort training other al-Qaeda members who participated in external operations on Western soil (such as the fifteen Saudi hijackers of the 9/11 plots) in aspects of Western society, mentality, and lifestyle.

130. OARDEC, "Verbatim Transcript of Open Session Combatant Status Review Tribunal Hearing for ISN 10019," United States Department of Defense, http://www.defenselink.mil/news/transcript_ISN10019.pdf, accessed 9 March 2012, p. 7.

131. "Profile: Amjad Farooqi," *BBC News*, 27 September 2004, http://news.bbc.co.uk/2/hi/south_asia/3692882.stm, accessed 3 December 2011.

132. "Ramzi Binalshibh," *GlobalSecurity.org*, 15 November 2006, http://www.globalsecurity.org/security/profiles/ramzi_binalshibh. htm, accessed 3 December 2011.

133. Among these projects were al-Qaeda senior activist Abu Khobab's efforts and an ambitious project aimed to produce anthrax conducted by al-Zawahiri and professionally headed by the Malaysian microbiologist Yazid Suffat. In addition, there were unconfirmed reports of consistent al-Qaeda efforts to achieve some level of nuclear capability, mainly vis-à-vis the network of Pakistani Abd al-Khan. See Deroy Murdock, "Terrorist Rogues Gallery," *NRO Weekend*, 27 September 2006, http://article.nationalreview.com/?q=YTQ1YWE1OT VkNTEyMGIwOGIwMmViYWEzYTFhYTIxZGU, accessed 30 March 2012; OARDEC, "Verbatim Transcript of . . . ISN 10024 (Khaled Sheikh Mohamed)"; "How Pakistan's Dr. X Sold Al Qaida Islamic Bomb,"

WorldNetDaily (WND), 17 August 2005, http://www.worldnetdaily.
com/news/article.asp?ARTICLE_ID=45812, accessed 30 March 2012.
134. "Abd al-Aziz al-Masri."
135. "Al Qaeda Goals and Structure," Combating Terrorism Center
at West Point.
136. Ali Sufan, personal interview.
137. Thomas Joscelyn, "Head of al Qaeda Victory Committee Survived Battle in Syria," 19 April 2014 at http://www.longwarjournal
.org/archives/2014/04/head_of_al_qaedas_vi.php?utm_source=rss&
utm_medium=rss&utm_campaign=head-of-al-qaedas-victory-com-
mittee-survived-battle-in-syria# . Accessed 12 June 2014.
138. Ibid.
139. For the meaning of "al-Sahab," see Peter Bergen, *The Longest
War: The Enduring Conflict Between America and Al-Qaeda*, New York:
Simon and Schuster, 2010, p. 199.
For the al-Sahab Foundation, see Evan F. Kohlmann, "Prominent Jihad Media Organizations in Central Asia," *The NEFA Foundation* 2009,
http://www.nefafoundation.org/miscellaneous/FeaturedDocs/nefa
jihadmedia0309.pdf, accessed 11 November 2011.
140. *United States of America vs. Usama Bin Laden, et al.* 2001 WL
102338 (S.D.N.Y. 6 Feb 2001) (No. S(7) 98 CR 1023 LBS), p. 211.
141. OARDEC, "Verbatim Transcript of . . . ISN 10024 (Khaled
Sheikh Mohamed)," p. 17.
142. "Al-Qaeda Media Committee," *GlobalSecurity.org*, 1 November
2006, http://www.globalsecurity.org/security/profiles/al-qaeda_me-
dia_committee.htm, accessed 3 December 2011.
143. "Mustafa Ahmed al-Hawasawi," *GlobalSecurity.org*, 1 November 2006, http://www.globalsecurity.org/security/profiles/mustafa_
ahmed_al-hawsawi.htm, accessed 3 December 2011.
144. "Adam Ghadahn," *GlobalSecurity.org*, 1 November 2006, http://
www.globalsecurity.org/security/profiles/adam_gadahn.htm, accessed 16 December 2011.
145. *Der Spiegel*, 29 January 2006.
146. Rohan Gunaratna and Aviv Oreg, "Al Qaeda's Organizational
Structure and Its Evolution," *Studies in Conflict & Terrorism*, Vol. 33, No.
12 (2010), p. 1044.
147. For the full responsibilities of the Administrative and Financial
Committee, see the Arabic version of "Al Qaeda Goals and Structure,"
Combating Terrorism Center at West Point, pp. 15–19.
148. "Shaikh Saiid al-Masri."

149. Cruickshank, "The Rupture: Could the Killing of Al Qaeda's no. 3, Mustafa Abu al-Yazid Sever the Ties Between the Terrorist Groups and the Taliban?" *Foreign Policy*, 3 June 2010.

150. "Abu Fadhl al-Makkee."

151. Kohlmann, "Dossier: Shaykh Mustafa Abu al-Yazid (a.k.a. 'Shaykh Saeed')," *The NEFA Foundation*, June 2008, http://www.nefafoundation.org/miscellaneous/FeaturedDocs/nefayazid0608.pdf, accessed 9 March 2012, p. 2.

152. "Key al-Qaeda Leader Killed in Pakistan," *News24*, 9 October 2010, http://www.news24.com/World/News/Key-al-Qaeda-leader-killed-in-Pakistan-20101009, accessed 9 March 2012.

153. "Al Qaeda Goals and Structure," pp. 15–19.

154. Ibid.

155. Ibid.

156. Ibid, pp. 19–22.

157. "Saif al-Adel," *GlobalSecurity.org*, 12 September 2007, http://www.globalsecurity.org/security/profiles/saif_al-adel.htm, accessed 26 February 2012.

158. Mussa, "Cairo papers," p. 2; CeifiT, "Terror Analysis: Abu Dahdah and Al-Qaeda's DAWA Apparatus," *CeifiT*, 29 April 2008, http://www.ceifit.com/?categoryId=27211&itemId=42270, accessed 30 March 2012.

159. *United States of America vs. Usama Bin Laden, et al.* 2001 WL 102338 (S.D.N.Y. 6 Feb 2001) (No. S(7) 98 CR 1023 LBS).

160. Bruce Riedel, "The Al Qaeda-Iran Connection," *Hot Air*, 29 May 2011, http://hotair.com/headlines/archives/2011/05/30/the-al-qaeda-iran-connection/, accessed 26 February 2012. Even though Abu Hafs' formal position was as a key theologian, it seems he used to possess a much higher status, probably as a committee leader. Three detainees, including KSM and two unidentified prisoners, said Abu Hafs opposed the strikes of 11 September and even wrote a letter to bin Laden, citing the Quran, to this effect. In our view, this episode reflects Abu Hafs' high status. See "Abu Hafs the Mauritanian," *GlobalSecurity.org*, 1 November 2006, http://www.globalsecurity.org/security/profiles/abu_hafs_the_mauritanian.htm, accessed 26 February 2012.

161. Report on al-Qaeda in Iran, Global Pathfinder 2 Database, International Centre for Political Violence and Terrorism Research, Singapore, 20 July 2012.

162. Yahiya al-Libi has emerged as a public face for al-Qaeda, appearing in more than a dozen lengthy Internet videos since 2006. His

claim to fame lies within his successful escape from a high-security U.S. military prison in Bagram, Afghanistan, in July 2005, along with three other al-Qaeda members. He styles himself as a theologian and has offered lengthy commentaries on a variety of political events, and hence is probably the new head of the Religious Committee. Whitlock and Ladaa, "Al-Qaeda's New Leadership."

163. "Al-Qaeda leader Abu Yahya al-Libi Killed in U.S. Drone Strike," *The Telegraph*, 5 June 2012 at http://www.telegraph.co.uk/news/worldnews/al-qaeda/9312536/Al-Qaeda-leader-Abu-Yahya-al-Libi-killed-in-US-drone-strike.html.

164. A major difficulty for KSM during the preparations for the 9/11 attacks was that the majority of hijackers were ignorant of Western mores. KSM organized special training in order to introduce them to the western way of life. See "Verbatim Transcript of Open Session Combatant Status Review Tribunal Hearing for ISN 10024 (Khaled Sheikh Mohammed)" at http://www.defenselink.mil/news/transcript_ISN10024.pdf and 9/11, accessed 17 February 2012; *The 9/11 Report*, p. 236.

165. Al-Zawahiri, who previously enjoyed good relations with the Iranian regime (which supported EIJ's struggle in Egypt in the 1990s), was the key figure in efforts to release the senior activists. Al-Qaeda's efforts to release these members became a key issue in the conflict between al-Qaeda's senior leadership from the Afghanistan-Pakistan border and the former al-Qaeda leader of Iraq, Abu Musab al-Zarqawi. The conflict involved al-Zarqawi's targeting policy, which included the Shiite population in Iraq and hence raised antagonism toward al-Qaeda in Iran. Al-Zawahiri, "Letter to Zarqawi," p. 9.

166. Joscelyn, "Osama bin Laden's Spokesman Freed by Iran."

167. Riedel, "The Al Qaeda–Iran Connection."

168. Report on al-Qaeda in Iran, Global Pathfinder 2 Database, International Centre for Political Violence and Terrorism Research, Singapore, 20 July 2012 .

169. Pepe Escobar, "Iran and al-Qaeda: Odd Bedfellows," *Asia Times Online*, 17 October 2003, http://www.atimes.com/atimes/Middle_East/EJ17Ak02.html, accessed 24 February 2012.

170. "Saad bin Laden" *GlobalSecurity.org*, 28 Nov 2006, http://www.globalsecurity.org/security/profiles/saad_bin_laden.htm, accessed 26 February 2012.

171. Bin Laden letter to Sheikh Atiya at http://www.ctc.usma.edu/wp-content/uploads/2012/05/SOCOM-2012-0000010-Trans.pdf.

172. "Al-Qaeda Spokesman in Iran," BBC, 17 July 2003, http://news.bbc.co.uk/2/hi/middle_east/3074785.stm, accessed 16 December 2011.

Abu Gheith was released in September 2010. Joscelyn, "Osama bin Laden's Spokesman Freed by Iran." In 2013 Abu Gheith was captured and extradited to the United States, http://www.nytimes.com/2013/03/08/world/middleeast/bin-laden-son-in-law-is-being-held-in-a-new-york-jail.html?_r=0.

4

Affiliated Groups

Al-Qaeda affiliated or associated groups refer to local organizations. They possess religious ideologies that are similar to al-Qaeda's ideology and promote internal jihad in their own countries in order to topple a secular regime, implement Islamic Sharia as the state constitution and law, and establish an Islamic Caliphate. Although there are more than fifty such groups operating in different parts of the world, we consider only the most significant three dozen groups. The majority of these groups have traditional contact with al-Qaeda, the "mother organization." Throughout their existence and mostly up to 2001, affiliated groups enjoyed significant financial and operational support from al-Qaeda. These groups received major support from al-Qaeda in the form of military training in al-Qaeda training complexes in Sudan (1991–1995), Afghanistan (1996–2001), and tribal Pakistan (2002–today).

In addition to this traditional cooperation with al-Qaeda, most of these groups were established following the success in the Afghan war and were headed by Afghan war veterans who returned to their home countries in the early 1990s after the war. As mentioned earlier, the Afghanistan arena was used as a melting pot for jihadi activists from different parts of the Islamic world. Islamic individuals far and wide, from Morocco to the Philippines and from Uzbekistan to Somalia, trained and fought against Soviet troops together in the name of the same radical Islamic ideology. These individuals maintained relations after returning to their homelands after the war with the Soviets ended in 1989. Veteran relations that were cultivated during the Afghan war are a key factor in the organizational cooperation between affiliated groups and al-Qaeda during the new era of Global Jihad that has characterized the last decade.

Since the U.S.-led coalition stormed Afghanistan following the 9/11 attacks in New York and Washington, some of these affiliated groups changed their targeting policy to include an international dimension.[1] In order to ease the pressure on al-Qaeda in Afghanistan and the Pakistani tribal areas after 9/11, a number of these groups diverted some operational efforts into the international arena and have attacked Western targets within their area of operations. In the early stages, this change in targeting policy was the result of veteran relations between individual mujahidin that were cultivated in Afghanistan. This policy change, predominantly based on personal relations, created antagonism among members of the local group, and in extreme cases caused a split within organizations. Hambali, as the military chief of JI, provided the use of JI infrastructure to his old friend Khalid Sheikh Mohamed (KSM) for al-Qaeda's external operations and faced antagonism from JI members. The influence of al-Qaeda's senior military commander, Abu Layth al-Libi, over several members of the Islamic Movement of Uzbekistan (IMU) regarding the international characteristics of IMU's targeting policy resulted in a split among pivotal IMU members and the creation of the Islamic Jihad Union (IJU).

In recent years, al-Qaeda's connections and collaborations with affiliated groups have become more formal. Since the U.S.-led offensive in Iraq in 2003, al-Qaeda leadership has established regional "al-Qaedas" that are based on local groups. The Algerian group, Global Salafist Group for Preaching and Combat (GSPC), became al-Qaeda in the Islamic Maghreb (AQIM), while al-Qaeda in the Arabian Peninsula (AQAP) and al-Qaeda in Yemen (AQIY) were established and eventually merged. In Iraq, Tawhid Wal Jihad changed its name to al-Qaeda in Iraq (AQI) and formed the Islamic State of Iraq (ISI), an umbrella organization for different Iraqi jihadi groups. Today, ISI is referred to as Islamic State of Iraq and Levant (ISIL), Islamic State of Iraq and Sham (ISIS), and the Islamic State (IS). In early 2012 al-Qaeda and the Somali group Shabaab al-Mujahidin merged.[2]

In both cases, motivated by veteran relations as well as the current more formal organizational cooperation, al-Qaeda's targeting policy influenced its associated groups, which have diverted some of their operational efforts from the domestic arena to the international arena.

The extent of "al-Qaedization" of a regional group indicates the level of its commitment to the Global Jihad ideology and the volume of its international activity. During the early 2000s, the personal relations between al-Qaeda seniors and local group leaders determined the level of international operational performance of local groups. In recent years, former al-Qaeda members have risen through the ranks of local groups and have thus channeled more efforts of these organizations toward international attacks.

Under these criteria, AQAP is a more significant threat than other local groups that conduct international attacks. AQAP leader Nassir al-Wuhayshi a.k.a Abu Bassir al-Yamani was Bin Laden's former personal secretary. AQAP has conducted numerous attacks against Western targets inside Yemen and even targeted at least four American aircraft outside the Arabian Peninsula since late 2009. Somalian Shabaab al-Mujahidin (al-Shabaab) is an emerging threat, whose rise has been directly attributed to the then increasing dominance of the late Harun Abdullah Fazul, al-Qaeda's most senior operational activist in the Horn of Africa, within the ranks of al-Shabaab. In contrast, none of the members within AQIM's leadership previously belonged to Al Qaeda. Consequently, AQIM's vast deployment in Europe has not been used operationally by al-Qaeda in spite of the public merge between the two organizations in 2006. Hence, the appointment of well-known al-Qaeda activists to senior positions within local organizations is the most significant indicator of the future activity of local groups in the international arena and international operations.

As this book is Western oriented, and thus focuses on Western perspectives of the threat derived from the Global Jihad, we choose in this chapter to focus discussion on local affiliated groups of al-Qaeda that have already included operations with international characteristics within their targeting policy. We will provide an overview of each organization in order to portray the potential risk of its activity, while focusing on the international characteristics of each group.

Since dozens of local groups enjoyed al-Qaeda's support in their domestic struggle, the potential of more groups to cross this Rubicon and undertake international operations is high. At the end of this chapter, we offer a brief assessment of groups that still refrain from internationalizing their activity yet have the potential of becoming international by using al-Qaeda's strategy in the international arena at any given moment should they decide to.

Jemaah Islamiyah of Southeast Asia (JI)

General Background

Jemaah Islamiyah (JI) is a radical Islamist organization that operates in Southeast Asia. Its political objective is to establish a *Daulah Islamiyah* (Islamic state) composed of Indonesia, Malaysia, the southern Philippines, Singapore, and Brunei.[3] JI wishes to implement Sharia as the only judicial reference in the region.

JI views jihad as the best method to achieve its goal. According to JI, jihad has become obligatory because Muslims have failed to defend their nations. The most preferred jihad is *jihad Musallah*, which means armed struggle. Armed struggle is to be carried out against the enemies of Islam: infidels, polytheists, and their supporters.

Even though JI was formally established as late as 1993, its roots date back much earlier. JI has its roots in Darul Islam (DI), an organization with a political Islamic agenda that has existed since the 1940s.[4] It was an anticolonial movement that became a political opponent of the Indonesian government after the colonial period.[5] The prominent founders of JI, Abu Baker Ba'asyir and the late Abdullah Sungkar, were inducted into DI in 1976. They were members of DI until 1993 when they broke away to form JI.

In 1971, Ba'asyir and Sungkar set up an Islamic boarding school or *pesantren*, which became the nexus for radical Islamic ideology in Indonesia. This *pesantren* school in Central Java, Indonesia, known as Pesantren al-Mukmin or Pondok Ngruki, taught many of the men who were arrested and linked to al-Qaeda.[6]

From 1978 to 1982, Ba'asyir and Sungkar were imprisoned in Indonesia for subversion. They fled to Malaysia in 1985 to escape another prison term and returned to Indonesia only in 1998 after the end of Suharto's regime. While in Malaysia, Ba'asyir and Sungkar promoted their vision for a regional pan-Islamic state, gathered like-minded Indonesians, Malaysians, Filipinos, and Singaporeans, and formed the JI. JI was established as a formal organization by Sungkar on 1 January 1993.[7] This event marked the formal institutionalization of a loose network that already existed years earlier.[8]

Years before the formal inception of JI, these groups in the loose network that had formed around Sungkar and Ba'asyir began conducting military activity. The constant persecution of Islamists and particularly DI members by Suharto's secular regime peaked with Ba'asyir and Sungkar's second escape, forcing the two to search for military capabilities for their followers. During the mid-1980s, Afghanistan was the center for radical Islamists looking for military capabilities and training. The jihad in Afghanistan shaped young DI members' worldviews, reinforced their commitment to jihad, and provided them with terrorist and guerilla training. All of JI's top leaders and many of the men involved in JI bombings trained in Afghanistan from 1985 to 1995.

More than 200 members from Southeast Asia trained in Camp Sadah in Afghanistan from 1985 to 1995. Camp Sadah was run by an Afghan mujahidin leader of Ittihad al-Islami al-Afghani, Abd al-Rasool Sayyaf. As JI was only founded in 1993, the first batches of mujahidin sent to Afghanistan for training were mostly DI members. Thereafter, all the Indonesian mujahidin in Afghanistan were JI members.

By May 1996, Sungkar and several Afghan veterans had consolidated the structure of JI. They documented it in the book *General Guidelines for the Jamaah Islamiyah Struggle*, also known by its Indonesian acronym *PUPJI*.[9] Most JI leaders returned to Indonesia after the end of Suharto's government in 1998, during the reform transition.[10] According to International Crisis Group's (ICG) assessment, in 2007, JI was composed of more than 900 members across Indonesia. It was assessed as being unlikely to grow but "retains deep roots and a long-term vision of establishing an Islamic state."[11]

Due to internal fighting between mujahidin factions in Afghanistan from 1993 to 1994, JI moved its military training to southern Mindanao in the Philippines. By late 1996, JI had gone through the Moro Islamic Liberation Front (MILF) to set up training facilities there.[12] Members of JI were first sent to Abu Bakar Camp of the MILF under the leadership of Salamat Hasyim, but later established their own camp in the region, Camp Hudaybiyah.[13] Training at Camp Hudaybiyah began only in mid-1997, after the formation of Mantiqi III. A military academy program and a short basic military training course known as Daurah Asasiyah Askariyah (DAA) were implemented. By late 1999, JI transferred its training camp in the Philippines to another location not far from Camp Hudaybiyah due to the "all-out-war" carried out by the Philippines' military on all MILF camps, including Camp Hudaybiyah neighboring camp, Camp Abu Bakar. The decision to move was given by the leader of Mantiqi III, who with the help of the MILF managed to get a new location for the camp that was named Jabal (Mount) Quba. DAA activities continued at Camp Jabal Quba. Small training camps were established later across Indonesia and Malaysia.[14] These camps however did not have the infrastructure of those in Mindanao.

JI has been capable of carrying out guerrilla and military operations, using small arms, antitank rockets, mortars, bomb construction, assassination techniques, and sniper activities. Its modus operandi includes constructing car bombs composed of ammonium nitrate and plastic explosives, which are directed at civilians and military targets, government (embassies, buildings), and foreign targets and infrastructure (maritime and aviation infrastructure).

JI's strategy is to create domestic and regional instability in order to oust secular governments in the region (Malaysia, Indonesia, and the predominantly Muslim part of the southern Philippines).

JI has adopted al-Qaeda's tactics and techniques. Like al-Qaeda, JI has conducted coordinated simultaneous suicide attacks against high-profile, symbolic, and strategic targets, inflicting mass casualties. Operational tactics include using truck bombs and suicide bombers. Among all associated groups, JI was, during the early years of the new millennium, operationally and ideologically the closest to al-Qaeda.

The internal operational activity of JI inside its vicinity of operations against local targets included attacks against diplomatic compounds and residences, churches, and Christian centers as well as financial facilities across the region.

Infrastructure Layout and Operational Capabilities

The Amir is the head of JI. His role is to lead the organization in every aspect. Four councils operate below the Amir, which are all appointed by him and subject to his control. One of the four councils, the Governing Council, is headed by a Central Command (*Qiyadah Markaziyah*) that exercises authority over the leaders of four Regional Commands (*Mantiqi*) and the heads of municipal cells (*wakalahs*).[15] Below the municipal cells are companies (*khatibah*); platoons (*qirdas*); and squads (*fiah*).

In practice, members of the Central Command are influential in setting policy and decision making regarding operations. They are not constrained by the formal hierarchy.[16]

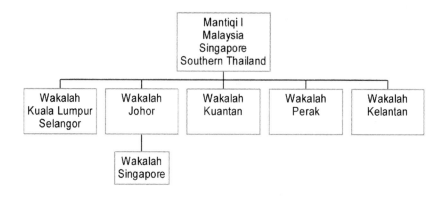

Chart 4.1.   Organizational Structure of JI.

SOUTHEAST ASIA

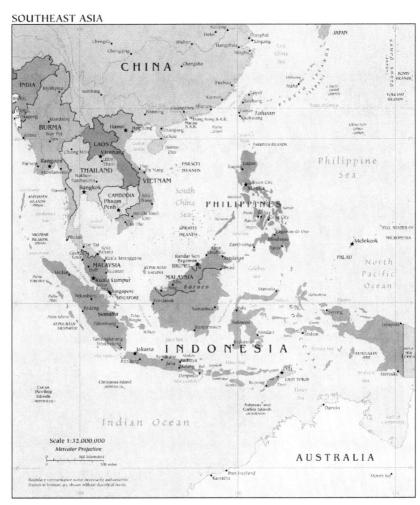

Map 4.1.   Geographical Sectors of Jl. Mantiqi 1-Singapore, Western Malaysia. Mantiqi 2-Sumatra, Jawa, Ambon, Lesser Sunda Islands. Mantiqi 3-Borneo, Sulawesi, the
Moluccas, southern Philippines, Thailand. Mantiqi 4-Australia, Irian Jaya.

Mantiqi I

Mantiqi I financed JI operations. Mantiqi I was based in Malaysia and covered Malaysia, Singapore, and southern Thailand.

Mantiqi I was initially led by Riduan Isamuddin, also known as Hambali, JI operations chief who was replaced by Ustaz Mukhlas in 2001.[17] Hambali was arrested on 11 August 2003 in Ayutthaya, Thailand. Mukhlas was Mantiqi I's leader until his arrest on 3 December 2002.

Singaporean Cell

The Singaporean cell was established by Ibrahim Maidin between 1988 and 1989. He was arrested in 2001. Mas Selamat Kastari assumed leadership until he was arrested in early 2003 in Bintan, Singapore.

Before JI was broken up by the Singaporean intelligence agencies, it had sixty to eighty members, twenty-five of whom were operational. Singapore JI leadership is subordinate to the Johor JI leadership. With the arrest of Mas Selamat Kastari, Singaporean intelligence agencies crippled the JI cell in Singapore. However, Mas Selamat Kastari escaped from prison on 27 February 2008.

Malaysian Cell

The Malaysian cell was established by Abdussalam bin Abu Thalaibi, and was subsequently headed by Abu Hanafiah and Abu Bakar Bafana. This cell actively recruited Indonesians and Malaysians. It was estimated to comprise about 200 members.

Five major responsibilities of the Malaysian cell included:

1. Acting as a conduit between al-Qaeda and JI.
2. Liaising with Kumpulan Mujahidin Malaysia (KMM) in Malaysia.
3. Establishing front companies that could be used to channel funds.
4. Being responsible for recruitment and education.
5. Helping establish Mantiqi IV (Australia).

Thai Cell

The Thai cell was led by Dr. Waedaoh, a forty-one-year-old owner of a drugstore in Narathiwat, Thailand. Members consisted of Maisuri Haji Abdullah, an Islamic religious teacher in southern Thailand; his son, Muyahi Haji Doloh; a Singaporean Chinese JI member known as Arifin Ali a.k.a. John Wong Ah Hung; and Samarn Waekaji, JI's operations chief in Thailand.

Hambali claimed to have had no success in dealing with southern Thai militants because they refused to help him blow up tourist spots in the country.[18]

Mantiqi II

Mantiqi II covered most of Indonesia, except for the islands of Borneo, Sulawesi, and Kalimantan. It was led by Abdullah Anshori a.k.a Abu Fatih, who remains at large. He assisted in recruiting volunteers for Afghanistan between 1985 and 1986.

He relinquished his leadership to Zuhroni a.k.a Nu'im, an Afghan veteran. Abu Rusdan was allegedly the head of the military wing in Mantiqi II. He was arrested in April 2002.[19]

Indonesian Cell

The Indonesian cell appears to be connected to Majlis Mujahidin Indonesia (MMI), which was established in 2000 by Ba'asyir and Irfan S. Awas. MMI's support base overlaps with that of JI in terms of membership as well as their *pesantren* support base.

The major role of the Indonesian cell is to provide spiritual and religious leadership. It is responsible for running a network of training camps in Sulawesi and in Balikpapan, Kalimantan.

We believe that the Indonesian cell was involved in the Christmas Eve bombings in Indonesia in 2000, the Bali bombing in 2002, and the Marriott bombing in 2003. In the instance of the Bali bombing, Mantiqi I provided planning and financial support. The planning of the Bali bombing took place in southern

Thailand in February 2002, while funds of $35,000 were received from Malaysia.[20]

Mantiqi III

Mantiqi III covered Mindanao, Sabah, Brunei, Sarawak, Kalimantan, and Sulawesi. It was responsible for military training.[21] Mantiqi III was reportedly led by an Indonesian, Mustopa a.k.a Pranata Yudha a.k.a Abu Tholut, an Afghan veteran and an instructor of explosives in Mindanao who was arrested in a raid on 11 July 2003 in Semarang.

In 2001, he was replaced by Malaysian Nasir Abbas, an instructor at a militant camp in the southern Philippines who was arrested on 23 April 2003. Mantiqi III appears to have had the most lethal capability among all Mantiqis. This Central Java cell had set performance targets as far as 2025 and had set targets with five different phases of development.[22] Since the arrest of its former leader Mustopa, a large batch of weapons and ammunition has been discovered, reflecting Mantiqi III's lethal capabilities and operational and targeting policy.

Philippine Cell

This cell was led by an Indonesian-born Afghan veteran and trainer, Fathur Rahman al-Ghozi a.k.a Mike. He was shot dead by Philippine soldiers in October 2003 while on the run, after escaping from a high-security prison. The Philippines was a major logistical hub for the JI network.

Responsibilities of the Philippine cell included:

1. To act as financial node for the transfer of funds to the MILF.
2. To act as a conduit between JI and MILF for training purposes.
3. To procure explosives, guns, and other equipment.

Mantiqi IV

Australian Cell

Mantiqi IV covered Australia and Irian Jaya, and was responsible for fund-raising. It was led by Abdul Rahim Ayub.[23] He first settled in Sydney, Australia, in 1997, and attempted, with the blessing of JI's spiritual leader, Abu Bakar Ba'asyir, to take control of a mosque at Dee Why on Sydney's northern beaches. Those efforts failed and Ayub moved to Perth. He was allegedly involved in induction activities. He fled Perth just four days after the Bali bombings and was arrested in Indonesia in July 2004. Before 1998, Ba'asyir and Sungkar visited Australia eleven times to promote JI's influence and activities under the respective aliases of Abdul Somad and Abdul Halim.[24] They focused their efforts on Perth, Melbourne, and Sydney.[25]

Mantiqi IV carried out numerous paramilitary training exercises in western Australia and the Blue Mountains in New South Wales, and attempted to recruit students from Curtin University in Perth.

Southeast Asian intelligence officials have disclosed that Hambali had recruited and trained a group to bomb the main stadium at Homebush during the Sydney Olympic Games.[26]

The Mantiqi structure is no longer functioning. Following a crackdown on the JI cells in Singapore and Malaysia, JI members held a meeting on 17 October 2002 to decide the future of Mantiqi I. It is believed that they decided that the strategic functions of all Mantiqi, especially Mantiqi I, should be temporarily paralyzed. There have been no indications thus far that the structure has been revived. According to seized documents and interrogations of detainees, JI has established a new structure in recent years. Diagrams of JI's new organizational structure are below. The new structure of JI has the following characteristics:

1. It is headed by the Majlis Qiyadah Markaziyah (the Central Command of JI).
2. It commands five divisions: *Dawa* (Propagation); Education; Economy; Information; and *Sariyah* (Military Corps).

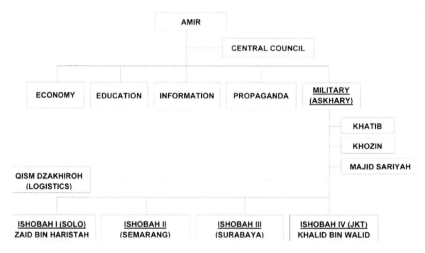

Chart 4.2. The New JI Structure.

3. The *Sariyah* (company) commands *Ishobahs* (groups, each about the size of a platoon) with several *majmuah* or units (one *majmuah* equals ten personnel).
4. There are four *Ishobahs*: Ishobah Jafar bi Abi Tholib covering Semarang, Ishobah Abdullah bin Rowwahah covering Surabaya, Ishobah Khalid bin Walid covering Jakarta, and Ishobah Zaid bin Haristah covering Surakarta.

Unlike the previous structure, where the Mantiqi were arranged to cover different countries in Southeast Asia, JI now appears more focused on its operations in Indonesia.

Raids and arrests conducted by Indonesian police from March to April 2007 revealed that JI may have reformed its military structure and constructed a new organizational structure for its military wing.[27]

The highest position in this structure is the *Qoryah*, or military commander. This position was held by Abu Dujana. Under him is an *ishobah*, a new term in the military wing of JI. This *ishobah* consists of several *majmuah* and has the same standing as the Qism Dzakhiroh, who handles logistics. A *Sariyah* is equivalent

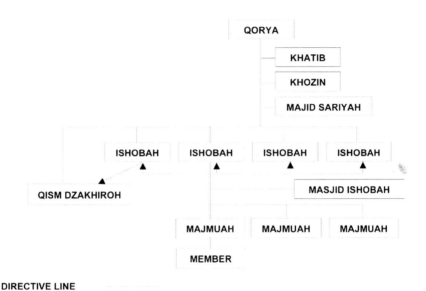

Chart 4.3.   New Military Division of the JI.

to one company or 100 people in standard military terminology. An *ishobah* is the size of a platoon. A *majmuah* is a squad of about 100 people.

JI has three categories of fighters:

1. Regular fighters who have undergone military training for four to six months.
2. Khos fighters, members of a special unit who have battle capabilities and weapons, and have undergone training for at least three years.
3. Istimata fighters who are trained to carry out *amaliyah istishadiyah* (suicide bombings).[28]

Lashkar Khos is believed to be a Special Operations Unit, established by Abu Bakar Ba'asyir to carry out assassinations and bombings. It came to public attention after the August 2003

Marriott bombing in Jakarta. It reports to the Central Command of JI. The members are drawn from individual cells, depending on the nature of the assignment. Lashkar Khos is the elite "special forces" in the network.

Lashkar Khos is believed to have been led by Hambali until his arrest. Indonesian police sources also reported that Mustopa, arrested in mid-July 2003, confessed to leading Lashkar Khos. Despite this report, Mustopa only commanded about fifteen men, which means he was probably the head of a subunit.[29]

As overall commander, Zulkarnaen a.k.a Aris Sumarsono, the Solo-based head of JI's military operations, had ultimate control over special operations. Zulkarnaen is now believed to be leading Lashkar Khos, whose members were recruited from some 300 Indonesians who trained in Afghanistan and the Philippines. Asmar Latin Sani, an alleged bomber whose severed head was found in the wreckage of the Marriott Hotel blast in Jakarta in August 2003, is believed to have been a Lashkar Khos militant working for Zulkarnaen. This unit is not a suicide brigade, although suicide bombers have been systematically recruited into JI.[30]

Funding

JI is largely a self-financing organization but also relies on external funding provided by al-Qaeda. JI collects *infaq* (charity in the name of Allah) from members and the general public.[31] JI also collects *zakat* (charity tithes) to help fellow Muslims, with 30 percent of the collection given to Ba'asyir.[32]

Many Singapore JI members had to contribute about 2 percent of their monthly salaries to JI, while in the latter half of the 1990s, the amount was raised to 5 percent. There were others who gave a fixed monthly sum.[33]

The group also used KOMPAK, a charity established to provide aid to the displaced, which became an important source of funds for the purchase of arms, and produced videos about Ambon and Poso used for JI recruitment purposes.[34]

External support comes primarily from foreign groups like al-Qaeda and the Moro Islamic Liberation Front.[35] KSM gave

Hambali a no-strings-attached U.S. $100,000 to spend on future operations, a departure from the normal practice of giving cash for specific missions.[36] Al-Qaeda was impressed with the Bali bombers' effective use of an earlier donation of U.S. $30,000 and thus saw U.S. $100,000 seed money as a productive investment.[37] Al-Qaeda has been accused of providing funding for the Australian embassy bombing in 2004.[38]

International Characteristics of Activities

The jihad in Afghanistan significantly shaped JI's worldview, reinforced its commitment to jihad, and provided it with terrorist and guerrilla training. All of JI's top leaders and many of the men involved in JI bombings trained in Afghanistan over a ten-year period, from 1985 to 1995. The process of sending recruits to Afghanistan began at least seven years before JI formally came into being. The first batch was sent to Afghanistan in early 1985. Following that, eight more batches of members were sent until 1993. Almost all members of the Central Command of JI were from the first wave of Afghan veterans.[39]

In the Singaporean case, at least eleven JI members detained in Singapore went to Afghanistan for training in al-Qaeda training camps. Preparations for their Afghanistan stint included religious and physical training, which were conducted in Negri Sembilan, Malaysia. In Afghanistan, an Academy of Military Education and Training (DikLat AKMIL) was created as part of the long-term strategy to produce highly skilled JI militants. The first two batches that were sent to Afghanistan encountered problems with the training as the instructors used English or Arabic as the medium of communication. However, the people from these two batches later became instructors for the subsequent batches and facilitated efficient training, as time was no longer wasted in translating what was taught.

JI also sent potential operatives to study in Islamic schools (madrassas) outside Southeast Asia. In 1999, Hambali set up a cell in Karachi, Pakistan, to train young Southeast Asian Muslims to become future JI leaders. Two Singaporeans who were being groomed to lead JI were arrested after returning from Pakistan. The pair were part of the same Pakistan-based cell, code-named "al-Ghuraba" or "the foreigners," which was broken up in September 2003 with the arrest of nineteen Indonesians and Malaysians.[40]

Supporting al-Qaeda Plots and Projects

11 September Attacks

As in many other cases, operational cooperation began as a consequence of the veteran relations cultivated during the Afghan war between individual jihad volunteers. In the JI case, it refers to the personal relations that developed between Khalid Sheikh Mohamed (KSM), a senior trainer and leader at Camp Sadah, and one of the DI trainees who arrived from Indonesia, Esam Radwan al-Din, also known as Hambali. The two maintained relations throughout the 1990s and were promoted in parallel within the ranks of their separate organizations. By the turn of the new millennium, KSM was al-Qaeda's chief of external operations, while Hambali became the leader of Mantiqi I and later the overall military chief of JI. Due to positive and enduring relations between the two figures, JI provided logistical and operational assistance for several al-Qaeda plots and attacks in the international arena. The first meeting that sparked preparations for the 11 September attacks took place in December 1999 in JI activist Yazid Sufat's apartment in Kuala Lumpur. Hambali arranged the meeting, which was attended by al-Qaeda operatives Nawaf al-Hazmi and Khalid al-Midhar, as well as Khalid bin Walid al-Attash and Abu Bara al-Yemeni.[41] Later on Yazid provided al-Qaeda activists Zacharias Mussawi with a recommendation letter that designated Mussawi as Yazid's company Infocus Tech's new representative in the United States. Mussawi used the letter to obtain an entrance visa to the United States and later on entered the United States and was enrolled in a flight training school in Oklahoma as part of al-Qaeda's second wave of attacks, planned to imitate the success of the 9/11/2001 attacks.[42]

Al-Qaeda's Anthrax Project

JI members had pivotal positions in al-Qaeda's ambitious anthrax project. JI involvement with the program began when al-Qaeda military chief Mohamed Atef, a.k.a. Abu Hafs al-Masri, turned to Hambali when al-Qaeda needed a scientist to take over the organization's biological weapons program. Hambali obliged by introducing a U.S.-educated JI member, Yazid Suffat, to Ayman al-Zawahiri in Kandahar. In 2001, Suffat spent several months heading the project of cultivating anthrax for al-Qaeda in a laboratory he helped to set up near the Kandahar airport.[43]

Singapore Plot

In December 2001, Singaporean authorities arrested thirteen JI members, eight of whom had trained in al-Qaeda camps in Afghanistan, who were planning to conduct bombings at strategic locations in Singapore, including the United States and Israeli embassies, the British and Australian high commissions, and several other buildings of large enterprises. This plot was coordinated with al-Qaeda, which appointed a Special Operations Unit operative from Canada, Mahmud Mansur Jabarah, to supervise JI preparations for the attack. Al-Qaeda probably provided the suicide bombers for the attack. The plot was dismantled by the Singapore secret service.[44]

Second Wave of a 11 September–Style Plot against the United States West Coast and Southeast Asia

JI members including Hambali were pivotal in KSM's plan of a 9/11-style suicide operation targeting a U.S. bank tower in Los Angeles in 2002. The plot was eventually dismantled.[45]

Four JI members led by Indonesian Mirsan Bin Arshad were directed by al-Qaeda's chief of external operations, Khalid Sheikh Mohamed (KSM), to begin preparations for a 9/11-style operation in the Far East. KSM provided funding for the operations as well. Following an intelligence tip the plot was dismantled and the activists arrested.[46]

JI's International Operations and Plots

As part of Hambali's international policy, JI conducted its own operations and plots with international dimensions, as follows.

Bali Bombing

On Saturday evening of 12 October 2002, at about 11 p.m. local time, a car bomb and suicide attack occurred at the Kuta tourist resort in the south of Bali in Indonesia. The explosions killed 202 people, including 164 foreign nationals, eighty-eight of whom were Australian. Hundreds were wounded. Investigations revealed that the attack was carried out by Indonesian JI members of Mantiqi I and was under Hambali's overall supervision.[47]

Marriott Bombing, Jakarta

On 5 August 2003 at around 12:45 a.m., a high explosive device planted in a Kijang van exploded at the entrance to the JW Marriott Hotel in the Mega Kuningan business district in South Jakarta. Twelve people including the bomber were killed, while 149 others were injured. Investigation into the attack linked Hambali and Noordin Mohd Top, a senior JI activist, to the attack. The suicide bomber was Asmar Latin Sani, most likely a member of the Lashkar Khos (Special Operations Unit) led by Zulkarnaen.[48]

Australian Embassy Bombing, Jakarta

On 9 September 2004 at about 10:45 a.m., a white Daihatsu truck loaded with explosives detonated in front of the Australian embassy in Jakarta. The center of the blast was the road just in front of the building. The attack killed nine people and injured about 182 others. All of the deceased were Indonesian. Investigation revealed that the attack was led by Noordin Mohd Top, who assembled the team using three networks: JI's East Java division; the informal alumni of JI schools in and around Solo and Central Java; and an offshoot of the old DI organization based in Banten and West Java Provinces.[49]

Bali Second Attack 2005

On 1 October 2005, a JI squad composed of three suicide bombers attacked three major tourist locations in Bali killing twenty people and injuring over 100. About 40 percent of the victims were foreigners.[50]

Ritz-Carlton and JW Marriot Attack 2009

On 17 July 2009, the JW Marriott and Ritz-Carlton Hotels in Jakarta, Indonesia, were attacked simultaneously by suicide bombers. Seven people died in the attack; only one of them was a local Indonesian. More than fifty people were injured. JI explosive expert Nooradin Mohd Top was blamed by authorities for the attack.[51]

Plot to Attack Israeli Targets in Australia

In 2000, Jack Roche, an Australian Islamic convert of British origin and a member of JI's Mantiqi IV, was personally instructed by bin Laden and KSM, in a meeting in Kandahar arranged by Hambali, to conduct reconnaissance of the Israeli embassy and other Jewish targets in the Australian capital, Canberra.[52]

Plot to Attack El Al Flight in Bangkok

In the summer of 2003, the Thai authorities dismantled a JI plot led by Hambali to attack El Al Airlines' commercial jets in Bangkok International Airport.[53]

APEC Summit Plot

On 16 May 2003, Thai authorities arrested and extradited alleged JI member Arifin Ali to Singapore after a tip-off from authorities there. The forty-two-year-old is said to have planned to bomb the APEC summit held in Thailand in October 2003. The plan was aborted following Arifin's arrest. During the summer of 2003, Thai authorities arrested and charged Arifin's associates. The three were arrested in Narathiwat Province as suspected members of a JI cell led by Arifin. The four Thai nationals planned to bomb five embassies and popular tourist spots in Bangkok during the APEC meeting.

A week after the Jakarta Marriott bombing, Riduan Isamuddin a.k.a Hambali was arrested in Ayutthaya, Thailand. During his arrest, the Thai authorities confiscated a number of explosive devices and weapons, which Hambali allegedly confessed were being prepared for use in a terrorist attack during the APEC summit.[54] In further investigations, Hambali confirmed that fresh attacks were being planned in Bangkok, with possible targets including U.S.-owned hotels, airlines, and popular nightclubs. Hambali admitted in other interrogations that he was preparing to bomb the backpacker area of Khao San Road and the embassies of the United States, Israel, and Japan, adding that he had already scouted the sites.[55]

Future Assessment

JI is believed to have significantly degraded in recent years, but is still capable of mounting attacks, particularly bombings. JI has been factionalized by long-running disputes over strategy, but these factions uphold loyalty to JI's fundamental goals and are determined to wage a violent campaign.

According to our assessment, JI will continue recent years' trends and focus its activity on the home front in Indonesia, and hence limit its international operations. Since the arrest of Hambali (the main JI point of contact with al-Qaeda), JI has refrained from operating outside the Indonesian arena. The second attack in Bali in 2005 was most likely JI's last attack aimed at foreign citizens. In addition, JI's pro-bombing faction has been severely crippled following the death of Dr. Azahari Hussein (2007) and Noordin Mohd Top (2009). Hence, we believe that the coming years will be a building and consolidation phase for JI, which means that it is unlikely to be interested in large, expensive international operations that could further weaken its support base.

We believe that JI will not stop its operational activity inside Indonesia, since it is able to gain mass support through jihad and internal jihad. We believe that JI's conflicting needs—for organizational stability during its reconsolidation phase and for public exposure of JI's ideology (jihad) through operational activity—will be overcome in ways that will shape JI's overall targeting policy for the coming years:

- It will focus its activity in Indonesia in order to consolidate its public image as an Indonesian entity, unlike a global terrorist organization like al-Qaeda with an international agenda.
- It will conduct small-scale operations in far and remote regions in order to evade Indonesian authorities.
- These operational activities will be directed against non-Islamic, nongovernmental targets likely to receive little opposition from the Indonesian people.

The resurgence of violence in Poso, central Sulawesi, since late 2006 presents the best opportunity to implement this strategy and reinvigorate JI. During the peak of the conflict between Christians and Muslims, groups from Java came to Poso and established training camps. Poso may once again become the training and operational ground for JI and also a fertile area for indoctrination and recruitment.

One should remember that JI still possesses operational and logistical bases throughout the region, which will enable it to regroup and regain its operational status as the region's largest terrorist threat after the consolidation phase:

- Individuals whom JI members trained in explosives and firearms are still at large and can train others.

- Explosives are available in Indonesia; assembled from large quantities of fertilizer and leakage from army stockpiles.
- Interrogation of JI suspects suggest that JI is larger than initially thought, with a leadership base that enables it to replace its losses and regenerate itself.
- A JI support network still exists in Indonesia, the southern Philippines, southern Thailand, Cambodia, Malaysia, and Pakistan.
- JI has conducted widespread training over decades, ensuring its capacity across the region to engage in acts of violence through small groups.
- Dozens of suicide bombers have been trained and can still be deployed even under the tightest security conditions.
- JI's move toward business ventures is a marked departure from its previous dependence on foreign sources of funds and criminal acts such as a bank robbery. It is uncertain if the JI-linked industries are contributing to jihad activities. These businesses are not intended as profit-making ventures for individuals but provide jobs for JI recruits. A steadier stream of income could make JI more lethal and resilient in the long run.

Al-Qaeda in the Arabian Peninsula (AQAP)

Al-Qaeda in the Arabian Peninsula (AQAP) is not just another al-Qaeda-affiliated group. AQAP should be differentiated from other affiliated groups that operate against Western targets. One may find a direct link between AQAP and al-Qaeda by observing the dimensions of its history, activities, and performance. AQAP shares the same historical background, ideology, military, and terror strategies and tactics as well as recruitment methods with Al Qaeda. AQAP's senior leadership also possesses direct links, past and present, with al-Qaeda's top leadership in the Afghanistan/Pakistan border zone and have themselves been members of al-Qaeda, in some cases in senior positions. AQAP is described by scholars and intelligence experts as an organ branch or the "right arm" of al-Qaeda and not as an affiliated group.[56] AQAP is an extension of al-Qaeda.

In this section, we will focus on the current status and activity of AQAP in Yemen. We will describe the formal layout of AQAP, the different characteristics of its military capabilities and deployment in Yemen, and its modus operandi in the domestic and international arenas. We focus on the Yemen landscape, terrain, and demographics which make the country a safe haven for the Global Jihad Movement.

We will analyze the similarities between al-Qaeda's deployment and operational characteristics in Afghanistan during the last fifteen years and AQAP's deployment and military activity in Yemen. In view of these similarities alongside past and present direct links between al-Qaeda and AQAP senior leadership, against the backdrop of al-Qaeda's reshuffling in the last eighteen months as a result of bin Laden's death and the release of senior leaders who had been in Iranian custody since 2003, we believe that the relocation of al-Qaeda (or at least dominant parts of its activity) to Yemen and integration between al-Qaeda and AQAP is closer than ever. These likely developments should be considered as the next reference of threat by Western intelligence and security communities, and reflected in their budgets and operational planning for the near future.

General Background—Historical Foundations and Development

The legacy of AQAP, like that of its "mother organization" al-Qaeda, goes back to the early 1990s with the deployment of American troops to Saudi Arabia upon the invitation of King Fahd before the first Gulf War in Iraq in 1991. Osama bin Laden regarded the presence of American troops, especially American female soldiers, in the land of the two holy places as humiliating for the entire Muslim world. Gradually, this U.S. presence in Saudi Arabia turned bin Laden's attention to the international arena and was the dominant factor in his decision to engage in external operations, making the United States his first priority target for attacks through the establishment of the World Islamic Front for Jihad Against the Jews and the Crusaders in 1998. The founder and leader of AQAP, Nassir al-Wuhayshi a.k.a Abu Bassir al-Yamani, referred to the same events of the 1990s and U.S. deployment in the region as the most important development that triggered the establishment of his organization:

As our beloved leader Sheikh Osama said: "With America entering into conflict with the sons of the land of the two holy places (Saudi Arabia), it will forget the terrors of Vietnam. And, by the will of Allah, the upcoming victory in the land of Hejaz and Najd will make America forget the horrors of Vietnam and Beirut, by the permission of Allah, Glorified and Exalted be He."[57]

"Our objectives are driving out the occupiers from the Arabian Peninsula and purifying its land from them, establishing the law of Shari'a, the establishment of Khulafa, spreading the call to the oneness of Allah, defending against the transgressors and helping the weak."[58]

AQAP was established in January 2009 as a merger between two major jihadi offshoots in Saudi Arabia and Yemen. The first group consisted of the remains of the Saudi cell of al-Qaeda's Special Operations Unit, composed mostly of Saudi nationals who were veterans of the anti-Soviet war in Afghanistan, combatants from subsequent conflicts involving Muslims in other regions, and graduates of terrorist training camps based in Afghanistan that operated in Saudi Arabia between 2003 and 2007.[59] This cell, which included senior al-Qaeda figures such as Yusuf Al U'yari, Abd al-Aziz Al Muqron, and Saleh al-Awfi, operated under the direct leadership of al-Qaeda Special Operations Unit chiefs during that period (KSM and his successor, Hamza Rabia).[60] It conducted suicide operations inside Saudi Arabia targeting foreign civilians and Saudi security forces and plotted ambitious operations in the international arena.[61]

The second group was composed of al-Qaeda operatives of Yemeni origin who regrouped in Yemen between 2005 and 2010. This group has been significantly strengthened with the 2006 prison break of the group's current leader, Nassir al-Wuhayshi a.k.a Abu Bassir, and twenty-two other members. In 2006, Abu

Bassir founded al-Qaeda in Yemen (AQIY).[62] Like Saudi Arabia, Yemen has been a traditional source of jihadists; hundreds of Yemenis fought against the Soviets in Afghanistan and were graduates of training camps in Afghanistan. These mujahidin returned to Yemen and were subsequently embraced by the government and regarded as heroes by many Yemenis.[63] During the Yemen Civil War of 1994, President Ali Abdullah Saleh used these mujahidin to defeat the southern secessionists.[64] Perhaps due to the mujahidin's success in the war that reinforced Saleh's regime, the Yemeni government subsequently turned a blind eye to radical Islamic activity. The USS *Cole* attack in 2000 turned U.S. attention to the growing extremist activities in Yemen. After the 9/11 attack, the United States enlisted the Yemeni government's help in the U.S.-led War on Terror. This fundamentally changed the relationship between the Yemeni government and al-Qaeda. The post-9/11 cooperation between the U.S. and Yemeni governments was successful in the assassination of al-Qaeda leader Ali Qaed Senyan al-Harthi in 2002 by missile attack from a predator drone with the assistance of the Yemeni government.[65] However, Yemen fell off the United States' scope as the United States focused on its battle against insurgencies in Iraq and Afghanistan. The Yemeni government turned a blind eye to the extremists as long as they refrained from initiating operational activities. Under these conditions, the new AQIY launched a spate of attacks on oil pipelines, security installations, and Western embassies.

In 2007, Saudi Arabia began an aggressive crackdown on the remains of al-Qaeda's infrastructure in the kingdom and largely dismantled al-Qaeda's Saudi cell. Due to this aggressive crackdown, many operatives fled to the more hospitable operating environment in Yemen to regroup, eventually leading to the merger of the two groups and the establishment of the unified AQAP.

AQAP envisions the establishment of an Islamic state through dismantling current systems operating throughout the Arabian Peninsula.[66] Fighting is prioritized due to the perceived humiliation of the Islamic nation in the different areas in the world. Yemen is considered the land of Allah and according to the Prophet Muhammad, a land from which 12,000 warriors would come to fight in the name of Allah.[67] According to AQAP, the elimination of foreign powers from the Arabian Peninsula would result in the decline of Western influence in global politics.[68] AQAP also perceives the Arabian Peninsula as an important key arena for liberating Palestine. Abu Bassir asserts this, alleging that Muslims had cleansed the Arabian Peninsula from all "infidels" during the first decades of Islam and before the liberation of Jerusalem.[69]

Infrastructure, Layout and Operational Capabilities

Even though AQAP wishes to operate throughout the Arabian Peninsula equally, there is no doubt that it mainly focuses its activity and deployment in Yemen. AQIY magazine *Sada al-Malahim* lists traditional, geopolitical, and operational reasons for prioritizing Yemen over Saudi Arabia:

> **First**: The people of Yemen and its inhabitants are the big majority as far as the number of inhabitants in the Arabian Peninsula is concerned. [. . .] The sum of all the people of the Arabian Peninsula—the Peninsula of the Muslims—and their center is approximately 35 million people, of which 25 million live in Yemen. That means that the number of inhabitants in Yemen is approximately 75% of the inhabitants of the Arabian Peninsula. This is one of the most important facts that must be understood—that the people of Yemen are the vast majority of the people of the Peninsula.
>
> **Second**: As far as the agriculture is concerned and [the question] of enough food, then the percentage of the fertile and productive lands in Yemen is also more than 75% of all the productive lands that have water and live on groundwater in the Peninsula [*sic*].
>
> **Third**: The fortified mountainous nature of Yemen makes her the natural secure fortress for all of the people of the Peninsula and moreover for the whole Middle East. She is the citadel where her people and Mujahidin can ask for shelter. This [fact] is stable along the military history of Yemen [*sic*]. The historic invasions were crushed on the rocks of her mountains

since ancient times, starting from the invasions of Portugal and Britain and later the Ottomans and the Egyptians in modern times. This, while the rest of the lands in the Peninsula are a flat desert, which does not provide strategic options for fighting and resisting [*sic*].

Fourth: The people of Yemen have strength, braveness and ability to fight. This is in addition to the fact that its land is fitted to fighting and the fact that it is a strong fortification in the face of the enemies. The tribal coherent structure, the strength, the braveness, the love for fighting that the men of Yemen have—all this is an obvious historic fact since ancient times.

Fifth: The spread of weapons and ammunition in Yemen, in all its forms. The formal statistics from two years ago talk about approximately 70 million pieces of personal weapons in Yemen. That is in light of the tribal traditions of which it is proud and the stocks which the communists left in the south of Yemen, as well as due to the prosperity of the weapon trades with the coasts that face the Horn of Africa and East Central Africa, where the remnants of weapons and ammunition are being piled up in enormous amounts, as a result of the revolutions and the wars which occurred in those areas. Hence, there are 70 million pieces of personal weapons, not to mention tens of thousands of pieces of heavy weapons, such as cannons, tanks, different rockets and enormous amounts of ammunition. [. . .]

Sixth: The open borders which enable free movement and military maneuvers, the mountains and the northern deserts go deep and provide roads to the rest of the Peninsula, in Najd, Hejaz, Muscat, Oman and the Gulf countries. These borders spread the length of 4,000 kilometers. And the coasts that overlook the islands and the sailors in the Red Sea, the bay of Oman and the Arabian Sea—these coasts' cumulative length is more than 3,000 kilometers and they control one of the most important maritime gates—the strait of Bab Al-Mandeb, through which most of the world's important trade between the east and the west passes, as well as through the Suez canal. These open borders that cannot be controlled provide margins of a very important military strategic maneuver that is not hidden of any person with sharp sight.

Seventh: The free nature of the people of Yemen, as is the case of the land. The tribes, the youth and the Islamic revival did not fall as prisoners into hypnotizing and psychological control. The cultural and scientific openness, the variety of directions and the fact that there are many ideological streams in general and [many] Islamic, religious and Jihadist schools in particular [sic]. The people of Yemen in general, and the youth of the revival together with the Mujahidin in particular, have a free nature.[70]

Learning from past mistakes to gain local mass support, AQAP religious ideologue Adel al-Abbab a.k.a. Murad al-Shishani addressed the Yemeni people in populist rhetoric. This use of vernacular jihad discourse displays and emphasizes the importance of Yemen for al-Qaeda as a potential safe haven.[71] While AQI damaged its own case through violent extremism that cost it support even among Iraq's Sunnis, AQAP fighters in Yemen are trying to foster peaceful relations with Yemen's Sunni tribes.[72]

Attitude toward the Yemeni Regime and Other Players in Yemen (for Details of Conflicts and Players in Yemen see Annex 1)

Neither AQIY, nor subsequently AQAP, saw any legitimacy in the Yemeni regime and called for the overthrow of Yemen's sitting president, President Saleh:

> Ali Abdullah Saleh is an infidel, for he opened espionage agencies against the Mujahidin, nay, against the Muslims in general, for the sake of the Zionist-Christian campaign. He is an infidel, for he protects the infidels and the pagans as the pagans of the Qarmatians. He is an infidel, for he provides help and protection to the blood-thirsty Americans, who are found upon the beaches and the shores and the islands of the Red Sea and the Arabian Sea, and he provides them with all their needs of food and fuel. He is an infidel, for his persistent stand with the secular governments against the formation of any caliphate that would rule according to Islam, as he had done with the Islamic courts-of-law in Somalia. He is an infidel, for he

protects the newspapers that insult Allah and the religion and ridicule the apostle of the Muslims, may Allah bless him and grant him salvation.[73]

In response to the enhanced U.S.-Yemeni cooperation in the crackdown on AQAP, the group doubled its efforts to attack state targets and threatened that "Anyone who stands with (Yemeni President) Ali Saleh and his government, and with the Crusader (Western) campaign is against our Muslim people, is our enemy and a legitimate target for us."[74]

AQAP has tried to gather support from south Yemen, which is seeking a separate state of its own. It has even reached out to the south's traditionally socialist and secular separatist movement, urging all Yemeni Muslims to unite against the Yemeni government.[75] AQAP's bimonthly magazine, Echoes of Epics a.k.a. Sada al-Malahim, discusses the situation in the south, stating oppression under the Yemen government.[76] In April 2009, Abu Bassir released a statement stressing his support for the southerners' campaign against the regime, and AQAP videos celebrated victories over the Yemeni Army in south Yemen.[77] However, there is no evidence yet of the southern Yemenis corroborating with AQAP.

Since 2010 AQAP has started referring to the rising internal tensions between Saleh's central government and the Shiite population of north Yemen. The fighting in the north between the Shiite group—led by Abdul Malik al-Houthi and also known as the Houthis—and the Yemeni military over the past seven years has left thousands of people dead. AQAP's media platform, al-Malahim, released an audio message by AQAP's religious ideologue, Ibrahim al-Rubaish, addressing the ongoing clashes between Houthis and Sunnis in the town of Dammaj, Yemen. AQAP calls on Sunnis to wage jihad against Houthis in Dammaj, and warns against a Shiite takeover of Yemen and the Gulf (of Aden).[78] AQAP's military chief, Qasim al-Rimi a.k.a. Abu Huraira al-Sanani, added:

As for targeting the Shi'a Rafidha in Sa'ada, it is because they involved themselves in the adoption of the American project which consists of tracking and going after al-Qaeda. Additionally, they have expanded inside the territories of Ahl as-Sunna, and as a result their actions have led to the humiliation of some [Muslims] [sic]. It even reached the point where they assassinated some of the Imams of a Sunni Masjid as well as arrested two brothers from amongst ours of whom are Mashoor al-Ahdal and Hussain at- Tais and then handing them over to Ali Salih's regime in exchange for 10 million Yemeni Riyals [sic].[79]

AQAP took further steps beyond this rhetoric and initiated military attacks targeting Shiites, peaking in November 2010 with two suicide car bomb attacks on Houthi religious processions, killing a total of twenty-five people.[80]

The Arab Spring and AQAP Reactions

An important development in the Middle East in 2011 was the Arab Spring, in which widespread protests all over the region challenged well-established regimes and which have so far led to the downfall of regimes in Egypt, Libya, and Tunisia. Yemen's Saleh regime faced a tremendous challenge to its authority during 2011 and the beginning of 2012. President Saleh himself was seriously wounded during one of the clashes but seems to have recovered and is still fighting to save his leadership.

The wave of uprisings sweeping the Arab world has left al-Qaeda and its affiliates with a major problem. The primary protests across countries in the Middle East bore secular characteristics that spontaneously adhered to Western styles of democracy, equality, freedom, justice, and women's rights that contradict Islamic fundamentalist beliefs. This new reality has challenged not only al-Qaeda's relevance but also the very need for it, as the same tyrants and their dictatorial regimes it has fought against for decades have toppled one after the other, under the pressure of peaceful and popular demonstrations. Al-Qaeda itself and its regional affiliates played no significant role in the popular protests that toppled the "apostate" rulers in a matter of weeks. Moreover, the fact that the uprisings succeeded without its participation, or the participation of any jihad group dedicated to armed activity, has undermined one of al-Qaeda's most fundamental ideological claims that tyrants can be ousted only by jihad and the force of arms.[81]

The leaders and ideologues of al-Qaeda and its affiliated groups have tried to minimize the damage to their importance by expressing support for the uprisings. They attempted to create the impression that the Global Jihad Movement triggered the protests, cultivating a narrative whereby it played a historic role in bringing about the Arab uprisings.[82] Al-Qaeda leader al-Zawahiri repeatedly claimed that the organization's attacks on the United States, especially the 9/11 attacks, were a key element in the historical development that culminated in the outbreak of the uprisings:

> The media loyal to America falsely claims that Al-Qaeda's strategy of [armed] conflict with the regimes has failed [sic]. This media is forgetting that Al-Qaeda, and most of the jihadi movement, concluded [as early as] 15 years ago that conflict with the [Muslim] regimes should be abandoned, and that focus should be placed on attacking on the leader of global villainess [i.e., the U.S.] [sic]. Thanks to this strategy, America, especially after the 9/11 attacks, ordered the Arab regimes to increase their pressure on their peoples and on their oppositions. This helped trigger popular action and anger, [ultimately] leading to the eruption of a massive storm. Sheikh Osama bin Laden used to stress this. [He said] that the more we pressured the Hubal of our age, namely America, the more it would weaken, and as a result, its agents would be weakened as well.[83]

At any rate, the outcome of the protests created a political vacuum and a leadership gap that drew Islamic outfits to the political field, which eventually made significant political achievements.[84]

The Arab Spring in the Middle East and especially its effect in Yemen did not bypass AQAP. Its leader Abu Bassir says that the revolts in Arab nations have "'blown America's dreams to the winds' and given Muslims 'a natural chance to rid themselves of the West's cross.'"[85] Anwar al-Awlaki, AQAP's most senior propagandist who was killed in a U.S. drone strike in 2011 in Yemen, painted the protests as "Islamic" by placing the protests within a radical Islamic context:

> The first and probably most important change that this monumental event brought is a mental one. It brought a change to the collective mind of the Ummah. The revolution broke the barriers of fear in the hearts and minds that the tyrants couldn't be removed. [. . .] [T]hat changing the client regimes in the Muslim world which have the entire Western world backing them politically, militarily and economically is unrealistic in this period of our struggle. The events of Algeria[86] which came after unsuccessful attempts by the Islamic movements in Egypt[87] and Syria[88] spread a spirit of defeatism amongst the Ummah. The long lives of the tyrants along with their amazingly long rule led to the belief that there was no hope in change. Twenty-three days in Tunisia and eighteen days in Egypt were enough to shatter that deep and long held belief. The Tunisian and Egyptian people proved to us that it can be done.[89]

Al-Awlaki continues:

> We do not know yet what the outcome would be, and we do not have to. The outcome doesn't have to be an Islamic government for us to consider what is occurring to be a step in the right direction. Regardless of the outcome, whether it is an Islamic government or the likes of al-Baradi, Amr Mousa[90] or another military figure; whatever the outcome is, our mujahidin brothers in Tunisia, Egypt, Libya and the rest of the Muslim world will get a chance to breathe again after three decades of suffocation. The crackdown that the Islamic movement in Egypt witnessed at the out-start of the Mubarak regime and that continued for the following thirty years would not be possible again in a post-revolution Egyptian government. The anti-Islam secular government of Tunisia that was the only Arab state to go as far as banning the niqâb would be impossible to repeat in a post-revolution Tunisia. In Libya, no matter how bad the situation gets and no matter how pro-Western or oppressive the next government proves to be, we do not see it

possible for the world to produce another lunatic of the same caliber of the Colonel. By the will of Allah those days are gone. Even if the upcoming governments wanted to continue with a policy of appeasing the West and Israel, they would not have the strength and depth of power that the previous governments had developed over the past three decades.[91]

Finally, al-Awlaki analyzes the events with direct reference to Yemen:

The fruits of what happened in Egypt are not exclusive to Egypt. In fact we might probably witness the greatest effect of what is happening in Egypt outside of Egypt. One such place might turn out to be Yemen. Yemen already has a fragile government and the events of Egypt are only going to add pressure on it. And any weakness in the central government would undoubtedly bring with it more strength for the mujahidin in this blessed land. Yemen would also represent another great opportunity for the West to show their hypocrisy of calling for freedoms while supporting a dictator just because they do not want Muslims to be ruled by Islam.[92]

Samir Khan, an American citizen who was influenced by al-Awlaki and joined AQAP, focusing on the operational gains of al-Qaeda and its affiliated groups from the Arab Spring, adds:

America since 9-11, has been focused on the fight with the mujahidin in Afghanistan, Pakistan, Iraq and now Yemen. It has devoted its resources and intelligence for the "fight on terror." But with what is happening now in the Arab world, America would no doubt have to divert some of its attention to the unexpected avalanche that is burying its dear friends. America has depended on these men for the dirty work of protecting the American imperial interests. They acted as point men that saved America the effort of doing it themselves but now with their fall, America would have to divert huge amounts of effort and money to cultivate a new breed of collaborators. This would force America, which is already an exhausted empire, to spread itself thin, which in turn would be a great benefit for the mujahidin. Even without this wave of change in the Muslim world, the jihad movement was on the rise. With the new developments in the area, one can only expect that the great doors of opportunity would open up for the mujahidin all over the world.[93]

Khan continues to direct his message to the populations of Middle Eastern countries and focuses on the solution and the necessary next steps:

> Your loyalty should be to Allah and His Messenger. [. . .] This implies that all matters of disagreement or in question should be referred back to the Qur'an and Sunnah. Turning to this law or that leader only leads to a great loss in the afterlife. [. . .]
>
> The revolution you have experienced in Tahrir Square, Alexandria and other places was not an end goal nor has it proved the correctness of its path. There is a time and place for everything. What doesn't change though are the principles. From these principles is the ultimate loyalty to Allah, The Almighty. [. . .]
>
> Today your people have found themselves in a new dilemma. Sure, the enemy may have left the seat of authority, but you now are faced with a complex interconnection between what is democratically acceptable and what is islamically acceptable. What America wants—and has even put forward as a condition for the next government—is the maintenance of the peace treaty with Israel. Adding to that, they have already expressed their dissatisfaction of the country falling under the rule of Islamists' or Muslims who fear their Lord [sic]. This is what is democratically acceptable, and allows life to go on quietly. At the same time, it will contradict the fundaments of Islamic law which is that peace treaties with an enemy whom it is individually obligatory [. . .] to repel are null and void. [. . .] It is the Shari'a way that will always lead to success in this life and the next no matter the trials.[94]

AQAP Infrastructure

AQAP infrastructure consists of four committees (divisions):[95]

- The Shura Council (Consulting Council), the highest authority of the organization.

- The Media Committee, which publishes *Echoes of Epics*, and since 2010, an English-language magazine, *Inspire*.[96] It develops marketing strategies for AQAP products and releases official statements, research papers, and studies issued by the other sections.
- The Military Committee.
- The Sharia (Religious) Committee.

There is little detailed information available on AQAP's command and control structure. The founder and leader of the organization is Abu Bassir, to whom members of the group pledge personal allegiance.[97] His deputy is Saeed al-Shihri a.k.a. Sheikh Abu Sufyan.[98] Qasim al-Rimi a.k.a Sheikh Abu Huraira al-Sanani is the military chief of the organization and heads the Military Committee.[99] Sheikh Abu al-Hareth Mohamed al-Awfi, a former Guantanamo Bay prisoner, was one of the senior field commanders of the organization until he became under Saudi custody.[100] Another senior military commander within the group was the late Jamil al-Anbari Aka Abu Saber al-Abyani, who headed AQAP troops in the Abyan region until his elimination in March 2010.[101]

The Sharia Committee includes individuals such as Ibrahim al-Rubaish and Khaled Batarfi a.k.a. Abu Miqdad al-Kindi. The chief of AQAP's Sharia Committee is Adel al-Abbab a.k.a. Abu al-Zubair, who is described as the preeminent figure concerned with the implementation of Sharia issues in AQAP's organizational hierarchy.[102] (For the full biography of AQAP senior leaders see Annex 4.)

Even though many pieces are still missing regarding the infrastructure and concrete hierarchy and layout of the organization, one may infer that AQAP's formal layout is identical to al-Qaeda's. The general subdivision into subjectual committees (religious, military, and media), the existence of an upper consulting body (Majlis al-Shura)—which operates as a kind of cabinet, the positions of Amir and a deputy as well as the pledge of personal allegiance—can all be found in the infrastructure of the "mother organization" al-Qaeda as well.[103] Moreover, Abu Bassir served for many years as bin Laden's personal secretary during the late 1990s and was influenced by al-Qaeda's model when establishing AQAP's internal infrastructure.[104]

We believe that AQAP comprises several other bodies that are yet to be confirmed as part of the formal layout of al-Qaeda. We can infer that an important body exists according to al-Qaeda's model of a Special Operations Unit designated and responsible for external operations. We believe that the main figure within such a unit would be Ibrahim al-Assiri, AQAP's explosives expert who was responsible for the construction of the explosive devices in the Christmas Day plot, the air cargo attacks, the attempts to blow up Western aircrafts in May and July 2012, and the foiled assassination of the Saudi prince Mohamed Bin Naïf, and was heavily involved in the execution of these operations.

AQAP Deployment in Yemen and Its Assessed Military Power and Capabilities

AQAP does not appear to have a significant conventional military capability. There is no consensus regarding the strength of AQAP's membership. Figures vary widely, ranging between fifty and 500. The Yemeni government claims that AQAP has around 200 to 300 members.[105] The majority of AQAP's members are experienced Arab fighters and graduates of the jihad arenas of Afghanistan and Iraq.[106] This enables the organization to manufacture and obtain highly developed military tools, such as the bomb that targeted Prince Mohammed Bin Naïf, the bomb in the attempted attack of a commercial Northwest jet flying over the Detroit, Michigan, airport on Christmas Day of 2009, and the bomb used in the air cargo plot against American cargo airliners in the autumn of 2010.

AQAP members are currently found mostly in Marib, a restless tribal province east of the Yemeni capital Sana'a. This wild, lawless province provides AQAP with the ability to conduct its activities almost undisturbed.[107] Protected by tribes wary of government interference, the group has established bases from which to launch fresh attacks.[108]

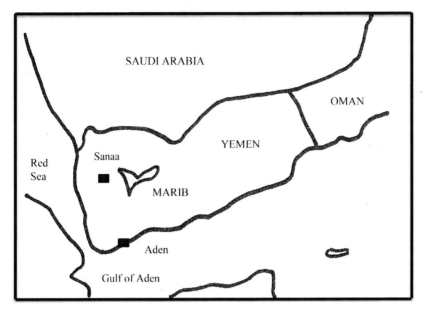

Map 4.2.   AQAP main area of deployment in Yemen.

Training Camps

AQAP has two training camps in Abyan, Yemen. The first is located in the Ahboosh Mountains, north of the city of Ja'ar.[109] The second camp is based in the al-Jaza area in the district of Mudiyah, in the southern province of Abyan.[110] Both training facilities are said to house several hundred fighters.[111]

AQAP Operational Activity
(Guerrilla and Terror) in Yemen

Inside Yemen, AQAP has adopted al-Qaeda's strategy. The group mounts violent attacks against foreigners and key instal- lations such as oil facilities and military targets in order to imple- ment its objectives. The group has vowed to attack oil facilities, foreigners, and security forces as it seeks to topple the Saudi monarchy and Yemeni government, and establish an Islamic

Caliphate.[112] AQAP's operatives have found new ways to bypass security measures and smuggle suicide bombers and explosives into even the most protected targets. Like al-Qaeda, AQAP possesses a deep understanding of the security paradigm and has developed tactics intended to exploit vulnerabilities in that paradigm in order to launch attacks.[113] (For AQAP's significant attacks in Yemen see Annex 2.)

International Characteristics of Activity

External Operations Originating from Yemen

AQAP's performance in external operations follows al-Qaeda's operational guidelines. Since its establishment in early 2009, AQAP has invested significant effort in conducting terrorist operations outside its traditional arena of operations in the Arabian Peninsula. In fact, AQAP is the only affiliate organization that has gone this far in adopting al-Qaeda's targeting policy beyond its base of deployment and activity.[114]

Within this framework of external operations there are two major strategies to which AQAP adheres:

- Planning and executing original AQAP operations mainly against U.S. aviation targets.
- Inspiring Western citizens of Islamic origin (or Muslim converts) and urging them to take action in the West, based on their own capabilities and initiative.

AQAP's original external operations include two ambitious plots targeting U.S. civil aviation:

The Christmas Day plot—On 25 December 2009, AQAP conducted its first operation outside the Arabian Peninsula. It involved Nigerian operator Umar Farouk Abdulmutallab, who smuggled explosives in a plastic bag stitched to his underwear and boarded a Northwest Airlines aircraft departing Amsterdam. The explosives failed to detonate and Abdulmutallab was arrested. Investigations revealed that Abdulmutallab was trained by the AQAP in Yemen and that the group provided him with the explosives for the attack.[115] On 28 December 2009, a jihadist website posted an alleged AQAP statement claiming responsibility for the attempted attack, saying that it was conducted in retaliation "after the savage bombardment of cluster bombs and cruise missiles launched from U.S. ships occupying the Gulf of Aden against the courageous Yemeni tribes in Abyan, Arhan, and Shabwa."[116]

Investigation revealed that Abdulmutallab lived in Yemen between 2004 and 2005 while studying at the Sana'a Institute for the Arabic Language.[117] He returned to the same school in August 2009 and stayed in Yemen until December where he met radical cleric Anwar Awlaki. Some reports indicate that Abdulmutallab may have been radicalized during this time or while studying abroad in London, where he graduated from the University College of London in 2008. In a detailed interview, Abu Bassir explained the reason behind the operation and its outcome:

> The operation of `Umar al-Faruq—may Allah hasten his release—is a strong blow to the coffin of the American economy and is a slap in the face of the American security apparatus. He reached his destination and was able to break through all of the strict security barriers after passing through a few airports and was searched in them. But through the blessing of Allah all security equipment failed to display his explosive device.
>
> The message we intended on sending to the Americans is: "America will never enjoy security until we live it in Palestine and it is not fair for you to enjoy life while our brothers in Gaza are going through a difficult life."

The fruits of the operation are many. Some of which:

- Great loss to the US economy which reached $41 billion and all of their security measures have gone with the wind.
- The fear which has spread throughout airports and security institutions has revealed to the American people that its security institutions are not to be counted upon.

- Delivering fear to the American people and creating a balance in fear and that security is not something that the government of Obama can control.
- Opening the door for many Muslim youth in the West who want to seek revenge from the Crusader states that are fighting Islam.[118]

The air cargo plot—In October 2010, based on intelligence from Saudi Arabia, Western security services recovered two explosive parcels hidden inside printers on board FedEx and UPS cargo flights en route from the Gulf region to the United States. AQAP claimed responsibility for the explosive parcels that were designed to explode in midair over U.S. land, as part of Operation Hemorrhage, intended to "cause maximum losses to the American economy."[119] AQAP also took credit for crashing a cargo jet in the Persian Gulf two months earlier.[120] An official communiqué released by AQAP claiming responsibility for the two attacks included a direct message to the U.S. leadership: "And we say to Obama: we pointed three attacks to your planes within one year, and we will continue Allah-willing to direct our attacks on the American interests and the interests of America's allies."[121]

The plot involved targeting Western economic interests. On 20 November 2010, AQAP released the third issue of *Inspire*, edited by former North Carolina resident Samir Khan. The magazine included an article titled "The Objectives of Operation Hemorrhage," examining the cargo plane bomb plot. Khan noted:

> The air freight is a multi-billion dollar industry. FedEx alone flies a fleet of 600 aircrafts and ships an average of four million packages per day. It is a huge worldwide industry. For the trade between North America and Europe air cargo is indispensable and to be able to force the West to install stringent security measures sufficient enough to stop our explosive devices would add a heavy economic burden to an already faltering economy. [. . .] So our objective was not to cause maximum casualties but to cause maximum losses to the American economy.[122]

This dimension of AQAP activity targeting economic interests resembles al-Qaeda's operational strategy to wage financial war on the West as small-budget operations force the West to invest billions of dollars in security measures.[123]

AQAP's cargo plot reflects its operational learning process: the ability to change tactics, adopt new operational strategies, and create new equipment and devices accordingly:

> After the operation of Brother Umar Farouk [the Christmas Day plot] we have been experimenting with ways to bring down airplanes. We have researched the various security systems employed by airports. We looked into X-Ray scanners, full body scanners, sniffing dogs and other aspects of security. The resulting bomb was a device that we were confident that, with the will of Allah, it would pass through the most stringent and up-to-date security equipment.[124]

Attempt to assassinate Saudi prince Naïf—Another plot, although it took place in AQAP's vicinity of operations, demonstrates again the group's creativity and operational innovation in overcoming tough security measures. The first major operation after the 2009 merger was conducted against Prince Mohammed bin Naïf, Saudi Arabia's security chief and head of the Saudi Prevention, Rehabilitation, and Post Release Care (PRAC) program. In August 2009, Abdullah al-Assiri, a wanted Saudi AQAP member, allegedly renounced terrorism and requested to meet the prince in order to repent and enter the country's rehabilitation program. The surrender of terrorists is a media event in the country's ideological battle against al-Qaeda. Reports indicate that al-Assiri traveled to Saudi Arabia from the Yemeni region of Marib, stating that he wanted to turn himself in to Prince Mohammed.[125] However, al-Assiri's surrender was a ploy to get close to Prince Mohammed who was targeted because of his key role in this ideological battle. After al-Assiri entered a small room to speak with Prince Mohammed, he activated an improvised explosive device (IED) hidden inside his anal cavity.[126] The resulting explosion killed al-Assiri but only slightly injured the prince. AQAP claimed responsibility for the failed attack in a statement posted on Islamist websites.[127]

Attempt to blow up American passenger jet (April 2012)—A British activist, who turned to be an intelligence agent, was able to infiltrate the ranks of AQAP, from whom he received an explosive device and was directed to activate it on board a commercial American jet.[128]

Attempt to blow up American passenger jet during the London Olympic Games—Recent reports (July 2012) originating from intelligence and security circles suggest that a Norwegian Islamic convert was sent by AQAP equipped with an explosive device to blow up an American passenger aircraft during the summer Olympic Games in London.[129]

Two AQAP recruiters of French nationality, the brothers Said and Cherif Kouachi, conducted a large-scale attack in the French magazine *Charlie Hebdo* headquarters in Paris during a morning editorial meeting, killing eleven journalists and wounding others. Among those killed at *Charlie Hebdo* was chief editor Stéphane Charbonnier, as well as other prominent cartoonists of the magazine. AQAP has officially claimed responsibility for the attack, suggesting it came as revenge after the magazine published cartoons of the Prophet Mohamed. It should be mentioned that AQAP included Charbonnier on its "wanted list" that was published in the tenth volume of the organization's "inspired" magazine two years before the attack.[130]

AQAP's external activities also involve inspiring Western citizens of Islamic origins (or Muslim converts) to take violent action in the West based on their own capabilities and initiative. The pivotal role of this activity has been conducted by al-Awlaki, a U.S. citizen and Islamist cleric of Yemeni origin, who was first publicly mentioned in reference to the 9/11 attacks as some of the attackers attended his sermons at the Dar al-Hijra mosque in Falls Church, Virginia, between 2000 and 2001. Al-Awlaki, an eloquent and persuasive ideologue, used his speeches, writings, and exchanges to lure, convince, trap, and control his followers to the extent that they were willing to kill and die for him. The rise in homegrown terrorism in the West is attributable in part to al-Awlaki.[131]

Al-Awlaki's ideas propelled secondary school students across North America and Europe to advocate, support, and participate in violence. Canadian and British intelligence services detected students as young as fifteen years old who had been engaged by Al-Awlaki. Many were counseled by elders, parents, teachers, and the security services, but a few have remained solidly committed to Al-Awlaki's ideals of death and destruction.[132]

Al Awlaki was adept in the use of the Internet. Although those inspired and instigated by al-Awlaki never met him face-to-face, his message found an audience and will resonate long after his death.[133]

It was only in June 2008 that al-Awlaki's activities came under the auspices of AQAP, as he built a relationship with Abu Bassir, who recognized his influence over Western Muslims, to conduct operational activities in their homelands based on their own capabilities and initiatives. Using the Internet, he provided answers to contemporary issues of injustice felt by Western Muslims. His message resonated because of its straightforward and brave tone and content. Awlaki demonstrated how effectively cyber media could be used to radicalize susceptible audiences.[134] (For the list of jihadists who were influenced by his message and turned to jihad see Annex 3.)

Although al-Awlaki's elimination by an American drone attack in October 2011 was a major blow to this tactic of rhetorical persuasion, AQAP and its supporters will continue al-Awlaki's legacy to influence Muslims in the West to turn to operational and radical activity. Shortly after AQAP confirmed al-Awlaki's death, jihadi forum members threatened to avenge his death by spreading his message on American forums and social media websites.[135] AQAP military leader Qasim al-Rimi promised to include in future publications of *Inspire* a special military section to propose effective operational measures that could be used by individuals to conduct terrorist attacks: "As for executing operations on the ground there [the West], this *Inspire* magazine thankfully works towards preparing great ideas for that matter, and soon if Allah wills, there will be a military section explaining what the Muslim should do in that field."[136]

Cooperation with External Elements

In addition to its original jihadi activity inside and outside the peninsula and its ever-growing influence over jihadi individuals especially in the West, AQAP has been maintaining contacts with regional jihadi groups around the globe. Ali Mohamud Rage, the spokesman of al-Shabaab, acknowledged that al-Shabaab has close ties to the Islamist rebels in Yemen,[137] and "Abu Jihad Al-Luzuni," apparently belonging to the Philippine jihad group, the Rajah Suleiman Movement (RSM), pledged allegiance to al-Zawahiri and other al-Qaeda-affiliated groups including AQAP.[138] Recent evidences recovered in Mali suggested a cooperation between AQAP and AQIM as well.

Parallels between AQAP and al-Qaeda, and the Climate in Their Jihad Arenas

AQAP views the characteristics of Yemen's land and terrain as a replica of the Afghan landscape. The long inaccessible mountainous chains in Yemen (a sharp contrast to the Saudi desert landscape), just like the Afghan mountains, provide AQAP with the ability to regroup and act almost freely like al-Qaeda did in Afghanistan. The existence of loyal Yemeni tribes in AQAP's deployment areas resembles the holy treaty between al-Qaeda and the local tribes in the Afghan mountains. Yemen is also full of operational opportunities in terms of availability of weapons and ammunition, similar to Afghanistan during and following the war with the Soviets.

Like the Pakistani madrassas, which attract many radical Muslims from all over the globe to come to Pakistan to study radical Salafi ideology, such radical learning centers exist and operate freely in Yemen as well. Iman University in Sana'a and the Sana'a Institute for the Arabic Language in the Yemeni capital are well known among radical Islamists especially in the West. Just like the madrassas in Pakistan, these Yemeni learning centers serve as fertile grounds of recruitment for AQAP.[139]

Most importantly, the lack of authority stemming from a weak central regime that has been losing the battle over Yemen for the last two decades to separatist groups in the south and north is similar to the climate in Afghanistan around the days of the emergence of al-Qaeda.

According to AQAP, recent regional developments in the Middle East have negated international intervention in Yemen as the U.S.-led Western powers are preoccupied with the outcome of the Arab Spring in countries across the region.

AQAP's ideology and legacy relies heavily on al-Qaeda. The leaders of the peninsula organizations previously held pivotal ideological and operational positions in al-Qaeda's hierarchy and vowed loyalty to al-Qaeda in numerous addresses since AQAP's establishment.[140]

AQAP's leadership has completely adopted al-Qaeda's international strategy and aspirations as it regards the fight against the United States, the West, and Israel as its chief priorities.[141] Abu Bassir calls for a fight in Yemen "so that we will be able to purify the [Arabian] Peninsula from the filth of the malicious occupiers and their treacherous collaborators, in order so that we can march toward our brothers in Gaza and Palestine [sic]."[142] He continues:

> We must stop the support for the Christian-Zionist campaign, kill every Christian we find in our lands, and destroy Western interests, until Europe and America shall stop aiding the Jews, stop the killing there, and order their collaborators among the treacherous leaders to open the border crossings to Gaza and Palestine.[143]

In another interview, Abu Bassir responds to a question about AQAP attacks on America and Americans:

> America is the one forcing us to target it. These heinous crimes which the human soul rejects such as the cartoons of the Messenger and holding celebrations and awarding those who curse the Prophet require us to target the Americans. In fact they require us to wipe them out of the map completely. America is a cancer that needs to be removed along with the West that is supporting this criminal behavior and are banning the niqâb of the chaste and pure Muslim women.[144]

Saeed al-Sherri, a former Guantanamo Bay detainee who has assumed a key leadership role in AQAP, ends one of his addresses with a quote from bin Laden: "America will not dream to have security until we live it practically in Palestine."[145]

AQAP leadership constantly reacts and responds to international jihadi issues such as the developments in jihadi arenas (Iraq, Somalia, Palestine, and Afghanistan) or the Prophet Muhammad cartoons.[146] AQAP leaders refer to AQAP as the new center of gravity for the overall jihadi movement and to Yemen as the new center of Global Jihadi activity. For example, they declare: "We pledge our allegiance to our brother Abu Bassir Nasir al-Wuhayshi, may Allah protect him and guide him well, so that we will serve as a buttress for the jihad to expand from the [Arabian] Peninsula to Palestine, Somalia, Iraq, Afghanistan, and all the Muslim countries [sic]."[147]

A few early indicators suggest that Yemen is becoming the preferred arena for training, as AQAP becomes the preferred training outfit by mujahidin from different parts of the world. Abu Hummam al-Qahtani, who was one of AQAP's most wanted men until he was killed, testified that he first arrived in Yemen in "search for good military preparation."[148] Further, areas or landmarks in Yemen belonging to countries involved in jihad arenas (other than the United States) have become prime targets for AQAP trainees. A young Yemeni and AQIY "martyr" Yasser Nasser al-Hamikany, who was denied access to Iraq and Afghanistan, was killed on his way to conduct an attack against the Ethiopian consulate in al-Bayda Province in retaliation to Ethiopian involvement in Somalia.[149]

As for military strategy and operational tactics, AQAP has adopted al-Qaeda's international targeting policy and has conducted operations and plots far from its base of operations, including on Western soil. AQAP is the only affiliated organization that has gone this far in adopting al-Qaeda's international aspirations. Moreover, AQAP is the only jihadi organization other than al-Qaeda to successfully execute an attack against a U.S. target in recent years, crashing a UPS cargo jet over the Persian Gulf in September 2010.

AQAP uses al-Qaeda's explosive charges tactics, as evidenced by the devices in the air cargo and Christmas Day plots, which contained pentaerythritol tetranitrol (PETN) as the explosive, directly linking AQAP's explosive expert, al-Assiri, to al-Qaeda's legendary bomb maker, Abd al-Rahman al-Muhajir.

In terms of recruitment, AQAP has been able to further advance and refine al-Qaeda's tactics. During the late 1990s, in order to conduct recruitment in the West, al-Qaeda laid down a vast network of logistical points of contact in important Western capitals under the cover of religious clerics.[150] AQAP was able to harness technological progress and the Internet exactly for that purpose. Through the activity of al-Awlaki, it reached out to thousands of potential new recruits living in the West, dozens of whom have joined and conducted attacks or devised plots based in most cases on their own initiation and capabilities.

Conclusion and Future Assessment

AQAP and Yemen as the New Hub for International Global Jihad Activity

Analyzing all the different dimensions of AQAP activity in the Arabian Peninsula it seems that the organization has completely adopted al-Qaeda characteristics and has the best potential among all Global Jihadi outfits to completely integrate with the "mother organization," which may eventually turn the Arabian Peninsula and especially Yemen into the new hub for the Global Jihad Movement.

AQAP sees the different characteristics of the land and terrain of Yemen as a replica of the Afghan landscape. The long inaccessible mountainous chains in Yemen are a sharp contrast to the Saudi desert landscape. Just like the Afghan mountains, inaccessibility provides AQAP with the ability to regroup and act almost freely just like al-Qaeda did in Afghanistan. The existence of loyal Yemenite tribes in AQAP's deployment areas resemble the holy treaty between Al Qaeda and the local tribes in the Afghan mountains. In addition Yemen is full with operational opportunities in terms of availability of weapons and ammunition just like Afghanistan during and following the war with the Soviets.

Furthermore—like the Pakistani madrassas which attract many radical Muslims from all over the globe to come to Pakistan and study the radical Salafi ideology, such radical learning centers exist and operate freely in Yemen as well. Iman University in Sana'a and the Sana'a Institute for the Arabic Language in the Yemeni capital are well known among radical Islamists especially in the West. Just like the madrassas in Pakistan these Yemenite learning centers serve as fertile incubators of recruitment for AQAP.[151]

And finally and most important the lack of authority of a central and weak regime that has been losing the battle over Yemen for the last two decades, to separatist groups in the south and in the north, is similar to the situation in Afghanistan around the days of the outbreak of al-Qaeda.

Recent regional developments in the Middle East prevents, according to AQAP, international interference in Yemen as the U.S.-led West is preoccupied with the outcomes of the "Arab Spring" in the different countries across the region.

AQAP ideology and legacy relies heavily on al-Qaeda. The leaders of the peninsula organizations held in the past pivotal positions, ideological and operational, in al-Qaeda hierarchy, and has vowed loyalty to al-Qaeda in numerous addresses since AQAP establishment.[152]

AQAP leadership adopted completely al-Qaeda international strategy and aspirations as it puts the fighting against the United States, the West, and Israel as its first priorities.[153] Abu Bassir al-Yamani called for a *"Fight in Yemen so that we will be able to purify the [Arabian] Peninsula from the filth of the malicious occupiers and their treacherous collaborators, in order so that we can march toward our brothers in Gaza and Palestine. We must stop the support for the Christian-Zionist campaign, kill every Christian we find in our lands, and destroy Western interests, until Europe and America shall stop aiding the Jews, stop the killing there, and order their collaborators among the treacherous leaders to open the border crossings to Gaza and Palestine."* In another interview Abu Bassir replies to a direct question referring to AQAP attacks on America and Americans: *"America is the one forcing us to target it. These heinous crimes which the human soul rejects such as the cartoons of the Messenger and holding celebrations and awarding those who curse the Prophet require us to target the Americans. In fact they require us to wipe them out of the map completely. America is a cancer that needs to be removed along with the West that is supporting this criminal behavior and are banning the niqâb of the chaste and pure Muslim women."*[154] Saeed al-Sherri, a former Guantanamo Bay detainee who has assumed a key leadership role in al-Qaeda in the Arabian Peninsula, ends one of his addresses with a quote of Osama bin Laden's words: *"America will not dream to have security until we live it practically in Palestine."*[155]

AQAP leadership reacts and response on a constant basis to international jihadi issues such as the developments in different jihadi arenas (Iraq, Somalia, Palestine, Mali Syria, and of course Afghanistan),[156] or the Prophet Muhammad cartoons.[157]

Moreover, AQAP leaders refer to AQAP as the new center of gravity for the overall Jihadi movement and to Yemen as the new center of the Global Jihadi activity. *"We pledge our allegiance to our brother Abu Bassir Nasir al-Wuhayshi, may Allah protect him and guide him well, so that we will serve as a buttress for the jihad to expand from the [Arabian] Peninsula to Palestine, Somalia, Iraq, Afghanistan, and all the Muslim countries. . . ."*[158]

A few early indications suggest that Yemen is becoming the preferred arena for training as AQAP becomes the preferred training outfit by Mujahidin (holy warriors) from different parts of the world. Abu Humam al-Qahtani, one of AQAP's most wanted men, testified that he first arrived to Yemen *"in the search of a good military preparation."*[159] Moreover, targets in Yemen belonging to countries involved in jihad arenas (other than the United States) have become prime targets for AQAP trainees. One of AQIY's martyrs, Yasser Nasser al-Hamikany, a young Yemenite that was denied exit to jihads in Iraq and Afghanistan, was martyred on his way to conduct an attack against the Ethiopian consulate in al-Bayda Province in revenge for Ethiopia involvement in Somalia.[160]

As for military strategy and operational tactics—AQAP has completely adopted al-Qaeda international targeting policy and conducted operations and plots far away from its base of operations and on Western soil. In fact AQAP is the only "affiliated organization" that has gone that far, which makes AQAP the flesh and blood of al-Qaeda. Moreover AQAP is the only jihadi organization (including al-Qaeda) that was able to execute an at-tack against a U.S. target in recent years far away from their own vicinity of operations, as it was able to crash a UPS cargo jet over the Persian Gulf in September 2010.

Tactically, AQAP used al-Qaeda's explosive charges tactics as the devices in the air cargo and Abd al-Farooq Mutaleb plots contained PETN as the explosive, directly linking AQAP explo-sive expert Ibrahim al-Assiri to his al-Qaeda operational mentor Abd al-Rahman al-Muhajer.

In terms of recruitment AQAP was even able to further develop al-Qaeda tactics into a more advanced and effective method. In order to conduct recruitment in the West al-Qaeda laid down during the late 1990s a vast network of logistical points of contact in important Western capitals under cover of religious clerics.[161] AQAP was able to harness progress and the Internet exactly for that purpose reaching through the activity of Anwar al-Awlaki to thousands of potential new recruitees living in the West of which dozens have actually joined and conducted attacks and plots based in most cases on their own initiation and capabilities.

Even on the logistical level AQAP has adopted some of the tactics used by al-Qaeda for fund-raising in the West using charitable foundations and Mosques operating mainly in the United States.[162]

Following the aftermath of the bin Laden assassination and the reshuffle of al-Qaeda seniors as a consequence, combined with the release of al-Qaeda leaders that were under Iranian custody for the last seven years, we believe al-Qaeda will try to find an-other alternative to the Afghanistan/Pakistan border zone which has served as the organization's main arena of deployment and center of activity since the American-led offensive in Afghanistan that followed the 9/11/2001 attacks. According to our assessment Yemen is the best alternative for such a move. First indication for this move may be seen in different reports, yet to be confirmed, about the arrival of al-Qaeda senior propagandist and one of bin Laden's close aids, Suleiman Abu Gheith, during 2010 to Yemen upon his release from over six years of custody in Iran.[163]

Furthermore one of AQAP's senior leaders, Adel al-Abbab, has referred directly to this issue and emphasizes the importance that al-Qaeda is putting on Yemen as a potential safe haven for their ranks.[164]

We believe that such a move will conclude with the complete integration of AQAP within al-Qaeda in Yemen and shall bring the united outfit back to peak operational strength, regarding all fronts, that bin Laden's organization enjoyed during the first years of the last decade.

At any rate we believe that the biggest operational concern for the West involving future activities of the AQAP depends on the organization's ability to integrate into Yemen's tribal communities and consolidate within a territorial base. This has been the key factor which enabled al-Qaeda to hide in Pakistan's tribal areas for the last decade.

We foresee the continuation of a terrorist campaign aimed at destabilizing the central regime in Sana'a while collaborating with secessionist tribes in the south.

We expect AQAP to continue targeting the Saudi state, as evidenced by its unsuccessful attempted assassination of Prince Mohammed in August 2009, the October 2009 shootout with AQAP operatives who had infiltrated the kingdom from Yemen, and the arrest of 113 militants (by Saudi security forces) said to be plotting attacks on oil operations and security facilities in the kingdom.

Both campaigns (Saudi and Yemen fronts) in the local arena will involve attacking economic targets such as the oil and tourism industries. We believe that AQAP will target the region's leaders, especially members of the Saudi royal family, as a terror tactic. Foreign official facilities such as embassies and convoys are also expected to become frequent targets of AQAP operations.

AQAP has developed significant capabilities to operate in international arenas far from its traditional vicinity of operations. We expect the organization to continue its attempts to target the civil aviation industry by striking both American passenger aircraft and cargo jets.

Annex 1—Yemen Conflicts Map

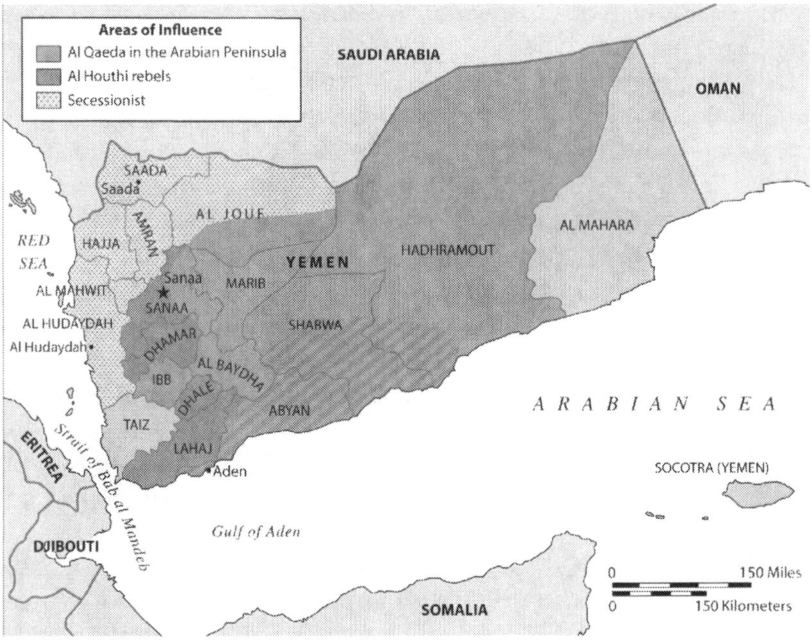

Map 4.3. Conflict Zone[165]

Annex 2—AQAP Prominent Attacks inside Yemen

- **July 2007**—AQIY used a suicide vehicle bomb in Mi'rib Province to attack the Queen of Sheba temple, killing nine people, mostly Spanish tourists.[166]
- **January 2008**—AQIY members were involved in the attack on a tourist convoy in Hadramaut, which killed two Belgian tourists and one Yemeni driver.[167]
- **April 2008**—AQIY was responsible for a mortar attack on the Haddah apartment complex in Sana'a which housed several U.S. embassy employees.[168]
- **July 2008**—AQIY has claimed responsibility for an attack against the camp of the central security forces in the Zanjabaar district in Abeen. The mentioned camp has

been widely known for its continuous tracking of Muja-hideen.[169]

- **September 2008**—AQIY attacked the U.S. embassy in Sana'a, killing at least eighteen, including one American. Reports indicate that vehicles, explosives, and small arms were used in the attack and that the suicide bombers were disguised in local Yemeni security force uniforms.[170]
- **March 2009**—AQAP suicide bombers killed four South Korean tourists and their local Yemeni guide near the ancient fortress city of Shibam. A week later, they followed this suicide bombing with a second attack against a convoy of South Korean officials who had traveled to Yemen to investigate the murders in Shibam.[171]
- **April 2010**—The British ambassador to Yemen escaped assassination after a suicide bombing of his security convoy on a narrow section of road on the way to the embassy in Sana'a. AQAP has claimed responsibility for the attack.[172]
- **June 2010**—AQAP attacked the high-walled, tightly guarded compound of Yemen's domestic intelligence agency in the port city of Aden, killing thirteen. [173]

Annex 3—Terrorist Attacks and Plots Conducted by Anwar al-Awlaki Influenced Groups and Individuals

Umar Farouk Abdulmutallab—Attempted to bomb Northwest Airlines Flight 253 over Detroit on Christmas Day 2009.[174]

Zachary Adam Chesser—Convicted on charges of communicating threats against the writers of the television show *South Park*, soliciting violent jihadists to desensitize law enforcement, and attempting to provide material support to al-Shabaab.

Nidal Malik Hasan—A U.S. Army physician who was in direct e-mail contact with al-Awlaki before conducting a shooting attack on Fort Hood in November 2009 that resulted in the deaths of thirteen U.S. servicemen.

Mohammed Hamid—A British citizen found guilty on three counts of soliciting murder and three counts of providing terrorism training. He has been accused of providing military training and inspiration to the 21 July 2005 bombers who attempted to repeat the attacks conducted two weeks earlier against the London transportation system. He was found guilty of organizing terrorist training camps and encouraging others to murder "nonbelievers."

Rajib Karim—A British citizen in e-mail contact with al-Awlaki, who asked him for advice about jihad arenas. al-Awlaki tried using Karim's position as a British Airways staff member to plant a bomb on board one of their aircrafts, and to provide information about airport security measures.

Farooque Ahmed—An American citizen influenced by al-Awlaki's lectures who attempted to collect and provide information to AQAP in order to assist in planning a terrorist attack on a transit facility.

Mahmood Alessa and Carlos Eduardo Almonte—American residents inspired by Awlaki's video sermons, who attempted to conduct an assassination outside the United States on behalf of al-Shabaab.

Betim Kaziu—An American citizen who was inspired, in part, by al-Awlaki's sermons and left for Egypt in 2009 and attempted to buy automatic weapons to be used against American troops serving overseas. Kaziu also attempted to join al-Shabaab in Somalia.

Colleen Larose a.k.a. "Jihad Jane" and Jamie Pauline-Ramirez—American citizens who followed al-Awlaki on Facebook. They were arrested on suspicion of conspiracy to murder Swedish cartoonist Lars Vilks, who had depicted Prophet Muhammad in a drawing.

Abdulhakem Mujahid Muhammad a.k.a. Carlos Bledsoe—An American citizen who conducted the fatal shooting at the U.S. Army recruiting office in Little Rock, Arkansas in 2009. Bledsoe claims he was a member of AQIY since 2007 and refers to al-Awlaki as his "Sheikh."

Roshonara Choudhry—A British citizen who stabbed her local Member of Parliament, Stephen Timms, for his support of the 2003 invasion of Iraq. During her interrogation, Choudhry admitted that al-Awlaki's lectures inspired her to act.

Aabid Hussain Khan—A British national, found guilty in possession of large amounts of al-Qaeda and other terrorism-related documents, among them al-Awlaki's sermons.

Other American citizens or residents who were influenced by al-Awlaki and intended to conduct terrorist acts but were apprehended by the authorities before they could execute their plans are **Dritain Duka, Shain Duka, Eljvir Duka, Serdar Tartar**, and **Mohamed Ibrahim Schnewer**.

The Toronto 18—A Canadian-based terrorist group composed of eighteen terrorists who in 2006 planned to carry out a series of attacks on various targets in Ottawa and Toronto. Four members of the group, Shareef Abdelhaleem, Fahim Ahmad, Zakaria Amara, and Asad Ansari, were convicted; seven pleaded guilty; and seven were cleared of charges. The group's members followed al-Awlaki's sermons in a makeshift training camp in Canada.

Annex 4—Biography of AQAP Senior Leaders

Nassir al-Wuhayshi a.k.a Abu Bassir al-Yamani

AQAP is under the leadership of Abu Bassir, a Yemeni who went to Afghanistan for military training sometime in 1996.[175] He is known to have served as bin Laden's personal secretary during his time in Afghanistan.[176] Given his association with bin Laden, Abu Bassir is most likely AQAP's strongest link to al-Qaeda's leadership in the FATA.[177] Abu Bassir fought at Tora Bora and in 2001 fled to Iran, where he was incarcerated and later extradited to Yemen for his role in the USS *Cole* bombing.[178] He broke out of a Sana'a prison with twenty-two others in the February 2006 prison break. Since becoming AQAP's leader, he has featured prominently on jihadist websites and forums. He has released videos calling on Muslims to rebel against Arab regimes, notably the government of Yemen under President Saleh and the Saudi royal family.[179] He has written many articles in *Echoes of Epics*.[180]

Saeed al-Shihri

The group's deputy leader is Saeed al-Shihri, a Saudi national who was a former inmate at Guantanamo Bay.[181] He traveled to Afghanistan in 2000 and fought the U.S.-led invasion of Afghanistan in 2001. He also served as an "al-Qaeda travel facilitator" in Mashhad, Iran, "where he would help al-Qaeda operatives enter Afghanistan."[182] He was detained in December 2001 near the Afghanistan–Pakistan border and transferred to Guantanamo Bay. In November 2007, he was repatriated to Saudi Arabia where he entered the Saudi rehabilitation program. He spent about six to ten weeks in the rehabilitation center and left Saudi Arabia for Yemen.[183] He was reported to have been involved in the September 2008 attack on the U.S. embassy in Sana'a.[184] He was reported by the Yemeni government to have been killed or captured on numerous occasions but these were later proven false. He has been active in giving statements on the Internet regarding AQAP's involvement in the 2009 Christmas Day plot and the call for a blockade in the Red Sea to cut off shipments to Israel.

Qasim al-Rimi a.k.a. Abu Huraira al-Sanani

Qasim al-Rimi is AQAP's military commander. He is responsible for the running of AQAP's training camp in Abyan Province.[185] He fought in Afghanistan during the U.S.-led invasion and trained at the al-Faruq camp there. He was incarcerated upon his return to Yemen in 2002. Rimi was one of the twenty-three escapees in the February 2006 prison break in Yemen. He was deputy to Abu Bassir before AQIY became AQAP in January 2009.[186] He was linked to the July 2007 suicide bombing that killed a convoy of ten Spanish tourists in Mareb Province.[187] Like al-Shihri, al-Rimi's death has been reported multiple times. Yemen's interior ministry said that he was killed along with six other al-Qaeda members on 16 January 2010.[188] However, AQAP

has stated on various websites that al-Rimi is still alive and rejected government claims that he was killed. *Inspire* published an
interview with al-Rimi in April 2011, indicating that he is alive.[189]

Ibrahim Hassan Tali al-Assiri

Al-Assiri is an explosives expert, whom U.S. counterterrorism officials believe is in charge of making the explosive
charges used in AQAP operations in the Arabian Peninsula and
the international arena.[190] Al-Assiri is suspected of building the
explosives used in the Christmas Day plot and the attempted
assassination of Prince Mohammed.[191]

Al-Assiri also probably constructed the two explosives that
were hidden inside printer boxes and exposed on board U.S.
cargo jets in Dubai and the United Kingdom in October 2010. Al-
Assiri's fingerprints were found on these devices, which originated in Yemen, where he is believed to be located. The devices
contained PETN as the main explosive, as in earlier attempts
involving explosives attributed directly to al-Assiri.[192]

Al-Assiri was born in 1982 and raised in Riyadh. He first
attracted the attention of the Saudi security forces when they
arrested him during his attempt to enter Iraq in order to join
Iraqi Islamist insurgents operating against the U.S.-led coalition
troops. Later, al-Assiri appeared on the Saudi government's
"85 Most Wanted" list for "participating in extremist activities
abroad" with "deviant groups."[193] Al-Assiri is believed to have
taken cover with Abu Bassir under the protection of local tribes
in the governorates of Shabwa and Mari.[194]

Adel Bin Abdullah Bin Thabit al-Abbab

Al-Abbab is the son of a Yemeni preacher who was formerly an imam of a mosque in Sana'a. Al-Abbab studied at the
Scientific Da'awa Centre for Sharia Sciences in Sana'a, which
represents the traditional Salafi ideology in Yemen. Al-Abbab
probably joined AQAP about the time of AQIY's regrouping
following the February 2006 jailbreak. In July 2007, Yemeni authorities arrested al-Abbab's father (who was later released) and
his three brothers in order to pressure him to surrender. Since

then, al-Abbab has featured in AQAP videos and his articles were published in *Sada al-Malahim*. He is considered to be the chief of the Sharia committee of the organization.[195]

Al-Qaeda in the Islamic Maghreb (AQIM)

General Background

Al-Qaeda in the Islamic Maghreb (AQIM) was established in 2006 as a result of an official merger between al-Qaeda and the ten-year-old local organization, the Global Salafist Group for Preaching and Combat (GSPC), which operated in Algeria since 1996.[196]

On 11 September 2006, al-Zawahiri, al-Qaeda's then second-in-command, announced the merger with GSPC in a videotaped address. GSPC leader Droukdel confirmed the alliance two days later, saying: "The United States can be overcome only by the Islamic United States . . . We advise our brothers in other jihadist movements to join this unity. Al Qaeda is the only organization able to unify mujahidin, represent the Muslim nation and speak on its behalf."[197] On 26 January 2007, the GSPC renamed itself the Tanzim al-Qaeda bi Balad al-Maghrib al-Islami, or AQIM.

Through this merger, AQIM pursues two simultaneous goals: Global Jihad and the creation of an Islamic state in Algeria. After officially merging with al-Qaeda in September 2006, AQIM adopted the Global Jihadist agenda. The group has extended its targeting policy and has begun to attack targets across Algeria's border as well as Western targets inside Algeria, in addition to continuing its local struggle to topple the Algerian government under President Abdul-Aziz Bouteflika and create an Islamic state in Algeria.

Infrastructure Layout and Operational Activity

AQIM is located in the following areas of Algeria:

- Province in Kabylie, in the mountainous region located east of Algiers in northern Algeria

- Desert road between Mali and Niger—the Menaka region
- Region II (Bourmedes, east of Algiers)
- Region V (northeast of Algiers)
- Region IX (a large part of southwestern Algeria, including the area surrounding Tamarasse)
- Other regions covering the remainder of Algeria

The group's main base is believed to be located in Kabylie, in the mountainous region located east of Algiers in northern Algeria.[198] Its stronghold is in Tizi Ouzou Province in Kabylie. In particular, the desert road between Mali and Niger, where the Menaka region lies, is a safe haven for the nationalist rebels and AQIM.

AQIM has divided Algeria into nine regions of operation.[199] Its most active areas of operation are Region II (Bourmedes, east of Algiers), V (northeast of Algiers), and IX (a large part of southwestern Algeria, including the area surrounding Tamarasse).

Organizational Infrastructure

AQIM is led by a supreme commander, considered as an Amir or prince, who gives direct orders.

Below the Amir operates the Ahl al-Hal wal-Aqd, or People of Authority, that comprises two branches: the Council of Notables and the Shura (Consulting) Council. The Council of Notables enlists top-level individuals involved in military actions or other violent tactics and the Shura Council comprises those versed in Sharia, medicine, communications, engineering, and politics. The Shura Council has a subsection to oversee various committees.

The decisions of the Council of Notables and the Shura Council, with the final authority of the supreme commander, are implemented by the leaders of each region of operation.

At the bottom level of the hierarchy are the fighters, which possibly includes a young militant wing, and Katibates (or companies), composed of up to 100 men who are employed for military engagement.

Abdelmalik Droukdel a.k.a. Abu Mussab Abdul Wadud, or Abou Mossaab Abdelouadoud, is the Amir. Droukdel succeeded Nabil Sahraoui as the leader of the then GSPC in 2004. He renamed the group AQIM and has pledged the group's allegiance to al-Qaeda.

The Council of Notables includes:

- Abu al-Hassan Rashid, a judge on AQIM's Shariah Council.
- Ahmed Abi Abdullah, finances.
- Salah Mohamed, propaganda.
- Younis al-Batini, leader of operations in the east.
- Asem Abi Hayan, leader of operations in the central region.[200]

Under Droukdel, there are nine leaders who are each in charge of one of the nine regions. Leaders at the regional level implement the decisions of the councils and the supreme commander:

- Region II is currently headed by Afghan-trained Abdelhamid Saadaoui a.k.a. Haitham Abou Yahya. It is located in Bourmedes, immediately east of Algiers.
- Region IX is headed by Mokhtar Belmokhtar a.k.a. Khalid Abu al-Abbas. Region IX covers a large part of southwestern Algeria, including the area surrounding Tamarasset. Belmokhtar's activities have taken him as far as Chad, Niger, and Nigeria.
- Amari Saifi a.k.a. Abderrazak El Para was the previous leader of Region V, which is located northeast of Algeria. After Saifi was captured in Chad in 2004, Mohamed Nekla a.k.a. Abdul Haq formally took over as the leader of Region V.

International Characteristics

Group affiliation   As GSPC, the group was a known affiliate of Global Jihadi groups, such as Tanzeem al-Qaeda fi Bilaad el Rafidain (al-Qaeda's wing in Iraq, headed at the time by Abu Mosab al-Zarqawi) and the International Islamic Brigade in Chechnya. These connections emerged because these groups were inspired by and vocally supported each other's attacks. These connections are not believed to include operational cooperation.

AQIM has engaged in logistical and operational cooperation with other regional groups such as the Libyan Islamic Fighting Group (LIFG), the Tuareg rebels,[201] and the Berber tribes in Boumerdes province, east of Algiers.[202]

Currently, AQIM is affiliated with other Global Jihad terror organizations and political movements, with al-Qaeda as its major affiliate.

Al-Qaeda

AQIM's link with al-Qaeda, including its historical progression, is relevant for security assessments because of AQIM's potential to implement al-Qaeda's ideology and wage attacks in the international arena. During his tenure, Hattab (the leader of GSPC until 2003) refused to meet with al-Qaeda representatives but soon after Sahraoui took over as leader in mid-2003, Sahraoui publicly announced GSPC's support for Jama'ah Qaidat al-Jihad a.k.a al-Qaeda for the first time. This informal alliance between the two groups has grown stronger over time. In June 2005, the Media Department of Tanzeem al-Qaeda fi Bilaad el Rafidayn, the Iraqi affiliate of al-Qaeda, issued a statement that included an endorsement of the Algerian mujahidin. In July 2005, the GSPC issued a communiqué calling on the al-Zarqawi-led group to target French nationals in Iraq. On 23 July 2005, the GSPC website congratulated al-Zarqawi's group on the abduction and murder of two Algerian diplomats in Baghdad, the capital of Iraq.

The GSPC–al-Qaeda merger was formalized on 11 September 2006 when al-Zawahiri announced that the GSPC had officially joined the al-Qaeda organization. The agreement signified GSPC's need to consolidate itself with a larger entity. More than a shared ideology, the alliance was necessary for GSPC's operational survival. The two groups enjoy a symbiotic relationship. As the al-Qaeda branch in North Africa, the GSPC gains legitimacy as a force in the Global Jihad arena and the struggle for an Islamic Caliphate, while al-Qaeda receives a base in North Africa, a pool of experienced militants, and potential access to militants and targets in Europe.

Finance

AQIM has received financial support from al-Qaeda since October 2002.[203] According to security and intelligence services, this support may have increased since September 2006.

AQIM's fund-raising methods in Algeria are primitive compared to the methods used by its European and North American support structure, which are better placed to exploit banking and modern technology. Kidnapping-for-ransom has been a key method for raising funds. The group's most famous and lucrative endeavor was the 2003 kidnapping of European tourists in southern Algeria by Amari Saifi a.k.a. Abderrazak El Para, the former leader of Region V. The kidnapping allegedly netted Saifi's cell around US$6 million in ransom money, some of which may still be held by several members. The group still favors kidnapping-for-ransom, but now focuses on abducting locals in the northern part of the country for much smaller payouts.

Other funding is derived from transnational smuggling. European cells assist fund-raising through drug dealing, counterfeiting money, and other illicit schemes. In Algeria, Belmokhtar uses his freedom of movement and knowledge of the Sahel region to traffic cigarettes, cannabis, and household goods. The Tuaregs (see Group affiliation, above) have been engaged in illicit commerce, including transnational trafficking, to supply AQIM. A total budget is not available at this time, but estimates of ransom monies paid suggest AQIM has been gaining several million dollars each year from kidnap operations.

AQIM also seeks funding from across Algeria's southern border. These funds are most likely acquired from AQIM's longstanding involvement with the "black economy"—smuggling, protection rackets, and money laundering across the borders of Mauritania, Mali, Niger, Libya, and Chad.

There has been recent speculation that AQIM and other al-Qaeda groups are working with the drug lords of Latin America, creating a lucrative source of income to finance attacks, inhibit economies, and deter intervention.[204]

Algerian expatriates and group members abroad, many residing in Western Europe, provide financial and logistical support to the group. Members abroad are also suspected of being engaged in criminal activities such as theft and car smuggling. Funding from criminal activities abroad may have extended to southern Europe and North America.

Operational Characteristics

Military capability Current estimates of the group's strength vary widely, from a few hundred to as many as 4,000 men. A more accurate number based on Algerian government reports puts the strength at about 1,000 men. The fighters have access to a range of weapons and are able to operate over large, remote areas of Algeria and its neighboring states.

AQIM has the capacity to target buildings and other infrastructure, including maritime vessels (see Local targets, below).

Advancing technology will likely enhance AQIM's military capability. It is experimenting with cell-phone detonators. GSPC was rumored to have purchased surface-to-air missiles, heavy machine guns, mortars, and satellite positioning equipment, all of which may be in AQIM's arsenal if in existence. Belmokhtar previously supplied AQIM with various armaments, in addition to setting up cells in the Sahel (far south in Algeria), Mauritania, and Mali.[205]

In January 2009, there was a poorly substantiated claim that AQIM was experimenting with chemical and biological agents. A U.S. intelligence official mentioned but could not confirm communication between AQIM and al-Qaeda regarding a base in Tizi Ouzou that was closed due to a failed nonconventional warfare experiment. AQIM refuted the claim on 20 January 2009.

The various weapons and possible technologies of AQIM have failed to translate into large, sustained attacks against multiple targets. However, the possibility of increased military capabilities remains.

Strategy Through its attacks, AQIM continues the practices of its parent organizations and al-Qaeda. AQIM uses targeted violence against security and military targets, foreigners, intellectuals, and administrative staff to assert control and implement its objectives. Terror attacks—assumed or confirmed to have been conducted by AQIM—have included attacks on military convoys, assassination, looting, arson, bomb attacks, and extortion (see Tactics).

Tactics AQIM uses a variety of tactics to implement its strategy. In general, AQIM employs a mix of armed guerrilla and terrorist tactics. In rural areas, it conducts classic guerrilla operations aimed mainly at government and military targets, and at times at civilians. The group employs large vehicle bombs in urban areas and has directed them at petroleum targets. Since the merger with al-Qaeda, AQIM has adopted synchronized attacks and suicide terrorism as part of its modus operandi.

Suicide attacks Suicide attacks were first carried out by the group in April 2007, about seven months after its merger with al-Qaeda.[206] The apparent change in attack methodology is linked to the merger, indicating al-Qaeda's influence over the strategy and religious ideology of the group, as no other group had committed a suicide attack in Algeria prior to AQIM.

AQIM conducted a series of suicide missions in August 2008. On 9 August, a suicide bomber rammed a truck filled with 200–300kg of explosives into the coast guard barracks in Zemmouri el-Bahri, Algeria.[207] On 19 August, a bomber drove an explosives-packed vehicle into a police training school in Issers, east of Algiers, killing forty-eight people and wounding forty-five others.[208] The next day, a military compound in Bouira and a hotel were bombed, leaving twelve people dead and thirty-one wounded.[209]

Raids and attacks Raids on military, police, and government convoys as well as other security apparatuses and official symbols of state are also a favored modus operandi where the civilian death toll is minimized. Presently, the group continues to commit small-scale terror operations against security forces in the country, especially in the mountainous Kabylie region.

Kidnapping and hostage taking AQIM also often conducts kidnapping and hostage taking. In recent years, the group has extended this tactic to include Western targets. On 22 January 2009, Edwen Dyer, a British national, was held hostage and executed. Dyer was kidnapped along with three other European tourists who were later released in exchange for the release of four imprisoned AQIM members.[210]

Under GSPC, one of the most significant instances of targeting beyond the national infrastructure was the kidnapping of thirty-two European tourists in 2003. Several hostages were rescued in an Algerian special forces operation, while others were transferred over the border to Mali by their captors. One hostage died from heatstroke. The German government is alleged to have paid around US$7 million (€5 million) to secure the release of the remaining hostages. Various factions of AQIM were involved in this hostage holding.[211]

Propaganda AQIM releases statements through the Internet, many of which are widely circulated on Arabic jihadist Internet forums. AQIM releases videos and still photographs on Islamic and Arabic websites and forums to address its supporters and promote its goals. In October 2009, AQIM allegedly established a new media wing, an audiovisual production subsidiary with exclusive rights over press release distribution. The name of this media company is "al-Andalus," a call to jihad in Andalusia.[212]

Training AQIM has been running secret paramilitary mobile camps in the Sahel region, most likely in northern Mali, where the Tuaregs have established a de facto autonomous region. These camps, though rudimentary, provide basic guerrilla training for recruits. The camps are used to train militants from Algeria, Mali, Morocco, Tunisia, Nigeria, and Mauritania.[213]

International Distribution

Several AQIM fighters from Algeria, Morocco, and Tunisia traveled to Iraq to gain combat experience and returned with knowledge on how to build car bombs and orchestrate suicide attacks. Some 20 percent of foreign mujahedeen fighters in Iraq are believed to be linked to AQIM.

The troop composition mentioned thus far is in addition to links that the group is suspected to have in European countries such as Italy, Spain, Germany, France, the United Kingdom, Portugal, the Netherlands, and Denmark. In recent years, authorities in these nations have made arrests of individuals suspected to have links to AQIM. In June 2008, Spanish authorities arrested eight men and detained a further ten from a local cell supporting AQIM.[214] In December 2007, French police uncovered a similar support cell outside Paris.[215] These intercontinental networks are mainly limited to logistical support, and not operational activities.

Targeting Policy

Local targets   In rural areas, AQIM mainly attacks government and military targets. AQIM has demonstrated its ability to infiltrate important government centers with decently sophisticated weaponry, an al-Qaeda trademark. Such attacks include false roadblocks against unsuspecting civilians and ambushes against convoys transporting military, police, or other government personnel. These attacks usually kill security forces and civilians, but do not threaten the existence or rule of the government.

In December 2005, GSPC claimed responsibility for a maritime attack on a vessel in Port Dellys, Algeria. The mission was undertaken with a remote-controlled device and resulted in one death.[216] GSPC, and now AQIM, have expressed no further interest in attacks on ports, and the increased security of port targets may have shifted its targeting policy.

Activity against Western Targets within the Sphere of AQIM Operations

AQIM conducts attacks against symbolic targets and Western interests. These include an attack on a bus transporting foreign workers affiliated with the U.S. oil company Halliburton in December 2006,[217] as well as an attack on the United Nations building a year later.[218] In addition, AQIM targets French targets in Algeria and the surrounding region.

In May 2006, Belmokhtar issued a statement of dissent, against the Algerian government and countries in the region. Belmokhtar expressed the group's desire to operate on a transnational level. The statement pledged support to al-Qaeda and warned against the establishment of U.S. military bases in Mali and Niger and future creation of bases in Mauritania and Algeria under the U.S. Trans-Saharan Counter-Terrorism Initiative (TSCTI). In December 2012, Belmokhtar left AQIM and established his own splinter organization, al-Mulathameen ("Masked") Brigade, also known as the al-Mua'qi'oon Biddam ("Those Who Sign with Blood") Brigade. In January 2013 the Brigade took more than 800 people hostage at the jointly owned Statoil, BP, and Algerian state oil company, Sonatrach, operated natural gas field Tigantourine near to Amenas in Algeria. Thirty-nine of the foreign national hostages were executed before the facility was stormed and recaptured by Algerian forces.[219] The brigade was listed by the U.S. State Department as a Foreign Terrorist Organization in December 2013.[220]

The organizational capability allows this evolving group to expand its activity to neighboring countries and establish nationwide representatives. Region IX has extended operations into Chad, Niger, and Nigeria. In June 2005, AQIM claimed responsibility for the Lemgheitty attack in neighboring Mauritania, in which at least fifteen soldiers were killed.[221]

Droukdel announced in an audio recording that AQIM would broaden its scope of targets to include all North African governments and Western interests in the Maghreb and France. Specific targets within North Africa potentially include NATO bases, petroleum industry–related resources, government buildings and security facilities, Western organizations operating in North Africa, and other Western assets. Droukdel also implied that Israeli interests, especially Jewish communities in North Africa, would be targeted.

- AQIM issued statements in 2005 and 2006, warning of attacks in countries surrounding Algeria, including Morocco, Mauritania, Mali, Niger, Nigeria, Senegal, and Chad.
- On 28 June 2009, Droukdel verbally attacked France for its ban on burkas and promised to retaliate by any means possible.[222]
- In July 2009, AQIM voiced its support for the Uyghur in China by threatening to attack Chinese workers in Algeria and surrounding areas, in retaliation for the Chinese government's alleged treatment of this Muslim group.[223]
- According to a report by the Council on Foreign Relations, AQIM has dispatched militants from North Africa to fight American and coalition forces in Iraq. The militants serve as suicide bombers and foot soldiers.[224]
- On 1 February 2008, AQIM attacked the Israeli embassy in Nouakchott, Mauritania.[225]
- Citizens of several European countries, among them Britons, French, Belgians, Germans, Austrians, and Italians, have been subjected to AQIM kidnap operations.[226]

The organization has not extended its terrorist activities beyond its vicinity of operations in North Africa, despite the vast international distribution of its cells, mainly in Europe and Canada, and despite al-Qaeda's expectations of such an extension following the merger.

Future Assessment

Attacks According to our assessment, AQIM's once localized attacks will continue to look outside the country. It is possible, although not imminent, that AQIM will attempt an attack in Europe, since it has claimed it will do so and since it has the capability to do so using its vast logistical infrastructure across Europe. Inside Algeria, AQIM will continue to focus its activity on governmental targets as well as Western targets, mostly American and French. Westerners in the Maghreb, especially along the Sahel line, will continue to be the preferred subject of kidnappings for prisoner exchange or ransom.

Weapons Interception of weapons caches suggested that the group may be in the process of developing more sophisticated improvised explosive devices (IED), which may include mobile phone detonators. These types of devices are more suited to urban areas, suggesting a possible expansion from the rural insurgency which the group has traditionally conducted.

Recruits, fighters, and alliances AQIM carefully balances individuals who wish to fight the West on both local and international fronts with others who would prefer to force change in Algeria. For fighters who cannot travel to Iraq, AQIM has encouraged the targeting of Jews, Christians, and apostates in the home regions. The merger with al-Qaeda further cultivated a culture of martyrdom, as this was the first proper sign that AQIM had been fully assimilated.

Future Cooperation with al-Qaeda

By joining with Al Qaeda, AQIM may be able to tap into al-Qaeda's wider international support base, from which AQIM may also receive ideological instruction as well as financial and logistical support. This could result in improvements to the group's existing training structure in the pan-Sahel region, such as its mobile training structure in Mali, which is utilized by members in the region. An upgraded facility will be able to provide training for al-Qaeda fighters from all over the world.

In the long run, cooperation between al-Qaeda and jihadi groups will unify and strengthen radical militant groups in the region ideologically and perhaps operationally. It will raise al-Qaeda to a commanding position in this growing cooperation, as it is the main organization rallying groups together.

Internal Dissent and Challenges

There is disunity within AQIM. In addition to internal dissent over hostages, AQIM has also seen defections. As operations expand, it is possible that more dissenters will emerge, as the group wrangles over its identity and leadership.[227]

The group's capabilities seem to have reduced over the years. The group may be able to sporadically execute attacks, but these attacks will not be significant enough to derail the Algerian peace process and amnesty program.

AQIM does not depend on popular support and does not need to pay significant attention to the local population. Its attacks will undermine any remaining support by the Algerian public. Although AQIM does not specifically target civilians, attacks inadvertently lead to civilian casualties and fatalities.

In addition, the Algerian government's reconciliation efforts are pulling men away from AQIM. Increased U.S. presence in the region and the U.S.-trained and supported security forces in and around Algeria also threaten the group's existence.

AQIM's training capabilities may be hindered by the Malines Tuaregs' recent announcement that they will combat cross-border smuggling. In Mali, representatives from the Tuareg, Arab, and Songhai communities united for the first time in ten years to help their government combat AQIM in the Sahel-Sahara. This unification may not necessarily eliminate the training structure altogether, due to the vast expanse of the region, the mobility of the structure, and the group's ability to defend itself there.

Lashkar-e-Toyba—(Army of the Pure) (LeT)

General Background

Lashkar-e-Toyba (LeT) is the militant arm of the Markaz Dawat-ul Irshad (MDI, renamed Jamaat-Ul-Dawa in early 2002), an Islamic fundamentalist organization following ultraconservative Ahl-e Hadith,[228] a branch of radical Sunni thought.[229]

LeT was formed soon after the founding of its parent organization MDI in 1987.[230] MDI was set up in Muridke, near Lahore in the Pakistani province of Punjab,[231] by Hafiz Mohammed Saeed, Zafar Iqbal, and Abdullah Azzam with the primary purpose as a center for religious preaching.[232] MDI soon distinguished itself as a hard-line fundamentalist organization following the Ahle-Hadith Movement.[233] While Prof. Saeed was in charge of military aspects (LeT), Prof. Iqbal was head of reform-oriented education (MDI).[234]

Initially, the MDI had a two-fold objective: to assist the Afghan mujahidin and to rid Pakistan of the alleged corrupting influence of Hinduism.[235] The MDI recruited volunteers to fight as mujahidin guerrillas against Soviet occupation of Afghanistan during the 1980s.[236] After the Afghan war, the group maintained close ties with the Taliban regime in Afghanistan, where it continued to train and educate its members until the U.S.-led campaign forced them to relocate.[237]

The earliest reference to MDI dates back to 22 February 1990, when it was launched during the inauguration ceremony of the Aqsa Maskar Maskar-e-Aqsa (the Aqsa Training Camo) at Tango in the Kunar Province of Afghanistan.[238] During the same year Aqsa Maskar was established near Muzaffarabad, the capital of Pakistan administered Kashmir to conduct training for Kashmiri jihadists.[239] Under the command of Abu Hafas, LeT Amir for Kashmir, LeT cadres began to infiltrate the Kashmir valley. Though the first encounter between the LeT and Indian security forces took place on 26 August 1992 at Rishighund, the formation of LeT as the armed wing of MDI was announced only in 1993.[240] LeT came into prominence along with the large-scale infiltration of its cadres into Jammu and Kashmir in 1993, in collaboration with the Islami Inquilabi Mahaz, a terrorist outfit based in Poonch district of Jammu and Kashmir.[241]

By 1997, LeT became the most active of all insurgent and militant groups in the Kashmir region. In that year, the largest group of terrorists killed in clashes with the security forces belonged to LeT.[242] During Nawaz Sharif's second term as prime minister of Pakistan, LeT became a greater priority for Pakistan's Inter Services Intelligence (ISI).[243] The then information minister Mushahid Hussain's visit to LeT headquarters in Muridke near Lahore is evidence of official patronage from Pakistan. Minister Hussain was accompanied by the governor of Pakistani Punjab Province, Shahid Hamid, and a host of provincial ministers.[244] Numerous reports have discussed LeT's involvement with official Pakistani armed forces in the Kargil conflict between India and Pakistan. LeT reportedly refused to withdraw from the Kargil-Drass sectors of Kashmir although a fifteen-group alliance, of which it was a key member, announced that it would "change positions" in the area after the Pakistani government ordered a retreat.[245] Reports suggest that the Pakistani army sent LeT cadres, the Harakat-ul-Mujahidin (HUM) and al-Badr, ahead of regular troops to occupy the ridges in the Kargil sector, after which the troops replaced them.[246] Before the Sharif government, under international pressure, made its formal decision to retreat, LeT cadres gathered in Rawalpindi on 18 June 1999 and warned the Sharif government that if it asked them to withdraw from the Line of Control (LoC), they would destroy the government.[247] LeT cadres alleged that they were promised that once entrenched in Kargil, they would proceed to take over the whole of Kashmir.[248]

The Kargil fiasco made LeT turn against the Pakistani government, especially after then prime minister Sharif banned the Muridke Convention of MDI. After Musharraf deposed Sharif in a military coup, he permitted MDI to hold its convention on 6–9 November 1999. Delegates from many countries, including India (Kashmir), Bosnia, Philippines, Myanmar, Chechnya, Saudi Arabia, Kuwait, the United Kingdom, France, the United States, and Afghanistan, participated.[249]

In a rally organized by the LeT at Aabpara Chowk in Islamabad in February 2000, Saeed made vicious anti-U.S. and anti-India speeches, and warned General Musharraf not to interfere with the Islamic madrassas, where "jihad," not terrorism, was taught.[250] He also declared that the Pakistani mujahidin groups operating in Kashmir would not tolerate any "ban" on their activities as demanded by the United States in return for a visit by then U.S. president Bill Clinton to Pakistan in 2000.[251] He described Kargil as the "first round" in the jihad against India.[252] He said that the post-Kargil "fidayeen attacks" on Indian military camps constituted the "second round" of "jihadi attacks" by the Lashkar mujahidin.[253] He declared that "very soon we will be starting the third round."[254]

On 26 December 2001, when United States designated the LeT as a terrorist entity, Saeed declared in a press conference in Lahore that the outfit had bifurcated.[255] MDI renamed itself Jamaat-al-Dawa (JD), with Saeed as its head.[256] Saeed claimed that JD would engage in political, organizational, and religious reformative activities, and that he would devote his time to preaching religion.[257] He said that the group had appointed Maulana Abdul Wahid Kashmiri as the new leader of its militant wing—which was to be the LeT[258]—and was shifting LeT headquarters from Muridke (Pakistan Punjab) to Muzaffarabad (Pakistan occupied Kashmir—PoK). This was a strategic move to escape legal prosecution, which would have become imperative after Pakistan banned the LeT on 12 January 2002.[259] It should be noted that officials in India and Pakistan consider JD and the LeT as one and the same entity. In January 2002, the Pakistani government targeted LeT in a major crackdown and rounded up many members.[260]

The United States designated the LeT as a terrorist organization on 26 December 2001.[261] It redesignated the LeT as a foreign terrorist organization in 2002, 2003, 2004, and 2005. Pakistan also designated the LeT as a terrorist organization on 12 January 2002.[262] Since November 2003, the Pakistani government has placed JD on its terrorism watch list.[263]

Objectives

The formal objectives of LeT are the liberation of Jammu and Kashmir, by merging Kashmir with Pakistan; and the creation of three separate independent Muslim homelands within India, by liberating Muslim majority areas in the north and south of India, respectively.[264] The means by which these are to be achieved is jihad. Saeed addressed the Lahore Press Club on 18 February 1996, stating, "The jihad in Kashmir would soon spread to entire India. Our Mujahideen would create three Pakistans in India."[265] He said in an interview in 1997, that "This will be accomplished" by arousing (Indian) Muslims "to rise in revolt . . . so that India gets disintegrated."[266] In 1999, Saeed said, "Kashmir is only our base camp. The real war will be inside India as we consider Himachal Pradesh (India) as the door to Jihad in India. Very soon we will enter India via Doda and unfurl the Islamic flag on Red Fort (New Delhi)."[267]

The LeT agenda, as outlined in a pamphlet *Why are we waging Jihad?* includes the restoration of Islamic rule over India.[268] The pamphlet describes jihad as being obligatory for taking back Spain, where the Muslims ruled for 800 years; the whole of India, including Kashmir, Hyderabad (in the Indian state of Andhra Pradesh), Assam (India), Nepal, Burma, Bihar (India), Junargarh (India); Palestine occupied by Israel; Hungary; Cyprus; Ethiopia; and Russia.[269] LeT also seeks to turn Pakistan into a pure Islamic state, and to wage jihad in Chechnya and Afghanistan, where non-Islamic governments are in power.

Areas of Operation

The LeT's primary area of operation is the Jammu and Kashmir region, which includes areas in India and the PoK. The group is known to have been active in other parts of India as well, such as New Delhi, Mumbai in the state of Maharashtra, and Hyderabad in Andhra Pradesh.[270] LeT was involved in several attacks and plots inside India, among them the attack against the Indian Parliament in New Delhi in November 2001 and the attack in Mumbai in November 2008, which resulted in the deaths of more than 160 civilians.

The main base of LeT and its parent organization, JD, is at Muridke, about forty-five kilometers from Lahore, in the Pakistan province of Punjab.[271] In December 2001, LeT shifted its headquarters from Muridke to Muzaffarabad in PoK. All the other LeT offices have also been shifted to areas in both Indian-held Jammu and Kashmir (IHK) and PoK. The group has offices throughout Pakistan and the main bases are in Lahore and Gujranwala district of Punjab Province, Karachi and Ferouz Pur in Sindh Province, Peshawar, the provincial capital of Khyber Pakhtunkhwa Province, the federal capital Islamabad, and Muzaffarabad, capital of AJK.[272] The LeT has more than 2,200 unit offices across the country[273] and over two dozen launching camps along the LoC in Kashmir.[274] Outside Pakistan, Kashmir, and India, the LeT is active in Bangladesh,[275] the United Kingdom,[276] Saudi Arabia, Dubai, Kuwait,[277] Iraq,[278] Australia,[279] the United States,[280] France,[281] and Spain.[282]

Organizational Structure

LeT's organizational structure is linked to that of its parent group, now known as JD, with most of the leadership working in dual capacities in both organizations. LeT, as the militant arm of JD, carries out jihad for the organization, while JD provides the ideological base.

The LeT has subdivided the Kashmiri region into districts, with each district commander in charge of military operations within his area of responsibility. Within Pakistan, the outfit has a network of training camps and branch offices, which conducts recruitment and fundraising, and provides military training for its cadres.

Under the Supreme Commander for Jammu and Kashmir (Zaki-ur-Rehman Lakvi), LeT has regional commanders for areas such as Srinagar, Bagh, Doda, and Muzaffarabad. According to sources in the Indian army, the LeT has formed four groups under new labels in the Indian state of Jammu and Kashmir: al-Madina for the group in charge of Srinagar district and its adjoining areas; Babul Hind Force for south Kashmir, including Anantnag district; Azam Jihad for areas in Doda and parts of Udhampur district; and al-Mansoorian for Jammu. Al-Mansoorian is also tasked with attacking security forces and other soft targets.[283]

Command Structure

Prof. Hafiz Mohammad Saeed: Amir, MDI; JD. Although Saeed has officially dissociated from the LeT, he retains de facto control over the organization.

Prof. Zafar Iqbal: Director, MDI, Muridke (Education Wing).

Amir Hamaza: Amir, Reformation and Invitation Wing.

Mulana Abdul Aziz Alvi: Amir, LeT (PoK).

Saifullah Mansoor: Amir, MDI, Sindh.

Zaki-ur-Rehman Lakhvi: Supreme Commander in the LeT, Jammu and Kashmir.

Abu Siddique: Organizer in the LeT, Jammu and Kashmir.

Abdul Rahman-ur-Dakhil: Commander in the LeT, Kashmir.

Abu Muslim Jarar: Supreme Commander, Jammu.
Abdul Rahman Makki (brother-in-law of Mohammad Saeed): In charge, Markaz Foreign Relations.
Sajid Mir: In charge of external operations.

The group has a socio-economic welfare wing named Dawat-e-Islami.

Operational

Military capability The exact strength of LeT cadres is unknown, but the organization has at least several hundred members in Pakistan, Kashmir, and India. The U.S.-based National Memorial Institute for the Prevention of Terrorism's (MIPT) Terrorism Knowledge Base (TKB) puts the total number of LeT cadres at approximately 300.[284] The U.S. Naval Postgraduate School (NPS) puts the total strength of LeT at "several thousand members in Azad Kashmir, Pakistan, in the southern Jammu and Kashmir and Doda regions, and in the Kashmir valley."[285] The U.S. State Department also estimates the number of LeT members at several thousand.[286] The *Friday Times* reported that there were 3,350 LeT activists.[287] According to a Pakistani Interior Ministry official, LeT's website states that "around 800 youngsters had embraced martyrdom while fighting the Indian army last year."[288] Willie Brigitte, who was arrested in Australia and deported to France, reportedly admitted that he received training at an LeT camp in Pakistan, where there were nearly 2,000 to 3,000 other mujahidin.[289]

Most of its members are unemployed youth and are recruited through government schools. Nearly 80 percent of the cadres are from Pakistan and some are Afghan veterans from the Afghan wars.[290]

The LeT successfully recruits thousands of committed young men by using its impressive organizational network, including schools, social service groups, and religious publications, to create a passion for jihad.[291]

LeT is secretive about the exact number of its cadres deployed in Kashmir at any given time. The Amir (Saeed) decides how many mujahidin need to be sent to the Kashmir valley. The decision depends on the number of deaths that have occurred. It also depends on operational requirements and the capacity of the organization inside Kashmir to absorb new fighters. What is known is that the LeT recruits and trains many more men than it requires in Kashmir at any given time.[292]

LeT terrorists operate in small groups of three or more persons, an operational strategy that allows them to conduct high-risk *fidayeen* attacks (penetrations in rural areas) against Indian security forces. In past operations, cadres used many kinds of arms and explosives, such as AK-47 assault rifles, light and heavy machine guns, mortars, and rocket-propelled grenades.[293] Interrogation of captured LeT cadres has revealed that members are proficient in bombmaking, using various kinds of explosives. An interrogation of an arrested LeT cadre in February 2003 by the Indian authorities revealed that LeT was planning to use "toy planes" to target army posts and leaders in order to conduct a "mini replica" of 11 September–type attacks in Jammu and Kashmir.[294] It reportedly acquired a fleet of four dozen such planes, capable of carrying 10–15 kilograms of RDX for carrying out attacks on army posts or helicopter gunships of the Indian Air Force.[295] Two such planes were recovered during 2002 from the Rajouri district of Jammu region. The "toy planes," which can be operated by a remote control, take a set trajectory and can hit a target within a range of 300 meters. The planes were reportedly being assembled at the group's main base at Muridke.[296]

Strategy The LeT uses guerrilla warfare to wear out and demoralize opponents who are militarily stronger. The group is known for its well-planned and well-executed attacks on Indian security force targets and for the dramatic massacres of non-Muslim civilians. The LeT also indulges in what it calls "the war of nerves." More than the number of security forces casualties inflicted by the LeT, the psychological impact of its attacks demoralizes the army.[297] LeT's intention is to gain publicity, generate fear, and to coerce allegiance and support from the local population. Non-Muslim civilian massacres are intended as a form of ethnic cleansing in the state of Jammu Kashmir. This has driven away substantial numbers of the Kashmiri Hindu population from the Kashmir valley. [298]

LeT cadres prefer to die in encounters with security forces than be caught.[299] Khalid Walid, an office-bearer of LeT, stated that LeT cadres prefer death to capture as a matter of policy. "Only those of our men are captured who faint during the fight. . . . Otherwise, we fight until death and do not surrender at any cost."[300] The LeT is believed to be opposed to suicide bombings. However, in many of the *fidayeen* attacks, where attackers burst into Indian army barracks, they have little chance of survival. LeT believes that fighters killed in the line of duty have embraced Shahadaat (martyrdom) while fighting in the name of Islam.[301]

Tactics LeT cadres use "hit-and-run" tactics to attack security force bases, military installations, air bases, and police stations. LeT hit squads typically move in small groups of fewer than ten members. The "self sacrifice"[302] squads termed as *"fidayeen"* work in smaller groups of two to five members to storm security force camps and bases, and police stations. LeT also targets Hindus and Sikhs at temple gatherings and weddings in Jammu and Kashmir, as in the murder of twenty-three people in Wandhama on 23 January 1988,[303] the massacre of twenty-five members of a wedding party in Doda, Jammu, on 19 June 1998,[304] and the Chattisinghpora massacre on 20 March 2000 where thirty-five people, mostly Hindus and Sikhs, were killed.[305] The group also plants bombs in buses and other places frequented by the public. LeT cadres also employ cruel methods such as beheading and disemboweling victims from security forces and non-Muslim communities.[306]

The extreme brutality evidenced by the indiscriminate massacre of civilians, including women and children, sets the LeT apart from other terrorist organizations operating in Kashmir.[307]

Training The LeT mainly trains its militants in training camps within Pakistan and across PoK and Afghanistan (until 2001). In PoK, some of its training camps are at Kotli, Sialkot Samani, and al-Aqsa near Muzaffarabad, the region's capital. All camps in Kashmir have been closed down, but one is still operating in Manshera (Northwest Frontier Province).[308]

Targeting policy LeT has been blamed for the massacre of Hindu civilians in the Kashmir region and other parts of India, the destruction of Hindu temples, and attacks in tourist and business areas (such as the Gateway of India and Zaveri Bazaar in Mumbai in August 2003).[309] LeT has always denied killing civilians.[310]

LeT has attacked Indian security forces, such as border police and infantry patrols. LeT also planned attacks against high-profile Indian leaders including Deputy Prime Minister L.K. Advani; Gujarat Chief Minister Narendra Modi; and Pravin Togadia of the Vishwa Hindu Parishad (VHP), a group of Hindu fundamentalists who seek the genocide of Muslims, Christians, and Sikhs.[311] Reports in the Indian media state LeT's plans to kill sport personalities like Sachin Tendulkar and Souray Ganguly.[312] The Indian government has claimed to have foiled attempts by the LeT to target software companies in Bangalore.[313] Indian analysts have expressed increasing concern of a possible LeT attack on U.S. diplomatic missions and U.S. naval ships visiting Indian ports.[314]

Since the U.S.-led coalition takeover of Afghanistan in November 2001, LeT has been upgrading its external operations targeting Western facilities. The structure and apparatus of LeT's external operations are not clear but cumulative reports suggest that LeT possesses a worldwide network in the United Kingdom, Spain, the United States, Italy, France, and India.[315] In its early stages, LeT provided its infrastructure to assist Al Qaeda's operations on Western soil.[316] In recent years, cumulative reports suggest that the organization has its own designated unit for external operations headed by Sajid Mir, which was responsible for Willie Brigitte's plot to target an Australian nuclear power plant in 2003 and the Mumbai attack in November 2008, which killed 164 people including many foreigners.[317]

Group affiliations LeT used to cooperate with several organizations that operated in south Asia, among them al-Barq[318] and SIMI.[319] As for Pakistani organizations, LeT collaborates with Jaish-e-Mohamed (JeM) and is part of the "Karachi Project."[320] In remote areas of terrorist operations, LeT is affiliated with al-Qaeda and the Taliban in Afghanistan,[321] as well as the Jemaah Islamiyah of Southeast Asia.[322]

Al-Qaeda and the Taliban

The relations and cooperation between LeT and al-Qaeda date back to the early days of the Global Jihad Movement in Afghanistan. LeT founder Saeed fought against the Soviet troops in Afghanistan,[323] probably within the ranks of Abd al-Rasool Sayyaf's "Itihad al-Islami al-Afghani" operating from Sadah Camp.[324] LeT was established to participate in the mujahidin fight against Soviet troops in Afghanistan. In the process, the outfit developed strong links with Afghanistan's mujahidin organizations. Reports suggest that MDI and LeT were members of bin Laden's World Islamic Front for Combat against the Jews and the Crusaders, formed on 23 February 1998. Bin Laden reportedly provided funds for the construction of a mosque and a special guesthouse inside MDI's Muridke complex near Lahore. Bin Laden was also reported to have addressed the annual conventions of the MDI via teleconference. During the annual conference at Muridke in November 1997, bin Laden spoke over the phone from Kandahar and reportedly said, "Those who oppose Jihad are not true Muslims."[325]

LeT has several Afghan nationals amongst its cadres.[326] The group once claimed that it had assisted the Taliban militia and al-Qaeda in Afghanistan during the fight against the U.S.-aided Northern Alliance in November and December 2001.[327] During the U.S.-led coalition offensive that followed the 9/11 attacks, Zayn al-Abidin Muhammad Husain aka Abu Zubeydah, a well-known Arab mujahidin leader in Afghanistan, was captured in an LeT safe house in Faisalabad in March 2002, suggesting that LeT members were facilitating the movement of al-Qaeda members in Pakistan.[328]

As previously mentioned, LeT cooperated operationally with al-Qaeda during the shoe bomb plot on December 2001, as LeT cells in Paris provided Richard Reid with the final necessary logistics before boarding the jet in Paris. Different indicators suggest that LeT may have collaborated with al-Qaeda in the Willie Brigitte case and the Mumbai attack as well.[329]

Jemaah Islamiyah (JI)

In October 2003, Singapore arrested two JI militants, Muhammad Arif bin Aaharudin and Muhammad Amin Bin Mohamed Yunos from Pakistan.[330] The pair were part of the Pakistani-based cell code-named "al-Ghuraba" or "foreigners."[331] This cell was set up by Hambali, the JI operations commander, in 1999 to train young Southeast Asian Muslims to become leaders of the group.[332] Amin also traveled from Pakistan to the southern Afghan city of Kandahar for full-time military training with al-Qaeda. Arif is alleged to have trained with the LeT in 2000 and 2001, after arriving in Karachi to join the al-Ghuraba cell.[333]

In September 2003, Pakistani authorities arrested Gun Gun Rusman Gunawan, Hambali's brother and a key leader of JI, from Karachi's Abu Bakar University, a madrassa affiliated with the Pakistani Ahle-Hadith Movement, LeT, and JD.[334] Gunawan's arrest led to the apprehension of five Indonesian and thirteen Malaysian students from Abu Bakar University and the neighboring Darasat ul Islamiah Madrasah, which is fully owned and operated by the LeT.[335]

Source of Supply and Finance

The LeT allegedly received supplies from the Taliban and al-Qaeda. According to Indian intelligence sources, it also receives arms and ammunition from Pakistani government agencies. The major source of its finance has been the Pakistani community in the Persian Gulf and the United Kingdom, Saudi dissidents, Islamic nongovernmental organizations (NGOs) and charities, and Pakistani and Kashmiri businessmen.[336] According to an Indian security official who investigated the cross-border funding of militants in Kashmir:

> Groups like Lashkar [LeT] and Jeish [Jaish-e-Mohamed, JeM] generally run on donations from rich Gulf and Saudis or on the

> Pakistani government's support. . . . The militant groups gen-
> erally get the guns and other arms and ammunition from the
> Government sources across the border. . . . They don't need to
> purchase it (arms and ammunitions) at all from open market.
> And they manage funds locally also. It is either consensual do-
> nations or extortion from local businessmen or ransoms. This
> is apart from *Hawala* channels. . . .[337]

One of the major sources of the group's finances has been the collection of funds through donations and public appeals. The group used to put donation boxes in many cities across Pakistan. Even after the group was banned by the Pakistani government in January 2002, the fund mobilization continued. On 14 October 2003, the U.S. Department of the Treasury issued orders to freeze the U.S. accounts of al-Akhtar Trust, a charity reportedly run by Jaish-e-Mohamed (JeM) in Pakistan, "providing a wide range of support to Al-Qaida and Pakistani based sectarian and jihadi groups, specifically Lashkar-e-Tayyiba, Lashkar-I-Jhangvi, and Jaish-e-Mohammed [*sic*]."[338] There were also reports about the associates of the trust "attempting to raise funds in order to fi-nance 'obligatory jihad' in Iraq."[339]

During the November 2003 Id festival (also called Eid) in Pakistan, the LeT was reported to have received charity contri-butions, mostly in the form of the hides of sacrificed animals, which were sold to raise 710 million rupees (about US$15.7 million).[340] Since the beginning of Ramadan (the Muslim holy month of fasting) in early November 2003, JD set up donation camps to collect donations.[341] In its 19 November 2003 issue, a Pakistan English language paper, the *Daily Times,* reported that the JD continued to collect donations despite a government ban.[342] It set up several camps in Chauburji, Samanabad, Allama Iqbal Town, Shadman, and Baghbanpura areas of Lahore city, capital of Punjab Province, seeking donations and selling JD publications, posters, stickers, and other material. A poster dis-played at the camps exhorted: "Help the Mujahidin with your money. They are defending your ideological and national fron-tiers with their blood." Ramadan is a profitable time for jihadi groups and seminaries soliciting donations, as a large number of Muslims pay their *zakat* (annual charity) and *fitrana* (poor dues related to the Id feast) then.[343] In March 2003, *South Asia Tribune* reported that LeT raised funds worth Rs. 1.4 billion from the Muslim community in Britain—allegedly, 675,000 Pakistani Muslims out of a total Muslim population of 1.6 million—in the name of Eid sacrifice.[344]

The LeT has invested in legal businesses, such as commodity trading, real estate, and the production of consumer goods.[345] The 17–23 January 2003 issue of the Lahore-based English weekly magazine, *Friday Times,* reported:

> The Jamaat-ud-Dawa (JD), formerly known as Lashkar-e-Toiba, is snapping up properties across Pakistan. Sources told the weekly that recent real estate purchases by the JD amount to about Rs.300 million [about US $ 6.7 million]. It has reportedly bought four plots of land in Hyderabad division (of Sindh) and six others in various Sindh districts. The total price tag is about Rs.200 million [about US $ 4.5 million]. Recent purchases in Lahore have cost it Rs.100 million [about US $ 2.25 million].[346]

Apart from donations from overseas Pakistani communities and from donation camps inside Pakistan, the LeT also solicits funds through a website under the name of JD. The site provides information on the group's activities.[347] In February 1999, major newspapers in Pakistan carried ads appealing for donations to LeT to support its activity in Kashmir.[348]

External Support

The LeT maintains ties to religious military groups around the world, ranging from the Philippines to the Middle East and Chechnya, and generates funds through its affiliates.[349] Its U.K. network allegedly raised funds for jihad in Kashmir, as revealed in the deportation trial of Shafiq ur Rehman, the Pakistani Muslim cleric from the mosque in Oldham, Lancashire; as well as from the admission of Mohammed Suhail, who worked for the British firm Railtrack and ran the Global Jihad Fund "to facilitate the growth of various jihad movements around the world by supplying them with sufficient funds to purchase weapons and train their individuals."[350] There are reports that LeT and Jaish-e-Mohamed (JeM) used to collect as much as £5 million (US$7.4 million) from British mosques annually in the name of Islam.[351]

There are also reports that LeT has strong links with Saudi Islamists and some members of the royal family. According to LeT's past claims, a significant portion of its funding comes from Saudi sources.[352]

Political Capability

LeT enjoys significant support from sympathizers in Pakistan. Its leadership had connections with key functionaries in the Pakistani government, especially in the military and intelligence setup. LeT believes that the liberation of Kashmir will pave the way for establishing Islam in Pakistan. Pakistan, which LeT considers "a moderate state," would be changed not through a revolutionary process, but by means of "a gradual reform through Dawa."[353]

Significant Events

Even though the majority of LeT's operational activity is limited to the Kashmir zone and along the LoC with India, the organization has conducted several attacks inside India's heartland in recent years:

- **22 December 2000**—An attack was carried out at Red Fort, New Delhi, by an LeT squad. Red Fort is a high-profile target as the seat of the Moghul Empire in India before British rule and as the site of the proclamation of India's independence from Britain on 15 August 1947. A two-member squad attacked an army camp within the Red Fort area and killed three people, two of whom were army regulars. In a message to the British Broadcasting Corporation (BBC), LeT claimed responsibility for the attack and described it as a suicide attack.[354] The attack occurred two days after the announcement of the extension of India's military cease-fire in Kashmir.

- **13 December 2001**—The Indian government accused the LeT of involvement in the attacks on the Indian Parliament in New Delhi.[355]
- **24 September 2002**—An attack on Akshardham, a unique cultural complex dedicated to world peace and harmony[356]in Gujarat, India, killed around twenty-eight people. Two heavily armed militants took position at a vantage location in the shrine with the greatest number of devotees. Their aim was to cause maximum harm to the civilian population. Though a letter found on one of the terrorists killed by security forces mentioned an unknown group Tehreek-e-Kasas to which the terrorist belonged,[357] it was subsequently revealed that the attack was masterminded by Abu Zubair, an LeT militant who was killed in an encounter with security forces on 23 September 2003.[358] The attack was reportedly planned in Riyadh, Saudi Arabia, as revenge for the killing of Muslims in the Indian Gujarat riots.[359]
- **29 October 2005**—A series of three blasts in New Delhi left fifty-nine people dead and nearly 210 injured. While the Islamic Inqilab Mahaz (Front for Islamic Uprising) claimed responsibility for the attack,[360] Indian authorities arrested Ghulam Muhammad Mohiuddin, an alleged Hizb-ul-Mujahedeen (HuM) member from Doda district in IHK, who confessed to aiding three LeT operatives in the attacks.[361]
- **26 November 2008**—The Mumbai attacks: more than ten coordinated shooting and bombing attacks were launched across Mumbai, India's largest city, by terrorists who invaded from Pakistani waters. The attacks, which drew international condemnation, began on 26 November 2008 and ended on 29 November 2008, killing 164 people and wounding at least 308.[362] The targets of the attacks were carefully selected and included places frequented by foreign nationals, such as the Taj Mahal, the Oberoi Trident hotels, and the Jewish Chabad House (Nariman House).

Hence, the list of casualties contained foreign citizens from the United States, the United Kingdom, and other Western states as well as Israel. The attack has been officially attributed to LeT.

Recent and Future Activities

There are reports that suggest that LeT has reorganized its structure based on al-Qaeda. It has expanded into business activities in order to augment its sources of income. Based on the interrogation of Walid bin Attash (a suspect in the USS *Cole* bombing arrested in Karachi in April 2003), LeT allegedly coordinates the supply of funds; suicide volunteers; and arms, ammunition, and explosives among pro–bin Laden networks across the world. Attash reportedly told interrogators that LeT had lent twelve suicide volunteers for missions against the United States in Iraq.[363]

The LeT maintains extensive ties with religious military groups all over the globe. Many terrorist suspects from outside Pakistan had stayed at Muridke and in LeT training camps. Willie Brigitte spent about six months at LeT training camps as did Abdul Qadeem Zaloom, a Saudi-based person with links to al-Qaeda.

LeT's alleged involvement with the Karachi Project may point to the future direction of LeT. According to our assessment, LeT will continue to provide its worldwide logistical infrastructure and its training centers in Pakistan for use by sister Islamist organizations in order to aid their activity, including international operations. We believe that LeT will refrain at this stage from initiating its own global operations against Western targets even though it vowed as early as 1998 to commit to Global Jihad and to wage operations against the United States and Israel.[364]

We believe that an exception to this policy is LeT's future operational involvement in Mumbai-style attacks in India that may include Western targets on behalf of a larger Pakistani alliance such as the alleged Karachi Project.

Abu Sayyaf Group (ASG)

The ASG aims to liberate Muslims in Mindanao from perceived oppression, tyranny, and injustice under the Christian-dominated Philippine government.[365] Since its inception, the ASG has advocated an Islamist ideology far more radical than the national principles of the Moro National Liberation Front (MNLF) and the Islamic principles of the Moro Islamic Liberation Front (MILF). The group aims to unify the predominantly Muslim provinces in the southern Philippines and establish an independent, purely Islamic state through armed struggle.[366] ASG founder Abd al-Razeq Janjalani intended to accomplish this objective through armed struggle instead of the gradual and peaceful process of Islamic proselytization embraced by Muslim groups such as the Tabligh Movement (a Muslim preaching organization).[367] ASG seeks its objective by staging bombings and kidnapping activities chiefly targeting Christians.

Unlike the MNLF and the MILF, which advocate an inclusive conception of the Bangsamoro state, the ASG aims to rid Sulu and parts of Mindanao of all Christians and non-Muslims. The group believes that any necessary method of purging Mindanao of Christians is justified because Islam calls Muslims to struggle against nonbelievers, particularly since ASG views such "enemies" to have deprived Muslims of their wealth and homeland. This anti-Christian enmity—an emotional outpouring rather than a rational approach toward its professed aims—was the principal motivation for ASG's initial wave of terrorist attacks. ASG also used these sentiments to rationalize its actions.

Observers note that when Khadafy Janjalani took over the ASG leadership in 1998, the group's priorities changed. It emphasized material interests over the radical religious-political objectives pursued under his brother, the founder of the organization, Abd al-Razeq Janjalani. Observers view that the group has abandoned its initial socio-political aims and has become a solely criminal-terrorist group that uses Islam to rationalize its mercenary activities. At present, the group's operations do not appear to be determined by any ideology. ASG has not issued statements related to Islam and did not refer to any belief or ideology in its recent kidnappings of local traders in the Basilan and Sulu regions of the Philippines.

History and Development

The ASG began its activity in 1991. Abd al-Razeq Janjalani, an Afghan war veteran and a former member of the MNLF, founded the ASG. The group combined radical Islamism with Moro (Mindanao) nationalism, aiming to unify Muslim provinces in the southern Philippines and establish an independent Islamic state.[368] Under Janjalani's leadership, a group of about ten MNLF members became increasingly drawn to the idea of waging *Qital* (combative) jihad. These MNLF members—which included Janjalani's brother, Hector; Edwin Angeles a.k.a. Yusuf Islam; Abdul Asmad; Yasser Igasan; and Isnilon Totoni Hapilon—later formed the ASG's core membership.

During the summer of 1991, the ASG established its headquarters, Camp al-Madinah Mujahideen, at Mount Kapawayan in Isabela, on the island of Basilan. By August of the same year, the group staged its first major terrorist attack when it bombed passenger ship MV *Doulos*, killing two foreign missionaries and wounding forty others. The incident also marked the first time that Janjalani used "Abu Sayyaf Group" to refer to his group, when he claimed responsibility for the bombing. In his statement, Janjalani warned Christian missionaries not to venture into the Muslim south again.

Since then, the ASG has staged bombings and kidnappings-for-ransom to gain publicity and acquire funds to sustain its operations. In February 1993, the ASG came to international attention when it kidnapped Charles Walton, a language researcher of the U.S.-based Summer Institute of Linguistics, who translated the Bible into local dialects.

Throughout the 1990s, despite the counter activity conducted by the Philippine army causing setbacks for the ASG, the group continued its terrorist activity, mainly kidnappings-for-ransom and bombings, and was able to increase its cadres mainly by recruiting senior MNLF operatives.

In 1995, the ASG gained notoriety when it set fire to the predominantly Christian town of Ipil, Zamboanga Del Sur, and conducted mass shootings, killing forty-one people. According to hostages taken during the attacks, the ASG warned of more attacks if the Philippine government continued alleged oppression and corruption.[369] The incident was followed by three separate incidents of kidnapping in Zamboanga: three Chinese executives from an unspecified Hong Kong company, an eighty-year-old woman and four family members of a Taiwanese resort owner, and an Italian priest.

The group was set to stage more kidnappings when the Philippine police killed ASG founder Abd al-Razeq Janjalani in a shoot-out in Basilan in December 1998. For a time, a power struggle among competing ASG commanders threatened to destroy the organization. However, Abd al-Razeq Janjalani's younger and less religious brother, Khadafy Janjalani, quickly moved in to succeed him.

Under Khadafy Janjalani's leadership, the ASG departed from armed political struggle to wanton kidnapping, with demands for ransom payments amounting to US$45,000 (PHP 1 million) for each hostage and beheadings when these demands were not met. The ASG continued to abduct Westerners for ransom as well.[370]

Financed by kidnap-for-ransom operations, the ASG targeted popular tourist resorts outside the Philippines, attacking several Malaysian diving centers and kidnapping staff members and tourists.[371]

The ASG experienced diminished operational capability in the wake of the 9/11 attacks, due to the Philippine and the U.S. governments' recalibrated approach to counterterrorism. This impaired the ASG's operational strength in terms of reducing its membership and capability to stage activities that required careful planning and execution, such as large-scale kidnappings. The group resorted to small-scale banditry at this time and remained elusive amid repeated and intensified military assaults.

In 2004, in order to assert its presence, the ASG extended attacks beyond the group's traditional area of operation. In

February 2004, the ASG executed its most devastating attack to date—the Super Ferry 14 operation. Investigations indicate that the ASG placed a television set containing an 8 lb (4 kg) TNT bomb on board the ferry, which sailed out of Manila for Cagey de Oro City with about 900 passengers and crew. When the ship was ninety minutes out of port, the bomb exploded, killing 116 people.[372] There are claims that the ASG bombed the passenger ship because the company that owned it, WG&A, ignored a letter demanding PHP 45 million (US$1 million).

In February 2005, the ASG again launched simultaneous bombings in Manila and key cities in the southern Philippines, Davao, and Zamboanga. The ASG announced that the bombings were the group's Valentine's Day presents to President Arroyo. The ASG operations planner warned that more "gifts" would come until justice was gained for the countless Muslim lives and properties allegedly destroyed by the Arroyo administration.

Since 2005, the ASG has suffered major setbacks inflicted by the Philippine army. In September 2006, Khadafy Janjalani was killed in a massive military operation in Sulu and on 16 January 2007, his successor Jainal Antel Sali Jr. a.k.a. Abu Suleiman was fatally wounded in a firefight.

Since then, remaining subleaders of the ASG—including Hapilon; Radulan Sahiron a.k.a. Commander Putol; and Gumbahali Abu Jumdail a.k.a. Abu Pula—and about 200 followers have been alternately evading and attacking pursuing government troops in Sulu and Basilan. While in their hideouts, the remaining ASG members look for opportunities to kidnap local traders or persons of interest.

A notable target was media personality Ces Drilon, who went to Sulu to interview Sahiron. On 11 June 2008, about forty ASG members kidnapped Drilon, two members of her news team, and a university professor in Sulu. Following negotiations for the ASG to not behead Drilon's group and for ransom payments amounting to US$445,000, the ASG freed the victims on 18 June 2008.[373]

A series of abductions of traders in Sulu and Basilan, including the kidnapping of Red Cross staff of different nationalities in Sulu, followed the highly publicized kidnapping, reinforcing the ASG as a key target of the country's counterterrorism efforts.

Area of Operation and Strength

Map 4.4.   The Philippines

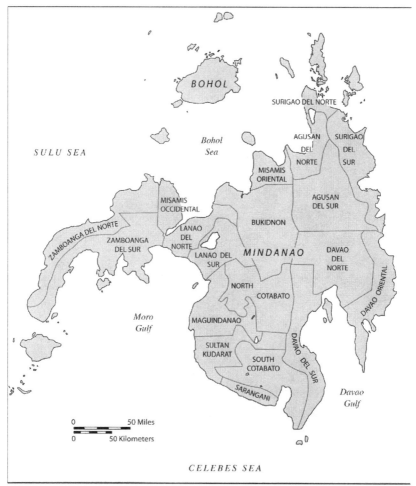

Map 4.5. Mindanao Island.

The ASG's areas of operations are Basilan, Sulu, Tawi-Tawi, Zamboanga Del Norte, Sarangani, Sultan Kudarat, North Cotabato, and Lanao Del Sur, all of which are within the island of Mindanao.

The Philippine military places ASG membership strength at fewer than 300, with half of its members also belonging to both the Sulu-based MILF and MNLF factions.

In terms of weapons, ASG fighters are well equipped with a wide range of small arms, which include AK47, M14, and M16 assault rifles; M203 grenade launchers; machine guns; and 90mm recoilless rifles and 60mm mortars.[374]

The ASG continues to be capable of staging bombings and kidnappings. Kidnap-for-ransom operations in particular indicate a strong desire by the group to raise funds crucial for its survival, despite a heightened government offensive. The group is believed to have bolstered its influence over surrounding communities by disbursing an undetermined amount of funds raised from kidnapping operations. This has enabled the group to access a robust information network in the area. The group's subleaders, which include Sahiron, Hapilon, and Indama, maintain bases of operation in Sulu and Basilan. These bases effectively shield the group from pursuing government troops, while also enabling them to reconsolidate and plan future attacks.

Command Structure

A document recovered by Philippine military intelligence from an ASG hideout in Sulu in August 2006 indicates a detailed organizational structure.[375] This organizational structure, prepared by Khadafy Janjalani in 2003, includes six major components. These are the Military, Civil and Media Sections; the Consultative Council; the Political Committee; and the General Budget. These units report to the group's Amir, Khadafy Janjalani.

1. The Military Section is "tasked to lead the ongoing war in Southern Philippines and implement *Shari'a* teachings."[376] The Military Section includes:
   i. The section leader
   ii. The Military Council: There is little information on the council except that it includes Moro leaders of the group's previous battles.
   iii. The "Battles and Camps" Team, responsible for selecting instructors and trainers, training camps, and mujahidin for leadership positions.

iv. The Supplies and Provision Team, comprising a team leader and six members. It is responsible for supplying provisions, surveillance and transport, military intelligence, and the development and planning management of subteams. All subteams are responsible for providing the ASG with a continuous supply of food, clothes, medication, transport needs, etc. They are also responsible for conducting surveillance against targets using sophisticated tools and gathering information on military targets.

2. The Civil Administration Section consists of:

i. The Educational Team, responsible for emphasizing jihad in all Islamic doctrines to promote monotheism and facilitate the spread of their religion.

ii. The "Implementing the Teaching of Islam Team" or *Hisbah*, in charge of keeping all ASG members on the "true path" to Islam.

iii. The Preaching Team, responsible for promoting and maintaining the tools of Islamic preaching, such as studies and research on Islamic doctrine as well as libraries, Islamic centers, madrassas (Islamic schools), and mosques. The team is also responsible for the welfare of students and preachers.

iv. The Rescue Organization Team, comprising legal entities that provide legal, social, or developmental aid to Muslims in the southern Philippines.

3. The Media Section consists of well-trained members responsible for relaying information through photography and other media. This section consists of the Photography and Montage, the Information and Communication, as well as the Editing and Directing subteams.

4. The Consultative Council includes top Islamic scholars who formulate policies and strategies to be adopted by the ASG. The council also decides general responsibilities, leadership appointments, and the group's budget.

5. The Political Committee consists of the ASG's official spokesperson, political planners, and political negotiators.

6. The General Budget is responsible for maintaining the group's financial resources and accounts as well as allocating funds for development or social projects.

Although the ASG did not fully adopt this crude organizational structure, the recovered document indicates the group's attention to details outlined for the specific tasks of the six major components in the structure. The organizational structure, which is reportedly shown to local and foreign prospective donors and/or active supporters, illustrates the group's intention to expand and organize membership to enable cohesion and efficiency.

In June 2007, the ASG's subleaders and about 200 followers reportedly chose Yasser Igasan to succeed Khadafy Janjalani as the group's leader. Reports from the Philippine military suggested that the ASG had chosen Igasan because of his close association with the Janjalani brothers as well as his terrorist training abroad, good educational background, and crucial connections with possible foreign financiers.[377] Observers had considered Hapilon, Sahiron, and Abu Pula as possible successors to Khadafy Janjalani.

Affiliated Groups

Within the local Mindanao arena, ASG cooperates with several local groups, such as the long operating MNLF and the MILF, that are struggling for the liberation of Mindanao.[378] More broadly across the Philippines, the ASG cooperates with the Rajah Suleiman Movement (RSM), as revealed in the investigations of the Super Ferry 14 and Valentine's Day attacks.[379] Links between the two groups are based on kinship rather than shared aims and beliefs. RSM leader Ahmad Santos, Khadafy Janjalani, and ASG commander Abu Suleiman are connected through their respective wives, the Dongon sisters Nurain, Zainab, and Amina.

Within the Southeast Asia regional arena, the ASG cooperates mainly with JI. Apart from sharing resources, both groups also exchange knowledge in terrorist techniques and tactics through frequent reciprocal visits, correspondence, and joint training.[380]

Al-Qaeda is the ASG's key partner in the international arena. As previously mentioned, this cooperation developed from Afghan war veteran relations between jihadi militants. The ASG–al-Qaeda cooperation is based on the relations that were cultivated in the Sadah camp of Ittihad al-Islami al-Afghani, which served as a melting pot of jihadi volunteers. The members of the Abd al-Rasool Sayyaf group included Abd al-Razeq Janjalani (who later founded the ASG in the Philippines), Hambali (who became the military chief of JI), Hafez Saeed (who became the founder and leader of LeT), and Khalid Sheikh Mohamed ([KSM] who became the chief of al-Qaeda's Special Operations Unit responsible for external operations). This melting pot of post–Afghan war operational collaboration was reflected in the planning of the Bojinca plot in 1994–1995. This plot was an ambitious attempt to crash a dozen American commercial jets over the Pacific Ocean in one day. The plot was led by KSM and his cousin Ramzi Yousef with Hambali as one of the main plotters. Janjalani provided the group with a safe apartment in Manila. ASG claimed responsibility for a "test attack" against Philippines Airlines Flight 434 en route from Manila to Tokyo that resulted in the death of a Japanese passenger. When KSM joined al-Qaeda in early 1999 as chief of al-Qaeda's Special Operations Unit for external operations, the informal relations become formal cooperation between al-Qaeda and the ASG.[381]

On 9 September 2001, KSM sent two al-Qaeda operatives to an ASG stronghold in order to train ASG members for future attacks against Western facilities in the Philippines. One of these plots, a suicide truck bomb attack against the Israeli and American embassies in Manila, was eventually dismantled by the Philippine authorities as it reached its final stages of preparations in early 2004.[382]

Finance

The ASG obtains most of its financial resources through robbery, piracy, extortion, kidnapping-for-ransom, blackmail, smuggling, and small-scale marijuana cultivation.[383]

The group has reportedly netted a windfall profit of about US$40 million in ransom payments from a series of high-profile kidnappings of Westerners and Filipino Chinese from the late 1990s to early 2001. The group also reportedly amasses PHP 45,000 (US$1,000) to PHP 68,000 (US$1,500) a month from "revolutionary taxes" that it demands from local businesses in Basilan and Sulu. In some instances, the group has demanded rice and other foodstuff as part of the payment. In May 2006, a report from the Philippine military revealed that the ASG had been sending extortion letters to several business establishments in Zamboanga City, demanding amounts ranging from PHP 2 million (US$40,000) to PHP 5 million (US$100,000). The ASG threatened to bomb these business establishments if they failed to pay.

"Revolutionary taxes" are part of a steady stream of funds that the group has been receiving from local politicians such as former Basilan governor Wahab Akbar and other secessionist groups such as the MILF, MNLF, and JI. [384]

In October 2007, the ASG was reported to have created a video calling for funds. According to these reports, the group posted the video on YouTube. Philippine authorities are still verifying sources of reports that through the video, the group has netted a significant amount of funds from foreign donors.

During the early 1990s, ASG received support from former terror-funding states such as Libya and Iraq. [385] Various reports from the Philippine National Police revealed that some overseas Filipino workers based in Saudi Arabia have transported funds to the ASG as well.

Operational Activity

Strategy The ASG does not appear to have an overall strategy to achieve its aims of unifying Muslim provinces in Mindanao and establishing an Islamic state. The group uses guerrilla tactics to harass and intimidate the Philippine government and its people. This approach has not gained popular support. In fact, in all its activities, the ASG has shown a disregard for the popular support crucial for the group to achieve its professed political and ideological goals. The group has also not undertaken Islamic social or development programs that could prepare the Muslim communities for the group's socio-political agenda of establishing of an Islamic state.

The group has recently carried out kidnapping-for-ransom activities in an effort to keep up with operational demands. Although these abduction activities are small, the frequency and the ease with which they are carried out has established the ASG as a key target of the country's counterterrorism agenda.

Tactics The ASG employs brutal and lethal tactics—such as the mutilation of Filipino soldiers' bodies or the beheading of hostages—to instill fear or maximize publicity. The group has repeatedly threatened to behead hostages in the course of its negotiations with the Philippine government, for example, in the abduction of Peruvian American Guillermo Sobero in May 2001.

The group motivates recruits with financial rewards. The ASG reportedly pays recruits from local communities to serve as security elements in ASG camps.

Training Arrested JI members in the Philippines have indicated that ASG leaders received basic infantry training and instructions in map reading and weapons handling from JI operative Rohmat a.k.a. Zaki.[386] ASG members also underwent deep-sea diving training with JI militants in July 2005 in Sandakan, Malaysia, in preparation for attacking maritime targets such as ports and commercial vessels.

Targeting policy Since 1991, apart from conducting raids and ambuscades against police and military outposts and convoys, the ASG has directed most of its attacks against Christian churches, Catholic priests, missionaries, and non-Muslim communities. For its kidnap-for-ransom operations, targets have included American, German, French, Malaysian, and Taiwanese citizens as well as Filipino Chinese tourists or traders.

During the mid-2000s, the group extended its vicinity of operations to the Philippine mainland by cooperating with the RSM. From 2001 to 2004, as a result of al-Qaeda's attempt to mobilize local groups against Western targets, the ASG was involved with an al-Qaeda-led plot to conduct suicide operations using truck borne improvised explosive devices (TBIED) against the Israeli and American embassies in Manila.

Terrorist Activity

- **1992**—The ASG hurled a bomb at a wharf in the southern city of Zamboanga where the MV *Doulos*, an international floating bookstore manned by Christian preachers, had docked. Two foreign missionaries were killed and forty other people were wounded.
- **1993**—The ASG kidnapped Charles Walton and freed him after twenty-three days.
- **April 1995**—The ASG attacked the predominantly Christian town of Ipil in Zamboanga. Gunmen razed the town center and killed fifty-three civilians and soldiers.
- **1996**—The ASG rebels kidnapped sixteen people in Mindanao and Trankeni Natural Resort, Lake Cebu.
- **1998**—The ASG abducted three executives from Hong Kong, an 80-year-old mother and four other family members of a Taiwanese resort owner, and an Italian priest in Zamboanga Del Sur.
- **2000**—The ASG raided two high schools and took forty-seven hostages, including a Roman Catholic priest from a church-run school in Sumisip town on Basilan Island and ten people from another school in Tuburan on the same island. They demanded the release of 1993 World Trade Center suspected bombers Ramzi Yousef and Omar Abdel-Rahman (The "Blind Sheikh") in exchange for the freedom of the remaining twenty-nine hostages.[387] The group also threatened to kill Americans in the Philippines.
- **April 2000**—The ASG kidnapped twenty-one foreigners from an island resort in Sipadan in Sabah, Malaysia. The group demanded PHP 1 million (US$45,000) for the release of each hostage.
- **July 2000**—German *Der Spiegel* journalist Andreas Lorenz and thirteen Christian preachers led by television evangelist Wilde Almeda of the Manila-based Jesus Miracle Crusade International Ministry were kidnapped in two separate incidents.
- **July 2000**—The ASG kidnapped three French journalists.

- **August 2000**—The ASG kidnapped American Jeffrey Craig Edward Schilling.
- **September 2000**—The ASG raided Pandanan Island near Sipadan and kidnapped three Malaysians.
- **May 2001**—The ASG attempted to attack Barcelo Pearl Farm beach resort in Samal Island but was stopped by the resort's security detail. The group took two hostages as it fled.
- **May 2001**—The ASG kidnapped twenty foreigners from the Dos Palmas Resort on Palawan Island. The group demanded PHP 1M (US$45,000) for the release of each hostage.
- **June 2001**—The ASG occupied the Jose Torres Memorial Hospital in Lamitan, Basilan, to get treatment for its members wounded in armed encounters with government troops.
- **February 2004**—The ASG bombed passenger ship Super Ferry 14, killing 116 passengers.
- **February 2005**—The ASG conducted three simultaneous bombings (the Valentine's Day bombings) in Metro Manila and the cities of Davao and Zamboanga, killing fifteen people and injuring several others.
- **August 2005**—The ASG conducted twin bombings in the cities of Cotabato and Koronadal in an attempt to divert military pressure from ASG leaders in MILF territories.
- **10 August 2005**—The ASG bombed two targets in Zamboanga City. The first bomb exploded in a parked minivan on Campaner Street in Zamboanga City. Thirty minutes later, a second blast tore through the second floor of a budget motel.
- **August 2005**—The ASG bombed the ferry MV *Doña Ramona*, wounding thirty people.
- **18 February 2006**—A bomb exploded in a bar outside an army camp in Sulu, killing one civilian and wounding twenty others. The Philippine military attributed the attack to the ASG.
- **27 March 2006**—An IED exploded on the ground floor of a two-story multipurpose cooperative store owned and

managed by priests of the Notre Dame of Jolo College, killing at least five people and wounding twenty others.

- **17 October 2006**—ASG subleader Furuzi and about ten of his men, armed with .45 pistols, ambushed a convoy of government troops in Tipo-tipo, Basilan, killing a soldier and wounding another.
- **10 January 2007**—Three bombs exploded in three places in Mindanao. The first bomb exploded in a marketplace in General Santos City, killing three people and wounding twenty-two others. Less than three hours later, a second bomb was detonated near a police outpost near Kidapawan City. The third bomb exploded in a dumpsite along a major street in Cotabato City. The attacks took place on the eve of the Association of Southeast Asian Nations (ASEAN) summit from 10 to 15 January 2007 in Cebu City.
- **10 July 2007**—Fourteen Marines were killed—ten of whom were beheaded—when they marched into MILF territory in Basilan in search of abducted Roman Catholic priest Gian Carlo Bossi and were fired at by ASG and MILF members.
- **February 2008**—The ASG kidnapped a female trader in Sulu.
- **May 2008**—The ASG kidnapped a businessman in Zamboanga City.
- **11 June 2008**—ASG gunmen held broadcast journalist Ces Drilon of ABS-CBN Broadcasting Corporation, her two cameramen, and a professor of Mindanao State University (MSU) after abducting them in Maimbung, Sulu. The widely covered hostage crisis involved the group's demand for ransom amounting to US$445,000, negotiations requesting the ASG not to behead Drilon's team and the alleged involvement of Sulu government officials in the abduction.
- **September 2008**—The ASG abducted five aid workers in the village of Cabangalan, Ungkaya Pukan, Basilan.
- **16 September 2008**—An undetermined number of ASG militants abducted two minors from their homes.

The group demanded PHP 1 million (approximately US$22,000) for the children's release.

- **28 November 2008**—Antiterrorism operatives foiled a possible bomb attack in Metro Manila after arresting two suspected ASG members, Sala Kasan Bairulla and his son Albasher Bairulla, in their safe house in Taguig City.
- **24 December 2008**—Twenty-one bystanders were injured when motorcycle-riding ASG suspects threw a fragmentation grenade outside a Jollibee restaurant in Isabela City, Basilan.
- **15 January 2009**—ASG militants kidnapped three workers of the International Committee of the Red Cross (ICRC) in Sulu. thirty-eight-year-old Swiss Andreas Notter, sixty-two-year-old Italian Eugenio Vagni, and thirty-seven-year-old Filipino Mary Jean Lacaba were aboard a Red Cross vehicle after inspecting a water sanitation project in Sulu provincial jail when kidnappers stopped them at gunpoint and abducted them. The abduction followed a series of kidnapping incidents during the previous months in Sulu and Basilan.
- **29 September 2009**—Two U.S. Navy soldiers and a member of the Philippine Marines were killed and two others were injured when a land mine exploded near a Marine detachment between the villages of Kagay and Luamsaing in Indanan, Sulu.[388]
- **13 April 2010**—The ASG extended its terror campaign to the heart of Basilan in Isabela City, setting off bombs at a Roman Catholic cathedral, a school grandstand and three other places, and clashing with government forces.[389] At least fourteen people were killed in the attacks.[390]

Islamic Movement of Uzbekistan (IMU)

General

The Islamic Movement of Uzbekistan (IMU) was founded in the early 1990s, when two Islamic radicals—twenty-four-year-old Tohir Yuldashev and twenty-two-year-old Jumaboy

Khojaev a.k.a. Jumaboy Namangani—led the establishment of Sharia-based vigilante groups in the Fergana valley in the then Uzbek Soviet Socialist Republic. Since its beginnings as a Sharia-based vigilante group, the IMU's objective has been to create an Islamic Caliphate in Uzbekistan, which would extend to the rest of central Asia and beyond, to include the Xinjiang-Uyghur autonomous region of China. To achieve this, the IMU seeks to overthrow the secular governments of central Asia, which IMU proclaims to be anti-Islam and pro-West.

On its official website www.furqon.com, the IMU stated the following objectives: "Leading the people from the ignorance to the bright and right path," "Cleaning Islam from different wrong stereotypes and habits," "Awakening sleeping hearts and cure their grievances," "Calling Muslim for abiding by the Islamic rules," "'Warning the Muslims from the anti-Islamic studies and streams," "Imposing the Sharia of Allah on the soil of Allah," "Deliverance from Hell and joining the Paradise community," "Reviving the Islamic Caliphate, which was enlightening the path of humanity in the thirteenth century," and "Liberating sacred places like Palestine and Arabia Steppe, stolen by the Christians and Jews."[391]

Since its inception, the movement has experienced changes, relocations, and major setbacks that include internal splits and assassination of the movement's most senior leaders. Throughout the years, the IMU has shown that it is capable of adjusting to new circumstances and has been able to rehabilitate its chain of command, relocate its base of activity to new locations, and continue its terrorist activity.

History and Development

The precursor organizations of the IMU were established between 1990 and 1992 in the Fergana valley. In the late 1980s, emissaries from Saudi Arabia, Afghanistan, and Pakistan visited the area in order to give financial and ideological support to the local Islamists advocating an Islamic state in the Fergana valley.[392] In April 1991, Yuldashev, a then prominent member of Islamic organizations that operated in the area, publicly demanded that Uzbekistan president Islam Karimov impose Sharia Law in the republic.[393] Yuldashev and Namangani fled to Tajikistan in 1992 to escape prosecution for their activities and joined the Tajikistan Islamic Renaissance Party in its fight against the central government. While Namangani stayed on to fight on the side of the Tajik Islamists until 1997, Yuldashev traveled to Pakistan, Afghanistan, Saudi Arabia, Iran, the United Arab Emirates, Turkey, and the Caucasus in order to gain ideological, financial, and logistical support and collaboration. From 1995 to 1998, with the support of Pakistan's ISI, Yuldashev procured grants from Pakistan's Jamiat-i-Ulama Islami and other Islamic parties to train young IMU members in Pakistani madrassas.[394]

In autumn 1997, IMU-affiliated militants conducted assassinations in the Fergana valley. Several local policemen, citizens, and businessmen were killed, beheaded, or robbed.[395]

In 1998, after setting up a base in Kabul, Afghanistan, Yuldashev and Namangani announced the creation of the IMU.[396] The group also declared jihad against President Karimov.[397]

Between 1998 and 2001, the movement relocated its base of operations to the Afghan arena under the auspices of the Afghan Taliban Movement. IMU members fought on the side of the Taliban against Ahmad Shah Massoud's Northern Alliance.[398] From Afghan land, the IMU made several attempts to infiltrate Uzbekistan in order to destabilize President Karimov's regime. On 16 February 1999, the IMU attempted a coup in Uzbekistan. The plot involved an assassination attempt on President Karimov and a series of simultaneous bombings in key locations across Tashkent. Six car bombs were detonated in Tashkent, which killed thirteen civilians and wounded 128 people. On 15 September 2000, the United States designated the IMU as a terrorist organization.[399]

The U.S.-led military campaign in Afghanistan in the autumn of 2001 resulted in the deaths of hundreds of IMU members, including its commander Namangani. From October to November 2001, the remnants of the organization crossed over to FATA, Pakistan, and settled down in Wana, capital of South Waziristan Agency. In early 2002, a group of discontented IMU members separated from the group and under guidance from al-Qaeda seniors established another jihadist group, the Islamic Jihad Union.[400]

The remaining IMU members under Yuldashev encountered difficulties in finding support and shelter amongst the Ahmadzai Wazir tribesmen in North and South Waziristan. In spite of his growing prominence among South Waziristan Islamists, Yuldashev lost his heroic status when his followers began targeting Pakistani army and government officials in late 2006, an act that was disapproved by the local tribesmen. After bloody fights between the local tribesmen and the IMU in March 2007, the latter was forced to take refuge in an area in South Waziristan that was under the control of Pakistani Taliban commander Baitullah Mehsud.[401] IMU militants operated in South Waziristan, particularly near the town of Kanigoram, until the Pakistani military campaign in autumn 2009 and the killing of Yuldashev by a U.S. drone attack in late August 2009.[402] IMU militants have been staging fierce resistance against Pakistani troops, by hiding in the mountainous zones of South Waziristan and in the upper agencies of the FATA, Pakistan, where they conduct land mine and sniper attacks on Pakistani troops using hit-and-run tactics.[403]

Organizational Structure and Leadership

From 1998 to 1999, the IMU created and developed its consultative body, the Oliy Shura (Supreme Council). The council's membership was composed of leading personalities in the movement—the Amir (Yuldashev), the commander (Namangani), the chairman and the press secretary (Zubair Abdur-Raheem), the chief of counterintelligence (Ali), the chief of intelligence (Abu Anas), the chief of internal police (Bilol), and the chief of the Sharia Department and publications (Sobithon).[404]

The organization has a Common Council which includes the auditor and the secretary of the Elders' Council as well as the heads of the Religious department, Construction Department, and Refugee Issues Section.[405]

In late 2003, the IMU created its media wing, Jundulloh (The Soldiers of Allah). It is presumed that the name was chosen after the death of Hasan Mahsum a.k.a. Jundulloh, the founder and ex-leader of the East Turkestan Islamic Movement (ETIM), who was in close contact with IMU leaders.

The Amir is the supreme leader of the IMU, whose orders are strictly followed. From 1998 to 2001, Amir Yuldashev controlled the IMU's counterintelligence, while Commander Namangani directed intelligence issues in tandem with Taliban representatives.[406]

After Namangani was killed in a battle near Kunduz, Afghanistan, by a U.S. air strike in November 2001, Yuldashev became the only leader of the movement until his death in the aftermath of a U.S.-drone attack in the Kanigoram area, South Waziristan, in the FATA of Pakistan on 27 August 2009.[407] Usmanjan Qari was reported to have taken over IMU leadership in September 2009 but this is uncertain as the IMU has remained silent about Yuldashev's death. On 31 May 2010, the IMU released a video which revealed that the organization was operating under four commanders: Abdul Malik, Usmon Hakimiy, Muso, and Abbas Mansur.[408]

On 17 August 2010, the IMU website released a statement by its spokesman, Fattoh Ahmadiy, in which he announced that all members of the movement would come under the new leadership of Usmon Odil. This was said to be in accordance with Yuldashev's last will.[409]

In April 2012 the IMU announced Usman Ghazi as its new Amir, taking over from Usmon Odil after he was killed in a U.S. drone strike in North Waziristan Agency in April 2012.[410]

Group Affiliation

In spite of its declarations that it is an independent organization, the IMU collaborated with government-linked, independent, and terrorist organizations and movements posing as the Islamic opposition to Uzbekistan's government. From 1992 to 1997, the IMU collaborated with the Tajik Islamic Renaissance Party, which was fighting against government troops. From 1998 to 2001, the IMU cooperated closely with the Taliban and the ETIM. When IMU moved to the FATA of Pakistan, it relied on the support of the banned Tehriki-Taliban-Pakistan (TTP), an umbrella militant organization of anti-Pakistan terrorist groups. At different stages during its early activity, characterized by frequent relocations until 2001, in order to obtain financial, logistical, and religious support, the IMU cooperated with influential representatives of the central Asian diaspora based in Afghanistan and some Arab countries, including high officials in Turkey, Chechen Islamic organizations, and the Saudi and Pakistani intelligence agencies. The IMU also recruited several hundred members of the Hizb ut-Tahrir (HUT), who fled central Asian republics in the late 1990s to escape government prosecution.

Finance

It is believed that the IMU supplied its financial needs by conducting illegal activities such as narcotics trafficking, robbery, and kidnap-for-ransom. From 1998 to 2000, under Namangani's leadership, IMU guerrillas were actively involved in the transport of heroin from Afghanistan to Tajikistan and on to Russia and Europe. In October 2000, the IMU reportedly collected US$2–6 million in ransom for the release of Japanese geologists. The money was reportedly paid to IMU guerrillas by Japanese officials though Kyrgyz official intermediaries.[411]

Initially, the largest share of funds came from wealthy Saudi businessmen of central Asian origin, which helped IMU leaders to build mosques and recruit youths. By 2001, the IMU had received over US$1 million in such donations. Since relocating to Pakistan's FATA, IMU has been sponsored by the Pakistani Taliban (TTP) and local Islamist donor organizations.[412]

Operational

The IMU's strategy is based on militant jihad ideology and activities. The group has been in limbo since late 2001 and operates mainly from Pakistan's FATA where it is regrouping for infiltration activities in central Asia.

There is no verifiable information on the IMU's actual strength as the numbers vary from several hundred to thousands, depending on the group's circumstances. The IMU reached its peak membership from 1998 to 2001 with about 1,500 to 2,000 members operating in close collaboration with the Taliban in Afghanistan. After the split of the movement in 2002, the group led by Yuldashev could not regain these early membership numbers because of poor resources and unclear strategy. Since the last counterterrorism campaign of Pakistani troops in the FATA in the summer of 2009, the IMU has suffered several casualties, especially among its leadership. At present, several IMU militant groups are operating separately in different parts of the FATA and northern Afghanistan.

During the 1999–2000 military incursions, IMU militants used various tactics including kidnap-for-ransom and sniper shooting. Since 2002, the IMU has conducted several robberies in South Waziristan, Pakistan, in order to sustain its budget. Beginning in 2009, the IMU launched more mine, rocket, and sniper attacks on Pakistani government troops alongside its hit-and-run operations. According to announcements in 2010 on its official website, the IMU's scattered militant groups are staging elusive resistance against Pakistani troops who are expanding the area of counterterrorist operations in the FATA. After retreating to the upper areas of the FATA, particularly to Kurram Agency, the IMU has reported its successes in killing Pakistani troops through sniper shootings, land-mine attacks, and ambushes. Part of its three-staged activities list from 12 December 2009 to 25 February 2010 includes the elimination of school and hospital buildings in the FATA to prevent their use as weapon stockrooms by Pakistani troops.

On 18 March 2010, the IMU distributed leaflets in the Mira shah area of North Waziristan in the FATA, in which they vowed to "free Pakistan from American clutches."[413]

The IMU targets government buildings and TV stations as well as government officials and law enforcement personnel. Until 2001, it was skilled in abducting foreigners for ransom as well.[414]

One of the IMU's main objectives is to provide consistent training for its members and prepare the young generation of mujahidin. IMU members received most of their military training during their battles in Tajikistan and Afghanistan. In Pakistan, IMU fighters systematically train themselves. Video footage of their training is part of the IMU's online propaganda.

Main Events

- **1990**—The creation of vigilante groups "Justice" and "Fighters for Islam" in Namangan city, Fergana valley, Uzbekistan.[415]
- **1998**—The creation of the IMU.
- **20 August 1998**—More than a dozen members of the group killed in Afghanistan in an American cruise missile attack against an al-Qaeda stronghold in Afghanistan in retaliation for al-Qaeda attacks against U.S. embassies in east Africa earlier that month.
- **16 February 1999**—First major bombing operations in Tashkent.[416]
- **1999–2000**—Failed military incursions into Uzbekistan through Kyrgyzstan and Tajikistan.[417]
- **Late 2001**—Namangani killed in U.S. air attack during Operation Anaconda; IMU moves to the FATA to regroup.[418]
- **2002**—Split into two groups. The establishment of the IJU.[419]
- **27 August 2009**—Yuldashev killed in U.S. drone operations. Group's partition into guerilla cells interconnected via radiophones.[420]
- **17 August 2010**—IMU website releases statements from the organization's spokesman Ahmadiy, its new leader Odil, and Yuldashev's will. IMU announces its further commitment to jihad.[421]

Islamic Jihad Union (IJU)

General Background

As a radical Islamic Uzbek group, IJU emerged as a splinter group of the IMU in 2002. The main objective of the group is to impose Sharia by conducting military jihad against the governments of Uzbekistan and other "anti-Islamic" countries like Afghanistan, Pakistan, the United States, and Germany. In line with al-Qaeda's agenda, the group is committed to participating in Global Jihad and focuses a significant amount of operational and recruiting efforts in the West, mainly among the Turkish migrant communities in Western Europe, first and foremost Germany as well as Turkic-speaking countries.

History and Development

The IJU was established in March 2002 in Mir-ali, North Waziristan, Pakistan, by splinters from the IMU. Najmiddin Jalolov, Suhayl Buranov, Kh. Ismoilov, and Ahmad Bekmirzaev, among others, were the founders of the new group, which took its initial support from senior al-Qaeda leaders, chiefly Abu Layth al-LIbi.[422] IJU's initial seed money came from al-Qaeda through its Libyan liaison.[423]

In the autumn of 2002, after training the first jihadists, the IJU began to plan its suicide operations in Uzbekistan under the operational leadership of Bekmirzaev. On 28 March 2004, nine IJU members died in an operational accident in the cell's safe house, a bomb-making factory in the Romitan district of Bukhara Province, Uzbekistan. As a consequence of the blast, all the operational plans of the IJU cell were accelerated, leading to the execution of several terrorist attacks in different parts of the country using suicide bombers (mostly females), from 29 to 31 March 2004. In the aftermath of these operations forty-six people died: ten policemen, thirty-three IJU members, and three civilians. Fifteen members of the group were detained.[424]

On 30 July 2004, IJU renewed its attacks in response to the trial of fifteen IJU fighters that was under way. Six people, two of whom were female IJU members, were tried in Uzbekistan, while sixteen other members of the IJU Kazakh cell were arrested in southern Kazakhstan. Three male suicide bombers simultaneously attacked the United States and Israeli embassies and the Uzbek General Prosecutor's Office in Tashkent. Four security personnel died and seven people were wounded in these blasts.

On 13 May 2005, a male suicide bomber was killed by security guards near the Israeli embassy, probably as part of the wider uprising of Islamists from the radical Akramiya group in Andijan city, Fergana valley, Uzbekistan. On the same day, IJU released a statement declaring jihad on the Uzbek government.[425]

As a consequence of IJU's failure to carry out significant attacks in Uzbekistan, IJU changed its strategy. Upon receiving assignments from al-Qaeda, the organization directed its focus on Europe, particularly on Germany, and began plotting against Pakistan.

From 2005 to 2006, the group plotted against German, American, and Uzbek targets in Germany using a local cell in Germany (Sauer land cell) composed of German converts to Islam and German citizens of Turkish origin. In December 2007, the IJU joined the fighting between local Taliban in the Swat region of the FATA and Pakistani armed forces.[426]

In 2008, the IJU shifted its activities back to Afghanistan and the group's trained fighters conducted several suicide attacks on NATO bases and coalition forces' convoys in the eastern part of Afghanistan.

The group lost dozens of fighters during the summer and autumn of 2009 in the FATA, which was mentioned by the remaining members in their exclusive online video footage in late 2009.[427] The group also lost its headquarters in Mir-ali, North Waziristan, Pakistan, and shifted its main location to the northern provinces of Afghanistan. The IJU is attempting to regroup, recruit new members, and raise funds by fighting alongside the Taliban and al-Qaeda.

During the autumn of 2010, IJU planned to conduct a large wave of Mumbai-style attacks in big cities in Western Europe. This plot was dismantled as ten European IJU activists (two British and eight Germans) were killed in Mir-ali during their training for the mission.[428]

Deployment

Since its inception in March 2002, the group has operated and coordinated its activities from its headquarters, located in Mir-ali, North Waziristan, FATA, Pakistan. Over the years, IJU has been deployed in Pakistan and the eastern provinces of Afghanistan. In the international arena, IJU cells operate in Uzbekistan, Kazakhstan, and Germany.

Group Affiliation

In spite of its independent status, the IJU was established and operates under the support and direction of al-Qaeda and Taliban leaders in Afghanistan and Pakistan. From 2005 to 2009, al-Qaeda's chief of the Religious Committee, Abu Yahiya al-Libi, was the contact person between IJU and al-Qaeda while IJU cooperated with the Haqqani network of Pakistani terrorists. The IJU also has close ties to Uyghur and Chechen Islamic radicals.[429]

Organizational Structure

Apart from the Amir, deputy, and several ideological posts in IJU's hierarchy, the rest of the fighters are referred to as "the jihadists." IJU'S Amir is responsible for the organization's operational planning, targeting policy, and military deployment. Specific operations are conducted by lower echelon cadres, who establish cells and are responsible for other aspects of operational activities.[430]

It seems that the organization has a specially designated unit for operations in the West. Within this framework, it is believed that IJU leader Qurashi specialized in training Germans to conduct attacks in Germany.[431]

Leadership

Najmiddin Kamolitdinovich Jalolov (1972–2009) was the founding Amir of the group. As a member of the IMU, Jalolov was trained in mines and explosives at al-Qaeda training camps and participated in operations in Afghanistan and Pakistan on the side of the Taliban. He was one of the organizers of the IMU terrorist attacks in Uzbekistan in 1999, and was convicted in absentia in 2000.[432] Jalolov was killed by a U.S. drone attack on 14 September 2009 in Mirali, FATA, Pakistan.[433] IJU field commander Ravshan a.k.a Muhammad Fotih, has succeeded him[434] and is the current leader of the group.[435]

Suhayl Buranov, born in 1983, is the Deputy Amir of the IJU, and is responsible for the group's communications. He received specialized training in mines and explosives in an al-Qaeda training camp in Khost and participated in operations in Afghanistan and Pakistan on the side of the Taliban. He was one of the masterminds of the 2004 suicide attacks in Tashkent.[436]

Finance

The initial seed money of the IJU originated from al-Qaeda through Abu Layth al-Libi.[437]

The group appears to be collecting money from sympathizers and supporters in central Asia, Afghanistan, Pakistan, Turkey, and Europe. Three people were detained in Germany in February 2010 because they had collected a total of €2,450 (US$3,339) since October 2009 and transferred it to a presumed IJU intermediary in Turkey.[438]

IJU provides members with a monthly salary of US$50–60. The annual budget of the group is unknown.[439]

Operational

Military capability The number of IJU fighters in North Waziristan has never exceeded 200. With the ideological and logistical support of al-Qaeda-affiliated terrorist groups, IJU has carried out several suicide attacks in Central Asia and has recruited Turkish and German citizens.[440]

Tactical characteristics IJU uses a myriad of operational tactics to conduct its jihadist and terrorist activities. Attacks by lone suicide bombers and coordinated strikes as well as small arms, mortars, and BM rockets were widely used in IJU's anti-NATO operations in Afghanistan and Pakistan.[441]

The latest planned IJU military operation in Western Europe was to be conducted in the style of the Mumbai attack—a sacrificial attack that included assaulting civilians by using rifles and light weapons, and probably barricading with hostages.[442]

IJU members use Internet cafés to stay in clandestine contact with operational leaders and the IJU leadership in Pakistan.[443] IJU recruiters also smuggle recruits across borders.[444] The IJU has, from time to time, conducted attacks to coincide with significant dates. Attacks in Uzbekistan have occurred on the anniversary of the 13 May Andijan terrorist uprising while attacks in Germany have coincided with the 9/11 anniversary.

Training The IJU consistently provides its members with training to stage bombings, rocket attacks, and one-on-one fights. The group also trains the children of current or deceased members in fighting and shooting.

Targeting policy In the FATA, the IJU attacks the Afghan National Army, coalition forces (mainly convoys), and Pakistani army troops. In Uzbekistan, the group attacks international (foreign embassies) and local targets. The group is very active in Europe, mainly in Germany with plots against local German targets. Germany also serves as IJU's main arena for recruitment. Many German citizens, of Turkish origin as well as Islamic converts, are operating in the FATA.

International Attacks and Plots

- **29–31 March 2004**—A series of suicide attacks across Uzbekistan resulted in the death of ten police officers, three civilians, and thirty-three IJU members.
- **July 2004**—Suicide attacks targeted the Israeli and American embassies and the General Prosecutor's Office in Tashkent.
- **13 May 2005**—A male suicide bomber was killed by security guards near the Israeli embassy in Tashkent.
- **2006–2007**—The Ramstein plot. On 4 September 2007, the German authorities uncovered and arrested an Islamic terror network that was plotting a series of terror attacks in Germany. The network was in the final stage of

preparation to conduct a massive car bomb attack on the Ramstein military air base used by the United States. The network was under surveillance from early 2006 and was known as the Sauer land group or Sauer land cell. The Sauer land cell was the most dangerous terror enterprise which originated in Germany and was composed of Muslims, many of whom were converts, who were radicalized in Germany and targeted locations inside the country.[445]

- **3 March 2008**—Turkish IJU member drove a vehicle borne improvised explosive device (VBIED) into a NATO compound in Paktika, Afghanistan, killing at least four people (two American soldiers and two Afghans).[446, 447]
- **31 May 2008**—An IJU-trained jihadist drove his explosive-laden car into a NATO convoy, killing a U.S. Marine and wounding three others.[448]
- **2005 to June 2008**—The group carried out over ten attacks on the NATO and Afghan National Army bases in Paktika, Afghanistan. Most of these attacks were conducted in coordination with the Taliban and al-Qaeda.[449]
- **October 2010**—An IJU plot to attack highly populated facilities such as stadium halls, train stations, and airports in central European cities, especially in Germany, was exposed. Several German converts who had undergone designated training in Waziristan and were to carry out the plot were killed, thus obscuring the current status of the plot.[450]

Assessment

Even though the IJU is relatively a small group, it is a good example of a local jihadi group operating in the international arena. It is an Uzbek national outfit that is deployed in the FATA under the patronage of al-Qaeda and the Taliban and is operationally and logistically active in Western Europe, mostly in Germany. In spite of its small number of activists, IJU poses a significant threat to Western forces and facilities inside the FATA and in the international arena. According to our assessment, the organization is rising in popularity among Uzbek nationals inside Uzbekistan and Turkish emigrants across Europe, especially Germany. In Germany, the group possesses a significant logistical infrastructure, which mainly provides the organization with new recruits. Based on these factors, we believe that the IJU will try to increase its activity on all fronts, particularly inside Uzbekistan, using suicide attacks against the West as well as international and local targets. By using new recruits, especially German Muslim converts, we believe that the group will try to extend its operational activities to more countries, including the United States and Israel as well as those in Western Europe.

Libyan Islamic Fighting Group (LIFG)

The Libyan Islamic Fighting Group (LIFG) is probably al-Qaeda's closest affiliate in Afghanistan. LIFG fighters were among the first to arrive in Afghanistan to fight the Soviets and many of them remained in the country after the war. LIFG members in Afghanistan collaborate with al-Qaeda and occupy leadership positions within al-Qaeda.

Background

Libya gained independence from Italy by the end of World War II and declared itself a constitutional monarchy under King Idris. On September 1969, Colonel Muammar al-Qadhafi staged a military coup d'état in Libya and established an Arab nationalist regime that adhered to an ideology of "Islamic socialism." Since then Qadhafi has been Libya's only leader until the recent "Arab Spring" uprising that resulted in the overthrowing of the Qadhafi regime during the autumn of 2011. His regime generated resentment among Islamic circles in Libya, which led to an Islamist revival since the late 1970s. This Islamist revival has been composed of several Islamist movements:

The Muslim Brotherhood

The Muslim Brotherhood first appeared in Libya in the 1950s. The king allowed it some freedom to spread its ideology, and the movement soon attracted local adherents.[451] Qadhafi took a less accommodating stance, regarding the Brotherhood as a potential source of opposition.[452] Soon after coming to power, he arrested several Brothers and repatriated them to Egypt. In 1973, the security services arrested and tortured members of the Brotherhood, who, under pressure, agreed to dissolve the organization. The Brotherhood remained silent throughout the remainder of the 1970s.

In the early 1980s, the Brotherhood (which by then had renamed itself the Libyan Islamic Group or al-Jemaah al-Islamiyah al-Libya) revived its aspirations to replace the existing secular regime with Sharia law through peaceful means, and was once again beginning to gather popular support. The group gained popularity through its charity and welfare work. The movement attracted members of the middle class and was especially strong in the eastern area of Benghazi, where the main tribes have traditionally opposed Qadhafi's rule.[453]

In the 1990s, political Islam received strong popular support in Libya. Economic mismanagement, falling oil prices, and international sanctions (imposed in 1992 as a result of Qadhafi's refusal to hand over two suspects in the 1988 Pan Am aircraft bombing over Lockerbie Scotland) contributed to chronic socio-economic malaise. With no other political alternative under Qadhafi's regime, the population was ripe for the radical approach of political Islam.[454] Not only did the Brotherhood garner greater support than before, new Islamic groups also emerged.

By the end of the 1990s, the authoritarian regime had eliminated organized Islamic opposition inside the country. However, Qadhafi has been unable to prevent the growing religiosity that had taken hold among the Libyan population, as it had across much of the Arab world. Increasing numbers of the population supported Brotherhood-type ideologies and aspired to the kind of Islamic alternative promoted by the Brotherhood, a form of passive resistance to the regime.[455] The Brotherhood was able to continue its activities, conducting annual conferences and preserving its political infrastructure and institutions as well as social and charitable activities.[456]

The Libyan Islamic Fighting Group (LIFG)—
Historical Development

The dominant Islamist group that has challenged the Qadhafi regime is the Libyan Islamic Fighting Group (LIFG). LIFG did not officially announce its formation until 1995, but initially developed as an underground jihadist movement formed in 1982 by Awatha al-Zuwawi. With no official name and under high security, the movement managed to spread and attract many followers throughout Libya over more than a decade.[457] Unlike the Muslim Brotherhood, it advocated military operations against the regime in order to overthrow Qadhafi and plotted attacks against senior figures in his government. By 1989, authorities had discovered the insurgency and arrested many of the rebels, including al-Zuwawi. Those who were not captured fled to Afghanistan.

The LIFG was engaged in long-term preparation for its military campaign. To strengthen combat skills, many LIFG members seized the opportunity in the 1980s to fight the Soviets in Afghanistan. There, they and other Libyans set up their own camp and underwent military training, at times instructed by al-Qaeda members.[458] It was then, while in exile in Pakistan and Afghanistan, that the movement began to morph into an identifiable organization. Besides military training, the Libyan recruits were also indoctrinated in Afghanistan by influential jihadist clerics such as Abdullah Azzam.[459] While the initial goal remained fighting the communist-led forces in Afghanistan, these recruits began to develop combat skills in anticipation of eventually fighting Qadhafi's regime.

Like other Muslims who had fought against the Soviet forces, many Libyans left Afghanistan between 1992 and 1993, following the Soviet withdrawal in 1989 and the emergence of the Afghan civil war that followed.[460] While some went on to aid militant groups in Algeria and Bosnia-Herzegovina, others, including LIFG members, became part of bin Laden's Islamic Army Shura (Consultative Committee), a platform he created in Sudan in order to coordinate his intended international militant alliance.[461] LIFG members who joined the Islamic Army Shura delivered lectures in Khartoum and maintained regular contact with LIFG members in Libya. Within this platform, LIFG members formed ties with operatives from various bin Laden affiliates, like the Algerian Armed Islamic Group (GIA) and the Egyptian terrorist group al-Gama`at al-Islamiyah.[462]

In Libya, the LIFG, led by Commander Abu Abdullah al-Sadek, was establishing its structure and developing the leadership skills of those in charge of cells and units throughout the country.[463] Throughout the 1990s, the LIFG continued to conduct military operations against the Libyan regime, including several failed attempts to assassinate Qadhafi. The Libyan regime fought relentlessly against the LIFG which suffered numerous losses including one of its founding fathers, Salah Fathi bin Suleiman a.k.a. Abu Abdurrahman al-Khattab, who was killed in a battle with Libyan soldiers near Darna in September 1997.[464]

Aggressive Libyan government operations throughout the country eventually crippled the LIFG's infrastructure within Libya and forced most of the remaining members to leave the country and resume operations in exile. As a result, many LIFG members, such as al-Qaeda associate Abu Anas al-Libi, engaged in political activity in the United Kingdom, where the organization established a robust underground support network.[465] Others fled to various countries in Asia, the Persian Gulf, Africa, and Europe, but Afghanistan once again became the preferred destination for LIFG members.[466]

Upon al-Qaeda's return to Afghanistan from Sudan in 1996, the LIFG ran at least two military training camps. Some of the training camps were shared by different terror groups and al-Qaeda affiliates, allowing the LIFG to form links with groups like the Moroccan Islamic Combatant Group (GICM). Past ties between the LIFG and al-Qaeda were strengthened during this time, as the two groups shared human and material resources. Over time, those ties appear to have had an ideological effect on the LIFG, as its leaders embraced a more radical anti-Western approach affiliated with al-Qaeda.[467]

After the U.S.-led invasion of Afghanistan following the 9/11 attacks, some LIFG members were captured, while many fled the country mainly to neighboring Pakistan.[468] Prominent LIFG commanders stepped forward to take over prominent positions within al-Qaeda's leadership and infrastructure in Afghanistan.

- Abu Faraj Al Libi became the overall chief of the al-Qaeda Military Committee (similar to al-Qaeda's chief of staff) until his arrest in the spring of 2005.[469]
- Abu Layth al-Libi was one of the senior military commanders of al-Qaeda, fighting the coalition and Pakistani troops. He was responsible for the Khost, Paktia, and Paktika Provinces until he was killed by U.S. forces in the spring of 2008.[470]
- Abu Yahiya al-Libi was the head of al-Qaeda's Religious Committee until his elimination by U.S. forces in a drone attack in May 2012.[471]
- During 2008–2009 Abdullah Sai'd was the head of internal regions (Afghanistan-Pakistan border zone) in al-Qaeda's Military Committee until he was killed by a U.S. drone attack.[472]
- Sheikh Atiya Allah was a prominent al-Qaeda senior leader who was considered to be very close to bin Laden and al-Zawahiri.[473] During 2010 he replaced the late Mustafa Abu Yazid (Sheikh Sai'd Al Masri) in a position akin to the CEO of al-Qaeda's Shura Council. Atiya Allah held this position until he was eliminated in an American drone attack during the summer of 2011.

In 2007, the LIFG was officially welcomed into al-Qaeda's fold in a statement released on the Internet by al-Zawahiri and Abu Layth al-Libi.[474] al-Zawahiri called for the overthrow of the governments of Libya, Tunisia, Algeria, and Morocco, while Abu Layth al-Libi urged Libyans to join the fight against Qadhafi, the United States, "and their brothers, the infidel of the West."[475]

When tallied in 2005, Libyan fighters were estimated to constitute 18.8 percent of foreign fighters in Iraq, second only to Saudi Arabia's 41 percent.[476]

While the external wing of the LIFG has increased its collaboration with al-Qaeda, the Libyan regime launched a conciliatory policy toward the LIFG inside Libya (2009). Reports suggest that Saif al-Islam Qadhafi, the son and then heir apparent of Muammar Qadhafi, held a clandestine series of negotiations in an attempt to achieve reconciliation between the Libyan state and the LIFG.[477] As a result of these efforts, in September 2009, LIFG leaders in Libya released a new "code" for jihad in the form of a 417-page religious document titled "Corrective Studies." The new code viewed the armed struggle against Qadhafi's regime as illegal under Islamic law and set down new guidelines for when and how jihad should be fought. It stated that jihad was permissible if Muslim lands were invaded, citing Afghanistan, Iraq, and Palestine as examples.[478]

Whether the LIFG are capable of assuming power in Libya after the Qadhafi era is unclear. While the group may have shifted its policy regarding its internal military operations as a consequence of the aforementioned negotiations with the Qadhafi regime, it maintains close ties with al-Qaeda, with some of its members holding senior positions within al-Qaeda. During the aftermath of the "Arab Spring" in 2011 several LIFG members in the northeast placed the organization under the National Transitional Council, the de facto Libyan government which commended the rebels in the Libyan civil war which eventually overthrew the regime and ended the Qadhafi era.[479] Authors believe that the LIFG will have a dominant role in determining the future politics of Libya. It seems that LIFG members, veterans of the jihadi arenas in Afghanistan and Iraq, will return to their homeland and use their operational experience to bring the jihad back to their homeland in order to instate Sharia law in post-Qadhafi Libya.

Shabaab Al Mujahidin—Somalia

General Background

The Council of Somali Islamic Courts (hereafter referred to as the Islamic Courts) created Shabaab al-Mujahidin (hereafter referred to as al-Shabaab) as a youth militant or special force in the years leading up to 2006. The Islamic Courts consisted of eleven individual courts in the south and east parts of Somalia that were dominated by the Hawiye clan. During the internal fighting in early 2006, the Islamic Courts and al-Shabaab defeated the U.S.-supported Alliance for the Restoration of Peace and Counter Terrorism.[480] Although the Islamic Courts created al-Shabaab, they have had a tense relationship with al-Shabaab's radical elements, especially as the Islamic Courts sought to uphold a positive international image. The Islamic Courts apologized for radical acts of violence committed by Al Shabaab, but that rhetoric did little to stem mounting international disapproval of al-Shabaab's "Taliban-like" actions in 2006.

When al-Shabaab was consolidating in 2006, it was supported by Mogadishu businessmen who were against many of the defeated warlords.[481]

Al-Shabaab has national and international aims. It aims to fight the government as well as Ethiopian supporters and implement Sharia law across Somalia. It also seeks to build an army that places an Islamic identity above clan loyalties. Al-Shabaab has stated that as part of the al-Qaeda network, it intends to wage jihad against the West and foreign interveners.

History and Development

Somalia has been plagued by instability, border skirmishes, warlords, and clan disputes from the 1960s. Muhammad Siad Barre led a military coup in 1969, declaring Somalia a socialist state, and governed until he was overthrown in 1991. For years following the fall of Barre, Somalia was dominated by clan-based violence and heavily armed warlords who divided up control over the capital Mogadishu. The prominent warlord during this stage was Mohammed Farah Aideed.[482] As in Afghanistan, Islamist forces participating in the overall violent chaos in the country gradually gained strength in Somalia by promising to end the reign of the warlords and swiftly reinstate law and order. One of the first such Islamist paramilitary organizations to emerge was the al-Ittihad al-Islami (AIAI, "the Islamic Union") in southern Somalia near the contested Ethiopian border.[483]

The United States and the UN sent troops and peacekeep-ers to restore stability and deliver aid. The United States ended its involvement in March 1994, following the deaths of eigh-teen U.S. Army Rangers whose helicopters were shot down by Somali insurgents in Mogadishu in the infamous Black Hawk Down incident 3–4 October 1993. UN peacekeepers left in 1995, having failed to achieve their objective. In 1996, Aideed died and was succeeded by Hussein, his son. By about 1999, the AIAI movement, founded by Sheikh Hassan Awes, was near bankruptcy and key AIAI functionaries such as Awes and Aden Ayrow had left Somalia in search of a safe haven in Afghani-stan. On 23 September 2001, the U.S. government blacklisted AIAI as a Designated Foreign Terrorist Organization under Executive Order 13224, which blocks the assets of organizations and individuals linked to terrorism.[484] Prior to its collapse, the AIAI's leadership established a new judicial system, the Islamic Courts, based on Sharia law and extending across several major Somali regions, including the key urban centers of Kismayo and Mogadishu. These courts loosely resembled the development of the Taliban in Afghanistan by offering much needed law and order through the rigid enforcement of puritanical religious interpretations. They formed a confederation in 2000 known as the Islamic Courts Union (ICU), which gradually consolidated influence over southern Somalia and Mogadishu.[485]

Al-Shabaab was founded between 2004 and 2006 as the militant wing of the ICU.[486] It was created by the Islamic Courts while they were attempting to unite Mogadishu, restore peace, and govern according to their religious vision after years of in-stability. In December 2006, Ethiopia launched an offensive in Somalia to unseat the Islamic Courts and force a regime change, providing an opportunity for al-Shabaab to engage in military action as the Islamic Courts disbanded the organization and fled the country.[487] Al-Shabaab's disjointed defensive against a for-eign invader appeared just, especially as it was waged primarily by Somalis.[488]

In the past few years, al-Shabaab has attempted with some success to evolve into a ruling authority in addition to waging ji-had. Its initial recruits were called to fight for Somali sovereignty and dignity.[489] The recruits, heavily scrutinized by al-Shabaab, hailed from poor and disenfranchised parts of Somalia.[490]

Since 2007, al-Shabaab has affiliated itself with al-Qaeda.[491] It became a formal part of al-Qaeda in February 2012.[492]

Al-Shabaab continues to oppose the current Transnational Federal Government (TFG) regime as well as external involvement by peacekeepers.

Area of Operations

By late 2007, the government was only effectively controlling 20 percent of Somalia, allowing significant space for al-Shabaab and other militants to develop. Although organized, al-Shabaab's areas of operation experience considerable friction that undermines its overall effectiveness and destabilizes it.[493]

Al-Shabaab has active cells in the Bay and Bookol region, south central Somalia and Mogadishu, and to a lesser extent in Puntland and Somaliland.[494] It is in control of Hiran Province, north of Mogadishu, although it lost the city of Bulo Burde to government forces in September 2009.[495] By late 2010 al-Shabaab was in full control of seven provinces in the south, including Lower Juba, Middle Juba, Gedo, Bay and Bakool, Lower Shabelle, and Middle Shabelle.[496]

From its stronghold along the Kenyan-Somali border, al-Shabaab trains its fighters and foreigners from different parts of the world as well as plans and conducts attacks in the Shabelle and Juba Provinces. Al-Shabaab directs operations in Mogadishu. It seeks control but does not have complete authority over the area. Controlling this stronghold is a primary goal for al-Shabaab and was a source of significant violence in 2010, including fighting near the presidential palace.[497]

In December 2009, al-Shabaab seized control of several islands on the far borders of southern Somalia, including Jolla, Guay, Mtaua, and Ras Kambouni. Al-Shabaab also gained control of the cities of Batoui and Kolbiyo, near the Kenyan border.[498] Al-Shabaab controls the port of Marka and commands other key posts near the Kenyan border. It controlled the port of Kismayo until 26 September 2009 when Hizbul Islam's Ras Kambouni Brigade and Anole (see Group Affiliation) forced al-Shabaab guerrillas to peacefully transfer control.[499] Kismayo is significant, not only because it is a port town, but because it was territory lost to the Ethiopians in the fighting between the end of 2006 and beginning of 2007.[500] On 20 December 2009, al-Shabaab also took control of Afmadoow, in Juba, following fighting with Hizbul Islam.[501] Near the Kenyan border, al-Shabaab also controls the towns of Diif and Dhobley.

Although slightly limited, al-Shabaab remained the dominant political factor in this area during the years that followed.

Organizational Infrastructure and Current Leaders and Commanders

Al-Shabaab is an organized hierarchy with independent components. It is headed by a ten-member Shura Council that decides all major objectives and operations. It is led by an Amir who, while significant, does not have sole authority. Below the council are several subdivisions covering traditional areas like politics, media, military operations, etc. Also under the Shura Council are the military branch, Jaysh al-Usra or the Army of Hardship, as well as the more judicial branch, Jaysh al-Hisbah, which upholds law and morality.[502]

Below the management levels is a regional division (see Area of Operations). Al-Shabaab appoints a political and a military representative for each region under its control. If this is a new region without al-Shabaab clan ties, a representative from a neighboring area will be brought in and appointed.[503] Regional commanders are free to pursue independent action without consulting the Shura Council.

The following is a list of members who hold prominent positions in the organization:

Sheikh Mohamed Mukhtar Abdirahman a.k.a. Abu Zubeyr a.k.a. Ahmed Abdi Godane (hereafter referred to as Godane) is currently al-Shabbab's official leader.[504] He is in questionable health as he was seriously wounded in an explosion at a Mogadishu safe house in May 2009.[505]

Sheikh Ali Mohammad Raghe a.k.a. Sheikh Ali Dhere (hereafter referred to as Dhere) is al-Shabaab's main spokesman and addresses the media regarding al-Shabaab's tactics.[506] He assumed this position in May 2009, after Mukhtar Roobow resigned.[507]

Sheikh Bare Mohamed Farah Khoje is also an al-Shabaab spokesman, but not as senior as Dhere.[508]

Abdighani Sheikh Muhammad is the spokesman in Kismayo, who issued warnings to Kenyan troops in November 2008.[509]

Mukhtar Roobow a.k.a. Abu Mansur (hereafter referred to as Roobow) oversees the Bay and Bokool regions and was formerly al-Shabaab's spokesman.[510] Roobow allegedly masterminded the October 2008 suicide bombings. Roobow was previously the leader of al-Shabaab from 2008 to 2009. Given Roobow's popularity and history with al-Shabaab, he could be a likely successor to Godane.

Hasan Hussein is a spiritual leader.[511] In July 2009, he was invited by the Bellevue Mosque in Gothenburg, Sweden to deliver a sermon. Although this engagement was protested by many in Gothenburg, it was an example of al-Shabaab's leadership and vision to reach out to individuals far from Somalia's borders.

Sheikh Abdirahman Abdi Shakur "Hudeyfi" is a member of the executive.

Sheikh Mukhtar Abdi Moussa is also a member of the executive.[512]

Qadi Abdullah Ahmad Muhammad heads the justice division.

Sheikh Hassan Yakub Ali is the information secretary for Kismayo.[513]

Harun Abdullah Fazul was al-Qaeda's most senior fugitive and its operational on-field chief of the attacks against U.S. embassies in the Horn of Africa in August 1998 as well as the attack against Israeli targets in Mombasa in November 2002. Different reports suggest that Fazul had become the new leader of the al-Qaeda cell in east Africa and was closely cooperating with al-Shabaab al-Mujahidin, using al-Shabaab activists for al-Qaeda suicide missions. This was reflected in the mutual attack in the Ugandan capital Kampala during the 2010 soccer World Cup final that resulted in the death of over seventy fans. Al-Shabaab al-Mujahidin officially claimed responsibility for the attack, while Fazul's operational fingerprints are all over it.[514] Recent reports suggest that Fazul was killed by another Somali militia during the summer of 2011.[515]

Other Notable Personalities

Several individuals were part at one time or another of the Mogadishu Command.[516]

Hassan Abdullah Hersi a.k.a. Turki a jihadist commander that oversees a stronghold in the Juba valley near the Kenyan border (see Area of Operations).[517] He served as a military commander and senior trainer, owing to his previous experience with al-Qaeda camps during the 1990s.[518]

Ibrahim Haji Jaama "al-Afghani," originally from Somaliland like Abdirahman, is a senior commander in Somaliland, Puntland, and the Ethiopian border area.[519] He also served in the Islamic administration of Kismayo and may be a spiritual leader.

Fouad Mohamed Shangole, a Swiss national, is a high-ranking commander serving in Mogadishu.[520]

Abdullah Uthman Jibril has been the field commander for the Gedo region, along with **Barre Muhammad Farah**.[521]

Sheikh Farah Muhammad "Abu Shureym" specifically commanded the Bardera region of Gedo.[522]

Harun Hussein Ibrahim has been the leader in the Gedo region.[523]

Abu Mansur al-Amriki has been the field commander in south Somalia and is suspected to be a former member of the U.S. military.[524]

Abdirahman Muhammad Ali "Filow" was the commander in the Lower and Middle Juba regions.

Sheikh Hassan Abd al-Rahman was the security chief in Shabelle.

Hassan Deerow was the commander of Baidoa.

Hassan Jibril Jama has been a field commander near the Kenyan border.

Sheikh Hassan Muhammad Abu Ayman commanded the Bay and Bakool regions.[525]

Khalif Adayle Abu Muhsin was the field commander of Hiwaye/Habr Gidir.[526]

Sheikh Abd al-Rahman Sirah has been the governor of the Wilayah of Shabelle.[527]

Sheikh Abdirahman Hassan Hussein is the governor of the Middle Shabelle region.

Sheikh Abdirahman Siro is the governor of the Lower Shabelle and was reported to have recruited child soldiers.[528]

Sheikh Abdullahi Mu'alim Ali "Abu Utayba" headed security for Mogadishu.[529]

Sheikh Ali Muhammad Husain is the governor of Banadiir region, which includes Mogadishu.[530]

Sheikh Ibrahim al-Maqdisi headed Treasury affairs in Shabelle.

Sheikh Sultan Muhammad al-Muhammad headed the Dawa of Shabelle.[531]

Ahmed Abdi Mohammed was named by the U.S. Department of State as a Specially Designated Global Terrorist in November 2001.

Issa Osman Issa was also named by the U.S. Department of State as a Specially Designated Global Terrorist in November 2001. Issa has served as an al-Shabaab commander in Somalia, and has recruited suicide bombers and led assaults targeting Ugandan peacekeepers. He is skilled in surface-to-air missiles,[532] and before al-Shabaab's creation, was one of the operatives who fired the surface-to-air missiles in the 2002 failed attempt to shoot down an Israeli airliner in Mombasa, Kenya.[533]

Muhammad Adan Kofi was the spokesman of the Islamic Courts and joined al-Shabaab in December 2008.

Former Leadership

Adan Hashi Ayro was the leader of al-Shabaab from 2007 to May 2008 and an alleged senior al-Qaeda member who was trained in Afghanistan.[534] He was killed in a U.S. military raid in Dusamareb, Somalia in May 2008.[535]

Roobow succeeded Ayro and led al-Shabaab from May 2008 to 2009.

Sheikh Ali Fidow led the Mogadishu Command, along with three others, and was the secretary of politics and regions. He was killed in a U.S. military helicopter raid in September 2009.[536]

Saleh Ali Saleh Nabahan was one of the most skillful and admired commanders of al-Shabaab, and one of the founding fathers of the organization. He was a Kenyan al-Qaeda activist who played an important role in the 2002 simultaneous attacks against an Israeli-owned hotel and an Israeli commercial jet on takeoff in Mombasa (fifteen killed, including three Israelis). Nabahan was personally responsible for launching the ground-to-air missile targeting the Israeli aircraft. He was killed by American forces in the autumn of 2009.[537]

Future Leadership

Roobow, a former al-Shabaab Amir as well as a prominent member and outspoken supporter of al-Shabaab's alliance with al-Qaeda, may replace Godane.

Awes is a possible candidate to lead or absorb al-Shabaab. Awes is the current leader of Hizbul Islam (see Group Affiliation) and has previously sought a merger with al-Shabaab.[538] While Hizbul Islam has voiced support for the merger, it prefers to maintain its own control over geographical areas with historical clan ties to Hizbul Islam members. The conflict over Kismayo will have a significant impact on the future relations between

Hizbul Islam and al-Shabaab. Should Hizbul Islam succeed in marginalizing or defeating al-Shabaab, Awes may emerge as the leader of all radical Islamic opposition groups in Somalia. Awes was the leader of the now defunct Islamic Courts and an active figure between 2008 and 2011 during Somalia's instability. Awes was trained in al-Qaeda camps during the 1990s, and participated in the Black Hawk Down incident in 1993.[539] He was named by the U.S. Department of State as a Specially Designated Global Terrorist in November 2001.[540]

Group Affiliation

Hizbul Islam   There is an uneasy rivalry between Hizbul Islam and Al Shabaab. Hizbul Islam led by Awes, was created in January 2009 in Somalia when three Islamic groups merged: Alliance for the Re-Liberation of Somalia-Eritrea, Jabhatul Islamiyah (the Islamic Front), and Anole. Hizbul Islam is dominated by the Marehan and Darod clans, whereas al-Shabaab's majority hails from the Hawiye clan. Through the history of its individual members and leaders, Hizbul Islam can also be considered a product of the Islamic Courts.

Hizbul Islam seeks to gain control of areas in Somalia, exemplified by its September 2009 takeover of Kismayo port, and has thus been interested in merging with al-Shabaab.[541] Awes announced the desired union to a crowd at the Aba Huraira Mosque in Bakaraha market in Mogadishu during June–July 2009.[542] This potential union was threatened however on 30 September 2009 when al-Shabaab declared war on Hizbul Islam over control of the port of Kismayo.[543] Hizbul Islam vowed to fight al-Shabaab in any part of Somalia and the two groups engaged in a bloody battle.

Historically, there have been other connections between the two groups. In February 2009, Hizbul Islam and al-Shabaab cooperated in an attack which killed some fifty African Union (AU) peacekeepers and wounded a further 300 people. They have also cooperated on other raids.[544] Hizbul Islam assists al-Shabaab in controlling the southern and many of the central provinces as well as in influencing Mogadishu region (see Area of Operations.)[545]

On 18 January 2011, al-Shabaab announced a merger with its former rival Hizbul Islam.[546]

Al-Qaeda

Al-Qaeda has the most internationally visible link to al-Shabaab since it became officially part of al-Qaeda on 1 February 2012.[547] The connection between the two groups began in the summer of 2006 when leaders from both organizations first voiced their support for each other.[548] In a speech that year, bin Laden voiced support for the Islamic Courts.[549] Two years later, Roobow told U.S. newspaper the *Los Angeles Times* in August 2008: "We will take our orders from Sheik Osama bin Laden because we are his students. Al Qaeda is the mother of the holy war in Somalia."[550]

There have been several videos linking al-Qaeda and al-Shabaab. The videos produced by al-Shabaab and al-Qaeda are similar in style and quality. Al Shabaab videos are hosted on al-Qaeda web forums and are reminiscent of the Algerian GSPC requesting integration with al-Qaeda.[551] Al-Shabaab activity has been referred to by al-Qaeda seniors:

- In January 2007, al-Zawahiri called on Somalis to use guerrilla tactics, suicide attacks, and roadside bombings to attack Ethiopian troops.[552]
- A September 2008 video showed an al-Shabaab leader pledging allegiance to al-Qaeda and encouraging young fighters to come to Somalia. This video featured Nabahan.
- In February 2009, al-Zawahiri praised al-Shabaab's seizure of the town of Baidoa and encouraged jihad against America.
- Turki, Indha Adde (former defense minister for the Islamic Courts prior to 2007), and Roobow featured in al-Qaeda propaganda videos.[553]

Eventually, in February 2012, al-Shabaab tightened its ties to al-Qaeda when its leader Ahmad Ali Godane aka Mukhtar Abu al-Zubair pledged total loyalty of his organization to al-Qaeda's leader, Ayman al-Zawahiri.[554]

Operatives from al-Qaeda are willing to travel, fight, and die for al-Shabaab's cause. Among the leading ranks of al-Shabaab were several of the most senior regional fugitives of al-Qaeda such as Nabahan, Issa, and Abu Talha al-Sudani. All three were wanted for their role in the mutual attack against Israeli targets in November 2002 and were killed by U.S. troops between 2008 and 2009.[555] As mentioned, Fazul used al-Shabaab assets and operatives for his activity, as reflected in the Kampala attack on 11 July 2010, demonstrating strong ties between the two groups.[556] AQAP has also allegedly assisted al-Shabaab.[557]

Lebanese Hezbollah

Hezbollah may be establishing ties with al-Shabaab. When al-Shabaab members returned from fighting in Lebanon (see Training) in August and September 2006, five Hezbollah members accompanied them to Somalia.[558] Although there is no conclusive evidence, we believe that this may indicate either a functional exchange and knowledge transfer between fighters, or that al-Shabaab is willing to counter opposing moderate Somali Sunni populations by engaging in any alliance possible, even a Shiite one.

Financial

Al-Shabaab fighters are concentrated in towns where it is possible to earn money as quickly as possible. Money also comes from pirate ransoms from the port of Haradheere,[559] or is sent by overseas supporters. It is believed that Hussein has used speaking engagements, including in Sweden, to recruit fighters and raise funds.[560]

Al-Shabaab receives the majority of its "long-term" financial support from the local mosques, imams, and communities that support the group.[561] They provide al-Shabaab with food, water, shelter, clothing, and moral support in exchange for justice and security. This support eases al-Shabaab's expenditure, enabling the group to purchase weapons.

In July 2009, Eritrea was accused by U.S. ambassador to the United Nations Susan Rice of arming and funding Islamist insurgents in Somalia.[562] Eritrea continues to face strong criticism from many nations for its alleged involvement in the Somali conflict. A 2006 UN report stated that Iran, Libya, Egypt, and several other countries in the Gulf region have been supporting insurgents in Somalia.

In addition, Somalian diaspora communities in Australia, Norway, Sweden, the United Kingdom, and the United States are supporting al-Shabaab with recruits and donations.

Given the group's known costs and the millions of dollars circulating, it is believed that al-Shabaab has an annual operating budget of about US$2 million.

Operational Characteristics

Al-Shabaab uses terror to mobilize the people of Somalia, but also seeks to build ties with the communities. Al-Shabaab is attempting to establish power sharing with the national government. In 2006, al-Shabaab made a series of town visits in order to preach at town meetings and hold discussions with clan elders.[563] It has built roads, organized markets, and distributed food and monies to needy towns. In November 2009, al-Shabaab announced the construction of a new bridge in the Lower Shabelle as well as the distribution of food, money, and other aid to immigrants from Mogadishu.[564]

Al-Shabaab implements retaliatory policies. Its March 2010 ban on science and English lessons in southern Afmadoow came after the schools ignored al-Shabaab's call for fighters and volunteers.[565]

Al-Shabaab militants terrorize local citizens by using scissors in the street to alter unacceptable hairstyles.[566] Al-Shabaab also performs judicial functions with "mobile Sharia courts," under which they conduct hand and foot amputations on convicted thieves.[567] Al-Shabaab also inspects women to check if they are wearing bras, a violation of Islam in its opinion. Women are whipped in public if found guilty.[568]

Al-Shabaab conducts public floggings and executions to instill fear in towns. This has been successful in controlling the south of Somalia. It also brutally murders spies and government informants. Al-Shabaab assassinated two alleged CIA spies in September 2009. Totally al-Shabaab's acts of violence have resulted in approximately one million displaced persons.

Al-Shabaab seeks to control ports, especially in the south, where the pirates present a lucrative alliance and directly interfere in the distribution of international aid to 3.2 million needy people in Somalia.[569] The August 2008 battle for the port of Kismayo displaced more than 35,000 people and the pending violence there is causing people to flee to the bush.[570] Previously, violence targeting the Ethiopian military caused some 400,000 individuals to abandon Mogadishu in late 2006.[571]

Al-Shabaab also expels international forces and assistance, including the U.S. humanitarian aid agency CARE, International Medical Corps, and Doctors without Borders. In January 2009, the UN World Food Program became the next organization to suspend operations, including the distribution of critical food supplies.[572] It is suspected that food aid from the UN is being diverted to al-Shabaab, corrupt contractors, and even local UN workers.[573]

Military Strength, Tactics, and Targeting Policy

Since its confrontation with the army in 2006, al-Shabaab has adopted more traditional guerrilla tactics and conducts operations in phases. It uses its regional commanders to conduct attacks, often alongside supporting organizations.

Al-Shabaab uses roadside bombs to harass AU peacekeepers.[574] Al-Shabaab targeted the Ethiopian army's supply lines in western Somalia in 2008.[575]

It has engaged in direct conflict with local clan militias, as in August 2008 when al-Shabaab fought the local forces in a bloody three-day battle to take over the southern port of Kismayo, which it held until September 2009 when Hizbul Islam took control.[576] It is also fighting a series of pitched battles against Hizbul Islam.[577] Its new alliance with al-Qaeda will likely result in additional suicide bombers, simultaneous bombings, and other trademark al-Qaeda moves.

After setbacks such as the successful defensive operation by the AU to protect an armory in Mogadishu in July 2009, al-Shabaab announced that it would change tactics to more traditional guerrilla-style suicide bombs and assassinations as with those they had used against Ethiopians in late 2008 and early 2009.

Fighters are recruited from inside and outside Somalia. The movement may have between 3,000 and 7,000 fighters, although the upper limit may include individuals technically belonging to other groups.[578] After a review of all publicly available ranges, the best estimate—including dedicated foreign fighters—puts al-Shabaab's strength at approximately 4,000 individuals. Al-Shabaab's initial recruits have historically been heavily scrutinized. At the beginning of the movement, they came from poor and disenfranchised parts of Somalia, especially in the south.[579] Al-Shabaab members are men between twenty and thirty years of age who are mostly uneducated, although there have been reports of male members as young as fourteen years old.

Al-Shabaab strives to recruit foreign fighters. UN Security Council documents estimate foreign fighters to number about 300. Fighters from Afghanistan, Eritrea, Pakistan, and Yemen are believed to operate in Somalia.[580] Kenyan fighters number several hundred, but are not particularly dedicated and frequently defect due to al-Shabaab's strict rules against alcohol, smoking, chewing khat, and extramarital relations.[581] Arab fighters are part of al-Shabaab units as well. In December 2006, twenty-five Arabs fought alongside other al-Shabaab members.[582]

Al-Shabaab also invests significant effort in external recruitment in the West, mainly from the Somali diaspora across the world. As many as twenty Somali Americans from ages seventeen to twenty-seven have been recruited from Minneapolis, Minnesota, the United States, and have traveled to Somali to train or wage jihad. A Somali American, Shirwa Ahmed, even completed a suicide mission in October 2008.[583] To enter Somalia, young Somali American recruits travel alone, routing through various cities to avoid arousing suspicion. The cost of such a ticket, some US$2,000, is usually financed by the organization or a sympathizer.[584]

Other foreign fighters entering Somalia in order to receive military training in al-Shabaab camps and gain combat experience along the lines of engagement are from the United Kingdom, Sweden, Norway, Israel (Israeli Arabs),[585] and Australia.[586]

Al Shabaab fighters are equipped with AK-47s and rocket-propelled grenades, and use land mines.[587] It is suspected that arms are being shipped through Eritrea.[588] Although al-Shabaab has weapons, it does not have enough to sustain operations in the long term without acquiring more from abroad or taking armories by force. It is unable to mount a standing battle against peacekeepers and conventional troops, and must rely on traditional guerrilla warfare.

Al-Shabaab uses suicide bombers, assassinations, IEDs, and other guerrilla tactics to conduct its operations. Suicide bombing is seen as taboo in Somali culture and is viewed by Somalis as an imported tactic.[589] There have been about a dozen suicide attacks in Somalia since the tactic was first used in 2006 until the beginning of 2010.[590]

Al-Shabaab has claimed responsibility for assassinating individuals, including military, government, and judicial officials across the country. It occasionally beheads individuals accused of spying for the Somali government or opposing the movement.[591] Al-Shabaab also conducts bombings, attempts to shoot down aircraft, mortar attacks, and kidnapping.[592]

Al-Shabaab targets western and foreign influences in Somalia. Since July 2009, al-Shabaab has altered its targeting policy and has used guerrilla tactics closer to those used against Ethiopians and AU peacekeepers in late 2008 and early 2009, as they proved effective in causing the foreign forces to withdraw. As a result, Somalia has seen a resurgence of suicide bombers—rather than conventional attacks on compounds—since early 2010. Following the May 2008 attack by U.S. forces that killed Ayro, al-Shabaab reciprocated by vowing to target all U.S., Western, and UN people and activities as well as any Somalis working or employed by the United States, the UN, or any regional collaborating nations.[593] Assassins linked to al-Shabaab have been responsible for the deaths of a peace activist, foreign journalists, and aid workers.[594] In February 2009, al-Shabaab activists murdered eleven Burundian AU peacekeepers and killed another fifteen in Mogadishu.

Al-Shabaab is keen to target any influence or soldiers of Ethiopia, a historic enemy. On 5 February 2008, al-Shabaab conducted twin bombings in the port city of Bossaso. Bossaso was chosen because Ethiopian soldiers and families frequent it for entertainment. This was the first attack in the Puntland region.

It also attacks people or forces affiliated with Transitional Federal President Sheikh Sharif Sheikh Ahmed, Prime Minister Omar Abdirashid Ali Sharmarke, and the national government.

Al-Shabaab has conducted several operations outside Somalia and waged operations and plots in Australia and Denmark. Its most famous attack is the 11 July 2010 World Cup final attack in Kampala.[595]

Al-Shabaab members are also sent to fight abroad. According to an official UN report yet to be verified, 720 handpicked al-Shabaab members were sent to Lebanon to fight the Israelis during the summer of 2006.[596] In November 2009, al-Shabaab declared the establishment of al-Quds brigade to conduct attacks inside Israel.[597]

Training

Al-Shabaab fighters typically undergo a six-week training course, either in a camp or former government building. Fish Trafico outside Mogadishu, formerly a police station, is one such camp.[598]

The camps divide recruits into small groups, then house and feed the trainees as well as provide medical treatment.[599] The men are taught to build strength and endurance through running, crawling, and jumping.[600] In particular, they must learn to shoot while running. Upon successful completion of the course, most men are sent to battle Somali government troops, Ethiopians, and AU peacekeepers in conflict areas.[601]

The better students go overseas for additional instruction. Occasionally, they are sent to Eritrea for advanced training in guerrilla warfare and explosives, including roadside bombs, suicide bombs, and car bombs. They are taught to deconstruct or cannibalize weapons systems and other arms for materials[602] and are trained for special operations.[603] Upon returning to Somalia, these foreign-trained al-Shabaab members impart their acquired knowledge to the rest of their camp or team.[604]

Foreigners are brought to the training camps to give weapons instructions. They are typically highly educated and from Egypt.[605] One instructor is rumored to be a white American.[606] Al-Qaeda may be training al-Shabaab members on weapons and the construction of roadside bombs, as well as providing al-Shabaab with funds for the purchase of such arms.[607]

By the end of the first decade of the new millennium al-Shabaab gave a great importance for the designated trainings of foreign fighters for operational activity overseas. Under the overall supervision of Harun Ali Fazul foreign fighters arriving mostly from Western countries were secluded from the rest of Shabaab fighters and received military and terror training, mostly in the construction of explosive devices, to be implemented in their home countries.[608]

International Operations and Plots

In Somalia

- **March 2007**—According to the ICRC, the worst fighting between peacekeepers/government forces and insurgents in fifteen years.
- **5 February 2008**—Al-Shabaab announced twin bombings in Bossaso in an Internet post. This was the first attack in the Puntland region, resulting in some twenty deaths and seventy injured persons.
- **July 2008**—Osman Ali Ahmed, head of the UN Development Program, was killed by gunmen in Mogadishu.
- **29 October 2008**—Five suicide bombers attacked the UN compound in Somaliland, the Ethiopian consulate, the presidential palace, and two intelligence facilities in Puntland.[609] One suicide bomber was Shirwa Ahmed from Minnesota, USA.
- **28 January 2009**—An al-Shabaab suicide attack killed some thirteen AU peacekeepers in Mogadishu.

- **4 February 2009**—Said Tahlil Ahmed, director of Horn Affric Radio, was killed by militants in Bakara market.
- **22 February 2009**—Eleven Burundian AU peacekeepers and fifteen others were killed in Mogadishu in a joint al-Shabaab and Hizbul Islam operation.
- **12 August 2009**—Two pilots and four aid workers were released after being abducted in November 2008.
- **17 September 2009**—Al-Shabaab suicide bombers attacked an AU base in Mogadishu and killed twenty-one people, including the deputy AU commander and sixteen peacekeepers. It is suspected that a Somali American, from Seattle, USA, was one of the suicide bombers.[610]

Outside Somalia
- **4 August 2009**—Five Melbourne members of al-Shabaab were arrested in Sydney for an imminent suicide plot to attack the Holsworthy army base with automatic weapons. The militants may have obtained a fatwa for the attack.
- **1 November 2009**—"Al-Shabaab" commander Abdifatah Aweys Abu Hamza threatened to transfer al-Shabaab fighters to the Middle East and announced, with this regard, the establishment of a new unit, "al-Quds brigade," designated to combat "the Zionist Entity."[611] Several months later, in early 2010, two Israeli Arabs, belonging to a self-made "Global Jihad" cell that operated in northern Israel and killed an Israeli taxi driver, were caught on the Kenyan-Somali border on their way to al-Shabaab training camps.[612]
- **1 January 2010**—A man with alleged ties to al-Shabaab and al-Qaeda broke into the house of Danish cartoonist Kurt Westergaard and attempted to murder him.[613]
- **11 July 2010**—Two suicide bombers attacked fans watching the World Cup final in Kampala. Over seventy people (locals and foreigners) were killed and about fifty were wounded. Al-Shabaab claimed official responsibility for the attack,[614] which was conducted in conjunction with al-Qaeda's east African cell led by Fazul.[615]

- **21–24 September 2013**—Al-Shabaab four-gunman squad attacked the Israeli-owned Westgate Mall in Nairobi, Kenya killing sixty-seven people, mostly local Kenyans, and wounding over 130. Al-Shabaab officially claimed responsibility for the attack.[616]

Assessment of Future al-Shabaab Activity

Al-Shabaab is a threat to regional countries and other nations far from its homeland. It is in an effective and advantageous position: operating in a porous nation while enjoying support from other Islamist organizations like al-Qaeda, and using a solid base of recruitment, ample funding, and control over large sections of Somalia. Al-Shabaab is in a strategic position in Africa, especially if piracy and other lucrative illegal enterprises continue to operate.

The future of popular support is uncertain. Early 2009 estimates predicted that the withdrawal of Ethiopian forces from Somalia would weaken the movement's popular support, especially as civilian casualties continued.

Clan militias and clerics began to actively oppose al-Shabaab in January 2009, expelling the group from Galgadud in central Somalia.[617] Sufi clerics are encouraging individuals to support the government and rebuild the nation.[618] Fatwas issued by Sufi clerics against al-Shabaab could undermine the group's popular support.[619] The International Crisis Group has reported the mobilization of orthodox Sunni Muslims in Somalia to repel al-Shabaab.[620] However, many Somalis are particularly weary of UN, AU, and foreign intervention and are open to "nationalist," extremist activity if it can provide peace and security.[621] A central government must demonstrate its ability to bring peace to Somalia and provide civil services to its provinces without direct Western intervention.

Amidst internal divisions and rivalries, al-Shabaab's leadership and command structure is likely to survive. Al-Shabaab does not rely on a figurehead to rally supporters and make operational decisions. The Shura Council, led by the Amir, has in the past shifted authority from one individual to another three times. Al Shabaab derives strength and sustainability from the foreign fighters that have joined its ranks, often in senior positions or advisory roles.[622]

Future Relationship with al-Qaeda

In 2008, analysts believed that al-Shabaab's ties to al-Qaeda were weak, but this changed during 2009, with fresh violence and pledges of allegiance to the global terror network that has been officially recognized by al-Qaeda in February 2012. There is serious concern that Somalia's borders and accessible 3,000 km coastline will harbor and facilitate radical groups seeking to exert influence over the region.[623] The operational cooperation between al-Shabaab and al-Qaeda via its east African cell poses a major threat to the region and to Western targets throughout Africa. An experienced and able stronghold of potential suicide bombers could turn Somalia into a fertile ground for large-scale, al-Qaeda-style terrorist operations. According to our assessment, the Kampala attack was the prelude to a wave of terrorist attacks across Africa that was followed by the Westgate Mall attack in Nairobi, in which suicide bombers or VBIEDs will be deployed against regional interests of the African nations which compose the African Union Mission to Somalia (AMISOM) peacekeeping force as well as Western facilities, primarily Israeli, British, and American targets.

Abdullah Azzam Brigades

General Background

The Abdullah Azzam Brigades is well known among jihadi military elements, counterterrorist agencies, and Global Jihad analysts.

During the first half of the 2000s, a group calling itself by that name issued numerous false claims of responsibility for different events (including events that were criminal in nature or due to mechanical malfunctions) occurring in the Middle East and hence was considered by agencies and analysts as unreliable.

During the second half of the 2000s, a new group began using this name and has been conducting terrorist activity throughout the Middle East. The new group, which originated from Saudi Arabia, is based on several al-Qaeda and Islamic activists who left the kingdom (some escaped Saudi prisons) and established an external military arm (outside Saudi land) named the Abdullah Azzam Brigades.

Infrastructure and Layout

All the Saudi leaders of the Abdullah Azzam Brigades are included in Saudi Arabia's 85 Most Wanted list. These Saudi leaders are settled in different locations across the Middle East. They have recruited locals, established local operational cells, and begun preparations for operational activities.

The different cells across the Middle East seem to be named after local jihadist heroes. They have begun conducting terrorist activities. The Lebanese branch of the group was the first to become operational. Named after the Lebanese 9/11 pilot Ziad Jarah, it probably consists of local Lebanese of Palestinian origin living in Palestinian refugee camps in Lebanon. It was led by the Saudi Saleh bin Abdullah bin Saleh al'Qarawi until his capture by the Saudis in 2012.[624] Qarawi was replaced by Majid al-Majid until the latter's death on January 2014.[625] The Abdullah Azzam Brigades/ Seraya (Platoon) Ziad Jarah has carried out several rocket attacks and plots along the Israeli-Lebanese border. A famous attack was carried out against the Israeli town of Nahariya on 13 September 2009.[626] The group has launched two more rocket attacks against northern Israel in November 2011 and on 22 August 2013.[627] Following the civil war that has erupted in Syria as a consequence of the "Arab Spring," the Abdullah Azzam Brigades/ Seraya (Platoon) Ziad Jarah directed most of its operational activity against the entities inside Lebanon that supports the Syrian president Bashar al-Assad troops in the conflict such as Hezbollah and Iran.[628]

On 28 July 2010, a Japanese oil tanker, *M Star*, was attacked in the Strait of Hormuz between the United Arab Emirates and Oman. In the days that followed, the nature of the event was not fully understood and it was initially considered a mechanical malfunction or even an earthquake. During the first week of August, authorities discovered that it was a terrorist operation involving a suicide bomber. A communiqué issued on jihadist forums on 3 August 2010 claimed responsibility for this attack on behalf of the Abdullah Azzam Brigades. The communiqué said that the bombing was carried out by a suicide bomber, Ayyub al-Taishan, pictured in an image attached to the communiqué, pointing to a laptop showing a tanker.[629]

This suicide attack on the Japanese tanker was the first operation of the Saudi cell of the Brigades. Named after the late al-Qaeda leader in Saudi Arabia, Yusuf al-A'yari, the cell had matured and was ready to operate. The target selection of the tanker was made in accordance with bin Laden's old call to attack oil facilities in order to undermine Western economic and infrastructural activity in the region.

Unconfirmed reports suggest the Abdullah Azzam Brigade has, in addition, an operational extension in Gaza. This extension named after Marwan Haddad[630] claimed responsibility for two rocket attacks against Israeli southern cities fired from Gaza.[631]

Group Affiliation

The Abdullah Azzam Brigades have close ties with al-Qaeda in Iraq (AQI) and AQAP and is mostly inspired by al-Qaeda's central leadership in Waziristan.

Future Activity

We believe that the tanker attack is a prelude to a series of attacks initiated by the Saudi branch of the Brigades. We expect it to conduct more operations in the region, which will probably be aimed at naval oil routes in the Gulf as well as oil facilities and hinterland oil fields along the Gulf States, Saudi shores, and maybe even in south Iraq. The Lebanese extension will probably continue to direct its operational efforts against Hezbollah and Iranian interests inside Lebanon using suicide bombing as their main modus operandi while conducting sporadic rockets attacks against the northwest part of Israel.

Other Islamic Militant Groups Operating in Local Arenas

As mentioned, our discussion of affiliated groups is limited to local groups that have internationalized their targeting policies to include Western targets. According to our assessment, there are additional local groups which have the potential to adopt similar international targeting policies in the near future. Below is a list of these groups which possess similar Islamic ideologies to the aforementioned affiliated groups and which are involved in violent conflict in their home states against local regimes:

The Pattani United Liberation Organization (PULO) is synonymous with the Thai separatist terrorist movement fighting against Thai governance of south Thailand. The PULO is a popular organization formed to represent the Malay people of southern Thailand's predominantly Malay provinces formerly known as the Malay Kingdom of Pattani, including the Pattani, Yala, and Narathiwat counties on the Thai-Malaysia border. The vast majority of Malay people in Thailand's south want to be annexed to Malaysia and conduct a large wave of terrorism against Thai authorities, military, and inhabitants of the region.[632]

The Rajah Suleiman Movement (RSM) is a radical Islamic movement that seeks to establish an Islamic state in the Philippines. It was founded in 1992 by Ahmad Santos, a Christian convert to Islam, and consists mostly of former Catholics who have converted to Islamic Salafism. Hence, most of the members do not have a southern accent or readily identifiable Islamic characteristics. This enables the group to operate inconspicuously in the main Philippine islands, which are predominantly Christian, including Luzon. The group cooperates with JI and the ASG, and took part in several attacks in the Philippines including the Super Ferry 14 attack in 2004.[633]

The Moro Islamic Liberation Front (MILF) is a separatist group that is violently operating in order to establish an Islamic state in the southern Philippines region of Mindanao.[634] The MILF was formed in 1977 when Hashim Salamat, supported by ethnic Maguindanaos from Mindanao, split from the Moro National Liberation Front (MNLF), advocating a more radical approach consisting of Islamic extremism in addition to national aspirations toward the Philippines government. The MILF has conducted military activity as well as terrorist attacks in Mindanao against the Philippine military and civilian populations.[635]

The Students Islamic Movement of India (SIMI) is a fundamentalist Islamist organization which advocates India's "liberation" by converting it to an Islamic state. SIMI, composed of young extremist students, has declared jihad against India in order to implement Sharia as the state law, either by forcefully converting everyone to Islam, or through violence. In recent years, SIMI has cooperated with sister movements in south Asia, including Pakistani and Bangladeshi groups.[636] SIMI has good relations with Middle Eastern groups including the Palestinian Hamas.[637]

The Jaish-e-Mohamed (JeM) is an Islamic extremist group based in Pakistan, formed in early 2000 by Masood Azhar upon his release from prison in India. The group's aim is to unite Kashmir with Pakistan. It is politically aligned with the radical Pakistani political party, Jamiat Ulama-i-Islam Fazlur Rehman faction (JUI-F).

Azhar's release from Indian imprisonment in December 1999 in exchange for 155 Indian Airlines hostages marked the formal establishment of the organization. The JeM's main area of deployment and operations is in PoK and along the LoC in that region. It is likely that the organization has extended its operational activity into the Indian heartland as well as against non-Islamic targets inside Pakistan's main cities. The JeM maintained several training camps in Afghanistan until the fall of 2001 and traditionally received external financial aid from bin Laden.[638]

Harakat-al-Mujahidin (HUM) is a Pakistani group that was formed during the 1980s and fought against the Soviet invasion of Afghanistan.[639] At the end of the Afghan war, HUM changed its location and focused operational activity in Kashmir, targeting mostly Indian targets.[640] During the first half of the 1990s, the group executed several kidnapping operations targeting Western tourists visiting Kashmir in order to pressure India into releasing HUM members held in Indian prisons.[641] In 1998, the group was one of the five groups led by al-Qaeda that founded The World Islamic Front for Jihad against the Jews and Crusaders.[642] Since 2000, HUM's activity in the Kashmiri arena sharply decreased. HUM's military is composed of thousands of armed supporters located in Azad Kashmir, Pakistan, and India's southern Kashmir and Doda regions. The group's main base is in Muzaffarabad, Pakistan. Most of its operational activity is in Kashmir and includes the use of light and heavy machine guns, assault rifles, mortars, explosives, and rockets. Like other Pakistani organizations, the group has changed its name several times and during the 1990s was operating under the name Harakat Ul Ansar (HUA) in order to avoid international sanctions.

The East Turkestan Islamic Movement (ETIM) is a jihadi terrorist organization operating in the western Chinese county of Xinjiang. ETIM is one of the more extreme groups founded by the Uyghurs, the Turkic-speaking ethnic majority in Xinjiang, who seek an independent state called East Turkestan. The group was established in 1993, but only began operating in 1997 when Hasan Mahsum assumed authority and reorganized the movement.[643] Mahsum moved ETIM's headquarters to Kabul, taking shelter in Taliban-controlled Afghanistan and cooperating with other jihadi terrorist groups that operated in Afghanistan, al-Qaeda first and foremost and the Islamic Movement of Uzbekistan (IMU) to a lesser extent. The group's infrastructure was crippled after the United States invaded Afghanistan in October 2001 and bombed al-Qaeda bases in the mountainous regions along the Pakistan border. Mahsum was killed in 2003 in an operation by the Pakistan army in the FATA.[644]

ETIM's primary goal is the independence of East Turkestan, and its secondary aim is to convert all Chinese people to Islam.[645] The organization focuses its operational activity in Xinjiang and has conducted several hundreds of attacks in the region since 1990 that include suicide operations in buses, markets, and government institutions as well as assassination of local officials, Muslim leaders, and civilians. According to official Chinese estimates, the overall number of casualties caused by ETIM until 2008 exceeds 500, including 160 dead.[646] In recent years, the organization has been operating outside its traditional Xinjiang arena—ETIM members were involved in two foiled plots in Dubai and Norway.[647]

Hizb-ul- Mujahedeen (HM) is one of the largest terrorist groups operating in Jammu and Kashmir and stands for the integration of the region with Pakistan. Since its formation, the HM has been promoting the Islamization of Kashmir.[648]

The HM was formed in 1989 in Kashmir as the militant wing of the Jamaat-e-Islami (JeI), in order to counter the Jammu and Kashmir Liberation Front (JKLF) which advocated complete independence of the state. Many early HM cadres were former JKLF members.[649]

HM is headquartered at Muzaffarabad in PoK, with an estimated cadre strength of 1500.[650] It has a substantial support base in the Kashmir valley; the Doda, Rajouri, Poonch districts; and parts of Udhampur district in the Jammu region.[651]

HM has conducted a number of operations against Indian military targets in Jammu and Kashmir. The group also occasionally strikes civilian targets in Jammu and Kashmir but has not engaged in terrorist acts elsewhere.

HM has contacts with Afghan Mujahedeen groups such as Hizb-e-Islami, under which some of its cadre have been alleged to have received arms training in the early 1990s.[652]

The Harakat-ul-Jihad-al-Islami (HUJI) is a Pakistan-based terrorist group with an affiliate branch in Bangladesh. HUJI's origins go back to the Afghan-Soviet war of the 1980s when Jamiat Ansar ul Afghani (JAA, the Party of the Friends of the Afghan People) was established by several seminary students from Karachi.[653] Toward the end of its Afghanistan engagement, the JAA renamed itself HUJI and reoriented its strategy to fight for the interests of Muslims in Jammu and Kashmir. HUJI's Bangladesh-based unit (formed in 1992), known as HUJI Bangladesh (HUJI-B), functioned in the initial years under the Jihad Movement in Bangladesh led by Fazlur Rahman, one of the signatories of the 23 February 1998 declaration of "holy war" under bin Laden's World Islamic Front for Jihad against the Jews and Crusaders.[654] HUJI belongs to the Deobandy school of thought and its recruits are indoctrinated in radical Islam. It draws inspiration from bin Laden and the Taliban. HUJI, like the other Pakistan-based terrorist groups, supports the secession of Jammu and Kashmir from India and its eventual accession to Pakistan through violence. It also propagates the idea of Islamic rule across India and the Islamization of Pakistani society. HUJI's cadre consists of around 500 to 750 members and its presence has been reported in more than twenty countries.[655] HUJI cooperates with other Pakistani outfits such as LeT and JeM, and is probably subordinate to the Pakistani intelligence unit's (ISI) direction. In Afghanistan, HUJI has traditional links to the Taliban and al-Qaeda, and some of its senior leaders such as Ilyas Kashmiri and his predecessor Amjad Farooqi were considered al-Qaeda's Special Operations Unit's operational points of contact in Pakistan.[656] The group is very active in Pakistan, mostly in the Karachi arena and the Jammu and Kashmir region. Several plots and attacks inside the Indian hinterland have also been attributed to HUJI.[657]

The Harakat-ul-Mujahidin al-Alami (HUMA) (Al-Alami, meaning international), formed in 2002, is an offshoot of the proscribed Deobandy terrorist group, the Harakat-ul-Mujahidin (HUM).[658] It is based in the Pakistani port city of Karachi.[659] The group is alleged to have been involved in several terrorist plots and attacks in Karachi, some of which were directed against international targets such as international hotels and the U.S. consulate.[660] The HUMA's links with al-Qaeda were established primarily through the proscribed Sunni group, Lashkar-e-Jhangvi (LeJ), and other terrorist groups like the HUM.[661]

Lashkar-e-Jhangvi (LeJ), an anti-Shia (Sunni-Deobandy) terrorist outfit, was formed in 1996 by a breakaway group of radical sectarian extremists of the Sipah-e-Sahaba Pakistan (SSP). The LeJ's political goal is to transform Pakistan into a Sunni state, primarily through violent means.[662] The entire leadership of the LeJ consists of jihadis who fought against Soviet forces in Afghanistan. Its cadres are estimated to comprise approximately 300 members, the majority being drawn from the numerous Sunni madrassas in Pakistan.[663] The LeJ has close links to the Afghan Taliban and its members fought alongside Taliban troops against the Northern Alliance. The LeJ is mostly involved with terrorist activity targeting the Shia population in Pakistan, first and foremost in Karachi.[664]

The Sipah-e-Sahaba Pakistan (SSP) is a Sunni sectarian outfit that has been alleged to be involved in terrorist violence, primarily targeting the minority Shia community in Pakistan. The group was established in 1985 and promotes an anti-Shia approach, aiming to destabilize Pakistani Punjab's feudal system and politico-religious developments in the 1970s and 1980s. Shias, a minority compared to the Sunni sect, were landowners with political and economic power in Pakistani Punjab. Violent sectarianism, embodied by the SSP, has been the most serious political challenge to the control of feudal interests.[665]

The SSP wants Pakistan to become a Sunni Islamic state under which Sharia is the state law and the Islamic Caliphate ruling system is restored.[666]

The SSP actively opposes the U.S.-Pakistan alliance formed in the aftermath of the 9/11 terrorist attacks, claiming that U.S. action was not a war against the Taliban but against Islam, and therefore it was essential for Muslims to declare jihad against the United States and its allies.[667]

According to different reports, the SSP is composed of 3,000 to 6,000 active members spread across Pakistan, especially in the Punjab region. The group also has branches outside Pakistan including in the United Arab Emirates, Saudi Arabia, Bangladesh, Canada, and England.[668]

During the 1980s and 1990s, the SSP had close relations with the Afghani outfits that fought against the Soviet troops and later with the Taliban regime that assumed authority in Afghanistan in 1996. Within this framework, SSP activists participated in the fighting against the Soviets and later against the Northern Alliance troops, and received military training in camps in Afghanistan.[669]

Important SSP links consisted of cooperation with Ramzi Yousef and KSM's group during the 1990s.[670]

Ansar al-Islam is a Kurdish Islamic group that operates in the Kurdish regions of northern Iraq. Ansar al-Islam possesses a radical Islamic ideology advocating Iraq as an Islamic state and Sharia as the state law.[671] The group was established in 2001 as a merger between two Islamic Kurdish groups. The group has close links with al-Qaeda in Iraq (AQI) dating back to the early days of the U.S.-led invasion of Iraq in 2003. The group was then the most important associate of al-Zarqawi, who became the most influential al-Qaeda operative in Iraq until his elimination by American forces in June 2006.[672] Ansar al-Islam consists of 600 to 700 operational activists.[673] Most of its operations are aimed at the local Patriotic Union of Kurdistan (PUK), the dominant group in Kurdistan, and its security apparatus. Some operational efforts are also directed against American and coalition forces. Ansar al-Islam uses various tactics in its operations including VBIEDs and suicide bombers. Ansar al-Islam, which changed its name to Ansar al-Sunna in 2003 and back to Ansar al-Islam in 2007, claims to be the second largest jihadi group operating in Iraq after AQI.[674] (For a detailed report on Ansar al-Islam, see chapter 5.)

Gama'ah Islamiyah Egypt, an Egyptian Islamic gang (Gama'ah Islamiah) established in the 1970s, is a prominent and effective Egyptian Islamic terror organization. At the peak of its activity during the 1990s, it was composed of several thousand active members and tens of thousands of supporters. The group's political aim is to topple the Egyptian regime, establish an Islamic state in Egypt, and implement Sharia as the state law. During the 1990s, the group was responsible for most of the terrorist attacks in Egypt, which have resulted in thousands of casualties. The most devastating attack of the group targeted foreign tourists in Luxor, in which about sixty tourists of different nationalities were killed. The spiritual leader of the group, Sheikh Omar Abd al-Rahman, is imprisoned for life in the United States for his involvement in the group's alleged plot to target New York in 1995. Since the late 1990s, Gama'ah Islamiyah Egypt officially announced a cease-fire with Egyptian troops and has complied with it since. A small faction of the group led by external leader Rif'ai Tah denounced this cease-fire and maintained the group's jihad agenda.[675] In 2003, the imprisoned leadership of the group renounced bloodshed. Several high-ranking members have since been released by Egyptian authorities and the group has been allowed to resume semilegal peaceful activities.[676]

Jeish al-Islam (The Army of Islam) is a Palestinian group in the Gaza Strip which comprises several dozen operatives who are ideologically affiliated with the ideas of Global Jihad and have contact with jihadi elements inside and outside Gaza. The group is headed by Mumtaz Durmush, a member of a powerful clan in the Gaza Strip. Mumtaz Durmush and Jeish al-Islam embrace the modus operandi of Global Jihad, including abduction of foreigners and attacks on recreation sites (such as Internet cafés), which they deem to be destructive to Islamic morals. Jeish al-Islam is one of the three organizations that claimed responsibility for the abduction of Israeli soldier Gilad Shalit (25 June 2006) and for the abduction of two Fox News reporters.[677] In March 2007, the group abducted BBC reporter Alan Johnston in Gaza. In exchange for Johnston's release, the group demanded the release of Sheikh Omar bin Mahmud a.k.a. Abu Qatada al Falastini—a prominent al-Qaeda affiliate in the United Kingdom—from British jail.[678] After 114 days in captivity, Johnston was released.[679] In 2010, the group was involved in a plot to abduct Israeli citizens visiting the Sinai Peninsula.[680] Egyptian authorities also claim that the group was behind the attack on the Coptic Church in Cairo on New Year's Eve of 2011.[681]

Palestinian Tawhid Wal Jihad is an Islamic group operating in Gaza. It is smaller than Jeish al-Islam and has been operating mostly along the Israel-Gaza border. In April 2011, the leader of the group, Hisham Saadini, was arrested by Hamas. The group retaliated by abducting and killing Vitorio Arigoni, an Italian peace activist and member of the "International Solidarity Movement" that has been located in Gaza since 2009.[682]

Asbat al-Ansar (League of the Followers) is a Sunni extremist group operating in Lebanon. The organization is composed of several hundred members, most of whom are Palestinian inhabitants of refugee camps in Lebanon's south, especially in the Saida area. The group possesses a Salafi approach and opposes Israel, the West, and non-Sunni Islamic sects in the internal Lebanese arena. The organization aspires to transform Lebanon into an Islamic state and implement Sharia as state law. The group was formed in the late 1980s and has since been involved in sectarian clashes in Lebanon. The group conducted several attacks and plots throughout the years against international targets in Lebanon that include Western diplomats and embassy compounds.[683] The group has close ties to al-Qaeda and mostly with al-Zarqawi of AQI.[684] The group has experienced splits and secessions throughout the years. In recent years, the group carried out several rocket attacks against Israel along the Israeli-Lebanese border.[685]

Fatah al-Islam is a Sunni Islamist group operating in the city of Tripoli in north Lebanon, composed of several hundred Palestinian activists from north Lebanon Palestinian refugee camps.[686] Fatah al-Islam was established between 2006 and 2007 in the Nahr al-Bared refugee camp in the outskirts of the northern Lebanese city of Tripoli. In early 2007, the organization initiated waves of attacks against the Lebanese army, which escalated into a full-scale collision between Fatah al-Islam and the military. Hundreds of people, many of whom were civilians, died in these three months of clashes before the Lebanese army was able to assume control of the camp. Fatah al-Islam is believed to be responsible for the 2007 attacks against UN peacekeeping forces deployed along the Israeli-Lebanese border. [687]

Fatah al-Islam's ideology is Sunni-Salafist, with an operational focus on Lebanon (the "infidel" regime and Western presence in Lebanon) and Israel. On a nonviolent level, it wishes to institute Islamic law in Lebanon. Aligning itself with the Global Jihad agenda, it also opposes the West and moderate, "apostate" Arab regimes, and supports attacks against them.[688]

Fatah al-Islam was formed by Palestinian militant Shaker al-Abssi, who is believed to be the original coordinator between Fatah al-Islam, al-Qaeda, and AQI.[689]

The group is composed of several hundred members of various nationalities.[690] In the past, the group has provided training and combat experience to foreign fighters, including Westerners from Europe and Australia.[691]

People Against Gangsterism and Drugs (PAGAD) was formed in 1996 as an Islamic militant group in Cape Town,

South Africa. It claimed to fight drugs and gangsterism but its members have been implicated in criminal and terrorist acts.

PAGAD's G-Force, operating in small cells, is believed to be responsible for killing many gang leaders and for a wave of urban terrorism—particularly bombings—in Cape Town. The bombings started in 1998, and include nine bombings in 2000. In addition to gang leaders, bombing targets included South African authorities, moderate Muslims, synagogues, gay nightclubs, tourist attractions, and Western restaurants. The most prominent attack during this time was the bombing of the Cape Town Planet Hollywood restaurant on 25 August 1998.[692]

PAGAD has been inactive in recent years.[693]

Al-Ittihad al-Islami (AIAI, The Islamic Union) is an Islamic group from Somalia and one of the more important allies of al-Qaeda in the Horn of Africa. AIAI was established in the early 1980s through the merger of Salafi groups. These groups enjoyed popularity in Somalia in the 1960s and 1970s, largely as a result of their attempts to regain lost Somali land after independence as well as their resistance to the Barre regime and Western influence. They gained the support of the Somali people through nationalist causes more than a common affinity for Salafism, an ideology which was widely unpopular in the country at the time.[694]

During the 1990s, the Barre regime was destabilized. AIAI openly denounced the Barre regime, and amid the onset of civil war and growing lawlessness, the organization shifted from spreading the message of Salafi Islam to engaging in armed conflict.[695]

As AIAI was fighting to establish an Islamic state in Somalia, al-Qaeda was sending funds, arms, and fighters to support the Islamists, and shared in the same goal—the creation of an Islamic state in Somalia. Responding to Operation "Restore Hope" under which U.S. troops entered Somalia, al-Qaeda engaged its own forces in Somalia and launched an al-Qaeda initiative named The Somalia Operation. Al-Qaeda sent its most prominent figures led by Mohammed Atef a.k.a. Abu Hafs Al Masri, the second-in-command of al-Qaeda's Military Committee, to Somalia in order to train locals in military tactics to be used in the civil war and against U.S. and UN forces. Under this initiative, al-Qaeda established several training camps in which most trainees were AIAI recruits. AIAI is believed to be responsible for the murder of eighteen U.S. military personnel on 3–4 October 1993, when three helicopters were shot down by al-Qaeda-trained Somali militants. Al-Qaeda donated as much as US$3 million toward the establishment of an Islamic state administered by AIAI.[696]

In the following years, AIAI was greatly weakened and completely disappeared from Somali politics by the late 1990s. Its members and leaders, however, continued to be very active in Somali politics and have served as members of the Islamic Courts. They also played a dominant role in the establishment of the new al-Shabaab al-Mujahidin group in the second half of the 2000s.[697]

AIAI is significant within the Global Jihad Movement. Al-Qaeda, its family, and the extended family views Somalia as an important arena for bases and training. More importantly, the personal relations between al-Qaeda's most prominent figures and AIAI senior activists cultivated during The Somalia Project is likely to shape al-Qaeda's future activity.

The Eritrean Islamic Jihad Movement (EIJM) began its activity in 1975 when a group of Islamist guerrillas split off from the Eritrean Liberation Front (ELF) that had been fighting since the beginning of the Eritrean independence movement. The EIJM was formally established in 1980. Since Eritrean independence in 1993, the EIJM (and its factions) has been the principal Muslim opposition group in Eritrea, seeking the violent overthrow of the ELF government led by President Isaias Afewerki.[698] EIJM's activists participated in the war in Afghanistan and probably continued to cooperate with al-Qaeda during bin Laden's relocation of his base of operations to Sudan in 1991–1995, mainly through Sheikh Abu Suhail (also known as Muhammad Ahmad). Abu Suhail participated in the Afghan jihad against the Soviets and is mentioned as the leader of the EIJM in documents captured from al-Qaeda in Afghanistan.[699]

The Moroccan Islamic Combatant Group a.k.a. Groupe Islamique Combattant Marocain (GICM) is a Moroccan radical

Islamist group that has been operating since the early 1990s.[700] The goals of GICM include establishing an Islamic state in Morocco and supporting al-Qaeda's war against the West.[701] The group appears to have emerged in the 1990s and is composed of Moroccan recruits who trained in armed camps in Afghanistan, including some who fought in the Soviet-Afghan war. Outside Morocco, the group has a significant presence among the Moroccan diaspora mainly in Europe and Canada.[702] The group's overseas cells operate on behalf of the group and conduct logistical activities to support the struggle in Morocco. They engage in trafficking falsified documents, recruiting new members, and smuggling arms.[703] As for international operations, the group was allegedly involved with planning the May 2003 Casablanca suicide bombings and the March 2004 Madrid train bombings. These allegations are yet to be proven.[704] The number of active members of the group is unknown and the group appears to have decreased its volume of activity in recent years.

Jama'a Ahl al-Sunna lil Daw'a wal Jihad aka Taliban al-Nigeri (The Nigerian Taliban) aka Boko Haram, which refers to itself as the Muhajirun (migrants) movement, first appeared around 2003. Like the Afghan Taliban whose name it adopted, Taliban al-Nigeri was composed primarily of religious students. Inspired by the Afghan Taliban's vision of an Islamic state ruled by an extremist interpretation of Islam, the Nigerian radicals abandoned Maiduguri and relocated to the rough bush of Yobe state near the border with Niger.[705]

In early 2004, descending from their wilderness retreat, the young militants raided the Yobe state capital of Damaturu, attacking police stations. Later that year, the militants tried to launch a guerrilla campaign around Gwoza, in Borno state near the Cameroonian border. Press reports indicated that the Nigerian militants wanted to establish an Islamic state and declared Muslims who opposed them to be "unbelievers" who deserved death.[706] Since 2010 the group, operating under the name Boko Haram, has executed numerous devastating attacks in Nigeria targeting governmental as well as Christian targets in the country, which has resulted in thousands of casualties, mostly civilians.[707]

Al-Qaeda and Affiliated Terrorist Organizations

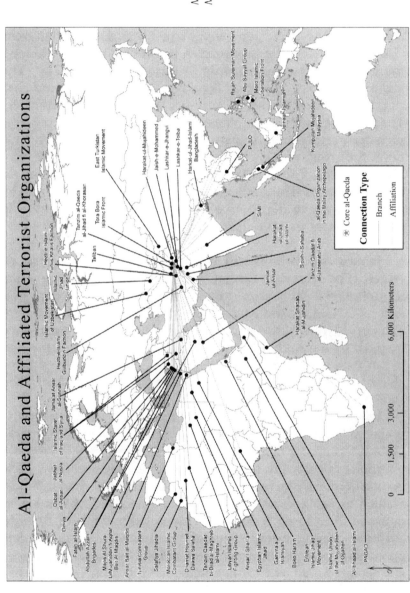

Map 4.6. © Richard M. Medina.

All of the abovementioned organizations have yet to conduct international attacks. They currently focus all operational efforts in the domestic arena, either attempting to topple secular regimes in their home countries or fighting a bordering enemy as in the case of the Palestinian outfits. Since they all possess radical Islamic ideologies, similar to al-Qaeda, the authors believe that in the near future, a significant number of these groups will divert some of their operational efforts to the international arena and include foreign targets within their targeting policy inside their current vicinity of operations. The latest developments and especially the outcome of the Arab Spring will open new windows of opportunity for some of these groups to abandon their terrorist agendas to regenerate their activity and direct it against external elements as well.

Notes

1. International terrorism here refers to either activity of a local group outside their home country or vicinity of operations (for example if the Abu Sayyaf Group [ASG] attacks the Philippine embassy in London), or operating internally against a third country's infrastructure or personnel (when the ASG conducted a terrorist operation aimed at the American embassy in Manila).

2. "Al-Shabaab Joining al Qaeda, Monitor Group Says," *CNN,* 9 February 2012 at http://articles.cnn.com/2012-02-09/africa/world_africa_somalia-shabaab-qaeda_1_al-zawahiri-qaeda-somali-americans?_s=PM:AFRICA.

3. Singapore Ministry of Home Affairs, *White Paper: The Jemaah Islamiyah Arrests and the Threat of Terrorism,* Singapore: Ministry of Home Affairs, 7 January 2003, pp. 3–4.

4. Singapore Ministry of Home Affairs, p. 6.

5. Ibid.

6. Maria Ressa, *Seeds of Terror: An Eyewitness Account of Al-Qaeda's Newest Center of Operations in Southeast Asia,* New York: Free Press, 2003, p. 48.

7. This information was obtained through JI detainee debriefing in Singapore and Indonesia. Also see, Sidney Jones, "Indonesia Backgrounder, Jihad in Central Sulawesi," *International Crisis Group (ICG)*

Asia Report, No. 74, Jakarta/Brussels, 3 February 2004, p. 2, where she authenticates the "Official Statement of al-Jamaah al-Islamiyah" (Pernyataan Resmi al-Jamaah al-Islamaah) of 6 October 2003, which cites the date of founding.

8. Jones, "Jemaah Islamiyah in South East Asia: Damaged but Still Dangerous," *ICG Asia Report,* No. 63, 26 August 2003, p. 2.

9. Pedoman Umum Perjuangan al-Jamaah al-Islamiyah (PUPJI).

10. Singapore Ministry of Home Affairs, p. 6.

11. "Indonesia: Jamaah Islamiyah's Current Status," *ICG Asia Briefing,* No. 63, Jakarta/Brussels, 3 May 2007, p. 1.

12. Jones, "Still a Real Threat," *Tempo* 6 (4), 14–20 October 2003.

13. The Hudaybiyah agreement in the Quran is referred to as an agreement to go to war.

14. Jones, "Still a Real Threat."

15. *Muntaqa* in Arabic literally means region. For details on *wakalahs,* see Bab III (Chapter 3), *Tandhim* (Organization), PUPJI.

16. Jones, "Jemaah Islamiyah in South East Asia," p. 1.

17. Interrogation deposition of Hashim bin Abbas, 13 December 2002 in "Jemaah Islamiyah in South East Asia," pp. 11–12.

18. Andrew Perrin, "Targeting Thailand: Are Islamic Militants Behind the Latest Wave of Attacks and Bombings in the Country's Restless South?" *TIME Asia,* 11 January 2004, http://www.time.com/time/magazine/article/0,9171,501040119-574944,00.html, accessed 9 April 2012.

19. "Achmad Roihan: This Is Not the Decision of the Organization," *Tempo* 6 (4), 14–20 October 2003.

20. "Ali Ghufron," *Global Jihad,* 23 October 2007, http://www.globaljihad.net/view_page.asp?id=509, accessed 9 April 2012.

21. Interrogation deposition of Hashim bin Abbas on 13 December 2002 in Jones, "Jemaah Islamiyah in South East Asia," pp. 11–12.

22. "Bombs in a Shoe Shop," *Tempo* 6 (4), 14–20 October 2003.

23. Interrogation deposition of Hashim bin Abbas on 13 December 2002 in Jones, "Jemaah Islamiyah in South East Asia," pp. 11–12.

24. Eddie Chua, "Abu Bakar Used Malaysian Passport to Enter Australia," *Malaysiakini,* 10 November 2002.

25. "Bashir Said Visited Australia 11 Times to Spread Jamaah Islamiyah Influence," *AFP,* 3 November 2002.

26 Mark Baker, Linda Morris, and Tom Allard, "JI Accused of Plot to Bomb 2000 Games," *The Sydney Morning Herald,* 4 Dec 2002, http://www.smh.com.au/articles/2002/12/03/1038712936708.html, accessed 16 April 2012.

27. Budi Setyarso, Imron Rosyid, and Ivansyah, "The Teacher's New Group," *Tempo Interaktif*, 10–16 April 2007.

28. "The General of Suicide Bombers," *Tempo* 6 (4), 14–20 October 2003.

29. Matthew Moore, "Jakarta Fears JI Has Suicide Brigade," *The Age*, 12 August 2003.

30. Interrogation deposition of Wan Min bin Wan Mat on 11 March 2003 in "Jemaah Islamiyah in South East Asia," p. 11.

31. Bab IV(Chapter 4), Article 8, point 4, PUPJI, Jones, "Jemaah Islamiyah in South East Asia," p. 1.

32. Ressa, p. 49.

33. Singapore Ministry of Home Affairs, *White Paper*.

34. Suryadi interrogation deposition in Abu Bakar Ba'asyir case dossier, referred to in Jones, "Jemaah Islamiyah in South East Asia," p. 20.

35. For discussion of the Southeast Asian Caliphate, see Jones, "Jemaah Islamiyah in South East Asia," p. 1.

36. Don Greenlees, "Still a Force to Be Feared," *Far Eastern Economic Review*, 22 January 2004, p. 14.

37. "Terror Before Us," *Tempo* 6 (4), 14–20 October 2003.

38. "Bin Laden Funded Australian Embassy Bombing: Report," *The Jakarta Post*, 2 August 2005. "Bin Laden 'Funded' Australian Embassy Bombing," *The Sydney Morning Herald*, 1 August 2005, http://www.smh.com.au/news/world/bin-laden-funded-australian-embassy-bombing/2005/08/01/1122748533388.html, accessed 16 April 2012.

39. "Achmad Roihan."

40. Karl Malakunas, "JI Arrests Have 'Dismantled' Cell: Minister," *The Age*, 18 December 2003, http://www.theage.com.au/articles/2003/12/18/1071337098888.html?from=storyrhs, accessed 12 April 2012.

41. Hazmi and Midhar were among the nineteen suicide bombers who eventually participated in the 9/11 attacks. KSM's original plan was to conduct mutual attacks on the U.S. East and West Coasts, but the plan was later limited to the East Coast. The four al-Qaeda members were personally selected for the operation from among al-Qaeda's ranks by bin Laden and Mohamed Atef.

For the full report about the Kuala Lumpur meeting, see The National Commission on Terrorist Attacks Upon the United States, *The 9/11 Commission Report*, 22 July 2004, http://www.gpoaccess.gov/911/pdf/sec7.pdf, pp. 155–60.

42. See http://cdn.historycommons.org/images/events/a017_infocus_letter_2050081722-13852.jpg.

43. The National Commission on Terrorist Attacks Upon the United States, p. 151.

44. "Singapore Cell," *Global Jihad*, 30 January 2009, http://www.globaljihad.net/view_page.asp?id=1357, accessed 14 April 2012.

45. Richard S. Ehrlich, "Bush Recalls the Capture of Hambali In Thailand," *Scoop*, 13 February 2006, http://www.scoop.co.nz/stories/HL0602/S00121.htm, accessed 14 April 2012.

46. "Verbatim Transcript of Combatant Status Review Tribunal Hearing for ISN 10024 (Khaled Sheikh Mohamed)" at http://www.defenselink.mil/news/transcript_ISN10024.pdf.

47. "Bali Bombings 2002," *Global Jihad*, 24 June 2007, http://www.globaljihad.net/view_page.asp?id=263, accessed 14 April 2012.

48. "Terrorism in Indonesia: Noordin's Networks," *ICG Asia Report*, No. 114, 5 May 2006, http://merln.ndu.edu/archive/icg/Terrorism-5May06.pdf, pp. 2–5.

49. Ibid, p. 5.

50. "Suicide Attack Leaves 22 Dead and Over 130 Injured," *The Guardian*, 3 October 2005 at http://www.theguardian.com/world/2005/oct/03/indonesia.alqaida. Accessed on 13 June 2014.

51. Berni Moestafa and Bambang Djanuarto, Bambang, "Jakarta Hotel Bombers Linked to Jemaah Islamiyah, Police Say," 19 July 2009 at http://www.bloomberg.com/apps/news?pid=newsarchive&sid=aslTMQuj6g4U. Accessed 13 June 2014.

52. Kate McGeown, "Jack Roche: The Naïve Militant," *BBC News*, 1 June 2004, http://news.bbc.co.uk/2/hi/asia-pacific/3757017.stm, accessed 14 April 2012.

53. "Militant Plot to Hit El Al Planes in Thailand: Thaksin," *The Sydney Morning Herald*, 25 September 2003, http://www.smh.com.au/articles/2003/09/24/1064083060742.html?from=storyrhs, accessed 14 April 2012.

54. "Hambali's Capture: PM—JI Plotted to Attack Apec Meet," *Asian Tribune*, 17 August 2003, http://www.asiantribune.com/news/2003/08/17/hambalis-capture-pm-ji-plotted-attack-apec-meet, accessed 16 April 2012.

55. Ehrlich, "Bush Recalls Capture."

56. Leah Farrall, "How al Qaeda Works: What the Organization's Subsidiaries Say About Its Strength," *Foreign Affairs*, March/April 2011, Vol. 90, No. 2, pp. 128–38.

57. "Interview with Shaykh Abu Basir," *Inspire*, Summer 1431/2010, pp. 13–14.

58. Ibid, p. 14.

59. Thomas Hegghamer, "Terrorist Recruitment and Radicalization in Saudi Arabia," *Middle East Policy*, Vol. 13, no. 4 (Winter 2006).

60. "Interview with Shaykh Abu Bassir," p. 13.

61. The most ambitious attempt of this cell was a plot to imitate the 9/11 attacks by hijacking commercial aircraft departing from Eastern European airports and crashing them into major London landmarks. Another plot involved a Saudi pilot who was tasked to divert his jet during routine maneuvers and crash it into a large hotel building in the southern Israeli city of Eilat. See Office for the Administrative Review of the Detention of Enemy Combatants (OARDEC), "Verbatim Transcript of Combatant Status Review Tribunal Hearing for ISN 10024 (Khaled Sheikh Mohamed)," United States Department of Defense, http://www.defenselink.mil/news/transcript_ISN10024.pdf; "In the Line of Fire by Pervez Musharraf," *The Times*, 26 September 2006, http://www.timesonline.co.uk/tol/news/world/asia/article650210.ece; Evan F. Kohlmann, "Al Qaeda's Committee in Saudi Arabia: 2002–2003," *Global Terror Alert*, December 2005, http://nefafoundation.org//file/qaidasaudi02-03.pdf, accessed 23 April 2012.

62. Michael Scheuer, "Yemen's Role in al-Qaeda's Strategy," *Terrorism Focus*, Vol. 5, Issue 5, 7 February 2008, http://www.jamestown.org/programs/gta/single/?tx_ttnews%5Btt_news%5D=4708&tx_ttnews%5BbackPid%5D=246&no_cache=1, accessed 23 April 2012.

63. Jeremy M. Sharp, "Yemen: Background and U.S. Relations," *Congressional Research Service*, 13 January 2010, p. 12.

64. Ibid, p. 13.

65. "Sources: U.S. Kills *Cole* Suspect," *CNN*, 5 November 2002, http://edition.cnn.com/2002/WORLD/meast/11/04/yemen.blast/index.html, accessed 14 April 2012.

66. "Al Qaeda in the Arabian Peninsula," *Yemen Times*, 22 March 2010.

67. Ibid.

68. Ibid.

69. Ibid.

70. "Excerpt from Al-Qaida in Yemen's (AQIY) Magazine: Sada al-Malahim April 2009," (CeifiT Ltd. trans. from Arabic) *The NEFA Foundation*, 20 April 2009, http://nefafoundation.org//file/NEFA%20AQIY%200409%20part%202.pdf.

71. Murad Batal al-Shishani, "Adel al-Abbab: Al Qaeda in the Arabian Peninsula's Religious Ideologue," *Jamestown Foundation*, Vol. I, Issue 3, 31 March 2010, http://www.jamestown.org/single/?no_

cache=1&tx_ttnews%5Btt_news%5D=36222&tx_ttnews%5BbackPid%5D=13&cHash=83cc90d89d, accessed 14 April 2012.

72. Ellen Knickmeyer, "Al-Qaida Takes Lessons Learned to Yemen," *NPR,* 27 September 2010, http://www.npr.org/templates/story/story.php?storyId=130163592, accessed 14 April 2012.

73. "Excerpt from Al-Qaida in Yemen's (AQIY) Magazine: Sada al-Malahim March 10, 2008" (CeifiT Ltd. trans. from Arabic), *The NEFA Foundation,* March 2008, http://www.nefafoundation.org/miscellaneous/NEFA_aqapmag0309.pdf.

74. "Al Qaeda Claims Attack in Yemen Oil Province: Web," *Reuters,* 7 August 2010, http://www.reuters.com/article/2010/08/07/us-yemen-idUSTRE6760PG20100807, accessed 14 April 2012.

75. Knickmeyer.

76. Barak Barfi, "Yemen on the Brink? The Resurgence of al Qaeda in Yemen," *New America Foundation,* 25 January 2010, http://www.newamerica.net/publications/policy/yemen_on_the_brink, accessed 14 April 2012.

77. Open Source Center, "Report on Al-Qaida's New Tactics in Yemen," *Al-Sharq al-Awsat Online in Arabic,* 22 July 2009, Document ID#GMP20090722825002; "New AQAP Video, Uploaded to YouTube before Its Official Release, Celebrates Victories over Yemeni Army in South Yemen," *The Jihad and Terrorism Threat Monitor,* No. 4236, 31 October 2011, http://www.memrijttm.org/content/en/report.htm?report=5760&param=APT, accessed 14 April 2012.

78. "AQAP Calls on Sunnis to Wage Jihad against Houthis in Dammaj, Warns against Shi'ite Takeover of Yemen and Gulf," *The Jihad and Terrorism Threat Monitor* 12 December 2011, http://www.memrijttm.org/content/en/blog_personal.htm?id=5615&param=GJN, accessed 14 April 2012.

79. "*Inspire* Magazine, Spring 2011: 'An Interview with Shaykh Abu Hurairah as-Sana'ani, the Military Commander of al-Qaeda in the Arabian Peninsula' March, 2011" (CeifiT Ltd trans. from Arabic) *The NEFA Foundation,* March 2011, http://nefafoundation.org//file/InspHurairah%20as-Sana'ani0411.pdf.

80. "Profile: Al-Qaeda in the Arabian Peninsula," *BBC News,* 14 June 2011, http://www.bbc.co.uk/news/world-middle-east-11483095, accessed 14 April 2012.

81. R. Green, "Putting a Spin on the Arab Spring: Al-Qaeda Struggles to Prove Its Relevance in the Era of the Arab Revolutions," *Free

Muslims Coalition, 11 October 2011, http://www.freemuslims.org/news.php?id=7128, accessed 14 April 2012.

82. Ibid.

83. "New Releases from Al-Qaeda's Media Wing Al-Sahab Celebrating 10th Anniversary of 9/11: Al-Zawahiri in Audio Message: 'Arab Spring' Will Be 'American Winter,'" *The Jihad and Terrorism Threat Monitor,* No. 4131, 13 September 2011, http://www.memrijttm.org/content/en/report.htm?report=5637&param=APT, accessed 14 April 2012.

84. The Islamic movement al-Nahada won the elections in the post–Zine El Abidine Ben Ali era and the early rounds of the general elections in Egypt resulted in the victory of the Muslim Brotherhood. The Muslim Brotherhood eventually secured the presidency with its candidate, Mohamed Morsi, winning the general elections in June 2012.

85. Abu Bassir, cited in Matthew Cole and Rym Momtaz, "Al Qaeda Leader in Yemen Pledges Allegiance to Zawahiri," *ABC News,* 26 July 2011, http://abcnews.go.com/Blotter/al-qaeda-leader-yemen-pledges-allegiance-zawahiri/story?id=14164884, accessed 14 April 2012.

86. Refers to the events in Algeria between 1992 and 1995 in which an Islamic party won the general elections that were revoked by the Algerian Army, which led to five years of internal clashes resulting in more than 50,000 people dead.

87. Refers to the violent campaign of the Egyptian Salafi Jihadi organizations of Gamm'aa Islamiyah and Egyptian Islamic Jihad which peaked with the assassination of President Sadat in 1981. This was followed by a tough and violent response by Sadat's successor Hosni Mubarak, which eventually crushed this campaign.

88. Refers to the Hamah massacres of 1982 in which Syrian president Hafiz al-Assad murdered more than 20,000 inhabitants of the city of Hama during a Muslim Brotherhood revolt against his regime in the city.

89. Al-Awlaki, cited in "AQAP's 'Inspire' Magazine: Shaykh Anwar al-Awlaki 'The Tsunami of Change' March 29, 2011," *The NEFA Foundation,* 29 March 2011, http://nefafoundation.org//file/InspireAwlaki 10311.pdf.

90. Two Egyptian secular candidates for presidency in the post-Mubarak era.

91. Al-Awlaki, cited in "AQAP's 'Inspire' Magazine: Shaykh Anwar al-Awlaki."

92. Ibid.

93. Khan, cited in ibid.

94. Khan, cited in "'Inspire' Magazine, Spring 2011: Samir Khan: 'The Egyptian' March, 2011," *The NEFA Foundation*, March 2011, http://nefafoundation.org//file/SamirKahnInspire311.pdf.

95. Al-Shishani.

96. "AQAP Calls on Sunnis to Wage Jihad against Houthis in Dammaj."

97. "AQAP Leader Unharmed In U.S. Navy Missile Attack in Southern Yemen," *The Jihad and Terrorism Threat Monitor*, 23 December 2011, http://www.memrijttm.org/content/en/blog_personal. htm?id=5647&param=GJN, accessed 20 June 2012; "Al-Qaida in Yemen: 'From Here We Will Begin and in Al-Aqsa We Shall Meet' January 2009" (CeifiT Ltd trans. from Arabic) *The NEFA Foundation*, January 2009, http://nefafoundation.org//file/FeaturedDocs/nefaqaidayemen 0209.pdf, p. 2.

98. "AQAP's 'Inspire' Magazine: 'Interview with Shaykh Abu Sufyan: The Vice Emir of Al-Qaida in the Arabian Peninsula' October 11, 2010," *The NEFA Foundation*, 11 October 2010, http://nefafoundation. org//file/InspireAl-Azdi1010.pdf.

99. "Al-Qaida in Yemen: 'From Here We Will Begin,'" p. 4.

100. Ibid.

101. "AQAP's Al-Malahim Media: 'Biography of the Martyr, The Commander Jamil al-Anbari (aka Abu Saber al-Abyani) April 4, 2011 [*sic*]," *The NEFA Foundation*, 4 April 2011, http://nefafoundation. org//file/Bio_Abu_Saber0411.pdf.

102. Al-Shishani.

103. Rohan Gunaratna and Aviv Oreg, "Al Qaeda's Organizational Structure and Its Evolution," *Studies in Conflict & Terrorism*, Vol. 33, No. 12 (2010), pp. 1053–64.

104. Ibid., p. 1056.

105. "Western Counter-Terrorism Help 'Not Enough for Yemen,'" *BBC News*, 29 December 2009, http://news.bbc.co.uk/2/hi/8433844. stm, accessed 20 June 2012.

106. "Profile: Al-Qaeda in the Arabian Peninsula."

107. Frank Gardner, "Is Yemen Becoming a Jihadist Plotter's paradise?" *BBC News*, 24 June 2010, http://news.bbc.co.uk/2/hi/pro grammes/from_our_own_correspondent/8755663.stm, accessed 20 June 2012.

108. "Profile: Al-Qaeda in the Arabian Peninsula."

109. Bill Roggio, "Al Qaeda Opens New Training Camp in Yemen," *The Long War Journal*, 13 November 2009, http://www.longwarjournal.org/archives/2009/11/al_qaeda_opens_new_t.php, accessed 14 April 2012.

110. Ibid.

111. Ibid.

112. "Profile: Al-Qaeda in the Arabian Peninsula."

113. "Ansar Al-Shari'a Newsletter Strengthens Suspicion of Connection to AQAP," *The Jihad and Terrorism Threat Monitor*, No. 4230, 27 October 2011, http://www.memrijttm.org/content/en/report.htm?report=5754&param=GJN, accessed 14 April 2012.

114. Out of the affiliated groups that include Western targets in their targeting policy, none have gone beyond their traditional vicinity of operations. Southeast Asian JI attacked foreign targets in Bali, Kuala Lumpur, and Jakarta; al-Shabaab attacked Western targets in Somalia Uganda, and Kenya; Pakistani Lashkar-e-Toyba (LeT) attacked Western targets in Mumbai; Pakistani Harakat Ul Jihad al-Alami (HUJA) attacked western targets in Karachi; and Mindanao Abu Sayyaf Group (ASG) has initiated several plots against Western targets in Manila.

115. Peter Baker, "Obama Says Al Qaeda in Yemen Planned Bombing Plot, and He Vows Retribution," *The New York Times*, 2 January 2010, http://www.nytimes.com/2010/01/03/us/politics/03address.html; reprinted in *The New York Times* (New York edition), 3 January 2010, A12.

116. Open Source Center, "Al-Qaeda in the Arabian Peninsula Claims Attempted Attack in US," *Jihadist Websites—OSC Summary in Arabic*, 28 December 2009, Document ID# GMP20091228535001.

117. Richard Spencer, "Detroit Terror Attack: Bomber Arrived on Student Visa to Study at Language Institute in Yemen," *The Telegraph*, 30 December 2009, http://www.telegraph.co.uk/news/uknews/terrorism-in-the-uk/6906963/Detroit-terror-attack-bomber-arrived-on-student-visa-to-study-at-language-institute-in-Yemen.html, accessed 17 April 2012.

118. "AQAP's 'Inspire' Magazine: 'Interview with Shaykh Abu Bassir: The Head of Al-Qaida in the Arabian Peninsula' July 11, 2010," *The NEFA Foundation*, 11 July 2010, http://nefafoundation.org//file/Abu-Basir_Inspire0710-.pdf.

119. AQAP Head of Foreign Operations, "The Objectives of Operation Hemorrhage," *Inspire* Issue 3, November 2010, p. 7; republished in *The NEFA Foundation*, 20 November 2010, http://nefafoundation.org//file/InspireOpHemmorhage.pdf.

120. On 3 September 2010, a UPS cargo jet crashed after taking off from Dubai International Airport. Until AQAP claimed responsibility, following its October attempts to crash two more cargo planes in mid-air, it was believed that the September crash was a result of a technical malfunction. See "Subject: Liquidation Devices Operations," *Inspire*, 5 November 2010, republished in *The NEFA Foundation*, http://nefa foundation.org//file/NEFA%20AQAPliquidation1110.pdf, accessed 18 April 2012.

121. Ibid.

122. Khan, cited in ibid.

123. Scheuer, *Through Our Enemies' Eyes: Osama Bin Laden, Radical Islam & the Future of America*, Washington, DC: Brassey's Inc., 2003, pp. 16–17.

124. "The Objectives of Operation Hemorrhage."

125. "Qaeda Names Man Who Tried to Kill Saudi Prince," *Al Arabiya News*, 30 August 2009, http://www.alarabiya.net/save_pdf.php?cont_id=83348&lang=en, accessed 14 April 2012.

126. Scott Stewart, "AQAP: Paradigm Shifts and Lessons Learned," *Stratfor*, 2 September 2009, http://www.stratfor.com/weekly/20090902_aqap_paradigm_shifts_and_lessons_learned, accessed 17 April 2012.

127. "Saudi Anti-Terror Chief Escapes Murder Attempt," *Al Arabiya News*, 28 August 2009, http://www.alarabiya.net/save_pdf.php?cont_id=83168, accessed 14 April 2012.

128. "Norwegian at Center of New al Qaeda Plot Fears" at http://www.cbsnews.com/8301-505263_162-57464755/norwegian-at-center-of-new-al-qaeda-plot-fears/.

129. Ibid.

130. "French Investigators Probing Claims *Charlie Hebdo* Gunman Had Links to 'Underwear Bomber' Who Plotted to Bring Down US Passenger Plane, as al-Qaeda Claim Responsibility," *Dailymail* 3 February 2015. http://www.dailymail.co.uk/news/article-2903938/I-defender-prophet-journalists-not-civilians-targets-Chilling-boast-terrorists-re-sponsible-Charlie-Hebdo-massacre-carnage-kosher-grocery.html.

131. Rohan Gunaratna, "al-Qaeda after Awlaki," *RSIS Commentaries*, No. 155, 27 October 2011, http://www.rsis.edu.sg/publications/Perspective/RSIS1552011.pdf, p. 1.

132. Ibid, pp. 1–2.

133. Ibid, p. 2.

134. Ibid.

135. "In a Continuation of Their 'Vengeance Raid,' Jihadis Take to Twitter to Spread Anwar Al-Awlaki's Message," *The Jihad and Ter-*

rorism Threat Monitor, 8 November 2011, http://www.memrijttm. org/content/en/blog_personal.htm?id=5551&param=GJN, accessed 14 April 2012.

136. "*Inspire* Magazine, Spring 2011: 'An Interview with Shaykh Abu Huraira as-Sana'ani, the Military Commander of al-Qaeda in the Arabian Peninsula' March, 2011."

137. "Al-Shabab Acknowledges Close Ties with Al-Qaeda in Yemen, Warns of Black Hawk Down Redux if U.S. Sends Troops," *The Jihad and Terrorism Threat Monitor*, No. 5108, 19 January 2010, http://www.memrijttm.org/content/en/report.htm?report=4319, accessed 24 June 2012.

138. "Jama'at Al-Tawhid Wal-Jihad in Philippines Asks Mujahideen Worldwide for Help Waging Jihad; Swears Allegiance To Al-Qaeda," *The Jihad and Terrorism Threat Monitor*, No. 4295, 17 November 2011, http://www.memrijttm.org/content/en/report. htm?report=5830&param=GJN, accessed 24 June 2012.

139. "Yemen Arrested 30 Militants," *Global Jihad*, 8 June 2010, http:// globaljihad.net/view_news.asp?id=1496, accessed 24 June 2012.

140. For example, see Cole and Momtaz.

141. Ibid.

142. "Al-Qaida in Yemen: 'From Here We Will Begin,'" p. 3.

143. Ibid.

144. "AQAP's 'Inspire' Magazine: 'Interview with Shaykh Abu Bassir."

145. "AQIY Leader Saeed al-Shehri: 'Repelling the Crusader Aggression' February 8, 2010," *The NEFA Foundation* 8 February 2010, http://nefafoundation.org//file/Nefa_AQIY0210Tape.pdf.

146. "Al-Qaida in Yemen: 'From Here We Will Begin,'" pp. 2–3; "Excerpt from 'Al-Qaida in Yemen' Official Magazine 'Sada al-Malahim' March 10, 2008" *The NEFA Foundation*, 10 March 2008, http://nefa foundation.org//file/nefaqaidayemen1008-2.pdf, p. 2.

147. "Al-Qaida in Yemen: 'From Here We Will Begin,'" p. 2.

148. "Excerpt from 'Al-Qaida in Yemen' Official Magazine 'Sada al-Malahim" January 12, 2008" (CeifiT Ltd trans. from Arabic), *The NEFA Foundation*, 12 January 2008, http://nefafoundation.org//file/ nefaqaidayemen1008-4.pdf, p. 2.

149. Ibid.

150. Abu Hamza al-Masri and Abu Qatada Al Falastini in London, Imad Baraqat Yarqas a.k.a. Abu Dahdah in Spain, and Mahmud Ould Salahi in Germany and probably other figures served as al-Qaeda points of contact in those countries and were responsible for spotting, drafting, and recruiting suitable new members into al-Qaeda. In this

way, members of the Hamburg cell comprised three out of the four pilots of the 9/11 attacks and were recruited in Germany by Salahi. See Gunaratna and Oreg, p. 1064.

151. http://globaljihad.net/view_news.asp?id=1496.

152. See for example http://abcnews.go.com/Blotter/al-qaeda-leader-yemen-pledges-allegiance-zawahiri/story?id=14164884.

153. Ibid.

154. Al-Qaeda in the Arabian Peninsula Al-Malahim Foundation for Media Productions "Inspire" Magazine, "Interview with Shaikh Abu Bassir: The Head of Al-Qaida in the Arabian Peninsula" Released: 11 July 2010 at http://nefafoundation.org//file/Abu-Basir_Inspire0710-.pdf.

155. Al-Qaeda in the Arabian Peninsula Sheikh Abu Sufian al-Azdi (a.k.a. Saeed al-Shehri), "Repelling the Crusader Aggression." Released 8 February 2010 at http://nefafoundation.org//file/Nefa_AQ-IY0210Tape.pdf.

156. http://nefafoundation.org//file/FeaturedDocs/nefaqaidayemen0209.pdf.

157. "Al-Qaidat al-Jihad Organization in the Arabian Peninsula: From Here We Will Begin and in Al-Aqsa We Shall Meet." Released 23 January 2009 (Translated by CeifiT) at http://nefafoundation.org//file/nefaqaidayemen1008-2.pdf).

158. Ibid.

159. "Excerpts from AQIY Formal Magazine 'Sada Al Malahim' January 2008" (Translated by CeifiT) at http://nefafoundation.org//file/nefaqaidayemen1008-4.pdf).

160. "Excerpts from AQIY Formal Magazine 'Sada Al Malahim' January 2008" (Translated by CeifiT) at http://nefafoundation.org//file/nefaqaidayemen1008-4.pdf.

161. Abu Hamza al-Masri and Abu Qatada al-Falastini in London, Imad Baraqat Yarqas aka Abu Dahdah in Spain, and Mahmud Ould Salahi in Germany and probably other figures served as al-Qaeda POC in those countries responsible for spotting, drafting, and recruiting suitable new members to al-Qaeda. In this way for example the members of the Hamburg cell comprised of three out of the four pilots of the 9/11 attack and were recruited in Germany by Salahi. See Gunaratna and Oreg P. 1064.

162. http://nefafoundation.org//file/rose_letter_cssw.pdf.

163. http://www.topnewspress.com/al-qaeda-leaders-are-leaving-iran-to-settle-in-yemen/871469/.

164. Murad Batal al-Shishani, "Adel al-Abbab: Al Qaeda in the Arabian Peninsula's Religious Ideologue" at *Jamestown Foundation* Publi-

cation: Volume: 1 Issue: 3 March 30, 2010 at http://www.jamestown. org/single/?no_cache=1&tx_ttnews%5Btt_news%5D=36222&tx_ttne ws%5BbackPid%5D=13&cHash=83cc90d89d.

165. http://www.google.co.il/imgres?q=yemen+conflict+map &hl=en&sa=X&qscrl=1&nord=1&rlz=1T4GGLR_enUS389IL389&b iw=1280&bih=554&tbm=isch&prmd=imvns&tbnid=nMHYuZZrt2 NkcM:&imgrefurl=http://www.propinoy.net/2011/04/23/under standing-islamist-militancy-in-a-pre-and-post-saleh-yemen/&docid =xqEowAnNvB9asM&imgurl=http://propinoy.net/wp-content/up loads/2011/04/Yemen_conflict_zones_800.jpg%253F9d7bd4&w=800 &h=529&ei=CLEGT7KmOofe8QOKxem9AQ&zoom=1&iact=hc&vp x=398&vpy=235&dur=4337&hovh=182&hovw=276&tx=118&ty=82& sig=113147507279942880764&page=2&tbnh=148&tbnw=208&start=21 &ndsp=10&ved=1t:429,r:1,s:21.

166. Scott Conroy, "Al Qaeda Suicide Bomber Kills 9 in Yemen," CBS News, 2 July 2007, http://www.cbsnews.com/stories/2007/07/02/ world/main3007189.shtml.

167. "Belgians Killed in Yemen Attack," BBC News, 19 January 2008, http://news.bbc.co.uk/2/hi/middle_east/7196186.stm.

168. Nidaa Abu-Al, "Attack Targets a Residential Complex in Sanaa, Yemen" http://www.pvtr.org/pdf/GlobalAnalysis/Attack%20Tar gets%20a%20Residential%20Complex%20in%20Sanaa%20Yemen.pdf.

169. http://nefafoundation.org//file/FeaturedDocs/nefaaqye men0608.pdf.

170. "What Governments Are Doing: Al-Qa'ida in the Arabian Pen- insula (AQAP)," Commonwealth of Australia 2011, 29 November 2010, http://www.ag.gov.au/agd/WWW/NationalSecurity.nsf/Page/ What_Governments_are_doing_Listing_of_Terrorism_Organisations_ Al-Qaida_in_the_Arabian_Peninsula.

171. "Tourists Die in Yemen Explosion," BBC News, 15 March 2009, http://news.bbc.co.uk/2/hi/7945013.stm.

172. Hugh Macleod, "UK Ambassador in Yemen Escapes Assas- sination attempt," The Guardian, 26 April 2010, http://www.guardian. co.uk/world/2010/apr/26/uk-ambassador-yemen-assassination-at- tempt.

173. http://www.npr.org/templates/story/story.php?storyId= 130163592.

174. Alexander Meleagrou-Hitchens, "As American as Apple Pie: How Anwar al-Awlaki Became the Face of Western Jihad," The Inter- national Centre for the Study of Radicalization and Political Violence, September 2011, p. 83.

175. Barfi.

176. Gunaratna and Oreg, p. 1056.

177. Ibid.

178. Barfi, p. 2. See also al-Wuhayshi's interviews with Abd Allah Haydar Shaa, at http://abdulela.maktoobblog.com.

179. David Kenner, "Yemen's Most Wanted," *Foreign Policy*, 8 January 2010, http://www.foreignpolicy.com/articles/2010/01/08/yemens_most_wanted?page=full, accessed 17 April 2012.

180. Ibid.

181. Ibid.

182. United States Department of Defense [government's unclassified files], Guantanamo, cited in Thomas Joscelyn, "Return to Jihad," *The Long War Journal*, 25 January 2009, http://www.longwarjournal.org/archives/2009/01/return_to_jihad.php, accessed 20 June 2012; Bill Roggio, "Yemen Captures Al Qaeda in the Arabian Peninsula's Deputy Leader," *The Long War Journal*, 18 January 2010, http://www.longwarjournal.org/archives/2010/01/yemen_captures_al_qa.php, accessed 20 June 2012.

183. Kenner, David.

184. Ibid.

185. Roggio, "Al Qaeda Opens New Training Camp in Yemen."

186. Kenner.

187. Ibid.

188. Mohammad Bin Sallam and Ali Saeed, "Five Al Qaeda Members Reported Dead/Religious Scholars Reject Foreign Military Intervention," *Yemen Times*, 18 January 2010, http://www.yementimes.com/defaultdet.aspx?SUB_ID=33416, accessed 14 September 2011.

189. "*Inspire* Magazine, Spring 2011: 'An Interview with Shaykh Abu Hurairah as-Sana'ani, the Military Commander of al-Qaeda in the Arabian Peninsula' March, 2011," pp. 1–4.

190. "Profile: Al Qaeda 'Bomb Maker' Ibrahim al-Asiri," *BBC News*, 31 October 2010, http://www.bbc.co.uk/news/world-middle-east-11662143, accessed 14 April 2012.

191. Ibid.

192. Ibid.

193. "Interior Ministry Issues List of Extremists Wanted for Extradition," *Information Office of the Royal Embassy of Saudi Arabia in Washington, DC*, 3 February 2009, http://www.saudiembassy.net/latest_news/news02030902.aspx, cited in "Profile: Ibrahim Al Assiri."

194. "Profile: Al Qaeda 'Bomb Maker.'"

195. Al-Shishani.

196. The GSPC was established in 1998 and was based on the foundations of the GIA, an Algerian Islamist group that conducted a large

wave of terrorist campaigns in the country between 1992 and 1997 in order to topple the Bouteflika regime, resulting in the deaths of approximately 25,000 civilians.

197. Kohlmann, "Two Decades of Jihad in Algeria: the GIA, the GSPC, and Al-Qaida," *The NEFA Foundation*, May 2007, http://nefa foundation.org//file/nefagspc0507.pdf, p. 21, accessed 18 April 2012.

198. Andrew Black, "Al-Qaeda Operations in Kabylie Mountains Alienating Algeria's Berbers," *Terrorism Focus*, Vol. 5, Issue: 16, 23 April 2008, http://www.jamestown.org/single/?no_cache=1&tx_ ttnews%5Btt_news%5D=4876, accessed 9 April 2012.

199. Camille Tawil, *The Al-Qaeda Organization in the Islamic Maghreb*, Washington, DC: Brookings Institution Press, 2011, p. 8.

200. "Al-Qaeda in Our Homes," *Asharq Al-Awsat*, 18 June 2008.

201. AQIM is closely linked to the Tuareg rebels and cooperates in kidnappings. Traditionally, the Tuaregs oppose the Malinese central government and have de facto control over the autonomous region in northern Mali. The convenient cooperation between the Tuaregs and AQIM may have been developed through business activities. The Tuaregs have been dealing in illicit commerce including transnational trafficking, a source of income for the group.

202. "Algeria Links AQIM With Tribes," *Middle East Newsline*, 29 September 2009.

203. Jonathan Schanzer, "Algeria's GSPC and America's 'War on Terror,'" *Policywatch* No. 666, 2 October 2002, and "Africa Terror Havens," Council of Foreign Relations, December 2003; cited in Girma Yohannes Iyassu Menelik, *Finances and Networks of Al-Qaeda Terrorists*, Germany: GRIN Verlag, 2009, p. 22.

204. "Islamic Militants Boost Role in Drug Trade," *The Washington Times*, 17 November 2009, http://www.washingtontimes. com/news/2009/nov/17/islamic-militants-boosting-role-in-drug-trade/?page=all, accessed 18 April 2012.

205. Nazim Fethi, "Belmokhtar Surrender Likely to Further Weaken al-Qaeda's Maghreb Branch," *Magharebia*, 28 April 2008, http://www. magharebia.com/cocoon/awi/xhtml1/en_GB/features, accessed 18 April 2012.

206. Assaf Moghadam, *The Globalization of Martyrdom: Al Qaeda, Salafi Jihad, and the Diffusion of Suicide Attacks*, Baltimore, MD: John Hopkins University Press, 2011, p. 159.

207. Zohra Bensemra, "Algeria Suicide Car Bomb Kills 6," *Reuters*, 10 August 2008, http://uk.reuters.com/article/2008/08/10/uk-alge ria-bombing-idUKLA45817720080810, accessed 18 April 2012.

208. Scott Stewart and Fred Burton, "Algeria: Taking the Pulse of AQIM," *Stratfor,* 24 June 2009, http://www.stratfor.com/weekly/20090624_algeria_taking_pulse_aqim, accessed 18 April 2012.

209. Steven Erlanger, "Blasts Kill 12 and Damage a Military Compound in Algeria," *The New York Times,* 20 August 2008, http://www.nytimes.com/2008/08/21/world/africa/21algeria.html, accessed 18 April 2012.

210. Matthew Weaver, "British Hostage Edwin Dyer 'Killed by al-Qaida,'" *The Guardian,* 3 June 2009, http://www.guardian.co.uk/uk/2009/jun/03/edwin-dyer-hostage-killed-al-qaida, accessed 18 April 2012.

211. Jeremy Keenan, "The Banana Theory of Terrorism: Alternative Truths and the Collapse of the 'Second' (Saharan) Front in the War on Terror," *Journal of Contemporary African Studies,* Vol. 25, No. 1 (January 2007), pp. 31–58.

212. Aimée Kligman, "Al-Qaeda Maghreb Group Out to Reclaim Europe's Grenada," *The Examiner,* 11 October 2009, http://www.examiner.com/foreign-policy-in-national/al-qaeda-s-maghreb-group-out-to-reclaim-europe-s-granada, accessed 18 April 2012; Kohlmann, "Al-Qaida in the Islamic Maghreb Spawns New Media Wing, 'The Andalus Foundation,'" *The NEFA Foundation,* 15 October 2009.

213. "Morocco Arrests 11 Terror Suspects," *Al Jazeera,* 28 December 2005; republished in *IslamicAwakening.com,* 28 December 2005, http://www.islamicawakening.com/viewnews.php?newsID=6691, accessed 18 April 2012.

214. Andrew Hansen and Lauren Vriens, "Al-Qaeda in the Islamic Maghreb (AQIM)," *Council on Foreign Relations,* 21 July 2009, http://www.cfr.org/north-africa/al-qaeda-islamic-maghreb-aqim/p12717, accessed 18 April 2012.

215. Ibid.

216. Kohlmann, "GSPC Claims Attack on Algerian Naval Vessels," *Global Terror Alert,* 25 December 2005, http://www.globalterroralert.com/library/north-africa/163-gspc-claims-attack-on-algerian-naval-vessels.html, accessed 18 April 2012; "Communiqué from the Algerian Salafist Group for Prayer and Combat (GSPC)," *Global Terror Alert,* 24 December 2005, http://www.globalterroralert.com/images/documents/pdf/1205/gspc1205-4.pdf, accessed 18 April 2012.

217. Jean-Luc Marret, "The GSPC/Al-Qaeda in Islamic Maghreb: A Mix of Low and High-Tech Capabilities," *Center for Transatlantic Relations,* 25 April 2007, http://transatlantic.sais-jhu.edu/bin/g/l/Marret_The_GSPC_Bouchaoui_CTR.pdf, accessed 18 April 2012.

218. "Algeria—Security," *GlobalSecurity.org,* 5 August 2011, http://www.globalsecurity.org/military/world/algeria/security.htm, accessed 18 April 2012.

219. Bill Roggio, "Nigerian Jihadist Identified as Commander of Algerian Operation," *Long War Journal* at http://www.longwarjournal.org/archives/2013/01/nigerien_jihadist_id.php#. accessed 13 June 2014.

220. "Newly Designated African Terror Group Targets Israel and Jews" at http://blog.adl.org/extremism/mulathamun-battalion-african-terror-fto-israel-and-jews, accessed 13 June 2014.

221. "Algerian Group Claims Mauritania Attack," *The Daily Star,* 8 June 2005, http://www.dailystar.com.lb/News/Middle-East/Jun/08/Algerian-Islamist-group-claims-Mauritania-attack.ashx#axzz1OleOYFOy, accessed 18 April 2012.

222. "Al-Qaeda Threatens France with Revenge over Burka Stance," *The Telegraph,* 1 July 2009, http://www.telegraph.co.uk/news/worldnews/europe/france/5700473/Al-Qaeda-threatens-France-with-revenge-over-burka-stance.html, accessed 18 April 2012.

223. Malcolm Moore, "Al-Qaeda Vows Revenge on China over Uighur Deaths," *The Telegraph,* 14 July 2009, http://www.telegraph.co.uk/news/worldnews/asia/china/5822791/Al-Qaeda-vows-revenge-on-China-over-Uighur-deaths.html, accessed 18 April 2012.

224. Hansen and Vriens.

225. See "AQIM: 'Statement on Attack on the Israeli Embassy in Nouakchott,'" *The NEFA Foundation,* 2 February 2008, http://www1.nefafoundation.org/miscellaneous/nefaaqim0208-2.pdf, accessed 20 April 2012.

226. For the full detailed engagement of AQIM in attacking Western targets see *NEFA foundation* at http://nefafoundation.org//index.cfm?PageID=58#D1081.

227. Also see Geoff D. Porter, "Splits Revealed inside Al-Qaeda in the Islamic Maghreb," *Terrorism Monitor,* Vol. 5, No. 7, 14 September 2007, http://www.jamestown.org/programs/gta/single/?tx_ttnews%5Btt_news%5D=4397&tx_ttnews%5BbackPid%5D=182&no_cache=1, accessed 20 April 2012.

228. Ahl-e-Hadith is a conservative strand of Sunni Islam in south Asia. It is another name for Salafism, of which WahHabism is a subset. It is the official Islamic school of thought practiced and propagated by the present Saudi royal family and the government. Ustaz Mohammed Haniff, personal interview, 13 June 2011.

229. Praveen Swami, "India's Most Wanted," *Front Line*, Vol. 19, Issue 2, 19 January–01 February 2002, http://www.frontlineonnet.com/fl1902/19020180.htm, accessed 20 April 2012.

230. American Foreign Policy Council, "Lashkar-e Toyba," *World Almanac of Islamism,* 14 July 2011, http://almanac.afpc.org/lashkar-e-taiba, pp. 1–2, accessed 20 April 2012.

231. Jayshree Bajoria, "Lashkar-e-Toiba (Army of the Pure) (aka Lashkar e-Tayyiba, Lashkar e-Toiba; Lashkar-i-Toyba)," *Council on Foreign Relations,* 14 January 2010, http://www.cfr.org/pakistan/lashkar-e-taiba-army-pure-aka-lashkar-e-tayyiba-lashkar-e-toiba-lashkar--taiba/p17882, accessed 20 April 2012.

232. Kaushik Kapisthalam, "Pakistan Faces Its Jihadi Demons in Iraq," *Asia Times,* 14 July 2004, http://www.atimes.com/atimes/South_Asia/FG14Df04.html, accessed 20 April 2012.

233. Šumit Ganguly ed., *The Kashmir Question: Retrospect and Prospect,* Abingdon, UK: Frank Cass, 2003.

234. Shujaat Bukhari, "Lashkar Moves to Give Struggle a 'Pure Kashmir Colour,'" *The Hindu,* 26 December 2001, http://www.hindu.com/2001/12/26/stories/2001122601431200.htm, accessed 20 April 2012.

235. B. Raman, "Lashkar-e-Toiba: Its Past, Present and Future," *South Asia Analysis Group,* No. 175, 25 December 2000, http://www.southasiaanalysis.org/%5Cpapers2%5Cpaper175.htm, accessed 20 April 2012.

236. "Terrorism: Lashkar-e-Tayyiba," *Center for Defense Information,* 12 August 2002, http://www.cdi.org/program/issue/document.cfm?DocumentID=1620&IssueID=56&StartRow=21&ListRows=10&appendURL=&Orderby=DateLastUpdated&ProgramID=39&issueID=56, accessed 20 August 2002.

237. "In The Spotlight: Lashkar-e-Toyba ('Army of the Pure')," *CDI Terrorism Project,* 12 August 2002, http://www.cdi.org/terrorism/lt-pr.cfm (expired link).

238. "General History of the Dispute: The Truth about Kashmir," *Army in Kashmir* http://www.armyinkashmir.org/history/history4.html (expired link).

239. Government of India, "Pakistan's Involvement in Terrorism Against India," p. 57.

240. Ibid.

241. "Brutal Terrorist Group Active in Kashmir—Lashkar-e-Toiba—"Army of the Pure," *Sreevideos.com,* http://www.sreevideos.com/indianews/library/weekly/aa122400c.htm; republished in *Hindu Vivek*

Kendra July 2001, http://hvk.org/archive/2001/0701/6.html, accessed 14 April 2012.

242. "Lashkar-e-Toiba," *BBC News*, 25 November 2002, http://news.bbc.co.uk/2/hi/south_asia/2510613.stm, accessed 21 April 2012.

243. "Lashkar-e-Toiba," *Kashmir Herald,* Vol. 1, No. 8 January 2002, http://www.kashmirherald.com/profiles/lashkaretoiba.html, accessed 14 April 2002.

244. Bukhari.

245. "Lashkar-e-Toiba Chief Vows to Continue 'War' in Kashmir," *Rediff,* 14 July 1999, http://www.rediff.com/news/1999/jul/14kash2.htm, accessed 14 April 2012.

246. Raman, "Badamibagh & After," *South Asia Analysis Group,* 19 November 1999, http://www.southasiaanalysis.org/%5Cnotes%5Cnote46.html, accessed 21 April 2012; cited in Caroline Ziemke, Satu Limaye, Kongdan Oh Hassig, and John T. Hanley, Jr., "Building a CATR Research Agenda, Proceedings of the Third Bi-Annual International Symposium of the Center for Asian Terrorism Research (CATR), March 1–3, 2006, Colombo, Sri Lanka," *Institute for Defense Analyses,* November 2006, p11.

Drawing on army updates, Ziemke et al. stated, "The Indian army assessed that 123 militants/mercenaries from various Tanzeems were killed and 50 are reported missing. The Tanzeems these militants belong to are Lashkar-e-Toiba, Harkat Ul Mujahideen and Harkat Ul Jihad-e-Islam." Army Update, 27 June 1999, http://meaindia.nic.in/warterror/kargil/upd2706-army.htm; cited in Ziemeke et al.

247. "Nawaz Sharif Government in a Tight Corner," *Sword of Truth,* Issue 26, 28 June 1999.

248. Ibid.

249. Mohammed Ahmedullah, "After the Coup," *Bulletin of Atomic Scientists,*Vol. 56, No. 1, Jan/Feb 2000, pp. 14–16.

250. Amit Baruah, "Militant Chiefs Warn Musharraf," *The Hindu,* 6 February 2000, http://hinduonnet.com/2000/02/06/stories/03060003.htm, accessed 21 April 2012.

251. Ibid.

252. Ibid.

253. Hafiz Saeed, quoted in Baruah.

254. Ibid.

255. Masood Hussain,"Lashkar-e-Toiba Shifts shop," *Tehelka,* 27 December 2001.

256. Wilson John, "Lashkar-e-Toiba: New Threats Posed by an Old Organization," *Terrorism Monitor,* Vol. 3, No. 4, 23 February 2005,

http://www.jamestown.org/programs/gta/single/?tx_ttnews%5Btt_news%5D=27599&tx_ttnews%5BbackPid%5D=180&no_cache=1, accessed 21 April 2012.

257. "Pakistan Freezes Militant Funds," *BBC News*, 24 December 2001, http://news.bbc.co.uk/1/hi/world/south_asia/1726813.stm, accessed 21 April 2012.

258. Ibid.

259. "Profile: Lashkar-e-Toyba," *BBC News* 3 May 2010, http://news.bbc.co.uk/2/hi/south_asia/3181925.stm, accessed 21 April 2012.

260. B. Muralidhar Reddy, "Crackdown Continues," *The Hindu*, 2 January 2002, http://www.hindu.com/thehindu/2002/01/02/stories/2002010201050100.htm, accessed 21 April 2012.

261. Aaron Mannes, *Profiles in Terror: The Guide to Middle East Terrorist Organizations*, Lanham, MD: Rowman & Littlefield, 2004, p. 68.

262. "Statement by External Affairs Minister Jaswant Singh on Pakistan President's Address on Terrorism," 13 January 2002, http://www.indianembassy.org/prdetail1187/statement-by-external-affairs-minister-jaswant-singh-on-pakistan-president%27s-address-on-terrorism, accessed 21 April 2012.

263. "Unfulfilled Promises: Pakistan's Failure to Tackle Extremism," *ICG Asia Report*, No. 73, 16 January 2004, extracts published in *Embassy of India*, http://www.embindia.org/eng/txt_icg_160104.html, accessed 21 April 2012.

264. Raman, "Lashkar-e-Toiba: Its Past, Present and Future."

265. Saeed's address to the Lahore Press Club on 18 February 1996, cited in Raman, "Lashkar-e-Toiba: Spreading the Jehad," *The Hindu*, 5 January 2001, http://www.hindu.com/businessline/2001/01/05/stories/040555ra.htm, accessed 21 April 2012.

266. Raman, "The Lashkar-e-Toiba (LeT)," *South Asia Analysis Group*, No. 374, 15 December 2001, http://www.southasiaanalysis.org/%5Cpapers4%5Cpaper374.html, accessed 21 April 2012.

267. Saeed, quoted in "Pakistani Terrorists Threaten to Unfurl Flag at Red Fort," *The Sword of Truth*, 14 December 1999, http://www.swordoftruth.com/swordoftruth/archives/newswatch/199951/news7.html (expired link). India celebrates its Independence Day every year on 15 August at the Red Fort in New Delhi.

268. "Who Are the Kashmir Militants?" *BBC News*, 19 February 2003, http://news.bbc.co.uk/1/hi/world/south_asia/1719612.stm, accessed 21 April 2012.

269. Seema Mustafa, "Jammu and Kashmir Rebels Advertise in Pakistan Papers," *The Asian Age*, 8 February 1999, republished in

Jammu & Kashmir, http://www.jammu-kashmir.com/archives/ archives1999/99february8.html, accessed 21 April 2012.

270. An LeT leader, Abdul Rahman Makki, claimed in a rally organized in Islamabad in February 2000 that the organization had a network in Hyderabad, which would become active in the next six months, and that they would be making a declaration of separation (from India). See Baruah.

271. Bajoria.

272. "Lashkar-e-Toiba: 'Army of the Pure,'" *South Asia Terrorism Portal,* http://www.satp.org/satporgtp/countries/india/states/ jandk/terrorist_outfits/lashkar_e_toiba.htm, accessed 21 April 2012.

273. Ibid.

274. Raman, "The Omens From the White House," *South Asia Analysis Group,* No. 381, 23 December 2001, http://www.southasiaanalysis. org/%5Cpapers4%5Cpaper381.html, accessed 21 April 2012.

275. Marri Ramu, "City a Vital Base for LeT's Covert Plans," *The Hindu,* 24 November 2002, http://www.hinduonnet.com/2002/11/24/ stories/2002112408460300.htm, accessed 21 April 2012.

276. "Muslim Cleric Faces Deportation," *BBC News,* 23 May 2000, http://news.bbc.co.uk/1/hi/uk/760342.stm, accessed 21 April 2012; "'Security Risk' Cleric to Be Deported," *BBC News,* 11 October 2001, http://news.bbc.co.uk/1/hi/uk/1593448.stm, accessed 21 April 2012; "Pakistani Cleric's Deportation Fight," *BBC News* 23 May 2000, http:// news.bbc.co.uk/1/hi/uk/759411.stm, accessed 21 April 2012.

277. Mainly for spotting, drafting, recruiting, and training of new activists. See Rajeev Sharma, "LeT Camps in Saudi Arabia, Kuwait," *The Tribune,* 11 January 2003, http://www.tribuneindia. com/2003/20030112/main4.htm, accessed 21 June 2012.

278. Kapisthalam.

279. Rafael Epstein, "Lashkar-e-Toiba Australian links," *AM,* ABC Local Radio, 5 November 2003, http://www.abc.net.au/am/con tent/2003/s982334.htm, accessed 21 April 2012, transcript; Epstein, "Willie Brigitte Proclaims His Innocence," *AM,* ABC Local Radio, 16 January 2004, http://www.abc.net.au/am/content/2004/s1026649. htm, accessed 21 April 2012, transcript; Norm Dixon, "How Willie Brigitte Became a 'Terrorist,'" *Green Left Weekly,* No. 561, 12 November 2003, http://www.greenleft.org.au/node/28747, accessed 21 April 2012.

280. "LeT Bigger Threat to US than Qaeda: US Intelligence," *The Economic Times,* 9 March 2009, http://articles.economictimes.indiatimes. com/2009-03-09/news/28446194_1_mumbai-terror-attacks-robert-mueller-intelligence-agencies, accessed 21 April 2012.

281. IANS, "Lashker-e-Toyba's France Based Leader arrested in Paris," *Newindpress.com,* 29 November 2002, http://www.newind press.com/Newsitems.asp?ID=IEH20021128100401&Page=H&Title=T op+Stories&rLink=0; republished in *Hindu Vivek Kendra,* December 2002, http://hvk.org/archive/2002/1202/6.html, accessed 21 April 2012.

282. Khalid Hasan, "Lashkar-e-Toyba Said to be Active in Spain," *Daily Times,* 10 February 2007, http://www.dailytimes.com.pk/de fault.asp?page=2007%5C02%5C10%5Cstory_10-2-2007_pg7_10, accessed 21 April 2012.

283. M. L. Kak, "Lashkar Operating Under Four Names," *The Tribune,* 25 July 2002, http://www.tribuneindia.com/2002/20020726/ j&k.htm#1, accessed 21 April 2012.

284. "Group Profile: Lashkar-e-Toyba (LET)," *MIPT Terrorism Knowledge Base,* http://www.tkb.org/Group.jsp?groupID=66, accessed 4 May 2007.

285. Geoffrey Kambere, Puay Hock Goh, Pranav Kumar, Fulgence Msafir "The Financing of Lashkar-e-Taiba" at http://www.nps.edu/ Academics/Schools/GSOIS/Departments/DA/Documents/CTX%20 Vol.%201%20No.%201.pdf, pp. 8–9. Accessed on 4 July 2012.

286. Katherine Shrader, "U.S. Pakistani Extremists Aid Terrorists," *Seattlepi,* 9 September 2005, http://seattlepi.nwsource.com/printer/ ap.asp?category=1104&slug=Jihad%27s%20Helping%20Hand; republished in *Militant Islam Monitor,* 14 September 2005, http://www.mili tantislammonitor.org/article/id/1076, accessed 9 April 2012.

287. "Jihad Recruitment is on the Rise," *The Friday Times,* 29 July 2003, http://www.pakistan-facts.com/article.php?story =20030729154610902, accessed 2 August 2003.

288. Ibid.

289. Wilson John, "Time to Decapitate Lashkar," *The Pioneer,* 20 July 2005; republished in *Observer Research Foundation,* 21 July 2005, http:// www.observerindia.com/cms/sites/orfonline/modules/analysis/ AnalysisList.html?index=240&level=1&id=1&cat=Pakistan, accessed 9 April 2012.

290. Zaigham Khan, "Allah's Army," *The Herald,* January 1998, pp. 124–25; excerpt reproduced in *Communalism Combat,* March 1998, http://www.sabrang.com/cc/comold/march98/neighbor.htm, accessed 9 April 2012.

291. Ibid.

292. Raman, "Markaz Dawa al Irshad: Talibanisation of Nuclear Pakistan (contd.)," *South Asia Analysis,* 26 July 1998, http://www.southa siaanalysis.org/%5Cpapers%5Cpaper6.html, accessed 9 April 2012.

293. "Profile: Lashkar-e-Tayyiba," *GlobalSecurity.org*, 9 July 2011, http://www.globalsecurity.org/military/world/para/lt.htm, accessed 9 April 2012.

294. K. P. S. Gill, "Cautious Engagement"; Ajai Sahni, "The Criminal-Terror Nexus, Again," *South Asia Intelligence Review*, Vol. 1, No. 30, 10 February 2003, http://www.satp.org/satporgtp/sair/Archives/1_30.htm, accessed 9 April 2012.

295. Lakshman Yadav, "ISI Toys with Sept 11–Type Terror," *Independent Media Centre—India*, 3 February 2002, http://india.indymedia.org/en/2003/02/3100.shtml, accessed 9 April 2012.

296. Ibid.

297. "Brutal Terrorist Group Active in Kashmir."

298. "Nearly 300,000 Kashmiri Pandits (original Hindu inhabitants of Kashmir valley) have been driven out of their ancestral homeland because of terrorist activities." "A Bird's Eye View of the Pakistani Terrorist Machinery," *Kashmir Information Network*, http://www.kashmir-information.com/Terrorism/machine.html, accessed 9 April 2012.

299. "Lashkar-e-Toiba: 'Army of the Pure,'" *South Asia Terrorism Portal*.

300. Khan.

301. "Profile: Lashkar-e-Taiba," *BBC News*.

302. The sole difference between self-sacrifice attacks and suicide operations is that during self-sacrifice operations the operator will likely be killed but in suicide operations the operator will definitely be killed.

303. Santosh Sinha, "Violent 'Army of the Pure,'" *BBC News*, 14 December 2001, http://news.bbc.co.uk/2/hi/south_asia/865818.stm, accessed 9 April 2012.

304. Ibid.

305. Ibid.

306. Raman, "The Lashkar-e-Toiba (LeT)."

307. "Brutal Terrorist Group Active in Kashmir."

308. Mohammad Amir Rana, personal interview, 5 January 2005.

309. "India Boosts Security after Blasts," *CNN* 26 August 2003, http://articles.cnn.com/2003-08-25/world/mumbai.blasts_1_students-islamic-movement-mumbai-masood-khan?_s=PM:asiapcf, accessed 9 April 2012; Ashrat Ansari, "2003 Mumbai Blasts: Court Awards Death Penalty to Three Convicts," *The Indian Express*, 6 August 2009, http://www.indianexpress.com/news/2003-mumbai-blasts-court-awards-death-penal/498708/, accessed 9 April 2012.

310. Ahmad Faruqui, "Negotiating Peace in Kashmir," *Chowk,* 18 June 2000, http://www.chowk.com/Views/Negotiating-Peace-in-Kashmir, accessed 9 April 2012.

311. Mohammad Shehzad, "The Apocalyptic Vision of Hafiz Saeed," *SikhSpectrum.com,* Issue No.10, March 2003, http://www.sikhspec trum.com/032003/hafiz.htm, accessed 9 April 2012.

312. "Terrorists Held," *The Hindu* 19 February 2002, http://www.hinduonnet.com/2002/02/20/stories/2002022003090100.htm, accessed 9 April 2012.

313. "Terrorism Related Incidents in Delhi," *South Asia Terrorism Portal,* http://www.satp.org/satporgtp/countries/india/database/Delhi_Incidents.htm, accessed 9 April 2012.

314. Raman, "Time to Be On our Toes," *The Week,* 17 July 2005, http://www.the-week.com/25jul17/currentevents_article10.htm, accessed 17 July 2005.

315. "The Network," *Global Jihad,* 22 November 2009, http://www.globaljihad.net/view_page.asp?id=1801, accessed 9 April 2012.

316. For example, see involvement of members from the French branch of Marqaz al-Dawa Wal Irshad (MDI, the civil branch of LeT) in Richard Reid's attempt to crash a passenger jet embarking Paris in December 2001. See "Testimony by Stephen Tankel Visiting Scholar, South Asia Program Carnegie Endowment for International Peace at the House Committee on Homeland Security Subcommittee on Counterterrorism and Intelligence," Washington, DC, 3 May 2011 at http://homeland.house.gov/sites/homeland.house.gov/files/Testimony%20Tankel%20(Revised).pdf.

317. LeT's designated external operations unit was exposed during the investigations into the Brigitte case of conducting operational reconnaissance in Australia and Pakistani American David Headley's involvement in the 2008 Mumbai attacks. See Sebastian Rotella, "The Man Behind Mumbai," *Pro Publica,* 13 November 2010, http://www.propublica.org/article/the-man-behind-mumbai, accessed 9 April 2012.

318 A group operating in Jammu and Kashmir in India. See http://www.start.umd.edu/start/data_collections/tops/terrorist_organization_profile.asp?id=4620.

319. The Student Islamic Movement of India is an Indian Islamic organization. See Ananthakrishnan G., "NIA Links SIMI to Lashkar-e-Toyba," *Times of India,* 30 December 2010, http://articles.timesofindia.indiatimes.com/2010-12-30/india/28271320_1_simi-men-students-islamic-movement-shaduli, accessed 9 April 2012.

320. The "Karachi Project" is an alleged project that observers and commentators believe has been led by the Pakistani Intelligence Service (ISI) at least since 2003. The "project" took place in a residential protected compound in Karachi where a conglomerate of anti-Indian fugitives and groups were working together to combine infrastructure, coordinate efforts, and carry out terror attacks in India in order to undermine and weaken Indian resolve and inflexibility over the Kashmir issue. This conglomerate includes the Indian Mujahideen, HuJI, Jamaat-ud-Dawa, the Sikh Babbar Khalsa International (BKI); Indian mobsters like Daoud Ibrahim; Pakistani groups like LeT and Jaish-e-Mohamed; and retired and serving Pakistani army officers like Colonel Shahid Bashir, former PAF pilot Nadim Ahmad Shah, and Major Sajid Mir. See "Karachi Project," *Global Jihad,* 13 April 2010, http://www.globaljihad.net/view_page.asp?id=1885, accessed 9 April 2012.

321. "Lashkar-e-Toiba: 'Army of the Pure,'" *South Asia Terrorism Portal.*

322. Wilson John and Swati Parashar, *Terrorism in Southeast Asia: Implications for South Asia,* New Delhi: Pearson, 2005, p. xii.

323. "Hafiz Saeed," *connect.in.com,* http://connect.in.com/hafiz-saeed/biography-516731.html, accessed 9 April 2012.

324. As mentioned, Sadah camp served as a melting pot for many jihad volunteers who later became key members of prominent jihadi terror organizations. For example, Khalid Sheikh Mohamed became al-Qaeda's head of special operations, Radwan Issam al-Din a.k.a. Hambali became JI's military chief, Abd al-Razeq Janjalani became the founder and leader of the ASG, and Hafez Saeed will become the founder and leader of LeT. See "Terror Analysis: Global Jihad Entities Cooperation—Where It All Began," *CeifiT,* 14 December 2008, http://www.ceifit.com/?categoryId=34115&itemId=60829, accessed 9 April 2012.

325. Raman, "Markaz Dawa al Irshad: Talibanisation of Nuclear Pakistan," *South Asia Analysis Group,* http://www.southasiaanalysis.org/%5Cpapers%5Cpaper5.html, accessed 21 April 2012.

326. "General History of the Dispute: The Truth about Kashmir," http://www.armyinkashmir.org/history/history4.html.

327. "Lashkar-e-Toiba: 'Army of the Pure,'" *South Asia Terrorism Portal.*

328. "Hafiz Saeed's Profile," *Hindustan Times,* 2 June 2009, http://www.hindustantimes.com/Hafiz-Saeed-s-Profile/Article1-417093.aspx, accessed 21 April 2012.

329. "Terror Analysis: Who is Responsible for the Mumbai Attacks?" *CeifiT*, 29 October 2008, http://www.ceifit.com/?categoryId=4
1112&itemId=59802, accessed 21 April 2012.

330. See Ministry of Home Affairs, "Singapore Government Press Statement on the Detention of 2 Singaporean Members of the Jemaah Islamiyah Karachi Cell," *Ministry of Home Affairs,* 18 December 2003.

331. Ibid.

332. Ibid.

333. Malakunas.

334. Kapisthalam, "Learning from Pakistan's Madrassas," *Asia Times,* 23 June 2004, available at http://www.atimes.com/atimes/South_Asia/FF23Df05.html, accessed 21 April 2012.

335. Ibid.

336. United States Department of State, *Patterns of Global Terrorism 2002—Israel, the West Bank, and Gaza Strip,* 30 April 2003, http://www.unhcr.org/refworld/docid/468107ad2.html, accessed 22 April 2012.

337. "Lashkar-e-Toiba," *Kashmir Herald.*
Hawala is a traditional method of transferring funds between different locations without using the formal banking system. These transactions are conducted with no records, making supervision of the *Hawala* impossible.

338. The Office of Public Affairs, "U.S. Designates Al Akhtar Trust: Pakistani Based Charity is Suspected of Raising Money for Terrorists in Iraq," *U.S. Department of the Treasury,* 14 October 2003, http://www.treasury.gov/press-center/press-releases/Pages/js899.aspx, accessed 21 April 2012.

339. B. Raman, "'Banning the Banned': Counter-Terrorism a la Musharraf," *South Asia Analysis Group,* No. 842, 20 November 2003, http://www.southasiaanalysis.org/%5Cpapers9%5Cpaper842.html, accessed 21 April 2012.

340. Wilson John, "Analysis: Lashkar-e-Toiba is New Al Qaida Face," *Observer Research Foundation,* 25 June 2003, http://www.orfonline.org/cms/sites/orfonline/modules/analysis/AnalysisDetail.html?cmaid=2564&mmacmaid=827, accessed 21 April 2012.

341. Asif Shahzad, "60 Offices, Seminaries Sealed in Punjab: Crackdown launched in Peshawar," *The Dawn,* 17 November 2003, http://archives.dawn.com/2003/11/17/top6.htm, accessed 21 April 2012.

342. Amir Rana, "JD Continues Raising Funds despite Ban," *Daily Times,* 19 November 2003, http://www.dailytimes.com.pk/default.asp?page=story_19-11-2003_pg7_2, accessed 21 April 2012.

343. Ibid.

344. Shehzad, "Banned LeT Collects Millions in Charity," *South Asia Tribune,* Issue No. 35, March 2003, pp. 23–29.

345. United States Department of State, *Patterns of Global Terrorism 2002.*

346. Raman, "Al Qaeda & Lashkar-e-Toiba," *South Asia Analysis Group,* No. 678, 3 May 2003, http://www.southasiaanalysis.org/papers7/paper678.html, accessed 21 April 2012; Raman, "LET: Al Qaeda's Clone," *South Asia Analysis Group* No. 729, 2 July 2003, http://www.southasiaanalysis.org/papers8/paper729.html, accessed 21 April 2012.

347. United States Department of State, *Patterns of Global Terrorism 2002.*

348. Mustafa.

349. United States Department of State, *Patterns of Global Terrorism 2002.*

350. See "UK Not So Golden Radical Islamist Oldies—Where Are They Now?" *Militant Islam Monitor,* http://www.militantislammonitor.org/article/id/386, accessed 20 June 2012.

351. "Pakistan: Madrassas, Extremism and the Military," *ICG Asia Report,* No. 36, 29 July 2002, p. 16.

352. Kapisthalam, "Pakistan Faces Its Jihadi Demons in Iraq."

353. LeT, quoted in Prakash Pillai, "Kashmir's Freedom Will Pave Way for Establishing Islam in Pak, Says Lashkar," *The Hindustan Times,* 2 February 2001, http://www.hvk.org/articles/0201/1.html (link unavailable).

354. "Govt Blames LeT for Parliament Attack, Asks Pak to Restrain Terrorist Outfits," *Rediff,* 14 December 2001, http://www.rediff.com/news/2001/dec/14parl12.htm, accessed 20 June 2012

355. "Police Hunt Red Fort Raiders," *BBC News,* 23 December 2000, http://news.bbc.co.uk/1/hi/world/south_asia/1083710.stm, accessed 20 June 2012.

356. "Temple Carnage: Terrorist Attack on Akshardham," *BAPS Swaminarayan Sanstha* 25 Sept 2002, http://www.swaminarayan.org/news/2002/09/akshardham/report.htm, accessed 20 June 2012.

357. Josy Joseph, "Letter Reveals Tehreek-e-Kasas Behind Attack; Advani Blames 'Neighbouring Nation,'" *Rediff,* 25 September 2002, http://www.rediff.com/news/2002/sep/25guj1.htm, accessed 20 June 2012.

358. "Lashkar Commanders' Killing Explodes a Many Myths," *The Daily Excelsior,* 24 September 2003, http://www.dailyexcelsior.com/web1/03sep24/news.htm#5 (expired link).

359. "Akshardham Plot Hatched in Riyadh," *Rediff* 30 August 2003, http://www.rediff.com/news/2003/aug/29akshar.htm, accessed 20 June 2012.

360. "Jihad Group Claims India Blasts," *Jihad Watch*, 31 October 2005, http://www.jihadwatch.org/2005/10/jihad-group-claims-india-blasts.html, accessed 20 June 2012.

361. Swami, "Breakthrough in Delhi Blasts Probe" *The Hindu* 9 November 2005.

362. Ian Black, "Attacks Draw Worldwide Condemnation," *The Guardian*, 28 November 2008, http://www.guardian.co.uk/world/2008/nov/28/mumbai-terror-attacks-international-response, accessed 20 June 2012.

363. Raman, "LET: Al Qaeda's Clone."

364. Raman, "Osama Bin Laden: Rumblings in Afghanistan," *South Asia Analysis Group*, 22 December 1998, http://www.southasiaanalysis.org/%5Cpapers%5Cpaper22.html, accessed 20 June 2012.

365. While the total number of Muslims in the Philippines only comprise 5 percent of the Christian-dominated population, the Muslim community composes 95 percent of the population on the island of Mindanao.

366. Rommel C. Banlaoi, "The Abu Sayyaf Group: From Mere Banditry to Genuine Terrorism?" *Southeast Asian Affairs 2006*, Singapore: Institute of Southeast Asian Studies, 2006.

367. Jeffrey M. Bale, "The Abu Sayyaf Group in its Philippine and International Contexts: A Profile and WMD Threat Assessment," Monterey Terrorism Research and Education Program, Monterey Institute of International Studies, December 2003.

368. In Afghanistan, Janjalani was trained by and fought within al- Ittihad al-Islami al-Afghani. The leader of this Afghan group was Abd al-Rasool Sayyaf. In his honor, Janjalani named the new group he formed in Mindanao as Abu Sayyaf.

369. "Hostage Says Kidnappers Called For End to Exploitation of the Poor," *Associated Press*, 2 January 1996.

370. Christina Mendez,"PNP: Sayaf Got p20-m from Palawan Hostages; Defense Sec Belies Report," *Philippine Headline News Online*, 11 March 2002, http://www.newsflash.org/2002/03/ht/ht002361.htm, accessed 20 June 2012.

371. "Pearl Farm Siege—2 Dead, 3 Hurt in Resort Attack," *Mindanao Times*, 24 May 2001.

372. Simon Elegant, "The Return of Abu Sayyaf," *Time Magazine*, 23 August 2004.

373. The entire case of Drilon abduction is extensively detailed in Maria Ressa's book *from Bin Laden to Facebook*, London: Imperial College Press, 2013.

374. Bale.

375. Documents Recovered by the Armed Forces of the Philippines in Oplan Ultimatum from ASG hideout, Sulu, September 2006

376. Ibid.

377. "Yasser Igasan Succeeds Janjalani as Abu Chief," *GMA News TV*, 27 Jul 2007, http://www.gmanews.tv/story/48531/Yasser-Igasan-succeeds-Janjalani-as-Abu-chief, accessed 20 June 2012.

378. "Southern Philippines Backgrounder: Terrorism and the Peace Process," *ICG Asia Report*, No. 80, 13 July 2004.

379. Banlaoi, "Suicide Terrorism in the Philippines: The Rise of the Rajah Suleiman Movement (RSM)," *IDSS Commentaries*, No. 109, 9 October 2006.

380. "Philippine Terrorism: The Role of Militant Islamic Converts," *ICG Asia Report*, No. 110, 19 December 2005.

381. For more information about the Bojinca plot and "Abd Rasul Sayaf graduate," see "Terror Analysis: Global Jihad Entities Cooperation—Where It All Began" at http://www.ceifit.com/?categoryId=341 15&itemId=60829. Accessed 13 June 2014.

382. Ibid.

383. "Philippine Terrorism: The Role of Militant Islamic Converts."

384. Angel Rabrasa, Peter Chalk, *Indonesia's transformation*, Santa Monica, CA: Project Air Force, and 2000 at http://books.google.co.il/books?id=zpsndWPR1xUC&pg=PA88&lpg=PA88&dq=%E2%80%9CRevolutionary+taxes%E2%80%9D++abu+sayyaf&source=bl&ots=usM0uqK-zG&sig=CZhvQnN97cHHNbnYhPapL1VsqYc&hl=en&sa=X&ei=H76YULumGYfIsgbFp4H4AQ&sqi=2&ved=0CCIQ6AEwAQ#v=onepage&q=%E2%80%9CRevolutionary%20taxes%E2%80%9D%20%20abu%20sayyaf&f=false, p. 88.

385. "Philippine Terrorists Claim Link to Iraq," *The Washington Times*, 4 March 2003, http://www.washingtontimes.com/news/2003/mar/04/20030304-085823-9114r/, accessed 20 June 2012.

386. "Philippine Terrorism: The Role of Militant Islamic Converts."

387. Both held in a U.S. jail for their involvement in terrorist events inside the United States.

388. Katherine Evangelista and Julie Alipala, "2 US Soldiers, 1 RP Marine Killed, 2 Hurt in Blast," *Philippine Daily Inquirer*, 29 September 2009, http://www.inquirer.net/specialreports/thesoutherncampaign/view.php?db=1&article=20090929-227485, accessed 20 June 2012.

389. Julie Alipala and Marlon Ramos, "15 Dead in Basilan Blasts," *Philippine Daily Inquirer* 14 April 2010, http://www.inquirer.net/specialreports/thesoutherncampaign/view.php?db=1&artcle=20100414-264133, accessed 20 June 2012.

390. Ibid.

391. www.furqon.com.

392. Sai'd Burhoniddin Qlich, *The Islamic Movement of Uzbekistan: Chronicle of Crimes,* 2009, www.stability.uz (now defunct).

393. At this stage, Uzbekistan was gaining its independence after the fall of the USSR and was looking for a national identity. Yuldashev demanded from Karimov that this identity should be an Islamic one with the full implementation of Sharia as state law.

394. Qlich.

395. Oleg Yakubov, *The Pack of Wolves: The Blood Trial of Terror,* Moscow: Veche Publishers, 2000, pp. 190–99.

396. Ahmed Rashid, *Jihad: The Rise of Militant Islam in Central Asia,* New Haven, CT.: Yale University Press, 2002, p. 148.

397. Ibid.

398. Syed Anwar, "Namangani Takes Charge of Taliban Frontlines," *Afghanistan News Center,* 8 November 2001, http://www.afghanistannewscenter.com/news/2001/november/nov8w2001.html, accessed 20 June 2012.

399. Yaqubov, *The Pack of Wolves,* pp. 159–80.

400. They acted mostly under the guidance of al-Qaeda's senior military commander Abu Layth al-Libi; Ronald Sandee, "The Islamic Jihad Union (IJU) October 14, 2008," *The NEFA Foundation,* 14 October 2008, pp. 1–2.

401. Raman, "Attacks on Uzbeks in South Waziristan," *International Terrorism Monitor,* No. 208.

402. Roggio, "Islamic Movement of Uzbekistan Leader Thought killed in August Strike in South Waziristan," *The Long War Journal,* 2 October 2009, http://www.longwarjournal.org/archives/2009/10/islamic_movement_of.php, accessed 20 June 2012.

403. IMU website, www.furqon.com, "Qaboilda-3" (In Tribal Areas—3). accessed 29 June 2012.

404. Mir Kaligulaev, Дорога к смерти больше, чем смерть или Опыт илюзорной биографии [The path to the death more than the death or Experience of illusory biography] England, UK: Black Qudrat Production, 2005, p. 141.

405. Erlan Satibekov, "Скорый суд над бывшим пресс-секретарем Джумы Намангани вызывает много вопросов [Rapid trial of the

ex-press-secretary of Juma'a Namangani is causing many questions]," *Fergana News*, 11 February 2003, http://www.ferghana.ru/article. php?id=1386, accessed 20 June 2012.

406. Satibekov.

407. Roggio, "Tahir Yuldashev Confirmed Killed in US Strike in South Waziristan," *The Long War Journal*, 4 October 2009, www. longwarjournal.org/archives/2009/10/tahir_yuldashev_conf. php#ixzz0wZ5w7KEq, accessed 20 June 2012.

408. IMU website, www.furqon.com, "Qaboilda-3" (In Tribal Areas—3).

409. See IMU website, www.furqon.com.

410. Jaccobd Zen, "IMU Announces Usman Ghazi as New Emir After Months of Deliberation," *Militant Leadership Monitor*, Jamestown Foundation, Volume 3, Issue 8, 21 August 2012, http://mlm.james town.org/single/?tx_ttnews%5Btt_news%5D=39791&tx_ttnews%5Bb ackPid%5D=539&cHash=ecec8979f447c4dc1d48a1a725ee6c2e.

411. Yakubov, *The Pack of Wolves*, pp. 159–80.

412. Qlich.

413. "Uzbek Group to 'Free Pakistan from US Control,'" *Daily Times*, 19 March 2010.

414. Hans-Inge Langø, "The Islamic Movement of Uzbekistan: Crackdown (2005–2010)," *Hegemonic Obsessions*, 10 March 2011, http:// hegemonicobsessions.com/?p=281, accessed 20 June 2012.

415. Langø, "The Rise of the Islamic Movement of Uzbekistan," *Hegemonic Obsessions*, 2 March 2011, http://hegemonicobsessions. com/?p=256, accessed 20 June 2012.

416. Ibid.

417. Ibid.

418. Langø, "The Islamic Movement of Uzbekistan: Factions and Resurgence (2002–2005)," *Hegemonic Obsessions*, 5 March 2011, http:// hegemonicobsessions.com/?p=266, accessed 20 June 2012.

419. Ibid.

420. Ibid.

421. Ibid.

422. Sandee, p. 2.

423. Ibid, p. 3.

424. Ibid, pp. 5–6.

425. Ibid, pp. 7–10.

426. Sandee, p. 15. With reference to the declaration by the IJU, 19 December 2007, www.sehadetvakti.com (now defunct).

427. The original video is located on the jihadist website, www. sehadetzamani.com.

428. Roggio, "8 Germans Killed in Oct. 4 Predator Strike in North Waziristan identified," *The Long War Journal*, 1 November 2010, http:// www.longwarjournal.org/archives/2010/11/8_germans_killed_ in.php, accessed 24 June 2012.

429. Guido Steinberg, "A Turkish al-Qaeda: The Islamic Jihad Union and the Internationalization of Uzbek Jihadism," *Strategic Insights*, July 2008, p. 6.

430. Sandee, pp. 2–3.

431. Roggio, "8 Germans Said Killed in Predator Strike in North Waziristan," *The Long War Journal*, 4 October 2010, http://www. longwarjournal.org/archives/2010/10/eight_germans_said_k. php#ixzz1cSQiUBnV, accessed 24 June 2012.

432. Sandee, p. 3.

433. Siobhan Gorman and Peter Spiegel, "U.S.: CIA Drone Kills 2 Al Qaeda Commanders," *Wall Street Journal*, 17 November 2009.

434. Alisher Siddiq, "Ўзбек 'жиходчи'лари бошсиз қолди [The Uzbek 'jihadists' lost their head]," *The Uzbek Service of The Voice of America*, 17 June 2009, http://www.ozodlik.org/content/article/1825256.html, accessed 29 June 2012.

435. Ibid.

436. Ibid.

437. Sandee, p. 3.

438. Yassin Musharbash, Marcel Rosenbach, and Holger Stark, "Mr and Mrs Jihad: Wife of Homegrown Terrorist Arrested over Fundraising Activities," *Spiegel Online*, 23 February 2010, http://www.spiegel. de/international/germany/0,1518,679723,00.html, accessed 24 June 2012.

439. Sandee, p. 13.

440. Siddiq.

441. Sandee, pp. 15–17.

442. Roggio, "8 Germans Killed in Oct. 4 Predator Strike in North Waziristan Identified."

443. Sandee, p. 4.

444. Yassin Musharbash and Marcel Rosenbach, "Sauerland Cell in the Dock: Germany Prepares for Homegrown Terror Trial" (Paul Cohen trans. from German) 16 April 2009, http://www.spiegel.de/in ternational/germany/0,1518,619381-2,00.html, accessed 24 June 2012.

445. "Sauerland Group," *Global Jihad*, 21 February 2011, http:// www.globaljihad.net/view_page.asp?id=2050, accessed 24 June 2012.

446. IJU press release on an attack carried out by the IJU in the Paktika region in Afghanistan on 3 March 2008, www.sehadetvakti.com/ (now defunct).

447. [Video of exploding the NATO compound in Paktika, Afghanistan, by the IJU], March 2008. http://www.nefafoundation.org/ multimedia-prop.html. Accessed 7 June 2010.

448. Ivan Watson, "Suicide Bomber in Afghanistan Kills U.S. Marine," *National Public Radio (NPR)*, 31 May 2008, http://www.npr.org/ templates/story/story.php?storyId=91029127, accessed 24 June 2012.

449. Sandee, pp. 16–17.

450. "12 Terror Suspects Arrested in Europe," *Global Jihad*, 5 October 2010, http://www.globaljihad.net/view_news.asp?id=1695, accessed 24 June 2012.

451. Allison Pargeter, "Political Islam in Libya," *Terrorism Monitor*, Vol. 3, Issue 6, 5 May 2005, http://www.jamestown.org/single/?no_ cache=1&tx_ttnews[tt_news]=306, accessed 29 June 2012.

452. Ibid.

453. Ibid.

454. Political Islam means the involvement of Islam and Sharia law in the day-to-day political management of the state. The Muslim Brotherhood (MB), al-Qaeda, and all its affiliate groups want to achieve this goal of political Islam. They differ regarding the ways to achieve it as MB uses different nonviolent means (preaching, social activity) to win the hearts of the people, while al-Qaeda and its affiliates (in the Libyan case, the LIFG) promote violent jihad against local regimes.

455. Pargeter.

456. Mohammed Aly, "Libyan MB Chairman: We Seek Civil Society-Inspired Reform," *Ikhwanweb*, 7 July 2007, http://www.ikhwanweb. com/article.php?id=929, accessed 24 June 2012.

457. Pargete.

458. Evan Kohlmann, "Dossier: Shaykh Mustafa Abu al-Yazid (a.k.a. 'Shaykh Saeed')," *The NEFA Foundation*, June 2008, http://www.nefa foundation.org/miscellaneous/FeaturedDocs/nefayazid0608.pdf, accessed 9 March 2012.

459. Ibid, p. 4.

460. "Interview with Neoman Bentoman," *Jamestown Foundation*, 15 March 2005, http://www.jamestown.org/news_details.php?news_ id+101 (expired link).

461. Kohlmann, "Dossier: Shaykh Mustafa Abu al-Yazid," p. 5.

462. Ibid, p. 6.

463. Ibid, p. 8.

464. Ibid, pp. 8–11.

465. Ibid, p. 11.

466. Ibid, p. 12.

467. Ibid.

468. Ibid, p. 17.

469. OARDEC, "Summary of Evidence for Combatant Status Review Tribunal—Al Libi, Abu Faraj," United States Department of Defense, 8 February 2007, http://www.defenselink.mil/news/ISN10017.pdf#1. From these allegations, one can conclude that he was the military chief of al-Qaeda at that time.

470. Craig Whitlock and Munir Ladaa, "Al-Qaeda's New Leadership," The Washington Post, 2006, http://www.washingtonpost.com/wp-srv/world/specials/terror/laith.html#profile, accessed 8 Mar 2012; Claude Salhani, "Jihad Turning Point?" The Washington Times, 5 February 2008, http://www.washingtontimes.com/article/20080205/COMMENTARY/189195617/1012/commentary, republished in FrontPageMag.Com, 7 February 2008, http://www.frontpagemagazine.com/readArticle.aspx?ARTID=29823, accessed 8 March 2012.

471. Al-Libi has emerged as a public face for al-Qaeda, appearing in more than a dozen lengthy Internet videos since 2006. His claim to fame was his successful escape from a high-security U.S. military prison in Bagram, Afghanistan, in July 2005, along with three other al-Qaeda members. He styles himself as a theologian and has offered lengthy commentaries on a variety of political events, and hence became the head of the Religious Committee. See Whitlock and Ladaa.

472. Sheikh Abdullah Saeed, "Signs of Victory are Looming over Afghanistan," Global Islamic Media Front Publication, http://223.25.242.81/showthread.php?p=12062 (expired link); republished at WorldAnalysis.net, 12 May 2009, http://worldanalysis.net/modules/news/article.php?storyid=629, accessed 24 June 2012.

473. Atiya Allah's position within al-Qaeda's senior leadership was fully exposed through a series of correspondences he held with al-Qaeda's Amir of Iraq, al-Zarqawi, on behalf of the al-Qaeda leadership. See "Letter Exposes New Leader In Al-Qaeda High Command," Combating Terrorism Center at West Point, 25 September 2006, http://ctc.usma.edu/harmony/pdf/CTC-AtiyahLetter.pdf.

474. Roggio, "Libyan Islamic Fighting Group Joins al Qaeda," The Long War Journal, 3 November 2007, http://www.longwarjournal.org/archives/2007/11/libian_islamic_fight.php, accessed 24 June 2012.

475. Ibid.

476. Christopher Boucek, "Libyan State-Sponsored Terrorism: An Historical Perspective," Terrorism Monitor Vol. 3, Issue 6, 5 May

2005, http://www.jamestown.org/single/?no_cache=1&tx_ttnews[tt_news]=305, accessed 24 June 2012.

477. Nic Robertson and Paul Cruickshank, "New Jihad Code Threatens al Qaeda," *CNN*, 10 November 2009, http://edition.cnn.com/2009/WORLD/africa/11/09/libya.jihadi.code/, accessed 24 June 2012.

478. Ibid.

479. " Islamic Militant Group Pledges Support to anti Gadafi rebels." *Irish Times*, 29 March 2011 at http://www.irishtimes.com/news/islamic-militant-group-pledges-support-to-anti-gadafy-rebels-1.585344. Accessed 14 June 2014.

480. Matt Bryden, "Washington's Self-Defeating Somalia Policy," *Center for Strategic & International Studies* (CSIS), 8 December 2006, http://csis.org/publication/washingtons-self-defeating-somalia-policy, accessed 24 June 2012.

481. "Extremist Splinter Group of Somali Islamic Courts Formed," *The Somaliland Times*, Issue 238, 12 August 2006.

482. Kohlmann, "Shabaab al-Mujahideen: Migration and Jihad in the Horn of Africa," *The NEFA Foundation*, May 2009, http://nefoundation.org//file/FeaturedDocs/nefashabaabreport0509.pdf, p. 1.

483. Ibid.

484. Ibid, p. 13.

485. Ibid.

486. "Al Shabaab," *CFR Backgrounder*, 27 February 2009.

487. "Violent Islamic Extremism: Al-Shabaab Recruitment in America," Hearing before the Committee on Homeland Security and Governmental Affairs, United States Senate, 11 March 2009.

488. "Al Shabaab," *CFR Backgrounder*.

489. "Former Members of Radical Somali Group Give Details of Their Group," *Voice of America*, 6 January 2007 (last updated 27 Oct 2009), http://www.voanews.com/content/a-13-2007-01-06-voa25-66764342/563884.html, accessed 24 June 2012.

490. "Al Shabaab," *CFR Backgrounder*.

491. "Al Shabaab," *CFR Backgrounder*.

492. "Al Shabaab," *CFR Backgrounder*.

493. "Al Shabaab," *CFR Backgrounder*.

494. "Al Shabaab," *CFR Backgrounder*.

495. "Al Shabaab," *CFR Backgrounder*.

496. "Al Shabaab," *CFR Backgrounder*.

497. "Al Shabaab," *CFR Backgrounder*.

498. "Al Shabaab," *CFR Backgrounder*.

499. "Somalia: Al Shabaab Withdraw from Kismayo," *Garowe Online*, 27 September 2009, http://www.garoweonline.com/artman2/

publish/Somalia_27/Breaking_News_Somalia_Al_Shabaab_with
draw_from_Kismayo.shtml, accessed 20 June 2012.

500. Roggio, "Al Qaeda-Linked Shabaab in Control of Southern Somalia."

501. "Al Shabaab Movement Controls the City of Afmadoow Somalia," *Mufakkirah Al-Islam,* 22 December 2009.

502. "Al Shabaab," *CFR Backgrounder.*

503. Ibid.

504. "Al Shabaab," *CFR Backgrounder;* Roque.

505. "Al Shabaab," *CFR Backgrounder.*

506. "Al Shabaab Vows Deadlier War Tactics," *Daily Nation,* 1 October 2009.

507. "Al Shabaab," *CFR Backgrounder.*

508. "Al Shabaab," *CFR Backgrounder.*

509. "Al Shabaab," *CFR Backgrounder.*

510. "Al-Shabah Spokesman Resign." http://www.hiiaan.com/news2/2009/may/al_shabah_spokesman_resign.aspx.

511. "Terrorutpekad till Göteborg," *Göteborgs-Posten,* 2 July 2009.

512. "Al Shabaab," *CFR Backgrounder.*

513. "Al Shabaab," *CFR Backgrounder.*

514. For more details concerning the 11 July 2010 Kampala attack and the operational cooperation between al-Qaeda and al-Shabaab that was exposed during the investigation of the attack, see "Secret Report Exposes Terror Network's Operations in Kampala Attack," *Daily Nation,* 23 September 2010, http://www.nation.co.ke/News/-/1056/1017114/-/11k9rajz/-/index.html; Steven Candia and agencies, "Uganda Detains Top al-Shabaab Commander," *New Vision Online,* http://www.newvision.co.ug/detail.php?newsCategoryId=12&newsId=732933 (link now unavailable).

515. For more details concerning the 11 July 2010 Kampala attack and the operational cooperation between al-Qaeda and al-Shabaab that was exposed during the investigation of the attack, see "Secret Report Exposes Terror Network's Operations in Kampala Attack," *Daily Nation,* 23 September 2010, http://www.nation.co.ke/News/-/1056/1017114/-/11k9rajz/-/index.html; Steven Candia and agencies, "Uganda Detains Top al-Shabaab Commander," *New Vision Online,* http://www.newvision.co.ug/detail.php?newsCategoryId=12&newsId=732933 (link now unavailable).

516. "Al Shabaab," *CFR Backgrounder.*

517. "The Rise of the Shabab," *The Economist,* 18 December 2008; "Al Shabaab," *CFR Backgrounder.*

518. "Al Shabaab," *CFR Backgrounder.*

519. Andrew McGregor, "Ricin Fever: Abu Musab al Zarquawi in Pankisi Gorge," *Terrorism Monitor*, Vol. 2, Issue 24, 15 December 2004.

520. "Al Shabaab," *CFR Backgrounder*.

521. "Al Shabaab," *CFR Backgrounder*.

522. "Al Shabaab," *CFR Backgrounder*.

523. "Al Shabaab," *CFR Backgrounder*.

524. "Al Shabaab," *CFR Backgrounder*.

525. "Al Shabaab," *CFR Backgrounder*.

526. "Al Shabaab," *CFR Backgrounder*.

527. "Al Shabaab," *CFR Backgrounder*.

528. "Al Shabaab," *CFR Backgrounder*.

529. "Al Shabaab," *CFR Backgrounder*.

530. "Al Shabaab," *CFR Backgrounder*.

531. "Al Shabaab," *CFR Backgrounder*.

532. "Chapter 5: Terrorist Safe Havens (7120 Report)," *Country Reports on Terrorism 2008*, U.S. Department of State, April 2009.

533. "Al Shabaab," *CFR Backgrounder*.

534. Amy Zalman, "Al Shabab (Somalia)," *About.com*, http://terrorism.about.com/od/groupsleader1/p/Al-Shabab.htm, accessed 1 October 2009.

535. "Al Shabaab," *CFR Backgrounder*.

536. "Al Shabaab," *CFR Backgrounder*.

537. "Al Shabaab," *CFR Backgrounder*.

538. Roggio, "Somalia's Shabaab, Hizbul Islam Seek Merger."

539. Roggio, "Al Qaeda-Linked Shabaab in Control of Southern Somalia."

540. "Al Shabaab," *CFR Backgrounder*.

541. Roggio, "Somalia's Shabaab, Hizbul Islam Seek Merger."

542. Ibid.

543. Mohamed Ahmed and Abdi Sheikh, "Somalia's al Shabaab Rebels Declare War on Rivals," *Reuters*, 30 September 2009, http://www.reuters.com/article/2009/09/30/us-somalia-conflict-idUS-TRE58T1S020090930, accessed 28 June 2012.

544. Roggio, "Somalia's Shabaab, Hizbul Islam Seek Merger."

545. Ibid.

546. "Al Shabaab," *CFR Backgrounder*.

547. "Al Shabaab," *CFR Backgrounder*.

548. Roggio, "Al Qaeda-Linked Shabaab in Control of Southern Somalia."

549. Ibid.

550. "Al Shabaab," *CFR Backgrounder*.

551. Nick Grace, "Shabaab Reaches Out to al Qaeda Senior Leaders, Announces Death al Sudani," *The Long War Journal*, 2 September 2008, http://www.longwarjournal.org/archives/2008/09/shabab_reaches_out_t.php, accessed 28 June 2012.

552. Nick Grace, "Shabaab Reaches Out to al Qaeda Senior Leaders, Announces Death al Sudani," *The Long War Journal*, 2 September 2008, http://www.longwarjournal.org/archives/2008/09/shabab_reaches_out_t.php, accessed 28 June 2012.

553. "Al Shabaab," *CFR Backgrounder*.

554. "Al-Shabaab Joining al Qaeda, Monitor Group Says," *CNN*, 9 February 2012 at http://articles.cnn.com/2012-02-09/africa/world_africa_somalia-shabaab-qaeda_1_al-zawahiri-qaeda-somali-americans?_s=PM:AFRICA.

555. Roggio, "Al Qaeda-Linked Shabaab in Control of Southern Somalia."

556. "Suspected Terrorist Killed in U.S. Raid in Somalia," *NPR* 15 September 2009.

557. "Al Shabaab," *CFR Backgrounder*.

558. UN Security Council, *Report of the Monitoring Group on Somalia Pursuant to Security Council Resolution 1676 (2006)*, 22 November 2006, S/2006/913, http://www.unhcr.org/refworld/docid/46cbf2e00.html, accessed 29 June 2012.

559. "The Rise of the Shabab."

560. "Al Shabaab," *CFR Backgrounder*.

561. Abdisaid M. Ali, "The Al-Shabaab Al-Mujahidin—A Profile of the First Somali Terrorist Organization," International Relations and Security Network (ISN), Center for Security Studies (CSS), ETH Zurich, 2 June 2008.

562. Susan Cornwell, "U.S.'s UN Envoy Warns Eritrea over Somalia rebels," *Reuters*, 29 July 2009.

563. "Somalia: To Move Beyond the Failed State," *ICG Africa Report*, No. 147, 23 December 2008.

564. "Al Shabaab," *CFR Backgrounder*.

565. "Al Shabaab," *CFR Backgrounder*.

566. Ali Musa Abdi, "No Splitting Hairs with al-Shabaab Fashion Police," *Mail & Guardian*, 23 February 2010, http://mg.co.za/article/2010-02-23-no-splitting-hairs-with-the-alshabaab-fashion-police/, accessed 29 June 2012.

567. Roque; Obed K. Katureebe, "Eritrea's Entry Changes Face of Somalia Conflict," *The Independent* [Ugandan], 21 July 2009, http://www.independent.co.ug/index.php/cover-story/cover-story/82-

cover-story/1290-eritreas-entry-changes-face-of-somalia-conflict, accessed 29 June 2012.

568. "Al Shabaab," *CFR Backgrounder*.

569. "The Rise of the Shabab."

570. "Somalia: Thousands Displaced as Insurgent Take Control of Kismayo," *IRIN*, 25 August 2008, http://www.irinnews.org/Report/79977/SOMALIA-Thousands-displaced-as-insurgents-take-control-of-Kismayo, accessed 29 June 2012.

571. "Al Shabaab," *CFR Backgrounder*.

572. "UN Pulls Out of Southern Somalia," *WikiNews*, Wikimedia Foundation, Inc., 8 January 2010 (revised ed.).

573. "Al Shabaab," *CFR Backgrounder*.

574. Frank Nyakairu, "About 300 Foreigners Fighting Somali Government-UN," *Reuters*, 15 May 2009.

575. "Al Shabaab," *CFR Backgrounder*.

576. "Scores Killed in Somalia Fighting," *Al Jazeera*, 23 August 2008, http://www.aljazeera.com/news/africa/2008/08/2008822133743544949.html, accessed 29 June 2012.

577. "Somalia: Al Shabaab Suffer 'Heavy Losses' in New Battles," *Garowe Online*, 7 October 2009; republished in http://allafrica.com/stories/200910080374.html, accessed 29 June 2012.

578. "Former Members of Radical Somali Group Give Details of Their Group."

579. Ibid.

580. "Eritrea's Entry Changes Face of Somalia Conflict."

581. Shashank Bengali, "Kenyan Islamist Recruits Say They Did It for the money," McClatchy, 18 November 2008, http://www.mcclatchydc.com/2008/11/18/56098/kenyan-islamist-recruits-say-they.html, accessed 29 June 2012.

582. "Al Shabaab," *CFR Backgrounder*.

583. Dan Ephron and Mark Hosenball, "Recruited for Jihad?" *Newsweek*, 2 February 2009.

584. "Al Shabaab," *CFR Backgrounder*.

585. Two operatives from a terrorist cell composed of Israeli Arabs from Nazareth were apprehended by Kenyan border passport control authorities while on their way to training in al-Shabaab camps in Somalia. See Roni Daniel and Yossi Mizrahi, "חוליית טרור פעלה הותר לפרסום: חוליית הטרור בצפון [Cleared for publication: The terrorist cell in North (Google trans. from Hebrew)]," *mako*, 28 June 2010, http://www.mako.co.il/news-military/security/Article-5a5e014906d7921004.htm, accessed 29 June 2012.

586. "Al Shabaab," *CFR Backgrounder*.

587. Nyakairu.

588. UN Security Council, *Report of the Monitoring Group on Somalia Pursuant to Security Council Resolution 1676 (2006)*.

589. "Violent Islamic Extremism: Al-Shabaab Recruitment in America."

590. "Al Shabaab," *CFR Backgrounder*.

591. Abdi Sheikh and Abdi Guled, "Fighting in Somali Capital Kills 17, Rebels Behead 2," *Reuters*, 11 March 2010.

592. "Al Shabaab," *CFR Backgrounder*.

593. "Violent Islamic Extremism: Al-Shabaab Recruitment in America."

594. Bryden.

595. "Al Shabaab," *CFR Backgrounder*.

596. UN Security Council, *Report of the Monitoring Group on Somalia Pursuant to Security Council Resolution 1676 (2006)*.

597. "Al Shabaab," *CFR Backgrounder*.

598. "Al Shabaab," *CFR Backgrounder*.

599. "The Rise of the Shabab."

600. "Former Members of Radical Somali Group Give Details of Their Group."

601. "Al Shabaab," *CFR Backgrounder*.

602. Ibid.

603. "Extremist Splinter Group of Somali Islamic Courts Formed."

604. "Extremist Splinter Group of Somali Islamic Courts Formed."

605. Bengali.

606. "The Rise of the Shabab."

607. "Extremist Splinter Group of Somali Islamic Courts Formed."

608. "Extremist Splinter Group of Somali Islamic Courts Formed."

609. "Suicide Bombers Strike in Somalia," *Sky News*, 29 October 2008, http://news.sky.com/story/644271/suicide-bombers-strike-in-somalia, accessed 29 June 2012.

610 "Suicide Bombers Strike in Somalia," *Sky News*, 29 October 2008, http://news.sky.com/story/644271/suicide-bombers-strike-in-somalia, accessed 29 June 2012.

611. "Assessing Al-Shabaab's Latest Threat towards Israel," at http://www.ceifit.com/?categoryId=25149&itemId=88260.

612. "Suicide Bombers Strike in Somalia," *Sky News*, 29 October 2008, http://news.sky.com/story/644271/suicide-bombers-strike-in-somalia, accessed 29 June 2012.

613. BBC News, 2 January 2010, http://news.bbc.co.uk/2/hi/europe/8437652.stm.

614. "Shabaab al-Mujahideen 'Statement Regarding the Blessed Kampala Operations' July 14, 2010." https://azelin.files.wordpress.com/2010/07/statemtnet-regarding-the-blessed-kampala-operations.pdf.

615. "Suicide Bombers Strike in Somalia," *Sky News*, 29 October 2008, http://news.sky.com/story/644271/suicide-bombers-strike-in-somalia, accessed 29 June 2012.

616. *The Guardian*, 4 October 2013, http://www.theguardian.com/world/interactive/2013/oct/04/westgate_mall-attacks-Kenya-terror#undedfined.

617. "Al Shabaab," *CFR Backgrounder*.

618. "Sufi Clerics in Somalia Support Unity Government," *Voice of America*, 18 February 2009.

619. Roque.

620. "Sufi Clerics in Somalia Support Unity Government."

621. Bryden.

622. Nyakairu.

623. Nyakairu.

624. Nyakairu.

625. Nyakairu.

626. LebanonJihad89, "These Are the True Mujahedeen in Lebanon 1/2," Online video clip. *Youtube,* 26 July 2009, http://www.youtube.com/watch?v=G51ZySRpWnk, accessed 29 June 2012.

627. "Al Shabaab," *CFR Backgrounder*.

628. "Al Shabaab," *CFR Backgrounder*.

629. "Abdullah Azzam Brigades," *CeifiT,* http://www.ceifit.com/?categoryId=23531&itemId=125602, accessed 29 June 2012.

630. It is not clear who is Marwan Haddad. The only Marwan Haddad mentioned in the history of Palestinian struggle is the brother of Wadia Haddad, the former late leader of the Popular Front for the Liberation of Palestine Special Operation Group—PFLP/SOG—that has replaced his brother after the latter's death back in 1978. As mentioned, the credibility of the existence of this extension is still doubtful.

631. Nyakairu.

632. See "Pattani United Liberation Organization (PULO)," *Global Security.org,* 11 July 2011, http://www.globalsecurity.org/military/world/para/pulo.htm, accessed 20 June 2012.

633. Roggio, "US Designates Rajah Solaiman Movement Terrorist Entity," *The Long War Journal,* 16 June 2008, http://www.longwarjournal

.org/archives/2008/06/us_designates_rajah.php, accessed 20 June 2012.

634. "Moro Islamic Liberation Front," *New York Times,* http://topics.nytimes.com/topics/reference/timestopics/organizations/m/moro_islamic_liberation_front/index.html, accessed 20 June 2012.

635. "Moro Islamic Liberation Front," *GlobalSecurity.org,* 11 July 2011, http://www.globalsecurity.org/military/world/para/milf.htm, accessed 20 June 2012.

636. "Students Islamic Movement of India (SIMI)," *South Asia Terrorism Portal,* http://www.satp.org/satporgtp/countries/india/terroristoutfits/simi.htm, accessed 20 June 2012.

637. Animesh Roul, "Students Islamic Movement of India: A Profile," *Terrorism Monitor,* Vol. 4, Issue 7, 6 April 2006, http://www.jamestown.org/programs/gta/single/?tx_ttnews%5Btt_news%5D=728&tx_ttnews%5BbackPid%5D=181&no_cache=1, accessed 20 June 2012.

638. "Jaish-e-Mohammed (JEM)," *FAS,* 3 May 2004, http://www.fas.org/irp/world/para/jem.htm, accessed 20 June 2012.

639. See HUM's official website at http://www.harkatulmujahideen.org/.

640. Ibid.

641. "Terrorist Organizations: Harakat ul-Mujahideen (HUM)," *terrorismfiles.org,* http://www.terrorismfiles.org/organisations/harakat_ul-mujahideen.html.

642. Ibid.

643. Shaukat Piracha, "China Asks Pakistan to Investigate Xinjiang Terrorists List," *Daily Times,* 17 January 2004, http://www.dailytimes.com.pk/default.asp?page=story_17-1-2004_pg1_2, accessed 20 June 2012.

644. "China: The Evolution of ETIM," *Stratfor,* 13 May 2008, http://www.stratfor.com/memberships/116428/analysis/china_evolution_etim (expired link).

645. "Turkestan Islamic Party (TIP): 'Why Are We Fighting China?'" (CeifiT Ltd trans. from Arabic), *The NEFA Foundation,* July 2008, http://www.nefafoundation.org/miscellaneous/FeaturedDocs/nefatip0409-3.pdf, accessed 20 June 2012.

646. Holly Fletcher and Jayshree Bajoria, "The East Turkestan Islamic Movement (ETIM)," *Council on Foreign Relations,* 31 July 2008, http://www.cfr.org/publication/9179/east_turkestan_islamic_movement_etim.html#p1, accessed 20 June 2012.

647. For Dubai plot, see Raffaello Pantucci, "Uyghurs Convicted in East Turkestan Islamic Movement Plot in Dubai," *Terrorism Monitor,*

Vol. 8, No. 29 (2010), http://www.jamestown.org/uploads/media/TM_008_68.pdf, p. 5; for Norway plot, see Edward Wong, "Chinese Separatists Tied to Norway Bomb Plot," *New York Times*, 9 July 2010, http://www.nytimes.com/2010/07/10/world/asia/10uighur.html?_r=1, accessed 20 June 2012.

648. "Hizb-ul-Mujahideen (HM)," *GlobalSecurity.org*, 11 July 2007, http://www.globalsecurity.org/military/world/para/hum.htm, accessed 20 June 2012.

649. Ibid.

650. Ibid.

651. Ibid.

652. Ibid.

653. "Harakat-ul-Jihad-al-Islami (HuJI) (Movement of Islamic Holy War)," *South Asia Terrorism Portal*, http://www.satp.org/satporgtp/countries/india/states/jandk/terrorist_outfits/HuJI.htm, accessed 20 June 2012.

654. Ibid.

655. Ibid.

656. For example, see "11 Pakistanis Charged over Spanish Plot," *Gulf Times*, 14 April 2005, http://www.gulf-times.com/site/topics/article.asp?cu_no=2&item_no=33376&version=1&template_id=39&parent_, accessed 20 June 2012; Sami Yousafzai, Ron Moreau, and Christopher Dickey, "The New Bin Laden," *Newsweek*, 23 October 2010, http://www.newsweek.com/2010/10/23/is-ilyas-kashmiri-the-new-bin-laden.html, accessed 20 June 2012.

657. "Harakat-ul-Jihad-al-Islami (HuJI) (Movement of Islamic Holy War)."

658. "Harakat-ul-Mujahideen Al-Alami(Huma)," *South Asia Terrorism Portal*, http://www.satp.org/satporgtp/countries/pakistan/terroristoutfits/HuMA.htm, accessed 20 June 2012.

659. Ibid.

660. Ibid.

661. Ibid.

662. "Lashkar-e-Jhangvi," *South Asia Terrorism Portal*, http://www.satp.org/satporgtp/countries/pakistan/terroristoutfits/lej.htm, accessed 20 June 2012.

663. Ibid.

664. Ibid.

665. See "Sipah-e-Sahaba Pakistan, Terrorist Group of Pakistan," *South Asia Terrorism Portal*, http://www.satp.org/satporgtp/countries/pakistan/terroristoutfits/Ssp.htm, accessed 20 June 2012.

666. Ibid.
667. Ibid.
668. Ibid.
669. Ibid.
670. During this period, Ramzi Yousef and KSM's group were very active in the international arena, targeting mostly American targets. In February 1993, the group conducted the first World Trade Center attack in New York in which six Americans were killed and over 1,000 injured. In January 1995, the group was hatching the Bojinca plot. In between these plots, the group was active in the sectarian violence inside Pakistan and even conducted terrorist operations on Iranian soil. SSP was mostly involved in the internal activity of Yousef and KSM's group and to a much lesser extent in the international arena. See Simon Reeve, *The New Jackals: Ramzi Yousef, Osama bin Laden and the Future of Terrorism*, Boston, MA: Northeastern University Press, 1999, pp. 50–51.
671. Kathryn Gregory, "Ansar al-Islam (Iraq, Islamists/Kurdish Separatists), Ansar al-Sunnah," *Council on Foreign Relations*, 5 November 2008, http://www.cfr.org/publication/9237/ansar_alislam_iraq_islamistskurdish_separatists_ansar_alsunnah.html, accessed 29 June 2012.
672. "Ansar al-Islam in Iraqi Kurdistan," *Human Rights Watch*, 5 February 2003, http://www.hrw.org/legacy/backgrounder/mena/ansarbk020503.htm, accessed 29 June 2012.
673. "Ansar al-Islam (AI) Partisans of Islam Helpers of Islam Supporters of Islam," *FAS*, 30 April 2004, http://www.fas.org/irp/world/para/ansar.htm, accessed 29 June 2012.
674. "Ansar al-Islam (AI)," *National Counterterrorism Center*, http://www.nctc.gov/site/groups/ai.html, accessed 29 June 2012.
675. "Al-Gama'at al-Islamiyya Jama'a Islamia (Islamic Group, IG)," *FAS*, 3 May 2004, http://www.fas.org/irp/world/para/ig.htm, accessed 29 June 2012.
676. "Al-Gama'a Al-Islamiyya vs. Al-Qaeda," *MEMRI Jihad & Terrorism Studies Project*, Special Dispatch No. 1301, 27 September 2006, http://www.memri.org/report/en/0/0/0/0/0/0/1887.htm, accessed 29 June 2012.
677. "The Army of Islam, a Radical Islamic Palestinian Terrorist group in the Gaza Strip, Claimed Responsibility for the Abduction of British Journalist Alan Johnston," *Intelligence and Terrorism Information Center*, 16 May 2007, http://www.terrorism-info.org.il/malam_multimedia/English/eng_n/html/islam_troops_e.htm, accessed 29 June 2012.

678. Ibid.

679. "BBC's Alan Johnston Is Released," *BBC News,* 4 July 2007, http://news.bbc.co.uk/2/hi/middle_east/6267928.stm, accessed 29 June 2012.

680. "מיידי לפיגוע התראה: סיני את לעווב [Immediate attack warning: Leave Sinai (Google trans. from Hebrew]," *News 1,* 11 November 2010, http://www.news1.co.il/Archive/001-D-253868-00.html, accessed 29 June 2012.

681. "Egypt Blames Gaza Group for Bombing," *Al Jazeera,* 23 January 2011, http://english.aljazeera.net/news/middleeast/2011/01/201112311414915283.html, accessed 29 June 2012.

682. "Hamas: Body of Kidnapped Activist Found," *Ynetnews,* 15 April 2011, http://www.ynetnews.com/articles/0,7340,L-4057173,00.html, accessed 29 June 2012.

683. "Terrorist Organization Profile: Asbat al-Ansar," *START,* http://www.start.umd.edu/start/data_collections/tops/terrorist_organization_profile.asp?id=4639, accessed 29 June 2012.

684. For many years, al-Ansar's leader, Abu Mohjen Asbat, was considered al-Zarqawi's second-in-command in Iraq. See "Terrorist Organization Profile: Asbat al-Ansar."

685. See "4 אל לפיגוע-פעילי לפיגוע בדרכם בלבנון נעצרו קאעידה [Four other al-Qaeda were arrested in Lebanon on their way to attack (Google trans. from Hebrew]," *News10,* 12 January 2006, http://news.nana10.co.il/Article/?ArticleID=219868, accessed 29 June 2012.

686. "Fatah al-Islam Announces Their Split from Fatah at the Nahr al Bared Palestinian Refugee Camp in Northern Lebanon," SITE Institute, 29 November 2006, http://siteinstitute.org/bin/articles.cgi?ID=publications230506&Category=publications&Subcategory=0 (link unavailable).

687. "Profile: Fatah al-Islam," *BBC News,* 15 August 2010, http://www.bbc.co.uk/news/world-middle-east-10979788, accessed 29 June 2012.

688. "Blast Hits Damascus, Turkey Sends Troops to Border," *Reuters,* 28 June 2012, http://www.trust.org/alertnet/news/blast-hits-damascus-turkey-sends-troops-to-border/, accessed 29 June 2012.

689. "Profile: Fatah al-Islam," *BBC News.*

690. "Fatah al-Islam : Leadership :Shehab al-Qaddour a/k/a Abu Hureira," *Fatah Islam,* http://www.fatahislam.com/leadership/abu-hureira.html (expired domain).

691. Fatima Rida, "From Beirut to Copenhagen" at http://www.i-m-s.dk/article/fatima-part-1. Accessed 4 July 2012.

692. "Pagad: Vigilantes or Terrorists?" *BBC News,* 13 September 2010, http://news.bbc.co.uk/2/hi/africa/923701.stm, accessed 29 June 2012.

693. Anneli Botha, "PAGAD: A Case Study of Radical Islam in South Africa," *Terrorism Monitor,* Vol. 3, Issue 17, 14 September 2005, http://www.jamestown.org/single/?no_cache=1&tx_ttnews%5Btt_news%5D=561, accessed 29 June 2012.

694. Kohlmann and Kohlmann, "Shabaab al-Mujahideen: Migration and Jihad in the Horn of Africa," pp. 13–20.

695. Ibid.

696. Ibid.

697. Kohlmann, "Shabaab al-Mujahideen: Migration and Jihad in the Horn of Africa," pp. 13–20.

698. Clint Watts, Jacob Shapiro, Vahid Brown, "Al-Qa'ida's (Mis) Adventures in the Horn of Africa" at http://www.ctc.usma.edu/wp-content/uploads/2010/06/Al-Qaidas-MisAdventures-in-the-Horn-of-Africa.pdf, p. 83. Accessed 4 July 2012.

699. Clint Watts, Jacob Shapiro, Vahid Brown, "Al-Qa'ida's (Mis) Adventures in the Horn of Africa" at http://www.ctc.usma.edu/wp-content/uploads/2010/06/Al-Qaidas-MisAdventures-in-the-Horn-of-Africa.pdf, p. 83. Accessed 4 July 2012.

700. "Chapter 8: Foreign Terrorist Organizations," *Country Reports on Terrorism 2005,* U.S. Department of State, 30 April 2006; republished in "Terrorist Organizations and Other Groups of Concern," http://www.investigativeproject.org/profile/139, accessed 29 June 2012.

701. Ibid.

702. Ibid.

703. Ibid.

704. Ibid.

705. J. Peter Pham, "The Return of the 'Nigerian Taliban,'" *World Defense Review,* 1 February 2007, http://worlddefensereview.com/pham020107.shtml, accessed 29 June 2012.

706. Abdullahi Bego [describing Nigerian insurgents in *Weekly Trust*], cited in ibid.

707. Haruna Umar and Bashir Adigun, "Boko Haram Prison Break: Radical Sect Frees 40 in Nigeria" at http://www.huffingtonpost.com/2012/06/25/boko-haram-prison-break_n_1624339.html retrieved on 4 July 2012.

5

Jihad Arena Offshoots[1]

According to Salafiya, a jihad arena is an area in which Muslims fight non-Muslims—an act deemed to be the obligation of all Muslims. Currently, Iraq, Afghanistan, FATA of Pakistan, Somalia, and Chechnya are considered as the traditional key jihad arenas. Since the eruption of the "Arab Spring" in the beginning of 2011 several more arenas in different parts of the Middle East have been accumulated to the traditional list. Among those one may find Libya, the Egyptian-ruled Sinai Peninsula, and above all Syria, as the civil war erupted in the country is currently considered the main jihadi arena in the world. These arenas attract many young, zealous Muslims from across the world to participate in the local struggles against "infidel invaders or regimes," thus creating a large concentration of trained and experienced warriors in each arena that will eventually, we hope, be looking to export their operational activities to the international arena when the war in the jihad arena will be over or will reach its concluded stages.

In this chapter we will focus our discussion on the jihad arena, not only as a military war zone in which jihadi elements play a significant role but as major hubs for jihadists with future implications as well.

Pakistan's Federally Administered Tribal Areas (FATA): Al-Qaeda's Center of Operations Today

Threat Landscape

When the U.S.-led coalition forces entered Afghanistan in 2001, al-Qaeda's membership numbered about 3,000. Today, al-Qaeda and other terrorists have shifted their focus from Afghanistan to FATA (also referred to the tribal area of Pakistan or the Af-Pak border region). Nonetheless, the number of foreign fighters in tribal Pakistan has sharply decreased due to Pakistani military operations and U.S. drone attacks.

According to Pakistani intelligence assessments, a group of about ninety hard-core members led by Ayman al-Zawahiri is spearheading the fight against the United States and its allies in FATA.[2] Although this assessment significantly downplays the overall number of al-Qaeda fighters operating in the FATA, the number of al-Qaeda fighters has been reducing dramatically since the 9/11 attacks and the U.S.-led offensive in Afghanistan. According to our assessment, the varying number of al-Qaeda troops in FATA is several hundred at any given moment.

In addition to working with tribal and mainland Pakistani groups, they also work with about 900 foreign fighters in FATA. Of the foreign fighters consisting of Tajiks, Uyghur, Turks, and other nationalities, Uzbeks number about 350.[3]

The foreign fighters work with about 15,000 Afghan and Pakistani insurgents on both sides of the border. About 60 percent of the fighters are from tribal Pakistan.[4] The tribal belt separating Afghanistan from mainland Pakistan has become the strategic epicenter sustaining the fight in the region and beyond.

The Context

Terrorism, guerrilla warfare, and insurgency comprise the preeminent national security threat to most countries in the early twenty-first century. The threat is spreading from conflict zones to neighboring regions and countries far away. Iraq, Afghanistan, and Pakistan are among the traditional best-known case studies. Al-Qaeda presents the most formidable threat on the spectrum of threat groups that includes Muslim and non-Muslim groups.

Afghanistan, facing international neglect after Soviet withdrawal, became the epicenter of terrorism until the U.S.-led coalition intervention. Since then, the center of international terrorism has shifted from Afghanistan to the tribal areas of Pakistan along the Afghanistan-Pakistan border region. Many of the major terrorist attacks attempted or conducted in the West after 9/11 were organized, directed, or inspired by the al-Qaeda senior leadership located in this rugged, inaccessible mountainous region.

Three profound developments characterize the post-9/11 global threat. First, after the U.S.-led intervention in Afghanistan, the center of terrorism has moved from Afghanistan to FATA. Today, FATA is the single most important base of al-Qaeda-led radical Islamic terrorist operations where leaders, trainers, and planners are located. Second, from FATA, al-Qaeda has directed the global battle that incorporates several jihad arenas, first and foremost in Iraq.

Third, by investing in sustained communication and propaganda from FATA, al-Qaeda has co-opted several like-minded groups in Asia and the Middle East. In place of a single al-Qaeda, there are several al-Qaedas—Tawhid Wal Jihad became al-Qaeda in Iraq, the Salafist Group for Call and Combat became al-Qaeda Organization of the Islamic Maghreb, al-Qaeda in the Arabian Peninsula (AQAP) and al-Qaeda in Yemen (AQIY) were established and eventually merged. Another formal merger took place between al-Qaeda and the senior leaders of the Libyan Islamic Fighting Group (LIFG) located on the Afghanistan–Pakistan border.[5] Jemaah Islamiyah's faction led by Noordin Mohd Top became the al-Qaeda Organization of the Malay Archipelago.[6] Formal mergers have been signed between al-Qaeda and the local groups of Shabaab al-Mujahidin al-Somali, and Jabhat al-Nusra in Syria.

Al-Qaeda has yet to achieve the long-term strategic significance of successfully carving out a semisafe haven in FATA. In addition to the inaccessible Afghan-Pakistan border emerging as the new headquarters of the Global Jihad Movement, al-Qaeda and like-minded groups are seeking to change the geopolitics of the region. In FATA, Muhsin Musa Matwali Atwah Muhsin Musa Matwal al-Qaeda, its associated groups, and self-radicalized homegrown cells have recruited globally and struck their enemies both through their operational networks and through inspired and instigated cells. Operating from FATA, groups trained in that region are mounting attacks in western China (Xinjiang), north India (Kashmir), Iraq, Algeria, Somalia, and other conflict zones. In addition, dozens of plots and attacks targeting Western targets around the globe have been initiated in FATA, mostly by al-Qaeda through its designated unit for external operations.[7]

FATA is the isolated region located along the 1,520-mile border separating Afghanistan and Pakistan. Spanning an area

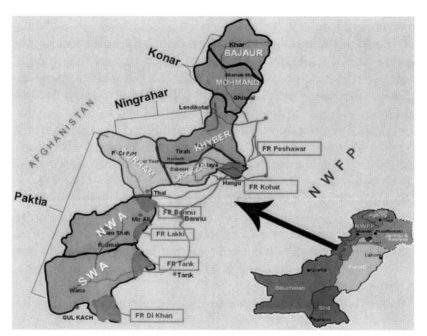

Map 5.1.   Tribal Pakistan.

of 27,220 km², FATA comprises seven tribal agencies—Bajaur, Mohmand, Khyber, Orakzai, Kurram, and North and South Waziristan.[8] FATA also has six tribal regions—Frontier Region (FR) Peshawar, FR Bannu, FR Kohat, FR D.I. Khna, FR Lakki Marwt, and FR Tank. While FATA has a population of 3.1 million, its adjacent Khyber Pakhtunkhwa Province, formerly known as the North West Frontier Province (NWFP), has a population of 17.5 million.

FATA has always been ruled by political agents. The Pashtu Wali or the Pashtun Code governs the way of life. They include the Hujra, the center of Pashtun society; Jirga, a council formed to settle conflicts; Malmastia, which regulates host/ guest relations; and Da khazoo dranaway, respect for females. Furthermore, they adhere to the principles of Jaba, to promise; Nanawatee, to seek mercy; Panah, to give shelter; Nang, to honor; and Badal, revenge.

These traditions and customs were affected by the steadfast Islamization of FATA in the 1980s and 1990s. The emergence of the Afghan Taliban, Mullah's first sovereign state, gave rise to like-minded forces in FATA. There was a resurgence of politico-religious parties and their militant wings. The number of Islamic schools (madrassas) including those preaching hatred grew dramatically. Nonetheless, an admirable security situation prevailed in FATA despite decades of conflict in neighboring Afghanistan and limited economic development.

To maintain control, Pakistan traditionally deployed five military and paramilitary organizations in FATA:

1. Frontier Corps—Deployed on the Afghan border
2. Frontier Constabulary—Deployed between FATA and settled areas
3. Police—Deployed in settled areas
4. Levies—Deployed in parts of the Provincially Administered Tribal Areas (PATA) or the Malakand Division.
5. Khassadars—Irregular forces based on inheritance, deployed in FATA.

Threat Displacement

After al-Qaeda was dislodged from Tora Bora in Afghanistan in early 2002, al-Qaeda retreated to FATA. After relocating to Waziristan, both al-Qaeda and the Afghan Taliban linked up with the Pakistani Taliban and other Pakistani mainland groups. These two entities survived by reaching out to their host, FATA's politico-religious parties. Thereafter, al-Qaeda used its historical affiliations as well as nurtured and built a clerical support base.

Al-Qaeda's deputy leader, Ayman al-Zawahiri, moved to Waziristan where he stayed for part of 2002, and eventually moved to Bajaur Agency. As his wife and two children were killed during U.S. attacks in Afghanistan, al-Zawahiri married a woman from the Mamond tribe in Bajaur Agency. Very similar to the manner in which Osama bin Laden had married a woman from Yemen to strengthen his ties to the Yemeni tribes, al-Zawahiri's marriage enabled him to develop strong tribal links to the leadership of Tehrik Nifaz Shariat Muhammadi (TNSM) in Bajaur Agency. Maulana Faqir Muhammad, also from the Mamond tribe, represented TNSM in Bajaur Agency. Similarly, al-Zawahiri built a relationship with Liaquat Hussein who ran the Ziaul Uloom Taleemul Quran seminary in Chingai in Bajaur Agency until his death in October 2006. Through these contacts, al-Zawahiri was able to avoid arrest and reconstitute the scattered al-Qaeda. As the de facto head of the Majlis Shura (Consultative council) of al-Qaeda, al-Zawahiri reestablished contact with al-Qaeda cells in Pakistan and overseas. He also built alliances with groups in the Arabian Peninsula, the Horn of Africa, Southeast Asia, and Iran.[9]

After the influx of foreign fighters in 2002, the situation in FATA began to change. Immediately after al-Qaeda and its associates retreated from Afghanistan to FATA, they began to plan attacks against coalition forces in Afghanistan. They were initially supported by multiple Pakistani groups that later formed The Talibani Pakistan (TTP). In addition to the Afghan Taliban, Hezb-e-Islami of Gulbaddin Hekmatiyar and the Haqqani network also joined them. As local Pakistani groups grew in strength, the Pakistani military responded by spawning an insurgency. As the Pakistani military had difficulties in mounting land operations to neutralize al-Qaeda and its associates in FATA, the United States conducted about 313 drone attacks from June 2004 until August 2012. The first U.S. drone attack killed Nek Muhammad and two of his associates in Wana, South Waziristan, on 18 June 2004. Nonetheless, the Pakistan government stated that the attack was mounted by the Pakistani security forces.[10] Nek, a staunch supporter of al-Qaeda and other foreign fighters, facilitated operations against U.S.- led coalition forces.

Abdullah Mehsud, a former detainee at Guantanamo Bay, replaced Nek Muhammad as the most significant leader in FATA. After Abdullah Mehsud's death on 24 July 2007, Baitullah Mehsud emerged as the most prominent leader in FATA. Under Baitullah Mehsud's leadership, Afghanistan and Pakistan experienced unprecedented levels of violence. Furthermore, al-Qaeda became more assertive, often using the Pakistani Taliban as its strike arm.

With the emergence of local militias in their support, Pakistan deployed its regular military in FATA. Since then, Pakistan has been facing an insurgency in FATA. In many ways, FATA drifted away from the state of Pakistan. Pashtun Wali, the system that governed the day-to-day lives of people in FATA, was shattered. Furthermore, faith in religion dwindled. In the name of Islam, "un-Islamic" acts were carried out by foreign fighters.

Threat Complexion

Almost all the terrorist and extremist groups that existed in Afghanistan during Taliban rule have redeployed their troops and facilities and now maintain a robust presence in FATA. al-Qaeda is providing the crucial knowledge and methodology to mobilize both foreign and domestic terrorist groups.

Traditionally, the tribes in FATA supported the anti-Soviet multinational Afghan mujahidin campaign (December 1979–February 1989). After the U.S.-led coalition intervention in Afghanistan in 2001, the tribes in FATA perceived Western intervention in Afghanistan as an extension of the past where non-Muslims occupied Muslim land. Henceforth, the hardliner Pashtu nationalists and the Islamists supported the fight against the United States and its allies. Like Sudan from 1991 to 1996 and Afghanistan from 1996 to 2001, for the jihadists FATA has emerged as the most important terrorist sanctuary in recent history. Fighting the U.S.-led coalition troops as well as the Pakistani army has transformed FATA into one of the more important jihad arenas in the world, and strategically, the most important one.

Today, FATA is of unprecedented significance to the international security and intelligence community for three reasons. First, the leadership of al-Qaeda, the Afghan Taliban, the Pakistan Taliban (TTP), the East Turkestan Islamic Movement (ETIM), the Islamic Movement of Uzbekistan (IMU), the Islamic Jihad Union (IJU), the Libyan Islamic Fighters Group (LIFG), and a dozen other groups are located in FATA. Both their operational and ideological leaders are protected by the Pakistani Taliban, a group that emerged after al-Qaeda and the Afghan Taliban moved to FATA in early 2002.

Second, FATA has become a sanctuary for research and development in explosives, training, and directing global operations. This includes attacks not only in Afghanistan and mainland Pakistan but the Middle East and the West. As long as FATA is a sanctuary, the attacks against coalition forces in Afghanistan will not stop. Furthermore, the spate of attacks in mainland Pakistan will continue. This includes the multiple assassination attempts on the former military ruler of Pakistan, General (R) Pervez Musharraf (1999–2008), and the successful assassination of former prime minister and chairperson of the Pakistan People's Party (PPP), Benazir Bhutto. The 7/7/2005 U.K. bombings and several other operations disrupted in the West including the liquid plot in August 2006 to blow up airplanes traveling over the Atlantic Ocean, were planned in FATA.[11] According to cumulative reports between 2009 and 2010, hundreds of Western citizens completed their designated training conducted by al-Qaeda's External Operations Unit in FATA and were sent back to their homelands to begin preparations for attacks.[12] Most of the operational activity of all the different entities of the Global

Jihad Movement in the international arena during 2010 could be directly attributed to elements deployed in FATA:

- Al-Qaeda's Special Operations Unit has launched plots in New York (Najibullah Zazi's plot to hit the New York subway system), north England (the mall plot), and Norway.
- The Islamic Jihad Union was planning to conduct Mumbai-style attacks in highly populated locations in major cities across Germany, targeting airports, train stations, sporting stadiums, and halls.
- It is not yet clear who was behind Faisal Shahzad's foiled attempt to conduct a devastating attack in Manhattan's Times Square in April 2010 using a vehicle borne improvised explosive device (VBIED) he constructed.[13] Was it a local initiative of a lone wolf or was it a conspiracy architected by the Pakistani Taliban? Shahzad's amateur performance suggests it was his own initiative as he was using gas cylinders as the explosive and fireworks as detonators. The fireworks would not have detonated the cylinders. His performance was also unprofessional. He detonated the fireworks, which were on the dashboard, and this hindered his vision because of the smoke. Hence, he parked at the first vacant spot, which was in the opposite direction to the traffic. He was in such a hurry to abandon the vehicle and leave the scene that he left his keys inside the ignition, which eventually led to his arrest. On the other hand, different and cumulative reports suggest TTP was behind the plot, trained him for the mission in FATA, and provided the funding needed. Since TTP has the know-how and the experience of making VBIEDs, as evidenced by its construction of dozens of such devices in the FATA combat zone, Shahzad's amateur performance on the scene might have been a deliberate message from TTP to U.S. decision makers not to interfere with TTP activity in FATA and Pakistan, as the group has the demonstrated ability to reach central Manhattan at any given moment.[14]

Third, al-Qaeda, working together with like-minded groups, has invested in sustained propaganda to radicalize the Muslim masses, including migrant Islamic communities in the West. Between 2007 and 2008, al-Qaeda and other elements deployed in FATA produced and distributed numerous propaganda publications, including magazines, online material as well as video and audio addresses on almost a daily basis. The aim of al-Qaeda is to politicize, radicalize, and mobilize Muslims worldwide into supporting and participating in the fight against the West. In the absence of a robust government response to counter al-Qaeda's message, Muslims are susceptible to extremist propaganda, which leads to support and participation in terrorism activity.[15]

Impact on FATA and Neighboring Regions

The population of FATA has suffered more than any other region of Pakistan. After al-Qaeda and the Afghan Taliban linked up with like-minded Pakistani groups and leaders, FATA emerged as a zone of sustained violence. The tribal belt has witnessed an unprecedented scale of violence and new tactics including suicide bombings, attacking *jirgas* (local leaders), killing women, beheadings, attacking mosques and funeral prayers, mutilating dead bodies, and targeted killing of rallying points or icons.

Seeking to exercise their control, Pakistani groups influenced by the ideology of al-Qaeda have killed over 600 tribal leaders in FATA.

Despite increased military and law enforcement personnel, the rate of crime has continued to increase. It has spilled over from FATA to settled areas, provincially administered tribal areas, frontier regions, and de facto tribal areas. The rise in violence and its spillover from 2007 to 2008 indicates a corresponding trend in 2009.

In addition to the number of military personnel fatalities since the beginning of the insurgency that has already exceeded 2,000, the number of law enforcement personnel fatalities has continued to rise steadfastly as well. After the Lal Masjid tragedy on 3 July 2007, both violence and the support for violence in FATA and the adjacent areas increased significantly.

Table 5.1.

OFFENSES	2007	2008	DIFFERENCE
Total Reported Crime	109475	114089	+4614
Against persons	8309	8830	+521
Kidnapping	669	810	+141
Assault on police	315	341	+26
Against property	1829	1959	+130
Vehicle theft	445	484	+39

FATA has suffered a double blow, losing both capital and skilled labor to other parts of Pakistan and overseas. The insecurity has caused economic activity to come to a near standstill. With utilities and other infrastructure destroyed, development funds have been diverted to law enforcement activities. The education system has suffered, gravely affecting the future of the region. In the Swat district of KP Province alone, over 200 schools have been destroyed and female education has been banned by the Taliban.

Al-Qaeda, the most hunted terrorist group in the world, has created another robust and resilient sanctuary in FATA. After the U.S.-led coalition's intervention in Afghanistan in October 2001 the core leadership of al-Qaeda made tribal Pakistan their new base. FATA became the new center of the operational activity of the Global Jihad Movement as dozens of jihadi entities—first and foremost al-Qaeda, the Afghanistan Taliban, and TTP—relocated their operational infrastructure to the region and directed internal and external operations from FATA.

As of 2008 the violence in Afghanistan has surpassed the violence in Iraq. Afghanistan witnessed a 33 percent rise in attacks in 2008.[16] In addition to its 36,000 existing contingent troops, Washington, DC, sent another 30,000 troops to Afghanistan in 2009.[17] Despite the increase of coalition forces in Afghanistan, the

Table 5.2.

Year	Police officers killed	Police officers injured
2006	25	31
2007	108	234
2008	166	300

terrorist threat there persisted. Afghanistan will regain its stability only when the terrorist enclave on the Afghanistan-Pakistan border is eradicated. FATA remains the epicenter of global terrorism, where al-Qaeda-led and al-Qaeda-driven threat groups plan, prepare, and execute global attacks.[18] The global threat will persist unless the international community assists Islamabad in dismantling al-Qaeda and the Pakistani Taliban infrastructure in tribal Pakistan. The proportion of attacks in Afghanistan by the Pakistani Taliban will increase with tribal Pakistan's influx of Pakistani fighters from mainland Pakistan.

Jihad Arena—Iraq

Over the past eleven years since the U.S.-led offensive on 20 March 2003, Iraq has become the world's largest hub for terrorist and insurgent activity in the international arena. Global elements, terror-sponsoring countries, regional elements as well as local Iraqi factors are the current players in the politically fragile Iraqi arena.

Since this study primarily refers to Global Jihad's Sunni elements, we will focus our analysis on the activity of radical Sunni groups that are currently deployed and operating in the Iraqi arena, first and foremost the al-Qaeda in Iraq (AQI)-led Islamic State of Iraq (ISI) insurgency coalition. Thus, we will exclude all other groups—militia, insurgency, and terrorist—that are also deployed and operating in Iraq. Iran-sponsored Shiite groups, non-ISI Baathist groups still loyal to the former regime of Saddam Hussein, national Iraqi groups, Kurdish groups (with the exception of the Islamist Ansar al-Islam) as well as militia and criminal gangs will not be part of our discussion.

General Background

Since independence, Iraq has been fighting to overcome its greatest challenge—political definition and secretarial unity. Iraq can be roughly divided into three regions:

- The south, where the population is predominantly Shiite.
- The center, where the population is predominantly Sunni.
- The north, where the population is predominantly Kurdish.

Since the late 1960s, the Iraqi military ruler Saddam Hussein (a Sunni) maintained Iraq as a unified state through violent dictatorship, which resulted in bloodshed, especially among the Shiite and Kurdish populations.

The U.S.-led occupation of Iraq in the spring of 2003 dramatically transformed the global, regional, and national threat landscapes. No invasion in contemporary times, including the Soviet invasion of Afghanistan in 1979, has had an equally profound national security impact as the invasion of Iraq. For Iraq, the invasion had multiple outcomes. The civil conflict produced human suffering, virulent ideologies, sectarian violence, internal displacement, refugee flows, extremism, and terrorism. The most enduring outcomes include (a) the origin and development of national and regional terrorist and insurgency groups, (b) the reorientation of other groups to develop ideological and operational links with external terror entities such as al-Qaeda and terror-sponsoring government entities in Iran, (c) the relocation to Iraq of external terrorist groups, notably al-Qaeda, and (d) the transformation of Iraq into a jihad arena which attracts many volunteers from across the Islamic world, and to a much lesser extent from the West, to participate in violent jihad alongside their brothers against the invading troops of the "infidels."[19] These outcomes still pose a threat to Iraq, the region, and the international community. Following the U.S. disengagement, Iraq presents a suitable climate and a fertile environment for the continuing arrival and presence of a diverse range of threat groups and external jihadi volunteers.

The Soviet invasion of Afghanistan radicalized a generation of Muslim youth. Its repetition by the United States in Iraq has radicalized a wider segment of the Sunni Muslim community.[20] Al-Qaeda, its associated groups, and affiliated cells extensively use new media technologies, notably the Internet, to radicalize the next generation of Muslims. The proliferation of ideas, technology, and tactics in Iraq in the real world and in cyber-space will sustain the global terrorist and extremist threat in the foreseeable future. While the greater threat stems from within Iraq, its immediate neighborhood of the Levant has been experiencing the impact of the Iraqi invasion. Securing the world, including future Iraq, from the fallout of the U.S. invasion of Iraq, will be a monumental challenge in the foreseeable future.

The U.S.-led invasion of Iraq created an uncertain global security climate, especially in the Muslim world. An unintended consequence of invasion was the emergence of Iraq as a global center for insurgent, terrorist, and extremist activity.[21] Another enduring outcome was the politicization, radicalization, and mobilization of a segment of Muslims worldwide, and their local and regional threat groups.[22] The U.S. invasion of Iraq created an anti-Western Muslim transnational support base facilitating the transformation of al-Qaeda into a global movement collectively identifying its struggle as violent jihad.

Global Jihad Presence in Iraq prior to the 2003 U.S.-Led Invasion

Global Jihad entities had established a presence in Iraq before the U.S. invasion of Iraq in 2003. A few radical Islamic groups located in the north of Iraq, notably the Islamic Movement of Kurdistan (IMK), developed links with the evolving radical Islamists in Afghanistan during the late 1980s and early 1990s.

Kurdish Elements

Poor governance led to the emergence of Kurdish separatist and subsequently Islamist groups in the 1980s.[23] During the Iran-Iraq War from September 1980 to August 1988, a segment of the Kurds in the north of Iraq did not support Saddam. In response, Saddam launched the al-Anfal campaign in Iraqi Kurdistan from 1986 to 1989. It resulted in the death of 30,000 Kurds in Iraq's Kurdish north and included the use of chemical agents.[24]

In response to Saddam's campaign, Kurdish Islamists from Iraq gathered in Dizly, Iran, to form the IMK in 1987. The founders of the group were the Abd al-Aziz brothers Osman, Ali, Sadik, and Omar, who were joined by Ahmed Kaka Mohamed, Sheikh Mohamed Barzinjy, Ali Papier, and other leaders. Iran's Ministry of Intelligence and National Security known as Etelaat supported IMK at its formation. Kurdish Islamists not only benefited from Iran but also from the developments in Afghanistan. Several dozen Kurds traveled to Pakistan and fought against the Soviets throughout the 1980s. Since 1988, leaders and members of the IMK have traveled to Peshawar. They were initially allied with Arab elements that fought against the invading Soviet troops, during which eight Kurds were killed, but subsequently formed Darul Akrad or the House of Kurds.[25]

Since its establishment, the IMK has cooperated with the evolving Global Jihad Movement that operated in Afghanistan and later relocated to Sudan. Many young Kurds traveled to Afghanistan to participate in the Soviet-Afghan war. They joined Abal al-Rasool Sayyaf's Ittihad-e Islami, Bara-ye Azadi-ye Afghanistan formed in 1981, and Abdullah Azzam's Maktab-al-Khidamat (MaK).[26] Educated in the Middle East, unlike the other Afghan commanders, Sayyaf worked closely with the Arabs and other foreign fighters including Kurds. One of the young Kurds that entered Afghanistan was Nashwan Abdulrazaq Abdulbaqi a.k.a. Abdul Hadi al-Iraqi from Mosul, a former major in Saddam's army.[27] He served as an instructor in Sayyaf's Sadah camp in Pakistan and later joined the emerging al-Qaeda. He rose through the ranks of al-Qaeda and by the early 2000s became the chief of the general section of al-Qaeda, which is responsible for the overall internal combat zone.[28] He was a member of al-Qaeda's Shura Council, the organization's highest decision-making body.[29] While several others like Abdul Hadi remained to serve the cause in Afghanistan, many returned to participate in Islamist movements in their own countries.[30] After al-Qaeda relocated to Khartoum, Sudan, in 1991, an al-Qaeda instructor visited northern Iraq and trained IMK activists. The training course conducted in 1992 was the first known formal contact between al-Qaeda and IMK. The links between al-Qaeda and IMK persisted throughout the 1990s. Intermittently, Iraqi Sunnis and Kurds traveled to Pakistan to either train or join al-Qaeda and the Taliban to fight against the Northern Alliance. Contact between northern Iraq and al-Qaeda occurred on several fronts. Through delegations and individuals who visited with bin Laden, IMK dispatched videos of the atrocities committed by Saddam in the north of Iraq and the suffering of the Kurds.[31]

The most prominent leaders of the IMK were Mullah Krekar; Abu Abdullah al-Shafi'i a.k.a. Warba Holiri al-Kurdi; Azo Hawleri; Ayyub Afghani; and Omar Baziany.[32] They became leaders of the Kurdish Islamist movements during the next decade. Together with the Afghan veterans, IMK members were determined to fight Saddam's regime. Supported by Etelaat, IMK reentered Iraq in 1989 and relocated to Halabja. IMK leaders exercised their influence by preaching jihad, showing photos and videos of their experience in Afghanistan, and recruiting members, supporters, and sympathizers to their movement. They claimed, "Allah succeeded us" and trained followers to fight the way they did in Afghanistan.[33] After recruiting several hundred Kurds from mosques, they fought against Saddam's rule from 1990. In 1991, during a Kurdish uprising against Saddam's rule, IMK joined forces with the Patriotic Union of Kurdistan (PUK), the Kurdistan Democratic Party (KDP), and other Kurdish secular groups. The unity among these rival groups was short lived. With the Kurdish returnees from Afghanistan and Pakistan joining IMK, a faction of the IMK adopted the ideology of jihad as a strategy. After IMK's Afghan veterans began to exercise their practices on the population, tensions emerged between the secular KDP and PUK with IMK.

Between 1993 and 1994, IMK started to spread its influence in Irbil, Halabja, and Sulaymaniyah. One of the first acts was conducted against a barbershop and involved throwing acid on the legs of female customers. Gradually, IMK came into conflict with PUK and KDP. Starting in 1994, PUK and IMK clashed and PUK, with the help of KDP, killed a few hundred members of IMK. Furthermore, disagreements developed within IMK, and IMK split into several factions that included the Salafiya group

(Mullah Krekar), the Jihadiya group (Ali Abdul Aziz), and the Kurdish Hamas (Omar Baziany and Mohomed Sofi), while Ali Papier remained one of the leaders of the IMK.[34]

Among other Kurdish groups opposed to Saddam, IMK too received U.S. assistance.[35] Gradually, IMK suffered splits under the leadership of Sheikh Ali Abd-Aziz, the brother of the IMK founder. In July 2001, IMK splinters—Kurdish Hamas and al-Tawhid (Islamic Unification Movement [IUM])—joined to form the Islamic Unity Front (IUF). In August, Second Soran Forces, another IMK splinter, joined them. After IUF was dissolved in early September 2001, Jund al-Islam (Soldiers of Islam) was established on 1 September 2001 under the leadership of Abdullah al-Shafi'i a.k.a. Mullah Wuria Hawleri, an Iraqi Kurd from the village of Gwer near Irbil. Jund al-Islam evolved into Ansar al-Islam on 12 December 2001. Najmeddin Faraj Ahmad a.k.a Mullah Mustapha Krekar, an Afghan war veteran who studied jurisprudence under Abdullah Azzam and was a close friend of Osama bin Laden, had returned to his home country when the war in Afghanistan was over, joined Ansar al-Islam shortly after 9/11, and became the leader of the group. Abu Abdullah Shafi', an Afghan veteran, became Ansar's deputy leader.[36] Other profound leaders of Ansar al-Islam were Assad Hammed Hassan a.k.a. Hawleri, the former leader of the Second Soran Unit, and Abu Abdul Rahman, an Afghan-trained explosives expert.

Both IMK and its splinters were operating between Halabja and Hawraman, along the Iraq-Iran border. Ansar al-Islam established itself in an enclave in northeastern Iraq, on the strategic Shinirwe Mountain overlooking the town of Halabja, near the porous border with Iran—an area outside Saddam's control. After its establishment, the group also seized the border town of Tawella, as well as the villages of Mila Chinara, Khak Kelan, Kharpan, Zardalhala, Hanadi, Dargashikhan, Balkha, Mishla, and Palyanaw. Over time, it expanded its influence, engaging in conflict with PUK, the established power in the region. After it relocated to Iraq, Ansar al-Islam controlled "a string of villages in the plains and mountains between the town of Halabja and the mountain ridge which marks Iraq's border with Iran." "The area has been dubbed as 'Iraq's Tora Bora' by some locals after the Al Qaeda stronghold in Afghanistan."[37] In September 2001, Ansar al-Islam committed the worst atrocity in the village of Khela Hama, near Halabja, when they captured and massacred forty-two members of PUK, which controlled the eastern half of Iraqi Kurdistan. Ansar al-Islam killed leaders, bombed restaurants, and desecrated Sufi shrines. In December, Ansar al-Islam killed 103 and injured 117 members of PUK who were returning home to celebrate the end of Ramadan, the Muslim holy month of fasting. Pictures of the killings were placed on the Internet.[38]

Starting early 2002, jihadi al-Qaeda affiliated operatives including al-Zarqawi, who relocated from Afghanistan via Lebanon and Iran as a consequence of the U.S. offensive that followed the 9/11 attacks, influenced both the modus operandi and targeting strategy of Ansar al-Islam. In April 2002, Ansar al-Islam attempted to kill Prime Minister Burham Salih, the head of the PUK-led Iraqi Kurdistan regional government.[39] In July 2002, Ansar al-Islam desecrated tombs of the Naqshbandi (Sufi) order. Kurdish society condemned this act. On 10 February 2003, Ansar al-Islam assassinated Shawkat Hajji Mushir, a founding member of PUK and a member of the Kurdish Parliament, along with two other Kurdish officials. Kurdistan suffered its first suicide bomb attack on 26 February 2003, when an Ansar al-Islam suicide bomber attacked government troops at a roadside checkpoint using a Land Rover taxi, killing two soldiers and the taxi driver.[40] The attack coincided with a conference of Iraqi opposition organizations on the post-Saddam political order, attended by Zalmay Khalilzad, President Bush's special envoy to the Iraqi opposition.[41] It is very likely that the attacker wanted to target the meeting. From this attack, it is clear that Ansar will become one of the most threatening terrorist groups to the coalition forces in Iraq.

After al-Qaeda's attack on 11 September 2001, the ideological and operational links between the Kurdish Islamists and al-Qaeda grew. After the U.S. coalition intervention in October 2001, a segment of the al-Qaeda leadership moved to tribal Pakistan and to Iran.[42] Under international pressure, Iran began to crack down on the al-Qaeda presence in Iran. A few hundred foreign fighters including al-Qaeda members moved through Iran and settled in northern Iraq, a "safe haven" from Saddam's atrocities protected by the West.[43] The Kurdish Islamists played a decisive role in providing a platform for the launch of an insurgency.

External Jihadi Elements—Abu Musab al-Zarqawi—Tawhid Wal Jihad Group

One of the consequences of the U.S.-led offensive in Afghanistan was the relocation of al-Zarqawi's group, Tawhid Wal Jihad, to northern Iraq. Al-Zarqawi ran a training camp in Herat in Afghanistan near the Iranian border with financial support from al-Qaeda.[44] Al-Zarqawi, a Jordanian citizen of Palestinian origin from the city of Zarqa (his alias al-Zarqawi refers to his hometown), established links with groups and individuals in the Levant. Most of the recruits of Tawhid Wal Jihad were from the Levant, including those living in Europe. Al-Zarqawi fled to Iran in late 2001 following the American offensive in Afghanistan. After the Iranians detained al-Zarqawi briefly, he relocated to Iraq in the late summer of 2002. Al-Zarqawi's host Mullah Krekar opposed unity moves by the parent IMK to join PUK and work with the United States in order to create an autonomous Kurdish state in the north of Iraq. Driven by al-Qaeda's ideology, Mullah Krekar and his followers initially wanted to create an Islamic state in the north of Iraq and subsequently the rest of Iraq.

With the help of Ansar al-Islam, al-Zarqawi settled in Halabja and established training facilities in the northern Kurdish areas outside Saddam-controlled Iraq. Benefiting from the protection of the U.S. northern no-fly zone, al-Zarqawi replicated the camp in Herat where he conducted training in poison (especially ricin) as well as explosives, his favored weapon. In addition to building a vast network in the Levant and Europe,[45] al-Zarqawi conducted operations and plots in Iraq, Saudi Arabia, Syria, Lebanon, and Jordan.[46] As a regional terrorist, al-Zarqawi traveled in order to establish networks, including a plot to conduct a chemical attack in Jordan that would have killed tens of thousands of people.[47] In May 2002, al-Zarqawi arrived in Baghdad for medical treatment and remained there for two months.[48] Western intelligence services assumed that Saddam "must have" collaborated with regard to al-Zarqawi's arrival or at least "known" about it, even though Saddam's involvement with the concrete facilitation of Zarqawi's return is not clear. [49]

Building the Case against Iraq

Even before 11 September 2001, U.S. political leadership was keen to invade Iraq. The U.S. intelligence community actively looked for links between al-Qaeda and Saddam as well as between Saddam and weapons of mass destruction (WMDs). They found none that were credible.[50] Saddam's security services dispatched serving Iraqi intelligence officers to join Islamist groups and report back on their plans and preparations. As the United States lacked an understanding of the threat groups, it misconstrued the presence of former and serving intelligence operatives within al-Qaeda-linked Kurdish Islamist groups as Saddam's links to al-Qaeda. To justify the invasion of Iraq, the White House influenced the assessments of the U.S. intelligence community. At least a segment of the international intelligence community still believes that Saddam worked with al-Qaeda and its associate groups in Iraq.[51] Addressing the U.N. Security Council on the U.S. case against Iraq on 5 February 2003, U.S. secretary of state Colin Powell said:

> [W]hat I want to bring to your attention today is the potentially much more sinister nexus between Iraq and the al Qaeda terrorist network, a nexus that combines classic terrorist organizations and modern methods of murder. Iraq today harbors a deadly terrorist network headed by Abu Mussab Zarqawi, an associate and collaborator of Osama bin Laden and his al Qaeda lieutenants. . . . We are not surprised that Iraq is harboring Zarqawi and his subordinates. This understanding builds on decades long experience with respect to ties between Iraq and al Qaeda.[52]

The misinterpretation of intelligence and the lack of understanding of the Middle East led the Bush administration to invade Iraq, an event that compounded the global terror threat.

Immediately after Powell's U.N. speech in which he referred to a facility manufacturing poisons and explosives at Khurmal, Ansar al-Islam invited journalists to visit and inspect the camp on 5 February 2003.[53] It is likely that the facility was used to experiment and train in the use of cyanide, ricin, and other poisons.[54] Commonly known as Ansar, the al-Qaeda-supported Kurdish Salafi group operated against both Kurdish secular groups and Saddam's regime. Even an International Crisis Group (ICG) report noted that there was little independent evidence of links between Ansar al Islam and Baghdad.[55] ICG judged that it would be very hard for people or military supplies to pass between Baghdad and the Ansar enclave because a secular Kurdish group hostile to both controls all the routes between them.[56]

The United States wrongly believed that Ansar al-Islam played a key role in linking al-Qaeda with the Iraqi government. When U.S. forces invaded Iraq, they were under the impression that Ansar was working with Saddam, and hence chemical, biological, radiological, and nuclear weapons (CBRN) could be used against them. In an attempt to build a case for the invasion of Iraq, U.S. leadership used counterterrorism intelligence that was questionable and uncorroborated. This included the debriefing of Abd al-Hamid al-Fakhiri a.k.a. Ibn al-Sheikh al-Libi, the leader of Khaldan Camp in Afghanistan, who was captured by the Pakistani government in early 2002. Although Ibn al-Sheikh was not an al-Qaeda member, he and Abu Zubeydah, the External Amir of Khaldan Camp, worked with al-Qaeda after their camp was shut down in 1999. As the CIA believed him to be uncooperative, they flew him to Egypt for further interrogation. Ibn al-Sheikh's claims contributed appreciably, if not totally, to the United States' reason and decision to invade Iraq, even though a month earlier the CIA assessed Ibn al-Sheikh's revelations as unreliable.[57] Powell told the U.N: "Al Qaeda continues to have a deep interest in acquiring weapons of mass destruction. As with the story of Zarqawi and his network, I can trace the story of a senior terrorist operative telling how Iraq provided training in these weapons to al Qaeda. Fortunately, this operative is now detained, and he has told his story."[58] After the U.S. invasion, Ibn al-Sheikh recanted claims of contact between al-Qaeda, Saddam's government, and al-Qaeda's training in WMDs provided by Iraq. On 22 November 2003, the Egyptian service returned Ibn al-Sheikh to the CIA. In January 2004, after U.S. interrogators presented Ibn al-Sheikh with new evidence from other detainees, he acknowledged that under torture in Egypt he had deliberately misled interrogators.[59] On 5 November 2005, the *New York Times* quoted the Defense Intelligence Agency stating:

> This is the first report from Ibn al-Sheikh in which he claims Iraq assisted al-Qaida's CBRN efforts. However, he lacks specific details on the Iraqi's [sic] involved, the CBRN materials associated with the assistance, and the location where training occurred. It is possible he does not know any further details; it is more likely this individual is intentionally misleading the debriefers. Ibn al-Sheikh has been undergoing debriefs for several weeks and may describing [sic] scenarios to the de briefers that he knows will retain their interest.
>
> Saddam's regime is intensely secular and is wary of Islamic revolutionary movements. Moreover, Baghdad is unlikely to provide assistance to a group it cannot control.[60]

Global Jihad Elements in Iraq During and Following the 2003 Invasion—Deployment, Performance, and Operational Activity

Prior to invasion, the western security and intelligence services working with KDP and PUK focused on developing intelligence on the threat groups in Iraq. They estimated that the Islamist troops in northern Iraq were composed of 300 to 400 Iraqi Kurds that were joined by 200 to 300 Arabs and other fighters who fled Afghanistan after the U.S.-led intervention in Afghanistan.[61] Their leader, Mullah Krekar, was the host to a few hundred Arabs including al-Zarqawi's troops.

At the time of the U.S.-led intervention in Iraq, several terrorist groups possessing radical Islamist ideologies were active and deployed in Iraq. The north of Iraq became a safe haven for several domestic and foreign groups. Ansar al-Islam, which has links to al-Qaeda and other Arab groups from Afghanistan, was the most structured terrorist group. Ansar al-Islam controlled Beriya, a tiny pocket of territory between Halabja and the Iranian border, an area around 80 km (50 miles) southeast of the PUK's administrative center of Sulaymaniyah.[62] Ansar al-Islam was the host to Tawhid Wal Jihad led by al-Zarqawi. Tawhid Wal Jihad relocated from Afghanistan after the U.S. intervention in 2001 and was composed of volunteers trained by al-Zarqawi from Lebanon, Syria, Jordan, and Palestine. The volunteers worked closely with Ansar al-Islam, which modeled itself on the Afghan Taliban.

During the U.S.-led invasion of Iraq, the first series of terrorist camps targeted by the coalition belonged to Ansar al-Islam. At that time, the United States believed that the camps were trying to develop crude chemical weapons and had links to al-Qaeda and Saddam's regime. U.S. Special Forces and air strikes supported by the PUK, a U.S. ally, attacked Ansar al-Islam hideouts. U.S. Tomahawk cruise missiles and warplanes from the Red Sea hit Khurmal as well as six mountain villages in northern Iraq on 21 March 2003.[63] With the exception of Abu Taisir al-Urduni, a specialist on poisons and al-Zarqawi's representative in northern Iraq, the strike failed to kill anyone of note. It is likely that more than 100 Ansar al-Islam members were killed. Significant documents including foreign passports and training manuals were recovered.[64] In a message "to the Muslims of Kurdistan, Iraq and the world," Ansar al-Islam leader Abu Abdullah al-Shafi'i threatened "martyrdom operations (suicide attacks) against the American and British Crusader forces."[65] The message claimed that "more than 300 martyrdom fighters have renewed their devotion to God" ahead of suicide attacks.[66] It declared that "We will make Iraq a cemetery for the Crusaders and their servile agents."[67] Most of their fighters dispersed to

Iran and regrouped on the border. Some Ansar al-Islam leaders, such as Abu Abdullah al-Shafi'i, Ayyub Afghani, and Sa'adoon Mohammed Abdul Latif a.k.a. Abu Wa'il, were seen in the Iranian border city of Sanandaj in June and July 2003, regrouping their fighters and recruiting men.[68]

After the U.S. invasion, the threat from the Kurdish areas of Iraq trickled to the middle of Iraq and subsequently to the rest of Iraq. From Iraq, the threat from Sunni groups spread to the region and beyond. As the Sunni groups were the best organized, many Baathists, especially former regime elements, and nationalists joined them. The Baathists and nationalists each organized and formed their own terror and insurgency groups. The threat from Shi'a groups, including those sponsored by Iran, spread from the south to the center of Iraq.

The threat groups in Iraq can be divided into four classes: the Baathists (pro–Saddam Hussein), the Sunni nationalists, the Sunni Islamists (pro-al-Qaeda), and the Shi'a Islamists (pro-Iran). The Sunni insurgency is not a monolithic threat.[69] Iraq's most powerful Sunni insurgent group, the Islamic Army (Al-Jeish al-Islami), was founded in February 2004.[70] The al-Qaeda-led Islamic State of Iraq (Dawlat al-'Iraq al-Islamiyah: ISI) was established on 15 October 2006.[71] Within the ISI, al-Qaeda in Iraq (AQI) was the largest entity.[72] In October 2007, twenty-three groups came together to form the Supreme Command for Jihad and Liberation led by former Iraqi vice president and deputy chairman of the Iraqi Revolutionary Command Council, Izzat Ibrahim ad-Douri.[73] The Sunni nationalists and Islamists feared the Shi'a dominated government of Iraq. The insurgency groups, including offshoots of the Baath Party, such as Jeish al-Fatih or al-Fatih Army, have assumed an outward Islamic character.[74] The Shi'a groups fought the Sunni groups and the U.S.-led coalition.[75] Two dozen well-structured groups worked with nearly 100 small- to medium-sized groups to make Iraq the site of the most violent conflict in the world. The insurgency peaked in 2006–2007, and declined thereafter. The U.S. military estimated the strength of the overall insurgent groups in Iraq to have ranged from 8,000 to 20,000, although Iraqi intelligence officials have issued figures as high as 40,000 fighters plus another 160,000 supporters.[76] At the height of the insurgency in Iraq, the two most lethal threat groups, AQI and Ansar al-Islam, had a numerical strength of 2,000–3,500 and 3,000–4,000 fighters, respectively. Of nearly 100 armed groups, al-Qaeda and al-Ansar belong to the strain of groups that are experienced, networked, and ideologically resilient. They are likely to last long after the other groups have been dismantled or abandoned violence.

Al-Qaeda Central Command's multiannual plan for Iraq was exposed in a letter sent from al-Zawahiri to al-Zarqawi in the autumn of 2005. Even if the letter's primary intentions were to subordinate al-Zarqawi to the overall strategy and agenda of al-Qaeda central, it also reflects a strategic plan of using the Iraqi arena to promote al-Qaeda and the Global Jihad's long-term aspirations. According to the letter, AQI's overall strategy comprises four stages. The first three are chronological and the fourth may be conducted in parallel to all stages:

- The first stage: Expel the Americans from Iraq.
- The second stage: Establish an Islamic authority or emirate, then develop it and support it until it achieves the level of a caliphate—over as much territory as possible to spread its power in Iraq, i.e., in Sunni areas, in order to fill the void stemming from the departure of the Americans, immediately upon their exit and before un-Islamic forces attempt to fill this void, whether it be those whom the Americans leave behind, or those among the un-Islamic forces who will try to take power. There is no doubt that this emirate will enter into a fierce struggle with the foreign "infidel" forces, and those supporting them among the local forces, to put it in a state of constant preoccupation with defending itself, to make it impossible for it to establish a stable state which could proclaim a caliphate, and to keep the jihadist groups in a constant state of war, until these forces find a chance to annihilate them.
- The third stage: Extend the jihad wave to the secular countries neighboring Iraq.[77]

- The fourth stage (this may coincide with the above three stages): A clash with Israel, because Israel was established only to challenge any new Islamic entity.[78]

Ansar al-Islam/Ansar al-Sunna

Since its inception, Ansar al-Islam has operated with experienced Kurdish and foreign fighters. With the aim of creating an Islamic state, Ansar al-Islam responded to the invasion by mounting attacks against Western, Iraqi, and Kurdish government targets, as well as foreign contractors starting in the Kurdish areas. On 22 March 2003, at the crossroads checkpoint outside the village of Khurmal, a suicide car bomb detonated, killing Australian journalist Paul Moran and four Kurds, and injuring dozens of other Kurdish *peshmerga* (local militia) and civilians, including correspondent Eric Campbell.[79] In Norway Mullah Krekar, the spiritual leader of Ansar al-Islam, justified the attack.[80] On 9 September 2003, three people were killed during an attempt to bomb a U.S. Department of Defense office in Irbil. As a group of Kurds operating with foreigners, Ansar al-Islam's operations were not limited to the north. As Ansar al-Islam wished to operate in the rest of Iraq, it changed its official name to Ansar al-Sunna (Supporters of the Tradition) on 20 September 2003. Ansar recruited Sunni Arabs in central Iraq to join the largely Kurdish group from the north of Iraq. Influenced by the Arabs that fought in Afghanistan, particularly Tawhid Wal Jihad, Ansar al-Sunna conducted graphic beheadings. In October 2004, Ansar al-Sunna released a video on its website which showed the beheading of a Turkish truck driver. The kidnappers on the video identified themselves as members of Tawhid Wal Jihad. Ansar's other tactics included vehicle- and human-borne suicide attacks, abduction, assassinations, IED attacks, rocket and mortar attacks, and roadside bombings. On October 2003, the Pentagon declared that Ansar al-Islam had become the principal terrorist adversary of U.S. forces in Iraq. As Ansar al-Islam started to operate in central Iraq, including Baghdad, Ansar's fighters were divided into six battalions: Nasr, Fat'h, Badr, Quds, Fida'iyun, and Salahudeen. Ansar fought in the "Sunni Triangle," north and west of Baghdad, the main battleground between U.S. troops and insurgents.

Tawhid Wal Jihad, operationally close to al-Qaeda, influenced Ansar al-Sunna's operational outlook. Ansar focused on conducting high profile attacks on symbolic and strategic targets, inflicting mass casualties and fatalities. In November 2003, Italian intelligence reported that an Ansar member helped to organize the truck bombings of the headquarters of the Italian military contingent in Nasariyah, southern Iraq. On 1 February 2004, Ansar's suicide bombers hit Eid (Festival) celebrations of PUK and KDP in Irbil, killing 109 and wounding 200. Both Ansar and Tawhid Wal Jihad vied for recognition by al-Qaeda. With al-Qaeda recognizing Tawhid Wal Jihad as a part of al-Qaeda, al-Zarqawi named his group "al-Qaeda in Iraq" in October 2004.

Due to the mounting daily killings of Shi'a Iraqis by AQI in September 2005, disagreements between AQI and Ansar developed, leading to a split in their alliance. Although AQI and its former host, Ansar al-Islam, started operating independently, Ansar maintained direct contact and communications with al-Qaeda. An Ansar leader, Abbas bin Farnas bin Qafqas a.k.a. Ali Wali, communicated with al-Qaeda leaders in Pakistan during 2005. However, Ali Wali was killed during a counterterrorism raid in Baghdad in May 2006.[81] In July 2007, Ansar al-Sunna was instrumental in forming an alliance of seven Sunni groups to prepare for the withdrawal of American and allied forces. In December 2007, Ansar al-Sunna formally declared itself as an offshoot of Ansar al-Islam.

Although over 100 large- to small-threat groups emerged in Iraq after the invasion, Ansar and AQI posed the biggest threat. Under the influence of al-Qaeda, they favored suicide attacks against high-profile, strategic, and symbolic targets. As most of their attacks were spectacular, they influenced the tempo of battle in Iraq and even inspired other groups in the region and beyond.

Tanzim Qaidat fi Bilad al-Rafidayn (al-Qaeda in Iraq)

In October 2004, Tawhid Wal Jihad renamed itself Tanzim Qaidat fi Bilad al-Rafidayn or al-Qaeda Organization in the Land of the Two Rivers, commonly known as al-Qaeda in Iraq.[82] After Tawhid Wal Jihad severed its ties with Ansar, the group came under greater influence from al-Qaeda. Led by al-Zarqawi, AQI emerged as the most violent terrorist group in the world. For information leading to al-Zarqawi's death or capture, the United States offered a reward of US$25 million, the largest amount offered for a terrorist's capture.

At AQI's peak in 2006, the total number of its combatants ranged between 2,000 and 3,500. AQI was responsible for the most suicide attacks and generally the most spectacular attacks in Iraq.[83] Although 90 percent of the group was Iraqi by 2006, foreigners constituted about 90 percent of its suicide bombers. AQI's key strength was the Majlis al-Shura Mujahidin fi al-Iraq (The Mujahidin Shura Council of Iraq), an umbrella organization of eight groups with AQI at its core.[84] On 15 October 2006, al-Qaeda established the Islamic State of Iraq (ISI) and calibrated it to serve AQI's interests. Twelve smaller militant groups and AQI operated within ISI's structure.[85] ISI received praise from al-Qaeda's leadership in Pakistan.[86]

Aside from attacking coalition and Iraqi security forces, the group has a confrontational policy against civilian Shiites and Iraqi nationalist resistance groups. Although al-Qaeda's leadership discouraged al-Zarqawi's actions, he refused to change his course, and the organization continues to conduct the same massacres as it did during al-Zarqawi's tenure and remains generally disliked among other militant groups in Iraq. These other militant groups have on many occasions appealed to bin Laden for intervention. However, al-Qaeda's leadership has instead supported the unpopular establishment of the ISI, which has tried to entice and coerce other militant groups to join the ISI entity.

AQI focused on vehicle- and human-borne suicide attacks. The group also conducts IED attacks, car bombings, and roadside bombings. However, the sheer scale of violence unleashed by AQI has sparked antagonism all over Iraq. With the Iraqi public providing intelligence to the government and to the United States, the group suffered the loss of key leaders. This led to AQI's steady deterioration, starting with the capture of al-Zarqawi's deputy, Hassan Mahmud Abu Nabha a.k.a. Milad al-Lubnani, in Lebanon in January 2006. Key arrests provided further intelligence, which led to al-Zarqawi's death in Baquba, Iraq, on 7 June 2006.[87] At the time of al-Zarqawi's death, the insurgency in Iraq was at its peak and continued at that pace for another year. His successor, Abd al-Munim Izzidine Ali Ismail a.k.a. Abu Hamza al-Muhajir a.k.a. Abu Ayyub al-Masri, was from the Egyptian Islamic Jihad, a group led by al-Zawahiri that had merged with al-Qaeda.[88] A former instructor at the al-Faruq camp in Kandahar from 1999 to 2000, Abu Hamza al-Muhajir fled Afghanistan, relocated to Iran, and was in Baghdad before the U.S. invasion in 2003.[89] A founding member of Tawhid Wal Jihad, he became an instructor on the making of improvised weapons and facilitated the travel of foreign fighters to Baghdad.

After al-Zarqawi's death, Abu Hamza al-Muhajir pledged allegiance to Abu Umar al-Baghdadi, who had just been declared Amir al-Mu'minin (Leader of the Faithful) of the newly formed ISI.[90] Despite Abu Hamza al-Muhajir reaching out to the Iraqis and their groups, which were fighting the coalition and Iraqi forces, AQI faced insurmountable challenges.[91] The backlash against AQI was the first permanent fracture within the insurgency. Although Abu Hamza al-Muhajir tried to appeal to the wider Iraqi population, the massacres of tribal leaders and civilians led to a decline in public support.[92] Unity among Anbar's twenty-five tribes over the high civilian casualties caused by AQI attacks initiated the group's decline. After questioning the authority and legitimacy of tribes in al-Anbar, an AQI member said: "This tribal system is un-Islamic. We are proud to kill tribal leaders who are helping the Americans."[93] The tribal formations included Hamza Brigade, created in 2004 and mainly made up of the Albu-Mahal tribe from the al-Qaim area of al-Anbar Province. The group has since been officially sanctioned by the Iraqi government under the name of Desert Protection Corps. Another tribal formation emerged in 2005 and was known as the

Tribal Council. The council was led by the powerful Albu-Fahad tribe from Ramadi. However, the council was severely weakened when AQI killed its leader, Sheikh Nasser Abdulkarim al-Miklaf, in January 2006. All of these tribal formations were either based on a single tribe or the tribes around one town or city. Due to their small and fragmented power base, these tribal formations were defeated and their leaders were often killed. This changed during the summer of 2006, when Majlis al-Shura of Inqath fi al-Anbar (The al-Anbar Salvation Council) was formed. Eleven tribes, which took part in The Awakening of al-Anbar Conference, formed this council. Each of the eleven tribes has formed its own armed formation. The Salvation Council claims to have a combined military force of 30,000 tribal fighters.[94] In September 2006, fifty-one tribal leaders from the Salvation Council, led by al-Shaykh Abd-al-Sattar Buzay Abu-Rishah, met with Iraqi prime minister Nuri al-Maliki. The Salvation Council asked the Iraqi government for help in combating the terrorists (AQI/MSC) in al-Anbar. Prior to this meeting, one of the main leaders of the al-Anbar Salvation Council, Sheikh Hamid Farhan, stated that the council's military formations had killed five AQI members, including the local leader in the town of Hit.[95]

This was followed by another clash in November, when forces from the Salvation Council battled AQI-led ISI near the town of Sofia in al-Anbar. The coalition forces assisted the tribal force with air and artillery strikes.[96] According to the leader of the Salvation Council, al-Shaykh Abd-al-Sattar Buzay al-Rishawi's forces from the Salvation Council had raided an AQI stronghold and killed fifty-five members while losing nine of its own.[97] By mid-February 2007, the tribes of al-Anbar had contributed 2,400 individuals to the local police force and 1,600 members to a new tribal force called the Emergency Response Unit. The Emergency Response Unit received training from U.S. forces in Iraq.[98] By February 2007, the United States cooperated with twelve tribes, up from three in June 2006.[99]

By February 2007, the Salvation Council had become such a threat to the forces of AQI-led ISI that the latter started a large terror campaign against al-Anbar Salvation Council leaders, members, and their families. In the middle of February 2007, more than twenty mourners traveling from a funeral in Fallujah were pulled from their bus and killed, due to their alleged family ties with members of the Salvation Council. During the same period, two suicide bombers struck, respectively, the blast wall outside and the house of tribal leader al-Shaykh Abd-al-Sattar Buzay al-Rishawi, who leads the al-Anbar Salvation Council. Five police officers and six civilians were killed in the attack, but their main target escaped.[100] In late February 2007, a suicide bomber detonated his truck outside a Sunni mosque in the town of Habbaniyah in al-Anbar province, killing at least thirty-nine people. The mosque was targeted because the Imam (prayer leader) of the mosque had spoken out against "extremists."[101]

The opponents of AQI argued that AQI was guilty of fratricide, and that its transnational goals in Iraq endangered the Iraqi people. On 27 October 2007 the Islamic Army of Iraq claimed that AQI "waged an attack in al-Shakhat (a part of al-Latifiyah) which resulted in the death of four unarmed citizens (as well as) an element of the Islamic Army with an insidious act and destroyed fourteen houses."[102] In 2007, the rivalry heightened. On 14 September 2007, AQI claimed that "Hamas in Iraq (a former faction of the 1920 Revolutionary Brigades) worked hard to uncover the weapons of the mujahidin and stood side-by-side with the occupiers and fought us."[103] However, Hamas in Iraq claimed that it "did not participate in any fight against the al Qaeda network and will never, ever cooperate with the occupiers."[104] The accusations continued. On 4 January 2008, Hamas claimed:

> Al Qaeda's fight against the resistance and mujahidin units . . . considered towards the benefit of the occupiers . . . put a drain on our youth and weaponry. The occupying forces were unable to enter Diyala until Al Qaeda paved the way for them by killing Sunnis and demolishing their homes, mosques, and hospitals. . . . Several individuals from the Islamic State of Iraq are responsible for killing commanders and fighters from our brigades in the Diyala province . . . killed them and mutilated them . . . killed our men's wives and children.[105]

After the United States reached out to the Iraqi Sunni groups, AQI's ISI started to fight the rival Sunni insurgent groups. These groups argued that AQI had started to

> terrorize the mujahidin under the pretext that their banners were agent banners, and it had the audacity to turn on the people of jihad and kill a number of the leaders of the Muslim Movement of the Mujahidin of Iraq, who, despite our reservations on them, should not be killed. They shot them in the back outside their homes, in their mosques, and amid their children.[106]

The main argument made by the rival Sunni groups was that AQI had distorted the resistance by fomenting sectarian conflict. On 15 April 2008, the Army of al-Mustafa, a breakaway faction of the ISI, claimed: "ISI threatened one of our field commanders with death for no apparent reason . . . we see no justification for the acts carried out by the brothers from the ISI—they have blackmailed us, threatened us, and seized the assets of the Army of al-Mustafa."[107]

After Zarqawi's death, ISI lost its strongholds in the Diyala and Salahudeen Provinces and in Kirkuk. Fighting continued in Nineveh, particularly in Mosul, between coalition forces and the ISI. The attacks in Mosul in 2009 included operations that targeted U.S. and Iraqi forces as well as militiamen of an Awakening Council in Latifiyah, Babil Province, as they waited to receive their salaries. The emergence of the Kurdistan Brigades demonstrated AQI's ambition to establish a foothold in the Kurdish areas. Pledging their allegiance to Abu Omar al-Baghdadi, the leader of the ISI, a representative of the brigades said:

> We are your brothers in the Kurdistan Brigades and we pledge our allegiance to the Islamic State of Iraq. . . . To the two Kurdish puppets, Jalal Talabani and Masud Barzani, I swear by God that we have no mercy or sympathy towards the traitors who sold themselves to the enemies of God. Your throats will be slit.[108]

The target of AQI-led ISI attacks shifted from coalition and Iraqi forces to the Awakening Movement. This caused fear, opposition, and revenge against the ISI. Due to declining support as well as increasing confrontation with the tribes of al-Anbar, the ISI moved most of its operations into Baghdad and Diyala Province. AQI has received some positive responses to Abu Hamza al-Muhajir's outreach and reconciliation efforts, especially in Diyala Province. On 4 October 2006, a statement from the Bubaz tribes referred directly to Abu Hamza's call for reconciliation between the Iraqi tribes and Muslim groups, by declaring "permanent reconciliation between the warring groups . . . [such] opens the field for the sons of the tribe to follow any faction or Jihadi brigade they wish to join in the quest for reward from Allah and destruction of the Crusader invade [sic]."[109]

In Baghdad and Diyala Province, AQI and especially the Iraqi Salafiya groups like Jaish al-Islami have managed to draw some support from local Sunni Arabs. Local Sunni Arabs perceive these groups as their only guardians against the Shiite death squads, who have confessed to killing thousands of Sunni Arabs. Despite these developments in Diyala and Baghdad, we assess that Abu Hamza al-Muhajir's outreach program has failed. The outreach program has not been able to woo major Iraqi resistance or militant Salafiya movements into the ISI. Instead, actions on the ground by AQI members have further alienated these actors.

The ISI remains the umbrella group of Sunni militant factions dominated by AQI.[110] Despite his speeches and networking efforts, Abu Hamza al-Muhajir has generally been unable to change the dynamics on the ground. On the ground, al-Zarqawi's uncompromising ideological legacy and the cycle of revenge still guides local AQI leaders, members, and supporters. The ISI remains active in the country; it announced its second "cabinet" formation in a video released on jihadist forums on 21 September 2009. According to the SITE Intelligence Group, the video, produced by ISI's media arm, al-Furqan, featured a spokesman for ISI's "Information Ministry" reading a statement from ISI leader Abu Omar al-Baghdadi about ministerial positions. The statement also gave assurance of the group's continued jihad activity as the ISI entered its third year. ISI announced its first cabinet formation in a video released on 19 April 2007, naming ten individuals as "ministers." The new list consisted of the following nine names:

- Sheikh Abu Hamza al-Muhajir—First Minister and Minister of War
- Sheikh Abdul Wahhab al-Mashadani—Minister of Shariah Affairs
- Sheikh Muhammad al-Duleimi—Minister of Public Relations
- Sheikh Hassan al-Jabouri—Minister of Martyr and Prisoner Affairs
- Sheikh Ustadh Abdul Razzaq al-Shemari—Minister of Security
- Sheikh Doctor Abdullah al-Qaysi—Minister of Health
- Sheikh Ustadh Ahmed al-Ta'i—Minister of Information
- Sheikh Engineer Usama al-Laheibi—Minister of Oil
- Sheikh Ustadh Yunis al-Hamadani—Minister of Finance

Despite the new cabinet and Abu Hamza's other efforts, AQI remains a fringe group, far removed from the mainstream Sunni-Iraqi militant groups. Nonetheless, AQI remains a significant group, especially due to its international links. It is one of the largest and best-funded militant organizations in Iraq. The group remains at the center of the ISI and is the single most influential Sunni militant group in Iraq.

By mid-2010, both Abu Hamza al-Muhajir and al-Baghdadi were eliminated by U.S. drone attacks. Following these losses, the ISI said its governing council had selected their replacements: Abu Bakar al-Baghdadi al-Husseini al-Qurashi as its caliph, or head, and Abu Abdullah al-Hassani al-Qurashi as his deputy and first minister. The names are most likely noms de guerre. The two leaders replaced Baghdadi, the former purported ISI head, and AQI leader Abu Hamza al-Muhajir, respectively.[111]

Response

Since the U.S.-led invasion of Iraq, the national, regional, and global threat landscapes have altered dramatically. In late

2003, when the coalition forces failed to provide the basic necessities to the public, the Iraqi insurgency took off and the public gradually turned against the occupying forces. Furthermore, the United States made a strategic error of dismantling the Iraqi military. Public support for trained Iraqis led to a sustained insurgency. Beginning in late 2003, three clusters of threat groups emerged: pro-al-Qaeda groups, pro-Baathist groups, and pro-Iran groups. With the influx of foreign fighters, Iraq emerged as the most violent theater in the world in 2004.

The United States wrongly perceived the biggest threat to Iraq to be the Baathists and not militant Islamists. L. Paul Bremer, the head of the Coalition Provisional Authority who dismantled the Iraqi army, and Condoleezza Rice, the then U.S. national security advisor and later secretary of state, failed to understand that the core threat stemmed from AQI-led ISI. While the White House and the U.S. State Department blamed Syria, the U.S. military and the CIA were aware of the threat but lacked support to focus on the real enemy. Sheikh Talal al-Gaood, a Sunni businessman who had close ties to Anbar's tribal leaders and led a group of Iraqis in early talks with the United States, was enraged by the "endless mistakes" of U.S. leadership.[112] He said: "You [Americans] face a Wahabi threat that you cannot even begin to fathom," and he derided White House "propaganda" about the role of Syria in fueling the insurgency.[113] The White House and the U.S. State Department blocked the U.S. military's attempt to co-opt Iraqi tribal leaders, an alliance that could have prevented the escalation of the insurgency and the widespread loss of lives and property.[114]

The turning point of the insurgency occurred when Sunni tribal groups led by tribal Sheikhs united to form clusters to protect their tribes from the ISI. With the steady increase in violence in Iraq and no assistance from Washington or the Shi'a dominated Baghdad government, the Sunni tribes reached out to the U.S. Marines for help. Although the United States was initially reluctant to assist them, Colonel John Coleman, the chief of staff for the First Marine Expeditionary Force, disregarded Washington's advice and went to Fallujah, a city in the heart of the Sunni triangle. He traveled there to assist the tribal leaders in fighting AQI after the killing of four U.S. security contractors in April 2004. A Saddam look-alike, who was a former general in the Iraqi army, aided coalition forces in Fallujah.[115] Although there was still resistance from Washington, the model for collaboration between the United States and the tribes was supported by Marine Lieutenant General James T. Conway, General David Petraeus, and Secretary of Defense Robert Gates. As U.S. understanding of Iraqi nationalism grew, the United States worked together with the Iraqi Sunni groups in its quest to defeat the ISI.

The balance of power shifted when tribes started to receive financial support, political guidance, and military advice from the United States. The U.S. politico-military strategy became more effective when the United States started to work with Iraqi Sunni groups in weakening the community support base that the ISI relied on. After Fallujah, similar efforts sprang up among army units patrolling in Tel Afar and in Ramadi where, five months after Coleman's Fallujah initiative, American military officers began tentative approaches to work with the Rishawi tribe and provide U.S. assistance.[116] Despite the killing of Ramadi's Sheikh Abdul Sattar Abu Risha in a car bomb attack in September 2007, the tribe strategy spread and even took hold in Babil Province's "Triangle of Death," the heavily fought-over area south of Baghdad.[117] Starting in early 2007, U.S. alliance with Babil's leaders, its former enemies, grew. By May 2007, the Babil tribes received U.S. funding including "$370 for each provincial policeman hired by Babil's Janabi tribe, a potent and influential force in southern and western Iraq."[118] When the Americans called for a meeting of the Awakening Councils with the Shia dominated Iraqi government on 25 June 2007, a suicide bomber penetrated three levels of security and killed twelve Iraqis, including six key members of the Anbar Salvation Council.[119] Despite AQI targeting several leaders and their families, the Awakening Movements in Iraq made a difference. A well-established counterinsurgency strategy of reaching out to local leaders and building relationships with them to marginalize other threat groups was effective in Iraq.

Within a year of the formation of the American strategy to pacify Iraq, the strength of the counterinsurgency groups grew to between 65,000–80,000 members.[120] Nonetheless, the coalition forces failed to restore peace and stability because Western public opinion turned against their deployment in Iraq. Although the Shi'a dominated government did not trust the Sunni tribes, Sunni leaders organized pockets of resistance against AQI and the ISI, starting in Anbar Province in 2005. The core was joined by Sunni groups that had previously worked with AQI. The groups joined the core after they realized that AQI did not have the interests of Iraq at heart. Although the "surge" helped in lowering violence, the Awakening Movement that began in Anbar Province and continued in Baghdad in 2008 was the most important reason for the insurgency's decline.[121]

Yet, following the withdrawal of U.S. troops from Iraq in 2011, the insurgency groups have reemerged and regained their operational activity resulting in violent clashes with the Iraqi central government and sectarian violence among the Iraqi religious and ethnical sects.[122] During June 2014 these conflicts escalated as the ISI (operating under its new name ISIS) offensive in the northern parts of the country resulted in the withdrawal of the Iraqi military and the seizure of important cities including Mosul , Iraq's second-largest city, and Tikrit , the hometown of former Iraqi leader Saddam Hussein, by ISIS troops.[123]

As ISIS troops fight their way toward the capital city of Baghdad, the resuming of full-scale civil war in Iraq is imminent.

The solution to the problem in Iraq came from the Iraqis themselves. In 2005 and 2006, the Iraqis became tired of AQI-led violence directed against Iraqis. Nonetheless, their resentment against AQI could be harnessed only after the United States was convinced that a partnership with the Iraqi Sunni tribes was the only way to stabilize Iraq. With the appointment of Lt. General David Petraeus, a counterinsurgency specialist, as the commanding general of the Multi-National Forces in Iraq in January 2007, U.S. strategy changed. Instead of conducting large-scale arrests, the kinetic operations became targeted. While using its force judiciously, the United States and its partners built local security forces. They rebuilt the utilities infrastructure, invested in the economy, and held elections which reinvigorated the political process. More importantly, the United States started to work with Sunni groups that had hitherto collaborated with al-Qaeda, and dramatically reduced violence in Iraq by 80 percent in 2007. A surge of troops enabled the United States to contain and limit the influence of al-Qaeda and other violent groups.

By October 2008, when Lt. General Petraeus handed over command in Iraq, he had built governmental capacity, developed employment programs, and improved daily life for Iraqi citizens.[124] Nonetheless, among the group of countries suffering from insurgency and terrorism, Iraq and Afghanistan continued to witness the highest levels of violence. As of 2009, the activity of Sunni and Shiite insurgent groups has been largely limited to attacks against coalition and Iraqi forces in areas of central and northern Iraq. In addition to Shi'a and Sunni groups, nationalist insurgent groups have mounted attacks.[125]

The Islamic Army in Iraq (IAI), Hamas-Iraq, JAMI, the Mujahideen Army, and the Shariah Committee of Ansar al-Sunnah came together for a joint project called the Campaign of the Iraqi Resistance in Support of Gaza. They claimed several attacks in the beginning and middle of January 2009 against U.S. forces in areas of Anbar, Baghdad, Kirkuk, and Salah al-Din Provinces.[126] Hamas-Iraq in particular and IAI also encouraged Muslim support for the Palestinian resistance. At the conclusion of the offensive in Gaza, the insurgent groups in Iraq congratulated Palestinians for their endurance. The al-Qaeda-affiliated groups, ISI and Ansar al-Islam, also offered support, not through attack campaigns, but via incitement of Muslims everywhere to attack U.S., Israeli, and Arab interests.[127]

External Jihadi Volunteers

Since April 2003, Iraq has become not only the hub of Islamic terrorism and insurgence activity but also the most important jihad arena. Iraq became the magnet for radical Islamic elements, attracting volunteers from all over the Islamic world as well as Muslims in the West to travel to Iraq and take part in the fighting. It is unclear exactly how many foreign mujahidin have arrived in Iraq since the beginning of the American-led invasion. According to U.S. military reports, up until the beginning of 2006, hundreds of foreign fighters in Iraq who have come from Saudi Arabia , Syria, Iran, Egypt, Sudan, Yemen, Libya, and other countries have been killed or captured by coalition forces.[128] These assessments were probably based on information revealed following the capture of 311 foreign mujahidin between April and October 2005.[129] The 311 captured mujahidin came from twenty-seven countries. The largest number came from Egypt (78), Syria (66), Sudan (41), Saudi Arabia (32), Jordan (17), Iran (13), Palestine (12), and Tunisia (10). Western countries were also represented. Two insurgents came from Great Britain and one each came from the United States, Denmark, Ireland, and France. The remaining countries were: Algeria (8), Libya (7), Turkey (6), Lebanon (3), Qatar (2), the United Arab Emirates (2), India (2), Macedonia (1), Morocco (1), Somalia (1), Yemen (1), Israel (1), Indonesia (1), and Kuwait (1).[130]

On 11 September 2007, coalition forces in Iraq raided a suspected al-Qaeda safe house in Sinjar, a western Iraqi town ten miles from the Syrian border. This operation recovered records documenting the backgrounds and flow of foreign fighters entering Iraq. The documents recovered in this operation included over 700 personal data files of external volunteers who had entered Iraq during the fifteen months between the spring of 2006 and the summer of 2007.[131]

Based on the figures of the Sinjar document, we assess that since the American-led offensive in April 2003 hundreds of foreign jihadi volunteers have been entering Iraq annually, accumulating to an overall total that exceeds 5,000.

Based on the Sinjar record and other raw documents, the Counter Terrorism Center (CTC) has conducted a thorough analysis on the external jihadi volunteers in Iraq and its key findings include:

Country of Origin

The majority of the foreign fighters in Iraq originate from Muslim states in the Middle East and North Africa:

- 41 percent Saudis
- 19.2 percent Libyans
- 8.1 percent Yemenites
- 8 percent Syrians
- 7.1 percent Algerians
- 6.1 percent Moroccans
- 1.9 percent Jordanians

Individual foreign fighters arrived from Egypt, Great Britain, France, and Sweden.[132]

Combat Use

Most of the external volunteers in Iraq were used as suicide bombers. More than half (56.4 percent [212 records]) of the volunteers in the Sinjar records consider themselves suicide bombers. These figures overlap with approximately 75 percent of the overall suicide attacks conducted in Iraq between August 2006 and August 2007.[133]

Budget Contribution

AQI relies heavily on funding transfer to Iraq by foreign fighters, especially those from Saudi Arabia. The mean contribution of Saudi fighters was equal to $1,088, far more than those of other fighters.[134]

Recruitment Methods

The majority (62.5 percent) of foreign fighters were recruited through local jihadi sympathizers (33.5 percent) and personal social networks (29 percent). Few were recruited directly via the Internet.[135]

Conclusion

The foreign fighters in Iraq share important similarities with their predecessors in Afghanistan. However, Iraqi volunteers have seen more combat than those in Afghanistan during the 1980s and they possess and perform better tactical skills and operational innovations.

Like their predecessors in Afghanistan, who helped to radicalize tens of thousands of jihadis across the world purely through their existence, we believe that Iraqi veterans will spread their operational heritage and influence over Muslim communities predominantly in the West.[136]

The Iraq war has increased jihadi radicalization in the Muslim world and the number of al-Qaeda recruits. Foreign fighters in Iraq have also acquired useful skills that can be used in future terrorist operations, including suicide tactics, organizational skills, propaganda, covert communication, and innovative IED tactics. Some AQI fighters that trickled out of Iraq have bolstered violent movements in Saudi Arabia and Lebanon. This trend will likely continue as Iraqi veterans would most likely prefer to join established jihadi groups in emerging jihad arenas such as Afghanistan, Pakistan, Somalia, Yemen, and recently Syria.[137]

Similar to Afghanistan's continued influx of jihadi volunteers after the departure of Soviet troops at the end of the Afghan war, U.S. withdrawal from Iraq did not end the flow of foreign fighters to Iraq. Iraq remains a viable arena for jihad, and became an international jihadi center dispatching warriors for operational activities in other needed locations, first and foremost Syria.

In particular, an ever increasing number of foreign fighters came to Iraq in recent years under the banner of the new version of the ISI—the Islamic State of Iraq and al-Sham (ISIS), determined to fight the Maliki government and the Sunni *sahwa* (awakening) movement that joined the United States last decade in standing up to AQI-led ISI. This trend—in conjunction with Iraqis fighting alongside ISIS in Syria and the group steadily seizing territory in western Iraq and eastern Syria—has effectively melted away the border. ISIS operatives now operate in both countries and view crossing the border as nothing more than going from one province in their "Islamic State" to another.[138]

Exporting Terrorist Operations from Iraq

Few terrorist operations that were conducted in the international arena in the last nine years originated from Iraq. Even though the Iraqi arena was composed of skilled and trained AQI militants, facilitators, explosive experts, suicide bombers, and foreign jihadi volunteers, the majority of their terrorist operations remained inside Iraq and did not spread to neighboring (excluding Syria) countries or the international arena. This trend was most likely the result of an al-Qaeda directive and policy to concentrate in Iraq at the first stage, which was enforced during 2005 through a series of letters between al-Qaeda's central leaders in Waziristan and AQI's commander at that time, al-Zarqawi.

As mentioned, al-Zarqawi had his own agenda and policy in Iraq that completely contradicted al-Qaeda's Central Command's agenda and even directives at important junctures. For example, al-Zarqawi's targeting policy against Iraq's Shiite population was completely rejected by al-Qaeda's command.[139] al-Zarqawi's external targeting policy raised antagonism among al-Qaeda's leadership as well, as its harsh outcome—the murder of dozens of innocent Muslims in these attacks—undermined al-Qaeda's legitimacy in the Arab world.

In April 2004, authorities exposed a large-scale AQI plot to attack key locations in the Jordanian capital, Amman, using several truck bombs. According to expert assessments, in case the plot had been carried out, tens of thousands of civilians would have been killed, since the bombs were to be composed of chemical ingredients alongside standard explosives.[140] In the second half of 2005, AQI initiated several plots and attacks outside Iraq. In August 2005, Turkish authorities dismantled an AQI plot to attack an Israeli cruise ship sailing the Mediterranean with a dingy full of explosives driven by a suicide bomber.[141] Later that month, an AQI squad conducted a mortar shelling of U.S. ships harboring in the Jordanian port city of Aqaba and the Israeli city of Eilat from the other side of the Jordanian-Israeli border.[142] On 9 November 2005, AQI executed three suicide attacks in Western hotels in Amman, killing over seventy Jordanians.[143]

On 8 June 2006, al-Zarqawi was eliminated by U.S. forces in Iraq. His successor Abu Hamza al-Muhajir was an Egyptian by origin and an EIJ member. Hence, Abu Hamza al-Muhajir was much more compliant with al-Qaeda's directives and orders. During his leadership, AQI halted most of its external operations and focused its activity inside Iraq, while its external activity, when conducted, followed the Central Command's plans and agenda. In a rare statement by Abu Hamza al-Muhajir describing the role AQI had in the foiled attempt to strike a London nightlife district and Glasgow International Airport in July 2007, he announced AQI's targeting policy in the international arena: "indeed we have already carried out many operations outside Iraq—one of which that should be particularly mentioned is the most recent operation in Britain, when part [of the mission] was carried out at the airport, and rest was a failure, due to a mistake committed by one of our brothers a few days before the operation, when he called to break the news that the operation was about to take place."[144] We believe that AQI's role in this operation was part of an overall al-Qaeda plan to attack facilities in the United Kingdom, most likely led and initiated by al-Qaeda central.[145] Another example of the cooperation between al-Qaeda and AQI in the international arena was exposed in the foiled attempt to conduct a terrorist attack during the World Cup games in South Africa. AQI activist Abdullah Azzam Salih Misfar initiated early plans to conduct a terrorist attack in South Africa aimed at Dutch and Danish teams and supporters, but these plans had not progressed past an introductory stage. Salih Misfar said, "I wrote the idea and sent it to Abu Hamza (Abu Ayyub Al Masri)," and the planning was said to have gone to al-Qaeda's deputy, al-Zawahiri, for approval.[146]

In late December 2010, a Swedish citizen of Iraqi decent, Taimur-al-Abdaly, conducted a suicide attack in central Stockholm. The investigation of this attack has yet to be concluded but early indicators suggest that Abdaly carried out the attack on behalf of the ISI.[147]

Future Assessment

Ideologues, including the al-Qaeda leader in Saudi Arabia, Yusuf al-A'yari, exploited Muslim sentiments by calling on Muslims worldwide to respond to the U.S. invasion. In "Crusader's War," an al-Qaeda blueprint for fighting in Iraq, al A'yari said, "If democracy is established in Iraq that will be the death of Islam."[148] Al-Qaeda propagated the idea of the invasion as an attack on Islam and Muslims. Al-Qaeda, like-minded groups, and their supporters will continue to highlight the existence of Muslim suffering, resentment, and anger in Iraq. There is anti-American sentiment among the Muslim population, with a narrow segment of that population being sympathetic to terrorism and extremism. As a result, there is growing ideological influence from al-Qaeda and its associated groups over territorial and diaspora migrant communities. The failure of the United States to contain the violence in Iraq has led to an increase in threat groups' influence in Iraq and overseas.

According to our assessment it seems that long after U.S. withdrawal, the wave of global extremism spurred by the violence in Iraq will persist. In contrast to the Saddam Hussein era, Iraq in the post-Saddam era will witness sustained violence that will affect Iraq's neighboring countries, the Middle East region, and the world. In an earlier generation, the disastrous Soviet invasion of Afghanistan spawned an ideology, and a pool of foreign fighters that continues to threaten international security. Likewise, the U.S. invasion of Iraq has created a plethora of threat groups that will be a source of domestic, regional, and global instability.

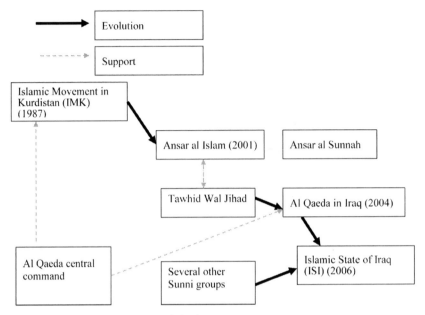

Chart 5.1. Evolution of al-Qaeda-linked groups in Iraq.

Appendix

Armed groups operating in Iraq
Insurgents
National Salafis
Islamic Army in Iraq
Sufi Naqshbandi Iraq
Iraqi Islamic Resistance Front
Jaish al-Mujahidin
Mujahideen Battalions of the Salafi Group of Iraq
Islamic Salafist Boy Scout Battalions
Mohammad's Army (a.k.a. Jaish-e-Mohamed).
Pan Arabian Nationalists
Nasserites
Jihadist Sunni Salafis

Islamic State of Iraq, an umbrella organization, com-
  posed of:
AQI
Jeish al-Fatiheen
Jund al-Sahaba
Katbiyan Ansar al-Tawhid wal Sunnah
Jeish al-Taiifa al-Mansoura
Monotheism Supporters Brigades
Sarayat al-Jihad Group
al-Ghuraba Brigades
al-Ahwal Brigades
Jamaat Ansar al-Sunna
Ansar al-Islam
Black Banner Organization
Asaeb Ahl el-Iraq
Wakefulness and Holy War
Abu Theeb's group
 Jeish Abu Bakar's group
BAATHIST REBELS AND INSURGENTS
Baathists
Fedayeen Saddam
The Return
General Command of the Armed Forces, Resistance,
  and Liberation in Iraq
Iraqi Popular Army
New Return
Patriotic Front
Political Media Organ of the Baath Party
Popular Resistance for the Liberation of Iraq
Al-Abud Network
MILITIA
Shi'a militia
Mahdi Army
Abu Deraa's Mahdi Army faction
Badr Organization
Sheibani Network

Soldiers of Heaven
Special Groups Criminals (Iraq)
Asa'ib Ahl al-Haq
Promised Day Brigades
Kata'ib Hezbollah
Sunni militia
Awakening groups
1920 Revolution Brigades
Jaish al-Rashideen
Islamic Front for the Iraqi Resistance
Hamas of Iraq
Kurdish militia
Peshmerga
Kurdistan Workers Party
Party for a Free Life in Kurdistan
Minority militia
Qaraqosh Protection Committee, an Assyrian Christian
  self-defense force
 Malik Al-Tawus Troop, a Yezidi self-defense force in
  northern Iraq[149]
Provincial control of Iraq in January 2007
Kurdish control
Sunni insurgent control
Shiite militia influence
Contested provinces

Jihad Arena—Chechnya

General Background

The First Chechen War was a violent conflict between Russia and Chechen rebels looking to establish a sovereign independent state in Chechnya, which lasted from December 1994 to August 1996. During the first stage of the conflict (1994–1995), the war mainly concentrated around the Chechen capital Grozny,

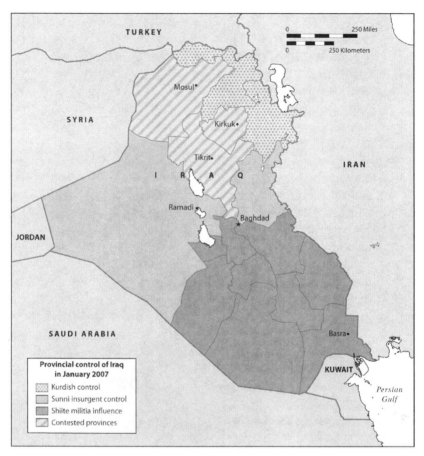

Map 5.2. The regional deployment of insurgent and terrorist groups operating in Iraq.

and was later extended to the mountainous area of Chechnya. During the second stage (1995–1996), Russian forces were set back by Chechen guerrillas in spite of Russia's overwhelming manpower, weaponry, and air superiority. A cease-fire between the two sides was achieved in 1996, followed by a peace treaty a year later, which lasted for three years. Estimates of the First Chechen War casualties vary between 40,000 and 130,000 deaths and over 200,000 injured. The majority of casualties were

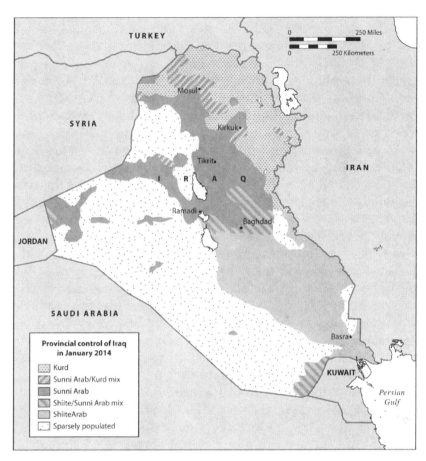

Map 5.3.   *Provincial control of Iraq January 2014.*[150]

Chechen civilians. More than 500,000 people were displaced by the conflict, which left cities and villages in ruins.[151]

On 26 August 1999, the Second Chechen War, or the War in the North Caucasus, was launched by Russia in response to the invasion of Dagestan conducted by a radical Wahhabi organization, the Islamic International Peacekeeping Brigade (IIPB), composed of local Chechen mujahidin, and Islamic foreign fighters. It had invaded Dagestan in support of local Dagestani Islamic rebels.

On 1 October 1999, Russian troops entered Chechnya, ended the de facto independence of the Chechen Republic, and restored Russian control over the territory.

In the early stages of the Second Chechen War, as in the First Chechen War, the Russian military was supported by local Chechen paramilitary forces, enabling them to overcome Chechen separatists and seize Grozny in February 2000. In May 2000, Russia established direct rule of Chechnya, but as time went by, local separatists rehabilitated their chain of command and operational activities and were able to inflict heavy Russian casualties and challenge Russian political control over Chechnya for several more years. The war in Chechnya was accompanied by large-scale terrorist attacks conducted by radical Islamist (Wahhabi) inspired Chechen elements against civilians inside Russian hinterland.[152] As of 2009, Russia has severely disabled the Chechen separatists and large-scale fighting has ceased. The Russian army no longer occupies the streets and the city of Grozny has undergone massive and rapid reconstruction. However, sporadic violence still exists and occasional attacks target Russian troops and regional government forces in the area as well as Russian civilians inside Russian hinterland.[153]

The exact death toll from the second conflict is unknown. Unofficial estimates range from 25,000 to 50,000 dead or missing, mostly civilians in Chechnya. Russian casualties are over 5,200 (the official Russian figure) and total at about 11,000. Recent estimates suggest that up to 75,000 people were killed during both Chechen wars.[154]

Radical Islamist (Mujahidin) Foreign Fighters in Chechnya and Their Influence

Although the war in Chechnya is regarded by many as an internal conflict within the Russian Federation, it has attracted a large number of foreign mujahidin.

During the eighteenth and nineteenth centuries, many Chechen and other North Caucasian inhabitants migrated to the Middle East, mostly to areas that are currently parts of Jordan,

Turkey, Syria, and Iraq. While Chechens in Turkey, Syria, and Iraq assimilated over time, today there still exists a unique community of around 8,000 Chechens in Jordan who have preserved their language and cultural traditions.[155]

During the early 1990s, it became increasingly common for Chechens in Jordan to visit their newly independent homeland. Sheikh Ali Fathi al-Shishani, an elderly veteran of the Soviet Afghan war and an ethnic Jordanian Chechen, arrived in Grozny and formed a Salafi Islamic Jamaat consisting of young indigenous Chechens and Jordanian Chechens. As the First Chechen War began, several Arab volunteers, veterans of the Afghan war, arrived in Chechnya, assisted by al-Shishani. Among them was Samir Salih Abdallah al-Suwaylim a.k.a. Ibn al-Khattab.[156] Khattab was a Saudi national veteran from the Afghan war who took part in the Tajik civil war in 1992.[157] As a result of a formal invitation from al-Shishani, Khattab formed a unit of eight experienced Arabs, all veterans of the Afghan war, who entered Chechnya in February 1995. Upon arrival, Khattab formed a military unit composed mostly of al-Shishani's troops. This company-sized unit was subdivided into sections headed by Khattab's deputies.[158]

Khattab allied with Chechen warlord Shamil Basayev and coordinated with the Chechen rebel command. Khattab and his commanders were able to conduct significant operations in Chechnya.[159]

As time went by, new mujahidin attracted by al-Shishani's propaganda volunteered to go to Chechnya and a total of eighty Middle Eastern Arab volunteers fought against the Russians during the first war (1994–1996).[160] Even though their military influence over the battlefield was negligible, their militant tactics and religious influence were to have an important impact on future Chechen combat.[161]

Even though the first war ended with a Chechen victory, Khattab was disappointed with the outcome as his vision of an Islamic state in the North Caucasus was unfulfilled. In order to overcome this gap, Khattab decided to continue with military activity and established several training camps that conducted religious and military training for trainees from the region. As a result, Khattab's troops were significantly reinforced at that time.[162]

As a consequence of Khattab's efforts, several Chechen separatist groups have integrated Islamic agendas into their primary objectives, alongside the goal of Chechen independence. According to press reports, this tendency was funded from outside Chechnya as millions of dollars per month were channeled into the region. At the same time, Chechen militants began participating in terror training in Afghanistan and were indoctrinated by the radical Islamic Wahhabi creed at various "learning centers" throughout Chechnya. Some reports suggest that as many as an average of 400 people underwent each of these two-month sessions, totaling, according to Russian authorities' estimates, at 2,500 recruits during the interwar period.[163] However, while Chechnya boasts a primarily Muslim population, the populace as a whole possesses only a weak allegiance to radical Islam. Today, most of the Chechen resistance groups continue to stress an independent Chechen state as their primary objective.[164]

Nevertheless, the impact of the external radical Islamic approach over local Chechen and other regional groups was far beyond their actual numbers as several newly established groups have integrated radical Islamic characteristics into their overall agenda as well as to their military tactics and operations.

The growing presence of these Islamic elements within Chechnya forced the secular president of the newly independent state, Aslan Maskhadov, to implement Sharia law and establish dozens of religious "courts" throughout the republic, under religious guidance from Sheikh Abu Omar al-Sayf, operating on behalf of the Sudanese Islamic model. Abdurrahman, a young Jordanian Chechen who succeeded al-Shishani as head of the Islamic Jamaat following his death in 1997, also provided religious guidance.[165]

Emerging Wahhabi influence as a whole and Khattab's jihadi group in particular played a pivotal role in leading to the outbreak of the Second Russo-Chechen War. The trigger was a military offensive in August 1999 initiated by the Wahhabi foreign fighters in Chechnya. Two thousand Wahhabi fighters stormed neighboring Dagestan in order to support local villages in their struggle against Russian troops that had been redeployed in the area to reestablish Russian sovereignty over the region. The military move led by Shamil Basayev and Khattab was religiously legitimized by fatwas (Islamic religious rulings) issued by Islamic clerics from Saudi Arabia and Pakistan, and was conducted under the slogan of combating world Zionism, an ideology that was far from the original aspirations of Chechen nationalism that provoked the outbreak of the First Chechen War in 1994.[166]

During the first week of the invasion, Wahhabi forces were successful, taking thirty-six villages from the Russians and declaring the region as "The Independent Islamic State of Dagestan." Soon after, the "Islamic Shura of Dagestan" was established as a governing body. The forces applied Sharia law over the occupied territory, selected Basayev as the region's overall commander, and declared war on Russia. These provocative moves triggered Russian retaliation. Supported by thousands of Dagestani police officers and villagers who rejected the presence of the Wahhabis, Russian forces stormed the Wahabi enclave in Dagestan and liberated it within weeks, forcing most of the Islamic fighters back to Chechnya. Vladimir Putin, the Russian prime minister, took advantage of the momentum of the Russian success in Dagestan to extend military maneuvers into Chechnya in order to uproot the social and political conditions that permitted the foreign invasion. Backed by strong public support, Putin ordered Russian-led attacks to continue in Chechnya, bombing Wahhabi strongholds in places like Vedeno, Urus-Martan, and Gudermes. What began as a rapid conquest of external land quickly turned into an internal defensive war for the Chechen Wahabis, soon defined as the Second Russo-Chechen War, which continues today.[167]

Soon, war dynamics and tactics adopted the characteristics of the foreign mujahidin modus operandi, as scores of bombings ravaged apartment complexes and shopping centers inside Russia, killing more than 300 people. These bombings were indicative of a future change in tactics. Even though Chechens engaged in terrorism during the first conflict, it was characterized by less frequency and brutality. Terrorist tactics such as hijacking airplanes and placing explosive devices in public places around Russia were deployed in order to frighten Moscow and attract the attention of the international community.[168]

During the second war, terrorism became the weapon of choice of the Chechen Wahhabis. Unlike the first war, mujahidin trained in Khattab's camps carried out hundreds of attacks both in Chechnya and inside Russian hinterland. While the perpetrators were mostly Chechens, their trainers were mostly Arab mujahidin. In 2003, Colonel Ilya Shabalkin, spokesman for the Russian forces in Chechnya, indicated that only about 200 foreign fighters were present in the region but highlighted their importance: "The Arabs are the specialists, they are the experts in mines and communications."[169] Forensic analysis of the land mines and detonators supported Shabalkin's claim, indicating that the designs and mechanisms of the devices used in Chechnya were identical to devices employed in the Middle East and other jihad arenas.[170]

Soon, Chechnya became the preferred jihad arena for jihadists from all over the world. In 2002, a small group of Arab mujahidin from al-Zarqawi's group Jund al-Sham were deployed in the Pankisi Gorge, a remote area of Chechnya-neighboring Georgia in order to provide Chechen fighters with shelter against Russian attacks and provide logistical support for Khattab's mujahidin fighting inside Chechnya.

Aside from technical expertise, Islamic clerics provided religious guidance and issued fatwas to support Khattab and his successors, Abu Walid and Abu Hafs al-Urduni, and to justify terrorist attacks and martyrdom operations.[171]

Chechnya became the new magnet for mujahidin mainly from Western European countries, as scores of Islamic fighters, following a long process of Islamic radicalization, traveled to Chechnya in order to conduct violent jihad and join the fighting against the Russians. Even the members of the Hamburg cell, who became the pilots in the 9/11 attacks, viewed Chechnya as their first priority for jihad and intended to go there before they were drafted for the operation by al-Qaeda.[172]

Moreover, Wahhabi influence and jihadi tactics are evident in the emergence of suicide attacks in Chechnya. While no suicide attack was conducted in the region before 2000, the Second Russo-Chechen War has been characterized by dozens of suicide attacks, many of which have been conducted by female suicide bombers, both inside and outside Chechnya. Scores of suicide attacks were conducted in Moscow's subway system, at a rock concert, and even against two Russian airliners. The more famous attacks—the brazen operation at the Dubrovka Theater and the siege of a school in Beslan—were conducted by ready-to-die fanatics trained by the Arab mujahidin. Russian authorities have alleged that most of these attacks had been planned and financed by Khattab and Abu Walid.

We believe that this change in modus operandi of the Chechen insurgency during the second war is due to the influence of Wahhabi fundamentalism on growing numbers of young Chechen men and women.

Local Chechen and Regional Groups with External Radical Islamic Influence

Islamic International Peacekeeping Brigade (IIPB)

The Islamic International Peacekeeping Brigade (IIPB) was established in 1998 by Shamil Basayev and Khattab. The IIPB is composed mostly of nationalistic, ethnic Chechen fighters as well as Arabs and other foreign fighters who adhere to an extremist Islamic doctrine. The IIPB has maintained operational bases all over Caucasia in Chechnya, Azerbaijan, Georgia, Russia, and Turkey. IIPB's main modus operandi is the use of explosives targeting Russian forces, occasionally using suicide tactics. Unlike other Chechen resistance groups, the IIPB's main objective is not only the creation of an independent Chechen state, but also to impose Sharia as Chechen state law.

The IIPB established training camps in southeastern Chechnya, which trained unemployed young Chechen men and Muslims throughout Russia for a jihad far greater in scope than originally envisioned by Chechnya's nationalist leadership.[173] Since 1999, the IIPB was responsible for several attacks against Russian military and civilian targets inside the Russian hinterland. IIPB's most famous and devastating attack was the seizure of Moscow's Dubrovka Theater on 23 October 2002.[174]

Riyad us-Saliheyn Martyrs Brigade

The Riyad us-Saliheyn Martyrs Brigade is a terrorist organization that promotes the creation of an independent Islamic republic in Chechnya as well as in other predominantly Muslim parts of Russia such as Dagestan, Kabardino-Balkaria, Ingushetia, Ossetia, and Tataria. The group, whose name means "requirements for getting into paradise," promotes a radical Islamic doctrine and some scholars believe that it possesses strong ties to al-Qaeda.[175] The group used widows of local Chechen fighters to conduct suicide attacks against the Russian military in Chechnya as well as civilian targets inside the Russian hinterland, including apartment buildings, trains, and aircraft. These widows, better known as the "Black Widows," conducted their first attack in December 2002, destroying Chechen government headquarters, killing seventy-two, and injuring 280 people. An attack in August 2003 targeting a hospital housing both civilian and military patients killed fifty-two and injured seventy-two, while the August 2004 attacks crushed two Russian airliners and bombed Moscow's subway system.

The group remains an active security threat in the region despite its setback following the loss of its leader Shamil Basayev in July 2006.[176]

Special Purpose Islamic Regiment (SPIR)

The Special Purpose Islamic Regiment (SPIR) was established by Arbi Barayev during the years of the cease-fire (1996–1999) between the two Russo-Chechen conflicts. The group's sole objective is the liberation of Chechnya from Russian dominance and the formation of an independent Chechen state. SPIR allied with other organizations that have been operating in Chechnya, including foreign Islamic groups. Following the collapse of the ceasefire in 1999, SPIR has expanded its operations, executing numerous attacks against Russian forces in Chechnya. Furthermore, SPIR played a significant role in the Dubrovka Theater attack in October 2002 alongside IIPB. As a result of Russian counter activity, SPIR has experienced frequent changes in its leadership. Amir Kazbek now leads the organization, which continues to conduct operations aimed to drive Russian forces out of Chechnya.[177]

Dagestani Shari'a Jamaat

The Dagestani insurgency, led by Rasul Makasharipov, has become part of the conflict in Chechnya. The group was established in 2002 under the name Dzhennet (Paradise). It is mostly active in the Dagestan region of Russia and has leaked into neighboring Chechnya. The group's objectives include the creation of an independent Dagestani state and implementation of Sharia as Dagestan state law. Dagestani Shari'a Jamaat mainly targets local Dagestani political figures as well as Russian security forces. In addition to operational activities, Dagestani Shari'a Jamaat invests heavily in propaganda, often claiming attacks on behalf of other groups; publicizing atrocities committed by Russian special forces in Chechnya; and publicly criticizing Russian policies and commenting on international political events, such as the Israel-Hezbollah War of 2006 and the execution of Russian diplomats in Iraq.[178]

Ingush Jama'at Shariat

The Ingush Jama'at Shariat is a Muslim separatist group composed of operational activists from Ingushetia and Chechnya, which aims to establish an independent Islamic state in Caucasia. The group has close ties to other active terrorist organizations in the region and was responsible for a series of arson attacks on homes occupied by "Russian colonists" throughout Ingushetia. The group, led by Amir Khabibulla, vowed to continue these kinds of attacks as long as its claims for independence in the Caucasus region were rejected by the Russians.[179]

Foreign Mujahidin Infrastructure

As mentioned, the founder of the Arab mujahidin forces in Chechnya, Khattab, also served as the group's first Amir. Khattab was killed in March 2002 and was succeeded by the Saudi Abu al-Walid. Under al-Walid's leadership, the mujahidin in Chechnya adopted a more global approach, adhering to al-Qaeda's agenda. Al-Walid issued several fatwas and political addresses to target U.S. interests in the region.[180] He was killed in April 2004 and was succeeded by Yusuf Amerat a.k.a. Abu Hafs al-Urduni (The Jordanian). Amerat has exploited his ties with al-Zarqawi in Iraq, who strongly supports the Chechen cause. They have expressed moral support for each other via jihadist websites. As some of the local inhabitants of Zarqawi's hometown of Zarqa are of Chechen origin, he has previously expressed his desire to fight in Chechnya.[181] Abu Hafs al-Urduni was killed in November 2006 and was succeeded by Muhannad, a citizen of the United Arab Emirates currently leading the Islamic Battalion.[182]

Since the outbreak of the Second Russo-Chechen War, the conflict in Chechnya has had a growing impact on the Global Jihadi Movement and has become a key jihad arena attracting hundreds of jihadi volunteers to the region.[183] Arabs, North Africans, Yemenis, and volunteers from Western countries such as France have traveled to Chechnya.[184]

The Chechen struggle attracted the interest of prominent jihadi elements operating in the international arena. Al-Zawahiri has displayed an interest in the development of jihadi events in the North Caucasus: "if the Chechens and other Caucasus mujahidin reach the shores of the oil-rich Caspian, the only thing that will separate them from Afghanistan will be the neutral state of Turkmenistan. This will form a Mujahid Islamic belt to the south of Russia."[185] Before al-Zawahiri's EIJ merged with bin Laden's umbrella group in 1998, he embarked on a fact-finding mission to Chechnya to investigate the establishment of a camp for his followers.[186]

Another example of the Global Jihadization of the Chechen War is evidenced by the Algerian GSPC's July 2006 address following Basayev's death, praising his role in fighting Russian forces in Chechnya.

Although the overall number of foreign Arab fighters in Chechnya has always been relatively small and never played an essential role in shaping the conflict, their influence over the war's characteristics was greater than their actual numbers. The players, tactics, and very nature of the Second Chechen War have been profoundly influenced by the activities of the foreign mujahidin who turned a national separatist conflict into a militant Islamist uprising, within the framework of the Global Jihad Movement.[187] Even if Chechen terrorism has yet to spread beyond Chechnya and Russia, the existing Wahhabi atmosphere as well as the growing operational presence of similar Global Jihad elements in the country suggest that it is only a matter of time before Chechen terrorism (by local and foreign veterans) is exported to the international arena, targeting the classic enemies of the jihadi movement, first and foremost the United States and Israel.

Jihad Arenas—the Aftermath of the "Arab Spring" in the Middle East

The term "Arab Spring" refers to dramatic events that emerged throughout the region in the beginning of 2011, changing dramatically the political landscape of many countries of the region, thus changing the entire region's political spectrum and stability. The Arab Spring emerged throughout the Middle East by modern, secular young citizens that searched for a better future for themselves. There was no Muslim Brotherhood or Salafi Jihadi presence at all in the events that provoked the Arab Springs riots that were aimed at the local and in most cases very corrupted regimes. Much of the process was nonviolent, without the involvement of al-Qaeda operatives or supporters, and was conducted under liberal slogans quite at odds with the organization's Salafist Jihadist orientation, directed at local and in most cases corrupted regimes. The slogans that characterized the Arab Springs were of Western style completely contradicted to those of the political Islam. Terms like democracy, justice, freedom, equality, gender issues, and woman liberations were heard throughout the Middle East and eventually led to the toppling down of several regimes. Yet, those events created a chaotic situation that vacuumed political elements that were traditionally organized into the political spectrum, while decreasing first and foremost the ability of the traditional law enforcement agencies to cope efficiently with the riots which provide new elements—radicals and jihadi—to revive and resume operational and violent activities. In many Middle Eastern countries the riots resulted in numerous breakouts from prison of political prisoners including thousands that were charged for jihadi and terrorist activities. These events have great impact on the political spectrum of many countries that mostly influence the current status and activities of the jihadi elements within their borders.

Egypt

The Muslim Brotherhood took advantage of the new democracy and won the general elections in Egypt in January 2012, and their leader Mohamed Morsi was democratically elected as president in May of the same year. Looking more deeply into the results of the Egyptian elections and the months that followed it reveals a more complicated picture. Since there were only two candidates in the final round—one from the Muslim Brotherhood and the other a member of the old Mubarak regime, the Egyptian average citizen had no real candidate that shared the values they went to the streets a year earlier in demand for a change. Thus the voting rate reached only 50 percent as about 900,000 Egyptian voters bothered to get out of their homes and went to the polls only to put a blank note. The final results showed a difference of only 800,000 votes in favor of the MB candidate Mohamed Morsi. These figures represent the atmosphere in Egypt that time among the secular. The young and seculars that went to the streets in search of a change and eventually toppled the corrupt Mubarak regime accepted the election of the Muslim Brotherhood candidate and referred to it as part of the democratic process they were searching for. Change has oc-curred and the democratization process in Egypt is irreversible, they believed. Encouraged by the figures of the election which reflects, they believed, the true support for political Islam in Egypt (about 25–30 percent only), they hoped to get ready and organize for the next round behind one elected candidate that will easily win the next round . Yet, the elected president Morsi and the MB tried to conduct several moves that would stop the democratic process and anchored Muslim Brotherhood leader-ship for life. As these maneuvers grew and the majority of Egyp-tians acknowledged, their revolution was being sort of stolen, they hit the streets again in million peoples' rallies all across the country, stimulating the military to conduct a coup d'état that has ousted the Muslim Brotherhood from power. We believe that the popular flames erupted in Egypt as a consequence of the coup d'état and the selection of General al-Sisi as the new presi-dent on June 2014 are going to gradually reduce mainly because of the MB's nonviolent DNA. Yet, the continuation of the cha-otic situation provided a large window of opportunities for the Salafi Jihadi terrorist elements to regain and significantly extend their operational activity aiming to destabilize the new military regime and the whole region. Their main hub of operation and logistic infrastructure is being deployed in a remote area that is far from the hand of the central regime, which is characterized by almost inaccessible terrain—the Tora Bora of Egypt—the Si-nai Peninsula.

Beside fighting the Egyptian military and police and creating a de facto radical Islamic enclave in this lawless land their de-clared strategic target is to drag Israel into the internal Egyptian conflict, thus destabilizing the Israeli-Egyptian peace accord.

Currently there are two major terror groups that are operat-ing in Sinai and along the Israeli-Egyptian border. One is Ansar Bait al-Maqadis (The supporters of Jerusalem)—a sinayan group that is based mostly on Islamic radical individuals from Sinai. This group claimed responsibility for dozens of attacks in the area in the last three years and is considered as the most active one in the peninsula. The group has conducted dozens of attacks against the Egyptian military and police in Sinai using all kinds of modi operandi. In addition they attacked foreign tourists as well as infrastructural facilities in Sinai such as the natural gas pipeline. The groups have launched rockets against the Israeli Red Sea coastal city of Eilat on several occasions and executed large-scale attacks along the Israeli-Egyptian border.[188] The activity of the group was singled out for public praise by al-Qaeda and its leader Ayman al-Zawahiri which called Mujahidin to come to Sinai and operate within the ranks of the group.[189]

The second group is the Majlis al-Shura LilMujahiddin Fi Aqnaf Bait al-Maqdis (Consulting Council for the Holy Warriors in the Outskirt of Jerusalem). In June 2012 two Salafi groups from Gaza—Tawhid Wal Jihad and Jaish al-Islam—along with two other small Salafi Jihadi groups from the strip, Jund Ansarallah and Ansar al-Sunna, teamed up to establish an umbrella organization called the "Consulting Council for the Holy Warriors in the Outskirt of Jerusalem" which unite the entire Salafi Jihadi elements operating in the Gaza Strip.[190] The new group has originated several rocket attacks from Gaza against Israeli settlements along the Israeli-Gaza border, yet since the overthrow of the Mohamed Morsi–led Muslim Brotherhood administration in Egypt in mid-2013 and the pressure imposed on the Palestinian Hamas that controls the Gaza Strip as a consequence, a significant part of the new umbrella group's operational activities were shifted to the neighboring Sinai Peninsula. The new group conducted several rocket attacks against Israeli territory including the launch of rockets against the Israeli southern city of Eilat which is mostly popular among Israeli and international vacationers. In addition the group was involved with several attacks against Israeli forces and civilians along the Israeli-Egyptian border in Sinai Peninsula.[191]

Libya

Arab Spring riots in Libya, which erupted in February 2011, quickly turned into a civil war between forces loyal to Libya's longtime dictator ruler Muammar Qadhafi and those seeking to oust his government. Many Islamists and jihadi elements played a major role in the Libyan civil war which ended with the overthrow of the Qadhafi regime and continued to possess a significant role in the post-Qadhafi-era Libyan political spectrum.[192]

The major element and the most violent group among the jihadi elements in Libya has been the Ansar al-Sharia Libya, which promotes the implementation of Sharia law all over Libya. The organization was involved in violent internal rivalries and conflicts among the rebels as well the destruction of Sufi shrines all over the country.[193]

The most devastating attack attributed to Ansar al-Sharia was the attack conducted against the U.S. consulate in Benghazi (northern Libya) on 11 September 2012, which resulted in the death of four American diplomats including U.S. ambassador J. Christopher Stevens. On 6 August 2013 a U.S. official charged the leader and founder of Ansar al-Sharia, Ahmad Abu Khatallah, for his role in the attack.[194]

As a result of the attack on the U.S. consulate, Ansar al-Sharia was forced to temporarily limits its presence, yet by the end of 2013 it has regained its activity in Benghazi.

In addition to the local jihadi Libyan elements which are currently enrolled in the political spectrum of the country, hundreds of foreign jihadi fighters, mostly from the Middle Eastern countries and veterans of the jihadi arenas of Afghanistan and Iraq, took part in the Libyan civil war[195] since many of them are still assessed to be present in the country.

Syria

As in Libya, the popular uprising of the "Arab Spring" quickly deteriorated into a full-scale civil war between the Bashar al-Assad regime and hundreds of rebel groups possessing of varied affiliation and political ideology all across Syria.

Unlike Egypt and Libya which are basically homogenous countries with an overwhelming majority of Sunni Muslim citizens, Syria has always been a much more heterogeneous community. Since the mid-1960s, the ruling sect in Syria is the minority Alawite which represents about 13 percent of the overall 23 million Syrian population. The biggest religious sect in Syria is the Sunni Muslims, which comprises 70 percent of the population. Other sects are Christians (9 percent) and Druze (3.5 percent).[196] In terms of nationalities, the Kurds in Syria compose about 7 percent of the population, mostly deployed in the north and northeast parts of the country.

The different elements which take part in the Syrian civil war have positioned themselves in accordance with their secretarial lines. On the one hand the Assad regime, that has relied solely on the Alawite sector, which traditionally compose the overall majority of the Syrian army command, while the insurgent groups that wish to topple him down heavily rely on the Sunni population of the country.

As was already mentioned, the insurgent groups include varied political and ideological approaches which can roughly be divided into three major parts: Syrian Nationalists, Islamists, and Salafi Jihadi elements.

Jabhat al-Nusra is a Salafi Jihadi outfit that has emerged during the sectarian civil war outburst in Syria as a consequence of the internal riots erupted in the country in 2011 as part of the "Arab Spring" aimed to topple down the Bashar al-Assad dictatorship regime. About 300 different military entities—groups, regiments, and platoons—became involved in the Syrian civil war within the framework of the so-called rebels, yet Jabhat al-Nusra distinguished itself with its unabashed Salafi Jihadi imagery and rhetoric. Overthrowing Assad represented only half of the battle and success would come only once the entire regime is replaced with an Islamic state following Salafi principles. Jabhat al-Nusra regularly takes responsibility for suicide attacks in civilian neighborhoods and is viewed by al-Qaeda as its favorite affiliate in Syria.

As of early 2013 al-Nusra is estimated to have around 5,000 members and the structure of the group varies across Syria in accordance with regional characteristics and capabilities; in Damascus the organization operates in an underground clandestine cell system, while in Aleppo the group is organized along semiconventional military lines, with units divided into brigades, regiments, and platoons. All potential recruits must undergo a ten-day religious training course, followed by a fifteen- to twenty-day military training program.

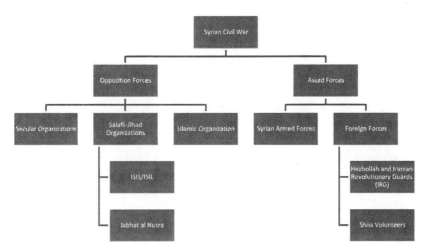

Chart 5.2.   Insurgent Groups in Syria by Ideological Affiliation.[197]

Al-Nusra contains a hierarchy of religious bodies, with a small Majlis-al-Shura (Consultative Council) at the top, making national decisions on behalf of the group. The leader of the group is Mohamad al-Jawlani.[198]

Islamic State of Iraq and al-Sham (ISIS)

In April 2013, the Islamic State of Iraq's (ISI) leader Abu Baker al-Baghdadi announced a merger between ISI and Jabhat al-Nusra forming one united organization, the "Islamic State of Iraq and al-Sham"[199]—ISIS.[200] In this statement Baghdadi announced the cancellation of the name Islamic State of Iraq and the cancellation of the name Jabhat al-Nusra, and the joining of the two under one name: the "Islamic State of Iraq and al-Sham." Unexpectedly Jawlani rejected the merger and pledged loyalty solely to al-Qaeda leader al-Zawahiri. As a consequence of the rejection ISIS started operating in Syria, excluding its operational activity from Jabhat al-Nusra, and based it totally on ISI foundations.

There are "significant differences" between Jabhat al-Nusra and ISIS; the ISIS tends to be more focused on establishing its own rule on conquered territory than in defeating the al-Assad government. The ISIS is far more ruthless in building an Islamic state, carrying out sectarian attacks, and imposing Sharia law immediately. Since mid-2013 ISIS has carried out dozens of suicide attacks in different parts of Syria and is currently considered as the most brutal element operating within the framework of the Syrian civil war. Both JN and ISIS include foreign fighters within their ranks, yet while JN is seen as homegrown by Syrians, the ISIS in contrast is described as foreign "occupiers" by many Syrians. In February 2014, Ayman al-Zawahiri announced that al-Qaeda was severing ties with the ISIS due to their brutal behavior toward the local population.[201]

Different sources have estimated ISIS manpower at about 7,000–10,000 well-equipped, experienced, and trained activists. Despite this relatively low number, ISIS became, since its deployment in Syria during April 2013, the most dominant operational factor among the insurgent groups, and the organization took control over a large part of Syria especially in the eastern and central provinces. ISIS uses the most brutal and lethal tactics both against its military enemies as well as the local civilian population.[202]

On 29 June 2014 ISIS announced the formation of the caliphate, changed its name to the Islamic State (IS), and named Abu Bakr al-Baghdadi as its caliph. Baghdadi is now to be referred to as "khalifah Ibrahim."[203] Since this announcement the new "Islamic State" was able to annex significant territorial gains, mostly in Iraq, through their summer 2014 military campaign, creating an IS territorial sequence on both ends of the border. IS offensive, which was characterized by harsh brutality, conducted mostly over the civilian population, and with rapid military advance which threatens the stability of the entire region, stimulated an American aerial military intervention and dramatic political changes in the internal Iraqi political spectrum with the sack of Iraqi prime minister Nur al-Maliki and the selection of a new prime minister, Haider al-Abadi.[204]

As in other regions, the Syrian conflict served as a magnet for foreign elements. While the Bashar al-Assad regime enjoys the support of its longtime allies Iran and Hezbollah many volunteers from dozens of countries and regions arrived on the scene and are fighting alongside the insurgent ranks. Unsurprisingly the vast majority of them find their way to the ranks of the Salafi Jihadi groups first and foremost ISIS, and Jabhat al-Nusra in a much lesser extent. Many of the foreign fighters arrive in Syria from Western countries. Estimates of the current numbers of Western foreign fighters vary between 1,200–3,000 and they are seen as one of the main future threats to the West homeland security upon their return home, equipped with operational know-how, ideological zeal as well as jihadi networking affiliation. Mehdi Namoush, a French citizen and a veteran of the ISIS in the Syrian civil war that conducted a most lethal assault attack in the Jewish Museum in Brussels in May 2014 (killing three people, two of them Israeli tourists), should be considered as only the initial case of this process.[205] In addition, it seems that ISIS's Internet fame and visual brutality influences lone wolves from the Western world. It should be emphasized within this framework that French attacker Amedy Coulibaly who conducted lethal attacks against French police and Jewish targets in January 2015, which resulted in the death of five French citizens and several more injured, has attributed his attack to ISIS.[206]

Notes

1. Sections of this chapter have been published previously as Rohan Gunaratna, "Al Qaeda: The Threat from Tribal Pakistan," *Pakistan's Quagmire: Security, Strategy, and the Future of the Islamic-Nuclear Nation,* Usama Butt, ed. New York: The Continuum International Publishing Group, 2010, pp. 157–74; and Gunaratna, "Terrorist Threat in Iraq: Origins, Development and Impact," *Beyond Iraq: The Future of World Order,* Singapore: World Scientific Publishing Co. Pte. Ltd., 2011, pp. 109–48.

2. As of January 2009, the intelligence community of Pakistan estimated the total number of Arabs serving in al-Qaeda in FATA at ninety. Personal visit to Pakistan, 17–23 January 2009.

3. Ibid.

4. U.S. assessments based on intelligence and debriefing of captives, January 2009.

5. Rohan Gunaratna and Aviv Oreg, "Al Qaeda's Organizational Structure and Its Evolution," *Studies in Conflict & Terrorism*, Vol. 33, No. 12 (2010), p. 1051.

6. "Indonesia: JI Militant Noordin Top's New Group," *Stratfor*, 1 February 2006, http://www.stratfor.com/memberships/50884/indonesia_ji_militant_noordin_tops_new_group?ip_auth_redirect=1, cited in Drew Davis, "Al Qaeda in the Malay Archipelago: A Case Study of the July 2009 JW Marriott & Ritz-Carlton Bombings in Jakarta, Indonesia," *Pax Americana Institute*, March 2010, p. 5.

7. Gunaratna and Oreg, pp. 1059–60.

8. Map of tribal Pakistan, provided by the Pakistani army to the International Centre for Political Violence and Terrorism Research.

9. Gunaratna and Syed Adnan Ali Shah Bukhari, "Making Peace with Pakistani Taliban to Isolate Al-Qaeda: Successes and Failures in Bangladesh," *Institute of Peace and Security Studies (BIPSS)*, Vol. 1, No. 2, Second Quarter, 2008, p. 3, http://www.bipss.org.bd/download/Vol1_%20No2_Second%20Quarter2008.pdf, accessed 23 April 2012.

10. Zulf Khan Afridi and Azka Jameel, "Operation in Wana: Wanted al-Qaeda Ally Killed," *Pakistan Times*, 19 June 2004.

11. "How the Threat Has Evolved," *Mi5*, accessed on 20 January 2015. https://www.mi5.gov.uk/home/the-threats/terrorism/international-terrorism/how-the-threat-has-evolved.html.

12. CeifiT special report "Is Al-Qaeda on the Brink of Conducting New Wave of Attacks in the West?" at http://www.upsite.co.il/uploaded/files/626_8230c8bf67553cd90811a026c3d14bbf.pdf.

13. Shahzad is an American citizen and accountant who is married with a daughter.

14. "United States of America Vs Faisal Shahzad" at http://s3.amazonaws.com/nytdocs/docs/333/333.pdf, pp 4–10. Accessed 18 June 2014.

15. Craig Whitlock, "Al Qaeda Growing Online Offensive," *Washington Post*, 24 June 2008 at http://www.washingtonpost.com/wp-dyn/content/article/2008/06/23/AR2008062302135.html. Accessed 17 June 2014.

16. Sayed Salahudeen, "Afghanistan Says Foreign Fighters Coming from Iraq," *Reuters*, 4 February 2009.

17. Karen de Young, "Afghan Conflict Will Be Reviewed: Obama Sees Troops As Buying Time, Not Turning Tide," *Washington Post*, 13 January 2009.

18. "Challenges the Nation Faces," *The Nation*, accessed 23 January 2015. http://nation.com.pk/columns/23-Jan-2015/challenges-the-nation-faces.

19. J. Mueller, "The Iraq Syndrome," *Foreign Affairs* (2005): 1–5.

20. "The U.S. and Afghan Tragedy: Remembering Recent History," *Foreign Policy* in Focus, accessed on 23 January 2015. http://fpif.org/the_us_and_afghan_tragedy/.

21. Gunaratna, "Terrorist Threat in Iraq: Origins, Development and Impact," *Beyond Iraq: The Future of World Order,* Singapore: World Scientific Publishing Co. Pte. Ltd., 2011, p. 110.

22. Ibid.

23. "Iraqi Kurdistan Profile," *BBC*, 20 January 2015, accessed on 23 January 2015. http://www.bbc.com/news/world-middle-east-28147263.

24. The most lethal event occurred from 16–17 March 1988 in Halabja, a town in the Sulaymaniyah governorate, located about ten miles from the Iranian border. Saddam's Iraqi forces used chemical weapons against the Kurdish civilian population.

25. Links between Al Qaeda and Kurdish Groups, Briefing by Security Service of Kurdistan, 14 February 2009.

26. Abdul Rabi Rasul Sayyaf, personal interview, Paghman, Afghanistan, 20 March 2008.

27. "Footage Showing Al-Qaeda leader in Afghanistan Abd Al-Hadi Al-Iraqi Downing an American Fighter Jet," *Al-Arabiya TV* (Dubai/Saudi Arabia), 29 May 2005, video footage.

28. Gunaratna and Oreg, p. 1057.

29. Ibid.

30. Sa'adoon Mohammed Abdul Latif a.k.a. Abu Wa'il, an Iraqi intelligence officer, also left Saddam's service and visited Afghanistan in 1999. He eventually joined Ansar al-Islam, the Kurdish Islamist group with links to al-Qaeda.

31. Of the 250 videotapes recovered by CNN in Afghanistan, at least two tapes were IMK or pro-IMK. "'Al-Qaeda Archive' Uncovered," *BBC News,* 19 August 2002, http://news.bbc.co.uk/2/hi/south_asia/2202670.stm, accessed 23 April 2012; Nic Robertson and Mike Boettcher, "Tapes Give Evidence of al Qaeda's Global Reach," *CNN,* 22 August 2002, http://articles.cnn.com/2002-08-22/us/terror.tape.main_1_al-qaeda-rohan-gunaratna-arab-fighters?_s=PM:US, accessed 23 April 2012.

32. Links between Al Qaeda and Kurdish Groups, Briefing by Security Service of Kurdistan, 14 February 2009. There are several photographs of these leaders in Afghanistan.

33. Head of Islamic Groups, Security Service of Kurdistan, personal interview, 13 February 2009.

34. When Mohomed Sofi was killed three weeks after the formation of Kurdish Hamas, Abu Musab al-Zarqawi, the leader of Tawhid Wal Jihad (later al-Qaeda in Iraq), appointed Omar Baziany as the Wali (chief Amir) of Baghdad.

35. On 5 February 1999, after consultations with Congress, the U.S. administration designated in Presidential Determination 99-13 the Islamic Movement of Kurdistan (IMK) as eligible to receive U.S. military assistance under the ILA. The support is referenced in the State Department's report to Congress in June 2000. Kenneth Katzman, "CRS Report for Congress: Iraq's Opposition Movements," Congressional Research Service, The Library of Congress, Order Code 98–179F, 27 June 2000.

36. Sunil Ram, "The Enemy of My Enemy: The Odd Link between Ansar al-Islam, Iraq and Iran," *The Canadian Institute of Strategic Studies,* April 2003. Another important leader was Abu Abdul Rahman, who had links to al-Qaeda and was killed in fighting in October 2001.

37. Jim Muir, "Al-Qaeda's Influence Grows in Iraq," *BBC News,* 24 July 2002, http://news.bbc.co.uk/2/hi/middle_east/2149499.stm, accessed 23 April 2012.

38. http://www.nawend.com/ansarislam.htm (expired URL), cited in Jonathan Schanzer, "Ansar al-Islam: Back in Iraq," *Middle East Quarterly,* Winter 2004, Vol. XI, No. 1, p. 43.

39. Country Information and Policy Unit, Immigration and Nationality Directorate, Home Office, UK, "COUNTRY ASSESSMENT – IRAQ October 2002." Accessed on 23 January 2015. http://www.justice.gov/eoir/vll/country/uk_cntry_assess/oct2002/1002Iraq.pdf.

40. Michael Ware, "Kurdistan: Death in the Afternoon," *Time,* 26 February 2003, http://www.time.com/time/world/article/0,8599,426910,00.html, accessed 23 April 2012.

41. Ibid.

42. Katherine Shrader, "Spy Chief Pushes for Action in Pakistan," *Associated Press,* 27 February 2007.

43. "Report of the Select Committee on Intelligence on Postwar Findings on Iraq WMD Program and Links to Terrorism and How They Compare with Prewar Assessments" at http://www.intelligence.senate.gov/phaseiiaccuracy.pdf p.86. Accessed on 16 June 2014.

44. Al-Zarqawi was not a member of al-Qaeda until late 2004. He was a Jordanian prisoner who was released following the general amnesty proclaimed in Jordan after the death of King Hussein in 1999. He arrived in Afghanistan and tried to join al-Qaeda but was refused. With the help of al-Qaeda, he moved to the Afghan city of Herat and

established his own organization, Jund al-Sham (the Soldiers of Sham), composed of activists mostly recruited from the Levant region (Syria, Jordan, Lebanon, Israel, and Palestine). See Gunaratna and Oreg, p. 1070.

45. "Transcript of Powell's U.N. Presentation," *CNN*, 6 February 2003, http://edition.cnn.com/2003/US/02/05/sprj.irq.powell.transcript/, accessed 3 May 2012. A Palestinian Jordanian, Adnan Muhammad Sadik a.k.a. Abu Atia was a graduate of Zarqawi's camp in Afghanistan who served in Pankishi valley in Georgia against the Russians in Chechnya. He was arrested in Azerbaijan and handed over to the CIA. Based on Abu Atia's interrogation, Powell remarked that at least nine North Africans were dispatched in 2001 to France, Britain, Spain, Italy, Germany, Russia, and elsewhere in Europe to conduct poison and explosive attacks. As of early 2003, 116 operatives, including the North African operatives, were arrested. Andrew McGregor, "Ricin Fever: Abu Musab al Zarqawi in Pankisi Gorge," *Terrorism Monitor*, Vol. 2, Issue 24, 15 December 2004.

46. On 28 October 2003, an executive officer of the U.S. Agency for International Development (USAID), Laurence Michael Foley, sixty-two, was shot several times in the chest and head while he walked toward his car in Amman, the capital of Jordan. "US Diplomat Shot Dead in Jordan," *BBC*, 28 October 2002, http://news.bbc.co.uk/2/hi/middle_east/2367311.stm, accessed 3 May 2012; Jean-Charles Brisard and Damien Martinez, *Zarqawi: The New Face of Al-Qaeda*, New York: Other Press, 2005.

47. From Iraq, Abu Musab visited Syria in 2002, where he organized finance, weapons, and training for his cell members in Syria and arranged for their departure for Jordan with instructions. It is very likely that he also traveled to Jordan. Jamal Halaby, "11 Terror Suspects Charged in Jordan," *Associated Press* via *Boston Globe*, 5 December 2002, http://www.boston.com/dailyglobe2/132/nation/11_terror_suspects_charged_in_Jordan+.shtml, accessed 12 December 2002 (expired URL).

48. Rowan Scarborough, "U.S. Tracked Top al Qaeda Planner's visit to Baghdad," *Washington Times*, 4 October 2002.

49. Sir John Scarlett, head, Secret Intelligence Service (SIS), personal interview (Gunaratna), UK, 2006. Before he became the head of SIS on 6 May 2004, Scarlett was chair of the Joint Intelligence Committee. "JIC Chief Concedes He Was Aware of Intelligence Staff's Worries over Dossier," *The Independent*, 24 September 2003.

50. Bob Drogin, *Curveball: Spies, Lies, and the Man Behind Them—The Real Reason America Went to War in Iraq*, Great Britain: Ebury Press,

2007, p. 319; Gunaratna, "Iraq and Al Qaeda: No Evidence of Alliance," *International Herald Tribune,* 19 February 2003.

51. Years after the invasion and after the intelligence archives on Saddam have been examined, a small group of people still believe that Saddam directed bin Laden. The unsubstantiated comments based on misinterpretation of the information derived during harsh interrogation remain uncorrected, thus propagating the myth. An Iraqi officer said, "Al Qaeda's strong relationship with Baath Party began in 1991 after Osama bin Laden visited with Saddam Hussein, the dictator, to collaborate between both parties." Iraqi Intelligence officer, personal interview (Gunaratna), February 2009. See also the accusation of Iraq's involvement in the 1993 WTC Bombing in Laurie Mylroie, *The War Against America: Saddam Hussein and the World Trade Center Attacks: A Study of Revenge,* Washington, DC: AEI Press, 2000.

52. "Transcript of Powell's U.N. presentation."

53. Borzou Daragahi, "Islamic Militants Show Press the Camp Powell Called Poison Site," *Associated Press,* 8 February 2003.

54. Damien McElroy, "Chemical War Threat by Iraq's Taliban," *The Telegraph,* 12 January 2003.

55. "Radical Islam in Iraqi Kurdistan: The Mouse That Roared?" International Crisis Group Middle East Briefing N°4, 7 February 2003.

56. "Radical Islam in Iraqi Kurdistan: The Mouse That Roared?."

57. CIA, *Iraqi Support for Terrorism,* September 2002. Ibn al-Sheikh is reported to have said that Iraq "provided" chemical and biological weapons training for two al-Qaeda associates in 2000, but "did not know the results of the training." He is also reported to have said: "Iraq—acting on the request of al-Qaeda militant Abu Abdullah, who was Muhammad Atif's emissary—agreed to provide unspecified chemical or biological weapons training for two al-Qaeda associates beginning in December 2000. The two individuals departed for Iraq but did not return, so al-Libi was not in a position to know if any training had taken place." CIA, *Iraqi Support for Terrorism,* January 2003.

58. "Transcript of Powell's U.N. presentation." The statement was made before and after the address to the world body. In Cincinnati in October 2002, Bush informed the public: "Iraq has trained Al Qaeda members in bomb making and poisons and gases." George W. Bush, "President Bush Outlines Iraqi Threat," Remarks by the President on Iraq, Cincinnati Museum Center—Cincinnati Union Terminal, Cincinnati, Ohio, 7 October 2002.

59. "Al Libi indicated that his interrogators did not like his responses and then 'placed him in a small box approximately 50cm x

50cm [20 inches x 20 inches].' He claimed he was held in the box for approximately 17 hours. When he was let out of the box, al Libi claims that he was given a last opportunity to 'tell the truth.' When al Libi did not satisfy the interrogator, al Libi claimed that 'he was knocked over with an arm thrust across his chest and he fell on his back.' Al Libi told CIA debriefers that he then 'was punched for 15 minutes.'" "Postwar Findings about Iraq's WMD Programs and Links to Terrorism and How they Compare with Prewar Assessments," Select Committee on Intelligence United States Senate 109th Congress, 8 September 2006, p. 81, quoting a CIA operational cable, 5 February 2004.

60. Defense Intelligence Agency, cited in Douglas Jehl, "Report Warned Bush Team About Intelligence Suspicions," *The New York Times*, 6 November 2005, http://www.nytimes.com/2005/11/06/politics/06intel.html, accessed 20 May 2012. (Original article is no longer available.)

61. These estimates are based on debriefings of captured Ansar members. About sixty Ansar members were trained in Afghanistan.

62. Elizabeth Rubin, "The Battle for Beyara: A Year of Training for 12 Hours of Fighting in Northern Iraq," *Slate*, 3 April 2003, http://www.slate.com/articles/news_and_politics/foreigners/2003/04/the_battle_for_beyara.html, accessed 15 May 2012.

63. Russell Skelton, "Need for That One Final Shot Was Fatal," *Sydney Morning Herald*, 24 March 2003.

64. C.J. Chivers, "Terrorist Manual May Link Iraqi Group to al Qaeda Information Found at Ansar al-Islam Training Center in Kurdish Enclave," *New York Times*, 27 April 2003.

65. "Ansar al-Islam Prepares for Suicide Attacks," *Daily Times*, 1 April 2003.

66. Ibid.

67. Ibid.

68. Eli J. Lake, "U.S. Negotiates Trade of Terror Suspects," *The Washington Times*, 9 May 2003.

69. The most prominent Sunni groups in Iraq were Salahudeen al-Ayyubi Brigades (JAAMI), al-Fatihin Army, 1920s Revolution Brigades, al-Qassas Brigade, Iraqi Jihad Union, Army of al-Mustafa, Dera Islam Brigade, Saad bin Abi Waqqas Brigades, The Kurdistan Brigades, al-Qaeda in Iraq, Army of the Victorious Sect, Army of Ahlus Sunna Wal Jamaah, Ansar al-Islam, Islamic Army in Iraq, Mujahideen Army, Hamas of Iraq, and al-Rashideen Army.

70. "Main Sunni Group Vows No Deal with US," *Agence France-Presse*, 7 January 2008.

71. Al-Qaeda in Iraq formed a coalition of Sunni groups that was composed of Jeish al-Fatiheen (Conquering Army), Jund al-Sahaba (Soldiers of the Sahaba), Katbiyan Ansar al-Tawhid Wal Sunna (Brigades of Monotheism and Religious Conservatism), Jeish al-Taiifa al-Mansoura (Army of the Victorious Sect), Monotheism Supporters Brigades, Sarayat al-Jihad Group, al-Ghuraba Brigades, al-Ahwal Brigades, Jamaat Ansar al-Sunna (formerly Jeish Ansar al-Sunna, Ansar al-Islam), ar-Rayat as-Sawda (Black Banner Organization), Asaeb Ahl el-Iraq (Factions of the People of Iraq), Wakefulness and Holy War, Abu Theeb's group, and Jeish Abi Baker's group.

72. "Al-Muhajir Pledges Allegiance to Al-Baghdadi, Threatens US, Europe," Jihadist Websites —Open Source Center Report, 11 November 2006. Although al-Qaeda in Iraq claimed its strength to be 12,000 fighters, its hard core was a few thousand fighters.

73. The Command consisted of the Army of the Men of the Naqshbandi Order, The Army of the Prophet's Companions, The Army of the Murabiteen, The Army of al-Hamza, The Army of the Message, The Army of Ibn al-Walid, The United Command of the Mujahideen in Iraq, The Liberation Brigades, The Army of al-Mustafa, The Army of the Liberation of Iraq, Squadrons of the Martyrs, The Army of the Sabireen, The Brigades of the Jihad in the Land of the Two Rivers, The Army of the Knight for the Liberation of the Self-Rule Area, Squadrons of the Jihad in Basra, Jihadist Squadrons of Fallujah, The Patriotic Popular Front for the Liberation of Iraq, The Squadrons of the Husayni Revolution of at-Taff, Squadrons of the Liberation of the South, Army of Haneen, Squadrons of Diyala for Jihad and Liberation, The Squadrons of Glory for the Liberation of Iraq, and the Kurdistan Liberation Army.

74. The Baathist groups are: Fedayeen Saddam (Saddam's Men of Sacrifice), al-Awda (The Return), General Command of the Armed Forces, Resistance and Liberation in Iraq, Iraqi Popular Army, New Return, Patriotic Front, Jihaz al-Iilam al-Siasi lil hizb al-Baath (Political Media Organ of the Ba'ath Party), Popular Resistance for the Liberation of Iraq, and Al-Abud Network.

75. The Shi'a groups were Mahdi Army (Jaish-i-Mahdi); its faction, Abu Deraa; Badr Organization (Badr Brigade/Bader Corps), the armed wing of the Supreme Council for the Islamic Revolution in Iraq (SCIRI); Jund As-Samaa (Soldiers of Heaven/Supporters of the Mahdi); Asaeb Ahl al-Haq (League of the Righteous People); and other special groups backed by Iran.

76. "Guide: Armed Groups in Iraq," *BBC News*, 15 August 2006, http://news.bbc.co.uk/2/hi/middle_east/4268904.stm#top, accessed 9 May 2012. The classified estimates reflect a similar range.

77. Institute for the Study of War, "Intercepted Document Discusses AQI's Strategy." Accessed on 23 January 2015. http://www.understandingwar.org/publications/commentaries/intercepted-document-discusses-aqis-strategy.

78. "English Translation of Ayman al-Zawahiri's letter to Abu Musab al-Zarqawi," *The Weekly Standard*, 12 October 2005, http://www.weekly standard.com/Content/Public/Articles/000/000/006/203gpuul.asp?page=2, accessed 9 May 2012.

79. "Guide: Armed Groups in Iraq."

80. From Iran, Krekar moved to Norway, where he and his family were granted refugee status in 1993 through the United Nations refugee resettlement program. While in Norway, he founded and served as an Imam for the Islamic Vision of Norway. Krekar was briefly detained in the Netherlands in September 2002, but managed to relocate to Norway where he continued to manage a robust Ansar network in Scandinavia.

81. "Terrorist Chemical Expert Killed; Firefighters Find Explosives," American Forces Press Service, U.S. Department of Defense, 8 May 2006, http://www.defenselink.mil/news/newsarticle.aspx?id=15837, accessed 9 May 2012.

82. Brisard and Martinez. This book provides a detailed account of the group.

83. In addition to coalition forces and foreign diplomats, al-Qaeda in Iraq targeted professionals, academics, and national and provincial government officials, especially military and police personnel.

84. "Statement of Mujahidin Shura Council on Establishment of 'Islamic State of Iraq,'" Open Source Center Report FEA20061015028735 15 October 2006.

85. Middle East Annual Assessment, International Centre for Political Violence and Terrorism Research, Singapore, 2006.

86. "Jihadist Website Posts Full English Transcript of Latest Al-Zawahiri Video," Open Source Center Report GMP20061221635002, 21 December 2006.

87. "Zarqawi 'Died of Blast Injuries,'" *BBC News*, 12 June 2006, http://news.bbc.co.uk/2/hi/5072104.stm, accessed 9 May 2012.

88. Unlike al-Zarqawi, Abu Hamza al-Muhajir maintained a low profile. High value detainees, personal interview (Gunaratna), Camp Cropper, December 2006.

89. "Identity of Zarqawi's Successor Still a Riddle," *AFP*, 18 June 2006.

90. "Al-Muhajir Pledges Allegiance to Al-Baghdadi, Threatens US, Europe," Jihadist Websites—Open Source Center Report, 11 November 2006.

91. Abu Hamza al-Muhajir followed Abu Musab's tradition of extensive use of multimedia communication. His messages aimed to galvanize Iraqis and terrorize the United States. In an audio speech posted on the Internet on 28 September 2006, he even called for the use of dirty bombs against U.S. bases in Iraq. "Al-Muhajir Pledges Allegiance to Al-Baghdadi, Threatens US, Europe," Jihadist Websites—Open Source Center Report, 11 November 2006. Furthermore, in an Internet post on 10 November 2006, Abu Hamza al-Muhajir made threats against the United States and Europe.

92. "Amir Gives Speech, Asks Each Muslim To Kill One American in 15 Days," Jihadist Websites—Open Source Center Report 8 September 2006. "Mujahidin Shura Council Issues Abu-Hamza al-Muhajir Audio Calling for Use of Dirty Bombs against US Bases in Iraq," Jihadist Websites—Open Source Center Report 29 September 2006.

93. "Interview of a Member of al Qaeda in Iraq," *BBC*, 18 September 2006.

94. "Iraq Chiefs Vow to Fight al-Qaeda," Iraq—Open Source Center Report, 28 September 2006; "Iraq Chiefs Vow to Fight al-Qaeda," *BBC News*, 18 September 2006, http://news.bbc.co.uk/2/hi/5357340.stm, accessed 15 May 2012; "Iraqi Tribal Leaders Vow to Fight Terrorist Groups," *Radio Free Europe*, 29 September 2006, http://www.rferl.org/content/article/1143726.html, accessed 9 May 2012.

95. "Ministry of Higher Education Found the Bodies of Four Employees of the Ministry, Including Three Bodyguards of Minister," Google trans. *Iraqi National News Agency*, 8 May 2007, http://www.wna-news.com/inanews/news.php?item.2365.15, accessed 9 May 2012.

96. "Iraq Tribe Says It Kills Dozens of Qaeda Fighters," *Reuters*, 26 November 2006, http://uk.reuters.com/article/2006/11/26/uk-iraq-qaeda-idUKPAR63032920061126, accessed 9 May 2012.

97. Ibid.

98. "Al Qaeda's Outrages Swing Sunnis to U.S.," *The Washington Times*, 17 February 2007, http://www.washingtontimes.com/news/2007/feb/17/20070217-123319-5645r/?page=all#pagebreak, accessed 9 May 2012.

99. Ibid.

100. "Attacks Kill 30 in Iraq, Mourners Gunned Down," *Reuters,* 19 February 2007, http://www.reuters.com/article/2007/02/19/us-iraq-bombs-idUSKHA72729620070219, accessed 9 May 2012.

101. Brian Murphy, "Blast May Hint at Growing Sunni Conflict," *Associated Press,* 25 February 2007.

102. "Islamic Army in Iraq (IAI) Selected Communiqués: (Oct. 27, 2007–Nov. 1, 2007)," *The NEFA Foundation,* 1 November 2007, http://www1.nefafoundation.org/miscellaneous/iaidigest1107-1.pdf, accessed 9 May 2012.

103. "Audio Statement from Abu Omar al-Baghdadi," *The NEFA Foundation,* 14 September 2007, http://nefafoundation.org/miscellaneous/FeaturedDocs/nefabaghdadi0907.pdf, accessed 9 May 2012.

104. "An Interview with 'Hamas in Iraq' (Former Faction of the 1920 Revolution Brigades)," *The NEFA Foundation,* 4 January 2008, http://www1.nefafoundation.org/miscellaneous/FeaturedDocs/nefahamasiraq0308.pdf, accessed 9 May 2012.

105. Ibid.

106. Canadian Coalition, http://canadiancoalition.com/forum/messages/19503.shtml. (Expired link.)

107. "Communiqué from 'Army of al-Mustafa,'" *The NEFA Foundation,* 15 April 2008, http://www.nefafoundation.org/miscellaneous/mustafaarmy0408.pdf, accessed 9 May 2012.

108. "'Kurdistan Brigades' Pledges Allegiance to Al Qaeda-Led Group," *CBS News,* 6 October 2008, http://www.cbsnews.com/8301-502684_162-4504531-502684.html, accessed 9 May 2012.

109. "The Shura Council of the Bubaz Tribes Issues a Statement of Reconciliation to the Mujahideen Groups in Iraq, Namely, the Mujahideen Shura Council," Site Institute, 6 October 2006.

110. Ahmed S. Hashim, "The Islamic State: From al-Qaeda Affiliate to Caliphate," *Middle East Policy Council* (Winter 2014), accessed on 22 January 2015. http://www.mepc.org/journal/middle-east-policy-archives/islamic-state-al-qaeda-affiliate-caliphate?print.

111. "Factbox—AQI Names New Leadership," *Reuters,* 16 May 2010, http://in.reuters.com/article/2010/05/16/idINIndia-48526820100516, accessed 9 May 2012.

112. Mark Perry, "US Military Breaks Ranks, Part 1: A Salvo at the White House," *Asia Times,* 23 January 2008, http://www.atimes.com/atimes/Middle_East/JA23Ak02.html, accessed 15 May 2012, p. 1.

113. Sheikh Talal al-Gaood, cited in Perry, p. 1.

114. The first round of talks started in August 2003, when tribal leaders met with U.S. military officials in Jordan. A second round of talks took place in Anbar Province in November 2004.

115. Brendan Miniter, "The Fallujah Brigade: How the Marines Are Pacifying an Iraqi Hot Spot," *The Wall Street Journal*, 1 June 2004. Miniter quotes Col. Coleman: "What they needed to do was drive wedges into the enemy ranks—divide and conquer. From studying the enemy, the Marines realized the insurgents can be separated into five disparate groups with widely varying goals: foreign fighters (some of whom are very skilled bomb makers), religious extremists, violent criminals released from prison by Saddam and willing to kill for money, Saddam loyalists (those Col. Coleman described as "bloody up to their elbows" in the old regime), and former military personnel."

116. Perry, p. 2.

117. Ibid.

118. Ibid.

119. Ibid.

120. Alissa J. Rubin and Damien Cave, "In a Force for Iraqi Calm, Seeds of Conflict," *New York Times*, 23 December 2007.

121. "Awakening Movement in Iraq," *New York Times*, 20 April 2009; Mike Lanchin and Mona Mahmoud, "Iraq Signs Up to Awakening Movement," *BBC*, 4 February 2008, http://news.bbc.co.uk/2/hi/middle_east/7226974.stm, accessed 15 May 2012.

122. Ashish Kumar Sen, "Al Qaida Drives Iraq towards Chaos; US Withdrawal Left Door Open to Secretariat Battle for Power," *The Washington Times*, 8 August 2013 at http://www.washingtontimes.com/news/2013/aug/8/al-qaeda-drives-iraq-toward-chaos/?page=all, accessed on 15 June 2014.

123. Ali Younes, "Iraq: An All-Out Sectarian War Is Looming; Sadam Hussain's Former Army Fighting Its Way Back?" *The Arab Daily News*, 14 June 2014 at http://thearabdailynews.com/2014/06/14/sectarian-war-looming-iraq-saddam-husseins-former-army-fighting-way-back/, accessed on 15 June 2014.

124. For instance, under Major General Douglas Stone, the head of Iraq's rehabilitation program, the United States rehabilitated and released over 10,000 detainees who had positive testimony of the United States' role in Iraq. Douglas Stone, personal interview (Gunaratna), 24 February 2009; personal observations based on the author's (Gunaratna) visits to Iraq.

125. inSITE: State of the Insurgency in Iraq, January 2009, 21 February 2009.

126. inSITE: State of the Insurgency in Iraq, January 2009, 21 February 2009.

127. inSITE: State of the Insurgency in Iraq, January 2009, 21 February 2009. Through al-Fajr Media Center on 9 January, ISI leader Abu Omar al-Baghdadi urged Palestinians, particular those outside Gaza, to strike U.S., Israeli and Arab interests. On 15 January Ansar al-Islam stressed that only jihad through guerrilla warfare and launching of rockets would affect change in Palestine, not democracy and diplomacy.

128. Alan B. Krueger, "The National Origins of Foreign Fighters in Iraq," Princeton University and NBER, 30 December 2006, http://www. aeaweb.org/annual_mtg_papers/2007/0105_1430_1601.pdf, p. 2.

129. Ibid, p. 3.

130. Alan B. Krueger, "The National Origins of Foreign Fighters in Iraq," Princeton University and NBER, 30 December 2006, http://www. aeaweb.org/annual_mtg_papers/2007/0105_1430_1601.pdf, p. 2.

131. Alan B. Krueger, "The National Origins of Foreign Fighters in Iraq," Princeton University and NBER, 30 December 2006, http://www. aeaweb.org/annual_mtg_papers/2007/0105_1430_1601.pdf, p. 2.

132. Ibid, p. 4.

133. Ibid, p. 5.

134. Ibid, p. 7.

135. Ibid.

136. Ibid, p. 9.

137. Peter Bergen et al., "Bombers, Bank Accounts, and Bleedout: Al-Qa'ida's Road in and Out of Iraq," ed. Brian Fishman. http://www. princeton.edu/~jns/publications/Sinjar_2_July_23.pdf.

138. Aaron Y. Zelin, "The Return of Sunni Foreign Fighters in Iraq," The Washington Institute, 12 June 2014 at http://www.washington institute.org/policy-analysis/view/the-return-of-sunni-foreign-fight ers-in-iraq, accessed on 16 June 2014.

139. Al-Qaeda was negotiating with Iran for the release of about ten prominent al-Qaeda leaders who had escaped Afghanistan to Iran in 2003 and were arrested by the Iranians. See Gunaratna and Oreg, p. 1052.

140. "Jordan Says Major al Qaeda Plot Disrupted," CNN, 26 April 2004, http://edition.cnn.com/2004/WORLD/meast/04/26/jordan. terror/, accessed 7 May 2012.

141. U.S. Department of State, Office of the Coordinator for Counterterrorism, "Chapter 8: Foreign Terrorist Organizations," Country Reports on Terrorism 2005, Washington, DC, 2006; republished in "Terrorist Organizations and Other Groups of Concern: Al-Qaeda in Iraq

(AQI)," 24 August 2007, http://www.investigativeproject.org/profile/124, accessed 7 May 2012.

142. Ibid.

143. Ibid.

144. "Al Qaeda Interview with Abu Hamza al Muhajir in Iraq," CeifiT Ltd. trans. *The NEFA Foundation*, 24 October 2008, http://nefafoundation.org//file/nefaabuhamza1008.pdf, accessed 7 May 2012.

145. Gunaratna and Oreg, p. 1052.

146. Ibid.

147. Bill Roggio, "Stockholm Suicide Bomber Trained for Jihad for 4 Years," *The Long War Journal*, 13 December 2010, http://www.longwarjournal.org/threat-matrix/archives/2010/12/swedish_suicide_bomber_trained.php, accessed 7 May 2012.

148. Gunaratna, "Terrorist Threat in Iraq: Origin, Development and Impact," *Beyond Iraq: The Future of World Order*, Amitav Acharya, Hiro Katsumata eds., Singapore: World Scientific Publishing Co. Pte. Ltd., 2011, p. 138.

149. "Special Groups (Iraq)," *Wikipedia: The Free Encyclopedia*, Wikimedia Foundation, Inc., 1 January 2012, http://en.wikipedia.org/wiki/Special_Groups_(Iraq), accessed 7 May 2012.

150. "How Can Militants Take Over Iraqi Cities," *BBC* 11 June 2014 at http://www.bbc.com/news/world-middle-east-25588623 . Accessed on 15 June 2014.

151. "Casualty Figures," *North Caucasus Analysis*, Vol. 4, Issue No. 5, 31 December 1969; republished in *Jamestown Foundation Chechnya Weekly*, Vol. 4, Issue No. 5, 20 February 2003; republished in David Johnson, ed., *CDI Russia Weekly*, No. 245, 21 February 2003, http://www.cdi.org/russia/245-14.cfm, accessed 7 May 2012; "First Chechnya War—1994–1996," *GlobalSecurity.org*, 11 July 2011, http://www.globalsecurity.org/military/world/war/chechnya1.htm, accessed 7 May 2012.

152. Alexander Pashin,"Russian Army Operations and Weaponry During Second Military Campaign in Chechnya," Moscow Defense Brief, Centre for Analysis of Strategies and Technologies (March 2002). Retrieved 29 May 2009.

153. Jonathan Steele, "It's Over, and Putin Won," *The Guardian*, 30 September 2008, http://www.guardian.co.uk/commentisfree/2008/sep/30/russia.chechnya, accessed 7 May 2012.

154. "Chechnya and the North Caucasus," *AlertNet*, 29 July 2009, http://www.trust.org/alertnet/crisis-centre/crisis/chechnya-and-the-north-caucasus?v=in_detail, accessed 7 May 2012.

155. Paul Tumelty, "The Rise and Fall of Foreign Fighters in Chechnya," *Terrorism Monitor* Vol. 4, Issue 2, 31 January 2006, http://www.jamestown.org/single/?no_cache=1&tx_ttnews%5Btt_news%5D=658, accessed 7 May 2012.

156. Ibid.

157. In Tajikistan, Khattab was commanding about twenty mujahidin, who composed about 50 percent of all the foreign fighters that were probably deployed at Abd al-Rasool Sayyaf's camp Sadah by the concluding stages of the internal Afghan war with the pro-Soviet Najibullah regime. Following the end of the Afghan war with the Soviets, the foreign fighters left Sayyaf's base in Sadah in search of new jihad arenas. While Khattab and his followers moved to Tajikistan and later to Chechnya, the other half of the foreign fighters consolidated a different group that was mostly occupied with external jihad and that waged spectacular terrorist operations against U.S. targets (the first WTC bombing, the "Bojinca" plot), led by Ramzi Yousef and Khalid Sheikh Mohamed (KSM), who became the mastermind of the 9/11 attacks. At one stage following the dismantling of the second group of Sadah graduates (Yousef and KSM's group) between 1995 and 1996, KSM made an attempt to go to Chechnya in order to join hands with Khattab. See The National Commission on Terrorist Attacks Upon the United States, *The 9/11 Commission Report: Final Report of the National Commission on Terrorist Attacks Upon the United States (9/11 Report)*, New York: Norton, 2004, p. 166, Web (hereafter referred to as *The 9/11 Report*).

158. Tumelty.

159. Tumelty. Khattab's commanders were his first deputy Abu Bakr Aqeedah, Hakim al-Medani, Abu Jafar al-Yemeni, Yaqub al-Ghamidi, and his then deputy and future Amir of foreign fighters, Abu Walid al-Ghamidi.

160. Ibid.

161. Ibid.

162. Ibid.

163. "Life and Times of Ibn ul Khattab," documentary released by the Ansaar News Agency, Birmingham, UK, 2002, cited in Lorenzo Vidino, "The Arab Foreign Fighters and the Sacralization of the Chechen Conflict," *Al Nakhlah,* Spring 2006, Medford, MA: The Fletcher School, 2006, p. 2.

164. Robert W. Kurz and Charles K. Bartles, "Chechen Suicide Bombers," *Journal of Slavic Military Studies*, 20: 529–47, 2007, p. 538.

165. Ibid.

166. Vidino, pp. 5–6.

167. Vidino, p. 5.

168. Ibid.

169. Colonel Ilya Shabalkin, quoted in Sharon LaFraniere, "How Jihad Made Its Way to Chechnya," *The Washington Post*, 26 April 2003.

170. Vidino, p. 5.

171. Ibid.

172. *The 9/11 Report*, p. 165.

173. http://fmso.leavenworth.army.mil/documents/chechen-suicide-bombers.pdf.

174. On 23 October 2002, several dozen suicide attackers took over the Dubrovka Theater in central Moscow, holding more than 900 spectators hostage for three days and demanding the complete withdrawal of Russian security forces from Chechnya. Following three days of negotiations, Russian special forces raided the building, killing all the terrorists and fatally wounding over 150 Russian hostages. Kurz and Bartles, p. 541.

175. http://www.start.umd.edu/start/data_collections/tops/terrorist_organization_profile.asp?id=3673.

176. Kurz and Bartles, p. 542.

177. Ibid.

178. Ibid, p. 543

179. Ibid, p. 544.

180. Tumelty.

181. Ibid.

182. "Commander Muhannad Assumes the Leadership of Arab Mujahideen in Chechnya," *Kavkaz Center*, 12 December 2006, http://www.kavkazcenter.net/eng/content/2006/12/12/6803.shtml, accessed 7 May 2012.

183. Vidino, pp. 1, 4.

184. Cerwyn Moore, "Foreign Fighters and the Chechen Resistance: A Re-appraisal," *Central Asia–Caucasus Institute Analyst*, 13 June 2007, http://www.cacianalyst.org/?q=node/4635, accessed 7 May 2012.

185. Ayman Zawahiri, "Knights under the Prophet's Banner," *Sharqi Al Awsat*, 5 December 2001.

186. Tumelty.

187. Vidino, p. 1.

188. Terrorist designation of Ansar Bait al-Maqdis by the U.S. government, http://www.state.gov/r/pa/prs/ps/2014/04/224566.htm. Accessed 15 June 2014.

189. Yoram Oreg Aviv Schweitzer, "Al Qaeda Odyssey to Global Jihad," INSS Memorandum 132, http://www.inss.org.il/uploadImages/systemFiles/memo134%20(4)_rev10April2014.pdf.

190. http://static.cejiss.org/data/uploaded/1383601365154531/CEJISS_Vol1_Issue2_full_version.pdf.

191. http://www.terrorism-info.org.il/en/article/20504.

192. Alison Pargeter, "Islamist Militant Groups in Post-Qadhafi Era," *CTC Sentinel*, February 2013 at https://www.ctc.usma.edu/wp-content/uploads/2013/02/CTCSentinel-Vol6Iss21.pdf. Accessed 15 June 2014.

193. Sharon Ward, "The Battle of the Shrines' Foreign Policy," 12 September 2012 at http://www.foreignpolicy.com/articles/2012/09/12/the_battle_of_the_shrines. Accessed on 15 June 2014.

194. Pete Williams and Richard Esposito, "US Charges Libyan with Role in Deadly Attack on Benghazi Consulate," *NBC News*, 7 August 2013 at http://www.nbcnews.com/news/other/us-charges-libyan-role-deadly-attack-benghazi-consulate-f6C10861451. Accessed on 15 June 2014.

195. Praveen Swami, Nick Squires, and Duncan Gardham, "Libyan Rebel Commander Admits His Fighters Have Al Qaeda Links," *The Telegraph*, 25 March 2013 at http://www.telegraph.co.uk/news/worldnews/africaandindianocean/libya/8407047/Libyan-rebel-commander-admits-his-fighters-have-al-Qaeda-links.html. Accessed on 15 June 2014.

196. "The Syrian Civil War: Breaking Down the Major Players," 6 March 2014 at http://recessiongrads.com/syrian-civil-war/.

197. Schweitzer, Oreg p. 46.

198. Quilliam Foundation, "Jabhat al-Nusra: *Jabhat al-Nusra li-ahl al-Sham min Mujahedi al-Sham fi Sahat al-Jihad*; A Strategic Briefing," http://www.quilliamfoundation.org/wp/wp-content/uploads/publications/free/jabhat-al-nusra-a-strategic-briefing.pdf.

199. Sham is the area including Syria, Lebanon, north Jordan, and northern Israel.

200. In some cases the group name is "The Islamic State of the Levant" or ISIL.

201. Yoram Schweitzer, Elior Albachari, Ilan Shklarsky, "Rifts in the Global Jihad Family in Syria," *INSS Insight*, No. 518, 18 February 2014 at https://www.inss.org.il/index.aspx?id=4538&articleid=661. Accessed on 14 June 2014.

202. Sarah Brick, "How Al Qaeda Changed the Syrian War" at http://www.nybooks.com/blogs/nyrblog/2013/dec/27/how-al-qaeda-changed-syrian-war/. Accessed 15 June 2014.

203. Bill Roggio "ISIS Announces Formation of Caliphate Rebrand as Islamic State," *The Long War Journal*, 29 June 2014 at http://www.long warjournal.org/threat- matrix/archives/2014/06/isis_announces_for mation_of_ca.php#ixzz3AXEFW92K. Accessed August 16 2014.

204. *Fox News*, 15 August 2014 at http://www.foxnews.com/world/2014/08/15/iraq-al-maliki-backs-new-prime-minister/.

205. The Meir Amit Intelligence and Terrorism Information Center, "News of Terrorism and the Israeli-Palestinian Conflict, 28 May–2 June 2014 at http://www.terrorism-info.org.il/Data/articles/Art_20653/E_085_14_2014481605.pdf, p. 12. Accessed on 16 June 2016.

206. Jane Onyanga Omara , "Video Shows Paris Gunman Pledging Allegiance to Islamic State," *USA Today*. 11 January 2015. http://www.usatoday.com/story/news/world/2015/01/11/video-gunman -islamic-state/21589723/.

6

Local Initiatives, Lone Wolves, and Homegrown Cells

In this chapter we will focus our discussion on the foot soldiers—what is known in the West as homegrown individuals and cells. In the previous chapters, we analyzed the performance of the different jihadi elements—al-Qaeda, local organizations, and jihad arenas—in a top-down approach by referring to formal infrastructure, connections, and roots. In this chapter we analyze and describe the homegrown individuals and cells, a phenomenon using a bottom-up approach. We examine individuals and their personal radicalization process up to the time that they executed attacks on behalf of their understanding of Islam.

Terrorism scholars and researchers often refer to "local jihadi initiatives," "lone wolves," and "homegrown cells" interchangeably. The term "homegrown cells" refers in general to all those individuals who are either citizens or longtime residents of Western countries which have adopted a jihadi ideology after a long process of radicalization and were able to implement it by executing an attack or plotting for it. All terrorist incidents and the vast majority of the plots conducted by jihadi elements since the 9/11/2001 attacks in New York and Washington on Western soil were perpetrated by "homegrown cells." Only in the 9/11 attacks, the attacking squads consisted of external Middle Eastern perpetrators that were penetrated into the United States in order to take part in the attack. Jihadi "local initiatives" and "lone wolves" are part of this homegrown cells phenomenon as they conduct operational attacks on behalf of the Global Jihad Movement and ideology. However, the key distinction between "local initiatives" and other individuals that are part of the homegrown cells is that the former, operating as lone wolves or as part of small cells, execute operational activities based on their own initiatives and personal capabilities. In contrast, other homegrown cells and individuals that have undergone the same radicalization process eventually implemented jihad by cooperating with more organized terrorist outfits such as al-Qaeda and other affiliated terrorist organizations, or by traveling to jihad arenas to join jihadi outfits operating there. This phenomenon of homegrown cells, overall its different components, predates the 9/11 attacks but developed significantly during the thirteen years that have followed.[1]

In 2004 al-Qaeda and the Global Jihad Movement have adopted the homegrown phenomenon, turning it into an operational ideology and a tactical militant doctrine. Mustafa Satmariam Nasser, better known by his nom de guerre of Abu Musab al-Suri, one of the important military strategists of the Global Jihad Movement, formulated a warfare doctrine called "death by a thousand cuts," which was published in a 1,600-page essay titled "The Global Islamic Resistance Call." In this pamphlet, al-Suri, urges the establishment of jihad activity at the individual level or the level of small, isolated cells. In this type of jihad, Muslims all over the world would operate independently of one another against Western targets and interests so that random and occasional violence would be perceived as a coordinated mass movement. According to al-Suri, continuous activity on the part of many cells, with each operating perhaps only once a month, would allow Global Jihad to reach an unprecedented number of attacks, many more than a single organization could ever hope to achieve. The sheer numbers would make life untenable for enemy countries and their citizens, and would encourage many other Muslims to join the struggle. Accordingly, al-Suri called on all Muslims, regardless of their geographical location, to join the struggle, thereby spreading the battlefields everywhere, turning every country and every city into a potential target for attack. The doctrine of individual jihad preached by al-Suri was recognized and adopted by Ayman al-Zawahiri and Anwar Awlaki and became the official warfare doctrine of the Global Jihad Movement. As a result, there was in fact a dramatic increase in the number of attacks, attempted attacks, and plots uncovered in North America, Western Europe, and Australia that had been planned or carried out by small groups or lone terrorists subscribing to a radical Islamic ideology and operating in the context of Global Jihad.[2]

The New York Police Department's (NYPD) Research Department conducted research into the radicalization process, referring to numerous test cases and relevant security episodes. This research centers on the radicalization process of individuals as they turn into homegrown cells. The research examines test cases from three continents (North America, Australia, and Europe) and focuses on individuals and cells that eventually conducted or planned terror attacks within the framework of the Global Jihad ideology.[3]

This chapter examines the process that an individual, in most cases a permanent resident of Australia, North America, or a Western European country, undergoes on his way to radical Islam and its most extreme interpretation, Salafiya Jihadiya. We explore the various factors that influence this process and the different indicators that arise throughout the individual's radicalization process. While not all who begin this process of radicalization become suicide bombers, a significant number do.

As we describe the radicalization process, we will refer to several test cases to support our findings:

- The 11 March 2004 Madrid train bombing—During Friday's early morning rush hour, seven explosive charges exploded on board seven commuter trains in the Spanish capital, causing 192 fatalities and over 1,800 injuries.[4]
- The Theo van Gogh assassination—On 2 November 2004, Dutch filmmaker and columnist Theo van Gogh was stabbed and shot to death on a street in Amsterdam. The assassination was conducted by Mohamed Bouyeri, a member of the radical Islamic Hofstadt cell, in response to

an article van Gogh had written which criticized the Salafi interpretation of Islam as well as a film he had produced promoting the same approach.[5]

- The Australian plot—Two jihadi cells operating in Melbourne and Sydney made a joint attempt to conduct suicide operations, targeting national symbols in Sydney and Melbourne. The plot was dismantled in late 2005 by the Australian Security Intelligence Organization (ASIO).[6]
- The "Toronto 18"—Crystallized in Toronto suburbs, the plot of a jihadi cell to attack Canadian national symbols and landmarks in late 2005 was dismantled by the Canadian Security Intelligence Service (CSIS).[7]
- The 7/7 London bombings—On 7 July 2005, four jihadi suicide bombers attacked three underground trains and a double-decker bus in the British capital, killing fifty-two people and wounding several hundred.[8]
- The Faisal Shahzad plot—In April 2010, Faisal Shahzad, a New York resident of Pakistani origin, parked a car full of explosives in Manhattan's Time Square, set to explode at midday. The charge failed to explode.[9]

According to the NYPD research, the radicalization process that an individual in the West undergoes comprises four phases:

1. Preradicalization
2. Search for self-identity
3. Indoctrination
4. Jihad: conducting a violent act[10]

First Stage: Preradicalization

The preradicalization stage reflects the world of the individual—his beliefs, lifestyle, attitude toward religion and Islamic faith in particular, social status, environment, and education before he begins his journey to radicalization.

It is not easy to determine the individual profiles of these radicals-to-be since their circumstances vary and are influenced by location, culture, and other factors. However, there are several profile attributes that are common among radicals-to-be at this stage:

Gender—All are male. Females are tasked with the birth and raising of jihad warriors. There are some cases of female involvement in jihadi activity such as Muriel Degauque, a Belgian female of Flemish origin who executed a suicide attack in an Iraq case,[11] yet those cases are considered as the exceptions to this general trend of male jihadists.

Age—Most are young people between eighteen and thirty-one years old. The majority are in their early to midtwenties.

Place of residence—They live, work, pray, and socialize within Islamic migrant communities from the Middle East, North Africa, the Indian subcontinent, and Southeast Asia.

Ethnic origin—The radicals-to-be are of various ethnic backgrounds. In most cases, they are second- and third-generation Muslim immigrants from the largest Muslim migrant community in their Western country of residence. Since the second half of the twentieth century, Western Europe, Australia, and Canada have been absorbing large waves of Muslim migrants from developing countries seeking a better life in the West.[12]

Two factors influence the choice of which Western country to immigrate to:

- Geographical proximity to their homeland.
- Cultural familiarity—Muslim migrants tend to migrate to the Western country that was the colonial power in their homeland.

Hence, the largest Muslim migrant community in Spain is from Morocco. In France, it is the Algerians. In Italy, it is migrants from Libya and Tunisia. In Austria, a new community of Bosnian immigrants emerged following the Balkan civil war of the early 1990s. In the Benelux countries, Moroccans and Tunisians form the dominant Muslim migrant communities, as Indonesians do in the Netherlands (Indonesia was ruled by the Dutch until 1948). The dominant Muslim migrant community in England is of Pakistani origin since India and Pakistan were formerly colonized (under the collective regional term "the Indian subcontinent") by Britain. Pakistanis also form the dominant Muslim migrant community in Canada, as Canada is a member of the Commonwealth. In Australia, most Muslim immigrants are from Lebanon, as the Australian government took in refugees from the Lebanese civil war of the mid-1970s.

Social status—Most come from middle-class families.

Education—In most cases, the radicals-to-be are at least high school graduates. In some cases, they are university students and graduates.

Religious affiliation—During the preradicalization stage, the vast majority of radicals-to-be may be considered moderate Muslims. They attend religious services in mosques only on holidays and special events such as weddings, and the vast majority of them are considered secular.

Criminal activity—During the preradicalization stage, the radicals-to-be possess no or minimal criminal records. The most common felonies are assault and personal use of light drugs such as hashish and marijuana. Their criminal activities and records are no different from the overall national average of youth involvement in criminal activity.

In summary, there are no remarkable characteristics that might attract attention or raise suspicion at this stage of their lives. They live like typical young people. They possess occupations common among youth; hang around in entertainment centers such as bars, clubs, pubs, restaurants, cinemas, and theaters; enjoy various sports; and in most cases, their male and female friends are from the same migrant community or are locally born.[13]

Below are profiles of famous radical Islamists who have either served time in prison for terrorism-related activities or conducted a suicide attack "in the name of Islam," which details their way of life prior to radicalization.

Faisal Shahzad, a New York resident of Pakistani origin, seemed at this stage of preradicalization to be well integrated into New York and Western society. He held an accounting position in a well-established international cosmetic firm. He had received his green card and was a legal resident in the United States. He had purchased a new house in Connecticut and his Pakistani American wife was expecting their first child.[14] The son of a Pakistani lieutenant colonel in the Pakistani Air Force, Shahzad had arrived in the United States several years earlier in order to gain a Western education. He was enrolled in the University of Bridgeport, Connecticut, studying computer application and information systems, and graduated in 2001. According to his classmates he showed "little interest in Islam."[15] In his free time, Shahzad liked to cook for his friends and spend time with them in New York's theme nightclubs.[16]

Fahim Ahmad and Sai'd Khaled were part of a terrorist cell that was dismantled by the CSIS as they were in the final stages of preparations to conduct large-scale attacks. During preradicalization the two were high school graduates from the Toronto suburb of Mississauga; they had assimilated into Western society and hung around in clubs with local Canadians.[17]

Jamal Ahmidan, a pivotal member of the cell in Spain that conducted the deadly attack on the Madrid train system in March 2004, had mostly assimilated into Spanish society in the preradicalization stage. His friends were secular, native Spanish who enjoyed sports, alcohol, and body piercings. Ahmidan was involved in a low level of criminal activity and was a junior member of a local network that traded hashish.[18] Jamal Zoukam of the same cell was a co-owner of a communication equipment store that sold cell phones. He enjoyed Western music, hung around disco bars, consumed alcohol, and was popular with the local Madrid women.[19]

Mohammed Bouyeri, who killed Dutch filmmaker Theo van Gogh in October 2004, was born in Amsterdam to Moroccan immigrant parents. He was regarded as a smart teenager and a promising young student. During the preradicalization period, he studied accounting and information technology at a local polytechnic institute in Amsterdam.[20]

Fadal Sayadi from Melbourne, who belonged to a cell that planned terrorist attacks targeting Australian landmarks in Sydney and Melbourne in 2005, was married and had worked during his preradicalization stage as a plumber in the city.[21] **Omar Belajam** from the same cell was a soap opera actor who appeared on several Australian productions (*Wild Side* and *Home and Away*).[22]

Mohamed Siddiq Khan from England, who was the cell leader of the 7 July 2005 suicide attacks that targeted the London transportation system and killed fifty-two people, had tried to suppress his Pakistani origins prior to radicalization. He introduced himself as Sid, shortened from his middle name Siddiq. Khan was a business graduate from Leeds University who joined the British Ministry of Industry and Commerce as a civil servant. Khan was married with a two-year-old daughter.[23] His cellmate **Shahzad Tanweer** was a member of a wealthy family. He was a graduate from Leeds Metropolitan University majoring in sports science. At an early age, he had a capital worth of US$200,000 and drove a Mercedes.[24] **Hussein Husseib**, another member of the cell, was introverted and the youngest of four siblings from a middle-class family. Even though he dropped out of school, he had achieved good marks. He was active in sports and played soccer and cricket at local clubs.[25] All three grew up in secular and relatively wealthy families and had assimilated into British society. They were graduates of the British public education system and focused their academic studies in modern, secular subjects. All three used to hang around clubs, pubs, and bars, and consumed alcohol and light drugs. All three became suicide bombers in the 7 July 2005 attacks.[26]

Nizar Trabelsi, who serves a life sentence in Belgian prison for his role in a dismantled plot to drive a VBIED into NATO headquarters in Brussels, was during his pre-radicalization phase the center forward striker of Fortuna Düsseldorf football club from the second division of the Bundesliga.[27]

Islamic Converts

Islamic converts are present in almost every plot and radical Sunni Islamic cell formed in the West. These converts, who were born non-Islamic, choose to convert to Islam and adopt the most radical interpretation of Islam, Salafiya, and later on the Salafi Jihadi approach. Operationally speaking, these converts have a Western appearance (look, dress, accent, speech, etc.) and hence do not attract the attention of local security and law enforcement agencies.[28]

Among those converts one may find:

Muriel Degauque, a Belgian native who conducted a suicide attack against an American convoy in Iraq, was an Islamic convert.[29]

Germaine Lindsey, a Jamaican-born teen, converted to Islam and became the fourth suicide bomber in the 2005 London attacks.[30]

Willie Brigitte, a French citizen and Islamic convert, conducted reconnaissance of a civil nuclear facility in Australia on behalf of Lashkar-e-Toyba and probably al-Qaeda.[31]

Richard Reid, a British Islamic convert of Jamaican descent, boarded an AA flight en route from Paris to Miami in late 2001 with explosive charges hidden in his shoes and attempted to ignite them midair.[32]

Jason Walters, a Dutch Islamic convert who led the Hofstadt group in the Netherlands, was the son of a Dutch woman and an African American soldier deployed in Holland.[33]

Steven Vikash Chand, from the Toronto cell that plotted to attack Canadian landmarks, was an emotionally unstable soldier in the Canadian army. He became Buddhist and later converted to Islam.[34]

Jack Roche, a British citizen, an alcoholic, and an Islamic convert, is serving time in an Australian jail for reconnaissance of Israeli targets as personally directed by bin Laden and Khalid Sheikh Mohamed.[35]

David Hicks, an Australian Muslim convert, was captured by American forces in an al-Qaeda training camp in Afghanistan following the 9/11 attacks.[36]

Second Phase: Search for Self-Identity

This phase is characterized by a search for personal identity. The catalyst of this phase is, in most cases, a cognitive event or crisis that challenges the individual's way of being and prompts him to seek new and different worldviews and ways of living.[37] To the individual, these personal crises are considered life changing—something that one will not ever recover from.[38] These crises include but are not limited to economic crises such as layoffs, rejections, or lack of career advancement; social crises such as discrimination, racism, and social and cultural alienation; political crises, where an individual feels affected by international conflicts involving Muslims such as the Israeli-Palestinian conflict, or the situation in Kashmir and, in recent years, Iraq and Syria; and personal crises such as relationship problems, the loss of a close relative or friend, etc., that occur in teenage years.[39]

Most teenagers who undergo Islamic radicalization blame their ethnic and religious background for the crisis. They then start to look for solutions to the crisis. These individuals initially look to their close friends and family, and when these fail to assist them, they start looking for solutions from the broader levels of neighborhood and community.[40]

The key establishments during this phase are known as incubators. This term refers to institutions or facilities that the individual goes to in his search for answers, which provide him with the necessary motivation and support to begin his journey of radicalization.[41]

The following list provides examples of incubators:

- Mosqus and Islamic centers—Individuals begin in central mosques preaching moderate Islam but soon move to the more radical Salafi mosques.
- Bookstores—The back rooms of the Islamic bookstores hold extremist literature and publications.
- Coffee shops
- Prisons
- Student associations
- Nargila smoking bars
- Gyms and fitness centers
- Halal butcher stores
- The Internet—This modern incubator provides easy access to Islamic extremist websites.[42]

In these incubators, individuals are not only exposed to radical Islam and Islamic material but they also meet others similar to them—young people, belonging mostly to the dominant Islamic migrant community, who have experienced some kind of crisis and are seeking a solution. The individuals bond and begin their communal journey of radicalization.

The indicators of this phase are:

- Adoption of the Salafi interpretation of Islam and joining a Salafi mosque.
- Estrangement and alienation from old social circles and joining a new circle of friends composed of new Salafis.
- Quitting smoking and alcohol consumption as well as abandoning Western styles of dress.
- Growth of a beard.
- Gradual adoption of a traditional Islamic outfit.
- Participating in voluntary social activities within the community.

Syrhan Farahat of the Spanish cell responsible for the 2004 Madrid train bombing arrived in Spain in 2000 having received an academic scholarship sponsored by the Spanish government. He abandoned his way of life due to a personal crisis. He began secluding himself from the outer world and moved into the M-30 Mosque, the most extreme Salafi mosque of Madrid, and did not leave its doors, speaking only about Islam and Islamic issues.

In Holland, Bouyeri suffered from a dual crisis: he was jailed for six months for involvement in a violent brawl and while he was in jail, his mother died from breast cancer. When he was released from prison, he changed his academic studies from accounting and information technology to social work. He began to conduct social work voluntarily at his community center. He started to wear a traditional Islamic outfit and to grow a beard. At this stage, Bouyeri spent a lot of time studying international conflicts involving Muslims, particularly the Israeli-Palestinian conflict. He began to attend the Al Tawhid Salafi Mosque of Amsterdam where his imam, an extremist cleric, strongly supported suicide bombings and the elimination of homosexuals from society by killing them. As Bouyeri became more and more radical, he tried enforcing Salafi ideology within his community center (banning of alcohol and female participants from events) and on this basis was expelled from the center.

In Canada, Ahmad, Khaled, and Zachariah Amara started to attend prayers at the Salafi al-Rahman Mosque in Mississauga. Amara's blog revealed his psychological and social processes. In this blog, Amara addresses regular teen problems. He most likely suffered from low self-esteem and wrote that he was embarrassed for being considered fat. During this stage, Amara published a poem on his blog regarding his search for "the light"—the right approach to life:

> Please someone find me
> I want to find the light
> but no one is there to guide me
> Open the door someone give me it's key [sic][43]

In Australia, the members of a Melbourne cell began attending prayers at a small Salafi mosque in Brunswick. The imam of the mosque was an extreme cleric who supported bin Laden and praised his activity and the activity of the Algerian GSPC.[44]

In England, Khan began to adopt a new Islamic identity. He quit smoking and drinking. He stopped attending bars and clubs. He started to grow a beard and began to attend religious prayers at the Salafi Mosque of the "Tabligh Jamaat" on Stanford Street in his hometown of Beeston. Khan volunteered for social activities within his community and worked as an assistant teacher for disadvantaged children from the Muslim community. He also volunteered as an assistant teacher at the Hamara Youth Access Point (HYAP), an Islamic charity. Tanweer stopped frequenting his favorite casino and started to grow a beard. Like Khan, he joined prayers at the Salafi Mosque of the Tabligh Jamaat on Stanford Street in his hometown of Beeston and volunteered at the HYAP. Husseib adopted a new Islamic dress code and volunteered at the HYAP. Lindsey's road to radicalization was stimulated by his difficult family background. Lindsey was born in Jamaica to a local father and a British mother who left the Caribbean island when Lindsey was one year old. Lindsey's father remained behind. Lindsey's mother moved frequently between male companions and locations. In 1996, when Lindsey was ten years old, his mother left a spouse and her home once more and converted to Islam. Germaine Lindsey converted with her. In 2000, his mother left him in England under the custody of Abu Faisal al-Jamaican, a radical imam, and moved to the United States with a new partner she had met.[45]

In the United States, political crisis was most likely the catalyst for the radicalization of the Times Square plotter Shahzad. In an e-mail he sent on 25 June 2006, he was disturbed by the wars in Iraq and Afghanistan, the plight of Palestinians, and the publication of satirical cartoons of the Prophet Muhammad in Denmark.[46] Shahzad had long been critical of U.S. foreign policy. A close relative said, "He was always very upset about the fabrication of the W.M.D. stunt to attack Iraq and killing noncombatants such as the sons and grandson of Saddam Hussein."[47]

Shahzad was influenced by the 2007 events in Islamabad's Red Mosque as tension between Sunni worshippers and Pakistani security services deteriorated into violent clashes. Shahzad used to pray at the Red Mosque during his visits home. According to senior American intelligence officials, the Red Mosque episode was pivotal for Shahzad, setting him on a course toward militant Islam.[48]

At the same time, Shahzad felt belittled at work and complained of a manager who "used to 'insult him.'"[49] According to his classmate, Shahzad felt that American Muslims were treated differently after the 9/11 attacks.[50] At this stage, Shahzad began dabbling in jihadist ideology, listening to the Internet sermons of Anwar al-Awlaki, the American-born radical imam, and Abdullah el-Faisal, a Jamaican extremist Islamic cleric operating in the United Kingdom.[51] On frequent trips home to Pakistan, Shahzad formed a new circle of friends. These visits were critical to his militant evolution. An anonymous administration official quoted in the New York Times indicated that Shahzad seemed to find a lack of "validation" from his family and work environment, finding it instead with "a bunch of like-minded brothers."[52] At home, Shahzad adopted religious habits. He prayed five times a day and avoided alcohol; visited mosques in Stamford, Norwalk, and Bridgeport, and pressured his wife to wear a hijab.[53]

Third Phase: Indoctrination

The third stage of radicalization is the indoctrination phase. This phase is characterized by a sharp growth in religious belief and total acceptance of Salafi ideology by the individual. At this stage, the individual has reached the conclusion that action in the form of militant jihad must be taken in order to support and promote Salafi objectives. The main goal at this stage is to use radical Islam to rationalize any violent action against anyone considered to be an "infidel," referring to everyone (Muslims and non-Muslims) who does not completely support Salafi ideology. Indicators of the Indoctrination Phase Are:

- **Leaving the mosque**—The individual deems the Salafi mosque not militant enough and no longer able to meet his needs. He considers it a place subject to supervision by local security forces, hence endangering his activity of waging holy war. In most cases, leaving the mosque is accompanied by sharp disputes with other attendants, as well as the imam of the mosque for more extreme individuals.
- **Politicization of new beliefs**—The individual analyzes global politics within a Salafi framework. Every act and international development is considered to be a scheme against the "pure" Islam. The world is divided between the enlightened (Salafi Muslims) and the ignorant (the rest of the world), who are deemed the ultimate enemy.
- **Exclusive interaction with a group of like-minded individuals**—The new group becomes the only world for the individual. He has completely abandoned his connection with former friends and in some cases, his family. The group becomes an intimate and exclusive society composed of individuals possessing the same psychological and sociological profile as well as ethnic beliefs and religious ideologies.
- **Continuation of activity in other locations (incubators and private homes)**—The dominant figure at this phase is the "role model." The role model serves as spiritual and operational mentor to the new group. In most cases, this person is significantly older than the group members, his ethnicity is different from the rest of the group (that belong to the dominant community), and he possesses deeper knowledge of radical Islamic ideology. The role model possesses operational experience and is a glorified jihadi veteran that took part in jihad in Afghanistan, Bosnia, Kashmir, or any other jihad arena.[54]

During the indoctrination stage, the group members that conducted the train bombing in Spain left the M-30 Mosque and continued their meetings in the private home of one of the group members, Faisal Aloush. Other members of the group led by Farahat were extremely influenced by the U.S.-led invasion of Iraq and its outcome.

In Holland, all the Hofstadt group members left al-Tawhid Mosque in Amsterdam and continued their activity in Bouyeri's private home. Bouyeri himself started to pay attention to the situation of Muslims in conflict regions in the international arena and discussed these issues with fellow jihadists around the world using Internet forums and chat rooms.

In Australia, the cell headed by its role model Barbinka left the Brunswick Salafi mosque in Melbourne and continued to self-learn the most extreme version of Islam without external and formal instruction. Barbinka considered Australian involvement in Iraq and Afghanistan as part of the infidel conflict with the "pures" and blamed the Australian government and Australians for electing it.

In Canada, the cellmates started to hold closed meetings in a special prayer room on the top floor of a building close to their school. They were influenced by the preaching of Jamal Qayum and begun to communicate with Muslims around the world through the web.[55]

In the United Kingdom, Khan and Tanweer left the Tabligh Mosque in Beeston as early as 2001. It was too moderate and apolitical for them. The two criticized the imam of the mosque, who was from the Indian subcontinent, for being unaware of the problems of second-generation immigrants in the United Kingdom. They left the mosque after a verbal dispute with other attendants of the mosque who wished to leave politics outside the mosque.

Khan and Tanweer continued their extreme religious activities and studies in the IQRA Islamic book center in Beeston and were soon joined by Husseib. In the back rooms of the center, they discovered Salafiya Jihadiya, far removed from the Islam they had practiced with their families. They conducted discussions over the status of Muslims in Kashmir, Chechnya, and Iraq and established Internet chat rooms where they discussed those issues. They produced propaganda DVDs in which they depicted

Islamic suffering in those places. They attended the lectures and sermons of the most extreme and radical clerics operating in the United Kingdom. The fourth cell member, Lindsey, was mostly influenced by his custodian, the radical cleric Abu Faisal al-Jamaican.[56] Lindsey attended many of his lectures and sermons and memorized his books and audio cassette recordings. Abu Faisal used to hold many of his conversations in IQRA back rooms. In IQRA the four 7/7 suicide bombers came together.[57]

In the United States, Shahzad increasingly engaged in radical Islamic ideas. His friends maintained that his Islamic devotion at this stage was not unique, but rather his Salafi interpretation of world events.[58] His 2006 e-mails echoed general Islamic slogans.[59] Shahzad subsequently became an admirer of radical Islamic thinkers and ideologues such as Ibn Taymiyyah and Abul Ala Maududy.[60] During his visits to Pakistan, Shahzad began to clash with his father and by 2009 he decided he no longer wanted to live in the United States.[61] After gaining American citizenship in April, he moved back to Pakistan while his wife and two children went to live with her parents in Saudi Arabia.[62]

Fourth Phase: Jihad

During this phase, the individual as part of the group makes a decision to fulfill his "Islamic" obligation and destiny by taking part in "jihad" and positioning himself as a mujahidin. The group begins with operational preparations to conduct "jihad."

This phase is characterized by:

- Total group loyalty and group thinking.
- Personal obligation by every member to perform "jihad."
- Operational preparation within a group framework.
- Relatively short time frame.

The indicators of this stage are:

- A search for rationalization for one's decision as well as a search for operational directions from external sources

such as prominent and extreme imams and their audio-
and videocassettes as well as the internet.
- Going abroad—The operational leaders and their role
  model travel abroad in order to cultivate ways of jihad.
- Group members undergo semimilitary training including
  navigation trips, camping, white-water rafting, paintball
  games, etc.
- Group members undergo additional changes of clothing,
  appearance, and behavior back to a modern and Western
  style in order to blend into mainstream Western society
  and avoid detection by the police or internal security services.[63]

Next, the group selects the location for "jihad." This stage
may have the greatest effect on the outcome of the group's attempt to wage jihad. There are two choices of location for jihad:

- **Jihad arena**—Iraq, Pakistan FATA, Chechnya, and Afghanistan used to be the main jihad arenas and many
  radicals choose to wage their jihad there. Somalia is becoming a popular arena as well; yet, since 2012, the current dominant jihadi arena is Syria. Cell members begin
  their search for logistical coordinators that are able to slip
  into those arenas.
- **Their own country**—conducting jihad in their country
  of residence. Once the newly radicalized group members
  choose to implement their jihadi duties in their own country of residence, they face two options to choose from:
  1. Connecting with a well-established and famous jihadi
     outfit in most, cases al-Qaeda for ad hoc cooperation for
     the execution of the attack—al-Qaeda is considered by
     homegrown cells in the West as the most professional
     jihadi entity. Hence, many radicalized individuals at-
     tempt to join the group in its main vicinity of activity
     along the Pakistan-Afghanistan border zone, undergo
     designated training, and then return to their country
     to conduct a large-scale attack based on the knowledge
     and support provided by al-Qaeda. In recent years, Ye-

men-based al-Qaeda in the Arabian Peninsula (AQAP) has been positioning itself as the new center of jihadi operational professionalism, which has attracted many Western homegrown groups and individuals to Yemen for training and operational tasking.[64]

2. Local initiatives—Another option is to conduct an attack in the member's home country based on the group's initiative, capabilities, and resources. These kinds of attacks are operationally characterized in most cases by popular methods such as stabbing, Molotov cocktails, riots, arsons, and solitary assassinations. Yet in some cases, "local initiative" groups or lone wolves are able to execute large-scale attacks as well.

After decisions have been made regarding the location and strategy of the attack, the group begins its operational planning and preparation. This stage is relatively short and includes:

- Target selection.
- Operational reconnaissance of the selected target.
- Renting of safe houses.
- Operational training.
- Making explosive charges.
- Executing the attack.

In Spain, the 11 March 2004 group members decided to conduct the attack based on their own initiative, capabilities, and resources. The decision to execute the attack was made in December 2003 in response to an anonymous call published on Islamic websites urging Muslims to attack countries that sent troops to Iraq. The document making the anonymous request was found on the hard disk of Farahat's computer.

Following their decision, the group members began with operational preparations.

Farahat downloaded instructions for making explosive charges from the Internet. Ahmidan used his criminal contacts to exchange hashish for explosives (dynamite) with a coal-mine guard in northern Spain. The group members rented a safe house in which they prepared the charges. On 4 March 2004, Zoukam provided the group with twenty cell phones that were used for detonating the charges. On 11 March 2004, the attack was executed.

In Holland, the Hofstadt group leaders decided to conduct jihad in October 2003 and began preparations. Walters most likely went to Pakistan for training while Samir Azouz planned to enter Chechnya. The two simultaneously began with target selection. During the spring of 2004, they received the approval of an Islamic cleric to target the Dutch government and police facilities. The slow progress of the operational preparations prompted Bouyeri to take action on his own. By the summer of 2004, Bouyeri had purchased a gun and went for sporadic training. On 2 October 2004, Bouyeri assassinated van Gogh, which led to the arrest of the rest of the group.

In Australia, the decision to wage jihad occurred in November 2005 and aimed to pressure the Australian government to withdraw its troops from Afghanistan. Activists from both cells (Melbourne and Sydney) underwent training in the Australian desert. The group members selected and conducted reconnaissance on symbolic targets (the Sydney Opera House, the Sydney Harbor Bridge, Melbourne Central train station, and the Sydney Stock Exchange Building). Large quantities of raw chemical materials, detonators, and batteries were purchased. The plot was dismantled by the Australian Security Intelligence Organization (ASIO) at the end of November 2005.

In Canada, at the end of 2005, the group members decided to wage jihad. Qayum, the role model of the group, went to Pakistan (formally to find a wife) and most likely underwent military training. On or around Christmas 2005, the cell members received semimilitary training in the countryside area around Toronto. Symbolic targets were selected (the Stock Exchange Building, the CN Tower of Toronto, and the Parliament House in Ottawa) and three tons of ammonium nitrate were purchased. The plot developed rapidly and was dismantled by the CSIS in early 2006.

In the United Kingdom, the cell leader Khan was able to establish access to al-Qaeda. The plot was conducted with the full control and training of al-Qaeda's Special Operations Unit, headed at that time by Hamza al-Rabia.

During a trip between late 2003 and early 2004, Khan decided to wage jihad. The initial purpose of the trip lay within the prior phase of indoctrination. Khan went to Pakistan with a large sum of money collected from donations in order to give it to the Pakistani terror group fighting in Kashmir. During this trip, Khan joined al-Qaeda and went through military training in one of the al-Qaeda camps still operating in Waziristan. In the spring of 2004, Khan went back to England and started forming the cell. On November 2004, Khan returned to Pakistan, this time accompanied by Tanweer. The two went through designated training provided by al-Qaeda's Special Operations Unit, headed then by Rabia. During this trip, the two were video recorded by al-Qaeda, in which they took credit for a suicide mission. The video was eventually broadcasted by Ayman al-Zawahiri after the London bombings were executed.

In February 2005, Khan and Tanweer completed their training and returned to England. They formatted the group from the wider circle of their radical friends and began with preparations for the attack. They took a white-water rafting consolidation trip to Wales and purchased the raw materials for making improvised explosives based on their training in Pakistan. The two rented a safe apartment in Leeds where they assembled the charges. The group members then selected the targets and conducted a thorough reconnaissance and dry run ten days prior to the attack.

On 7 July 2005, Khan, Tanweer, and Hussein left the safe apartment in Leeds and drove a Ford Fiesta to Luton train station. In Luton, they were joined by Lindsey and boarded a commuter train to London's King's Cross station, a main junction for several London subway lines. Here, they split up. Tanweer executed his suicide attack on the circle line between Liverpool station and Aldgate east. Lindsey's attack occurred on the Piccadilly line between King's Cross station and Russell Square. Khan's attack was on the Piccadilly line near Edgware Road. Husseib failed to detonate his explosive charge due to a battery malfunction and was evacuated onto the street with other commuters due to the other explosions. He went to a store and bought a new pack of batteries, assembled them to the charge, boarded a double-decker bus, and blew himself up in Travistock Square.[65]

In Pakistan, United States resident Shahzad received specific training from the banned Pakistani Tehrik-e-Taliban Pakistan (TTP), a militant umbrella group of more than forty anti-Pakistan terrorist organizations operating in FATA, on how to build a bomb that he planned to detonate in the United States.[66] After training, Shahzad returned to the United States and continued to communicate with the militant group from whom he received the funds needed for the plot.[67] In early 2010, Shahzad begun with concrete preparations for the attack as was detailed in his trial:

"Shahzad rented an apartment in Connecticut and purchased the necessary components for his bomb—fertilizer, propane, and gasoline, from various stores in Connecticut and obtained significant quantities of fireworks from a store in Pennsylvania.[68] Wanting to select the busiest time for pedestrian traffic in Times Square, he used the Internet to collect concrete, real time intelligence of the square, which enabled him to decide on the most effective location to place his VBIED in order to have the maximum damage and casualties.[69] On 24 April 2010, a week before the attempted bombing, Shahzad bought a Nissan Pathfinder and installed black window tinting to make it difficult to see into the vehicle which he used to deliver the bomb to Times Square.

As May 1st approached, Shahzad, applying the training he had received from the TTP, single-handedly assembled the bomb at his residence in Connecticut. During the late afternoon of May 1st, he loaded the bomb into the rear area of the Pathfinder . . . [and] drove . . . [to] Times Square at about 6:00 p.m. He parked the Pathfinder near the southwest corner of 45th Street and Seventh Avenue. He then lit the bomb fuse, which led to the three different detonating components of the bomb (fertilizer, propane, and gas). Shahzad had designed the bomb to detonate between two and a half minutes and five minutes after the lighting of the fuse."[70]

After lighting the fuse, Shahzad got out of the Pathfinder and walked toward Grand Central terminal and boarded a train back to Connecticut.[71] Shahzad was apprehended two days later at the John F. Kennedy International Airport as he was trying to flee the United States.

Virtual Logistics

As communication means especially, the Internet, have been developed, the operational dependence on traditional logistic support for operational activity has sharply decreased. A zealous jihadist can find today online all the information he needs in order to implement the operational activity he chooses to execute. We have already discussed the mental support people like Anwar al-Awlaki provide for online jihadists which have resulted in some of them executing attacks on Western soil. In recent years the logistical support has turned in addition to new directions and included other dimensions of the operational act:

AQAP has published in its *Inspire* magazine detailed instructions on how to construct explosive charges using pressure cookers. In April 2013 two U.S. residents of Chechen origin that went through the described radicalization process used the AQAP recipe to bomb the Boston Marathon, killing three spectators and injuring hundreds.

AQAP Instruction for Making an Explosive Charge as Was Published in *Inspire* Magazine

Many posts in different jihadi Internet platforms provide specific instructions on how to get to Syria. One of these posts provided the foreign fighters with the following information:

> When arriving in Istanbul get a visa. Not needed for Turkish passports. When getting the visa people who are travelling together should separate. Then you go separately through passport control. Join each other again in the baggage-claim area.

> *After you collect your luggage you can do two things:*
> *Option 1: Take a flight to Adana from Istanbul, takes about an hour.*
> *Option 2: You can take a cab to the bus station (OTOGAR). You take a bus to Adana, takes about eight hours. This option is the safest one. . . . When you arrive in Adana call the brothers. . . . After arriving in Adana in the evening you can stay in a hotel when brothers say so. The next day take the bus to Antakya. When arriving in Adana in the afternoon or during the day then you take the bus to Antakya (before you leave first call the brothers again). After arriving in Antakya call the brothers for further instructions.*[72]

An American Jew that had converted to Islam and adopted jihadi approach even marked Jewish facilities and community leaders as preferred targets of attacks and provided tactical information about their locations and private home addresses.[73]

Conclusion

Al-Qaeda, its affiliated allies, and inspired elements base their operational and logistical networks in the West solely on homegrown cells. As discussed, all but one of the attacks, plots, and attempts orchestrated by the different elements of the Global Jihad Movement since 9/11 in the West were perpetrated by homegrown cells.[74] As a consequence of a long and thorough radicalization process, homegrown cells and individuals operated on Western soil on behalf of all the different elements of the Global Jihad Movement. The common denominator of these activities has always been that the operators were born or resided and were educated for a significant part of their lives in a Western country such as the United States, Canada, Western European countries, and Australia. While the organizational affiliation behind the attack or plot varies, the operational executers are always homegrown cell members or homegrown individuals. Homegrown cells are regarded by jihadi elements as a key operational asset and as valuable ready-made individuals who speak Western languages, in most cases hold genuine documentation, and most importantly, are familiar with Western mentality and lifestyles. Even Osama bin Laden emphasized this asset in the "Abbotabad papers" when he directed AQAP leader Abu Bassir al-Yamani to "[c]oncentrate on the Yemeni emigrants who come back to visit Yemen and have American visas or citizenship and would be able to conduct operations inside America."[75]

As for the future performance of local initiators in the West, be it small cells or lone wolves, we expect occasional, random, and sporadic ad hoc violence and terrorist acts that are based on the individual initiative and capabilities of the perpetrators. The majority of this kind of violent activity will contain popular characteristics such as arson, use of Molotov cocktails, vandalism, and in extreme cases, stabbing and assassination. In rare cases, these kinds of attacks may be lethal with a high number of casualties.

In the previous chapters and throughout the book we have portrayed the Global Jihad threat. We emphasized the ideological foundations and occasional diversions of the ideology and its implementation into operational activity. We have mapped all the different elements operationally involved in conducting military and terrorist operations against the West and laid down their organizational layout, hierarchy infrastructure, and operational capabilities. We have focused large amounts of our discussions on the internal relations among and between the different players composing the "Global Jihad" camp, as central al-Qaeda—bin Laden's original force, crystallized in the hills and trenches of the Afghan war against the Soviets during the 1980s—has been functioning as a vanguard, leading a huge camp of followers and as a locomotive that harnesses local affiliated organizations, inspired groups and lone wolves, as well as offshoots from jihadi arenas into the tracks of a complete and global war against the U.S.-led western world.

On 1 June 2011, the U.S. Navy elite SEAL unit stormed Osama bin Laden's safe house in Abbotabad, Pakistan. Based on concrete and reliable intelligence the unit's warriors were able to locate bin Laden, identify him, and kill him. Numerous documents, papers, and computer files were seized during the operation. About a year later, U.S. authorities published some of these documents which illustrate and reflect the hard and challenging task of leading this huge and diverse camp of the "Global Jihad" Movement in the preferred direction. More than that, the "Abbotabad papers" serve as a mirror to the mostly challenging junction point the Global Jihad camp is experiencing today, some three years after the elimination of its ultimate leader, Osama bin Laden. As the U.S.-led manhunt of al-Qaeda central seniors continues[76] successfully, and with the coming effects of the "Arab Spring" and the changes in the Middle East authoritarian (and mostly secular) regimes in the entire region, it seems that the challenge—overall its different dimension—to the Global Jihad Movement is at its peak.

Ideology strategy and politics—bin Laden's legacy and even sort of his will was clear. Throughout the "Abbotabad papers" bin Laden directed his ideology and its derivative targeting policy against the West (external and Global Jihad) —first and foremost the United States. Probably based on religious directions he received from distinguish Saudi clerics,[77] bin Laden ordered his followers in the years before his death to simply refrain from any operational activity that is not targeting Western targets, first among them Americans. In a letter to AQAP leader Abu Bassir al-Yamani, bin Laden directed: *"Therefore, any arrow and mine we have should be directed against Americans, disregarding all other enemies, including NATO, and concentrating on Americans only."*[78] Bin Laden took even further steps and limited operational activities against the United States and its Western allies to the international arena and Western soil and allowed operational activity in "Muslim Land" only in cases of "self defence."[79]

The diversion of all operational capabilities and efforts to Western soil and against Western targets (U.S.) is the basic ideological legacy bin Laden has left behind.

On the other hand and in accordance with al-Qaeda's protocol, bin Laden's successor as the new leader of al-aeda is his former deputy Ayman al-Zawahiri. As was extensively discussed in chapter 2, Zawahiri is the ultimate candidate and the most zealous supporter of the internal jihad ideology—meaning that all operational efforts and capabilities should be directed in the internal arena against the current regimes and in order to eventually gain authority in different Muslim countries—first and foremost Egypt, Syria, and Iraq—and to implement Shari'a as the state's law. This dissonance between bin Laden's external jihad legacy and Zawahiri's internal jihad basics is further deepening as it comes when winds of change blow all over the Middle East and political vacuums have to be fulfilled in countries like Egypt, Libya ,Tunisia , Syria, and potentially in Yemen, Bahrain, and even Jordan, Lebanon, and Saudi Arabia. It should be clear that al-Qaeda was a nonfactor in the outburst of the "Arab Spring." So did all the other elements of the Global Jihad Movement possess the Salafiya Jihadiya approach. Popular demonstrations that eventually led to the downfall of three authoritarian regimes so far (Tunisia, Libya, and Egypt), and a most bloodied civil war in Syria, erupted throughout the Middle East over socio-economical issues and were led by young, educated, and mostly secular and spontaneous activists. Even though jihadi leaders—first among them Zawahiri—have been trying to take the credit for the events, it is totally clear that the original demonstrations were far remote from jihadis. The slogans under which the demonstrations were held were composed mostly of Western and non-Islamic slogans such as equality before law, justice, freedom, women's status, and women's liberty and equality. Yet, the success of the Arab Spring in toppling the above-mentioned regimes created a political vacuum which produce an atmosphere that is much more convenient for organized political players ,that already possesses of structured leadership and traditional organized bases of supports, such as the Muslim Brotherhood. The main question for the near future with regard to al-Qaeda and the other Global Jihad elements is could al-Qaeda and Global Jihad camp under Zawahiri leadership refrain from interfering internally in the changing world of the Muslim countries first and foremost Egypt? And if not what level of legitimacy could "internal jihad policy" gain as it absolutely contradicts the legacy of the all-out legendary leader Osama bin Laden?

Early indications suggest that Zawahiri is trying his best to carefully maneuver between these approaches. In his recent 2012 statements while publically supporting internal operation,[80]

Zawahiri admiringly eulogizes bin Laden and his legacy and heritage.

As a test case that reflects the entire picture in the region, these questions are mostly effective in the pro-revolution Egypt. Since the general elections held in May 2012, the country has been under the rule of the Muslim Brotherhood that had to be pragmatic and adopt "real politics" in their day-to-day activity in order to maintain day-to-day life in Egypt, which is totally dependent on external support from the West, and in order to increase their base of support within the divided Egyptian population toward the next round of elections in a way that would maintain their leading position.[81] On the other hand, the "real politics" approach of the Muslim Brotherhood is completely rejected by the jihadists that call for a full and instant implementation of the Islamic Shari'a as the new state law and the revoking of the 1979 peace treaty with Israel.

We believe that this kind of ideological duality between internal and Global Jihad is going to be the main characteristic of the al-Qaeda-led Global Jihad Movement in the coming future. As regarding internal jihad the direction is still vague, we strongly believe that the Global Jihad Movement led and harnessed by al-Qaeda will continue and even intensify its operational efforts against Western targets first and foremost the United States, harnessing the hate and antagonism to the United States that has been spread all over the Muslim world in the last two decades. The violent events and massive demonstrations that followed the release of the "innocence of Muslims"[82] are indicators for this volatile atmosphere against the United States all over the Muslim world, that can be sparked in a matter of hours.

Operationally speaking—we strongly believe that al-Qaeda and its affiliated allies and inspired elements will continue to base their operational and logistical networks in the West solely on homegrown cells. As was extensively discussed in chapter 5, the attacks, plots, and attempts in the West orchestrated by the different elements of the Global Jihad Movement since 9/11 were by homegrown cells and individuals.[83] Following a thorough and long radicalization process, homegrown cells and individuals operated in Western soil on behalf of all the different elements of the Global Jihad Movement as the common denominator of these activities has always been the fact that the operators were either born, resided, educated, or lived at least a significant part of their life in Western countries such as the United States, Canada, Western Europe, and Australia. The London 2005 bombers on behalf of al-Qaeda; Nigerian Abd al-Faruq al-Mutaleb, who tried to blow up a commercial flight in U.S. skies on Christmas Day 2009 on behalf of AQAP; Faisal Shahzad, who assembled a VBIED and parked it in Manhattan's Times Square on April 2010 on behalf of TTP: or Mohamed Boyari, who stabbed Dutch publicist Theo van Gogh to death and had operated alone—are all homegrown cells or individuals.

The homegrown cells are considered by the jihadi elements as operational assets and regarded by the Global Jihad Movement as ready to make individuals who speak Western languages and in most cases possess genuine documentation and most importantly, are familiar with Western mentality and lifestyle. Even Osama bin Laden emphasized in the "Abbotabad papers" this asset when he directed AQAP Leader Abu Bassir al-Yamani to "concentrate on the Yemeni emigrants who come back to visit Yemen and have American visas or citizenship and would be able to conduct operations inside America."[84]

As for a specific operational threat, we strongly believe that despite the setbacks al-Qaeda has been experiencing, caused by the personal manhunt of the United States, it still possesses significant operational capabilities. It is clear that al-Qaeda would invest large efforts in conducting big and spectacular attacks in the United States to revenge bin Laden's death. We cannot rule out the possibility that al-Qaeda would try to use non-conventional or even cyber warfare in executing this attack. One should not ignore in this regard the disturbing report that has been admitted by two mostly senior al-Qaeda military operators during their interrogation in 2004–2005. Both Abu Faraj al-Libi—the former head of the al-Qaeda Military Committee (equivalent to the minister of defense) that was apprehended in 2005—and Sharif al-Masri—a former regional command leader in al-Qaeda's military that was arrested in 2004—claimed that al-Qaeda is possibly possessing a nuclear bomb that was located (2004) in Europe and that al-Qaeda was conducting efforts to transfer the nuclear device into U.S. soil and keep it there. Sharif al-Masri believes in this regard that if bin Laden were to be captured or killed, the bomb would be detonated in the United States in revenge.[85] The current status of this nuclear plot is not clear.

With regard to the second element of the Global Jihad camp—the local affiliated organizations—we identify al-Qaeda in the Arabian Peninsula (AQAP) as the more potentially lethal terrorist threat to Western countries. We assess that the aviation industry—both passengers and cargo jets—will continue to be the first priority target for the Hejazi group using innovative tools and tactics to overcome different security measures. We assess that another threat, even if in a lesser extent to the Western world, derived from the terrorist activities of al-Qaeda in the Islamic Maghreb (AQIM), Somali Shabaab al-Mujahidin (SAM), and Islamic Jihad Union (IJU) especially in Western large metropolises. Lashkar-e-Toyba (LeT) is probably the most professional terrorist entity among the al-Qaeda-affiliated local organizations within the jihadi camp and is capable of executing large scale operations, Mumbai 2008–style, at any given moment. We assess that any external operation (outside the Kashmir arena) will target Western targets as well as American and Jewish/Israeli facilities.

Jihadi offshoots, especially veterans of the Syrian civil war, and also from Iraq (AQI) and Pakistan (TTP) have a very high potential threat for future lethal attacks on Western soil.

Occasionally we expect random and sporadic ad-hoc terrorist acts in Western countries, conducted by inspired homegrown cells and individuals that are based on the self-initiative and capabilities of the perpetrators. The vast majority of this kind of violent activity will contain popular characteristics such as arson, throwing of Molotov cocktails, vandalism, and in extreme cases, stabbing and assassinations. Yet in rare cases these kinds of attacks can also turn into mostly lethal ones with dozen of casualties.

As for the operational counter of jihadi terror activity, we support the continuation of the determined manhunt of al-Qaeda senior leaders all over the world and especially in Waziristan led by the U.S. forces. No doubt that this activity presents al-Qaeda with the biggest challenge for the continuation of its operational activity and even its physical existence as long as the United States gets closer to the "bottom of the barrel."

In addition we strongly recommend the intensification of the global operational cooperation in countering jihadi activity. As long as the jihad is global so should be the counter jihad. We strongly support the reduction of intelligence-based limitations thus providing maximum sharing of information between states. We believe that only a vast share of information between states will provide a clearer and more complete intelligence picture.

The most relevant and important suggestion for countering jihadi activity refers to countering the homegrown cells and interrupting the radicalization process. As was already mentioned, all the terrorist attacks, plots, and attempts that have been conducted by the different jihadi elements on Western soil since 9/11/2001 were physically executed by homegrown cells and individuals that have gone through the radicalization process. The first and initial stage of interrupting the radicalization process is to be able to spot and identify individuals involved in it, in as early stages as possible. Only after spotting and identifying these individuals will we have the ability to use different sets of tools to interfere and interrupt the radicalization process.

As was extensively discussed in this chapter, all the different stages of the radicalization process are full with early indicators and suspicious signs. We strongly recommend Western countries to learn these indicators and teach the local-level law enforcement personnel (mainly local and communal police) with these indicators, thus equipping them with the basic tools of identifying an individual involved in the radicalization process.

Only after spotting we may move on to countering. As countering involves operating within local and in most cases peaceful Islamic communities we believe that countering activity should initially attempt to encompass, contain, and redirect instead of just dismantle. For example, in some cases local police were able to spot an individual that was in the second phase of radicalization—the search for the self-identity. Authorities may simply arrest him and send him to jail. Yet we recommend, initially, to involve his family members or send him a moderate Imam to teach him the moderate path and interpretation of Islamic belief. Authorities will want, we argue, to involve as many members as possible, from within the local Islamic community in this countering process. The Singapore experience for example took further steps in this regard as officers placed within the Muslim communities were themselves Muslims. This move by the Singaporean authorities turned out to be mostly effective and productive.

At the same time a determined and unforgivable war should be declared against the different "incubators" which promotes jihadi extremism. Activities of radical imams operating in the West, which support jihad and violence, should be restricted, and extreme clerics should be either expelled or arrested. Extreme mosques that promote jihad or provide a stage for radical clerics or radical activity should be closed. Western authorities should intensify supervision of other facilities that adhere to jihad. Jihadi websites should be revoked and access should be denied. Again, we suggest that this activity should be conducted with significant involvement of local members of the different Islamic communities, as at the bottom line the struggle should be limited only against Islamic extremism and extremist interpretation of the Islamic holy book, the Quran, and not against Islam or peoples of Islamic origin in general. According to all studies and researches only a very small percentage of the members of the local Islamic communities living in the West share these extreme approaches.

Thus, states should be very strict and selective in focusing their CT activity against the extremists alone, otherwise it will gain no legitimacy from the local communities and will soon turn to be counterproductive, only accelerating the volume of extremism and radicalization among Islamic communities.

Despite a Global War on Terrorism (GWOT), Global Jihad Movement poses a major challenge for the security of the world. Jihadis are closer than ever to achieve a territorial sequence to establish a new enclave of jihadi land in the Middle East, stretching from Iraq into Syria. Stability in the original jihad arena of Afghanistan and the marginal territories of its Pakistani neighbors faces great challenges following the U.S. withdrawal from the area. Africa is becoming a huge hub for jihadi activity. New regions in Nigeria, Mali, and elsewhere in the Sahel have emerged in addition to the traditional areas of the Maghreb and the African Horn.

The actual conducting of jihadi terror is changing, yet never diminishing or even reducing. From a centralized characteristic of a uniorganization style (al-Qaeda) that conducted the vast majority of the operational jihadi activity in the international arena, we now face new characteristics of a multiorganizational style as many elements—affiliated organizations and inspired individuals—are currently carrying the torch of jihad by conducting terrorist activities with international characteristics.

At the home front—the campaign against Islamic radicalization and extremism seems to be a great failure. Several antiradicalization programs have been deployed in different Western countries, yet it seems to have only limited impact as the numbers of Western jihadi volunteers that have been traveling to Syria illustrates. Has the Global War on Terrorism campaign returned to square one? Yet it is clear that it is still far away from achieving its strategic objectives in reducing the level of threat derived from the terrorist activity of the Global Jihad Movement.

Notes

1. Yoram Oreg Aviv Schweitzer, "Al Qaeda Odyssey to Global Jihad," INSS Memorandum 132, http://www.inss.org.il/uploadImages/systemFiles/memo134%20(4)_rev10April2014.pdf.

2. Schweitzer, Oreg p. 30.

3. Mitchell D. Silber and Arvin Bhatt, "Radicalization in the West: The Homegrown Threat," New York: New York City Police Department, 2007, http://www.nyc.gov/html/nypd/downloads/pdf/public_information/NYPD_Report-Radicalization_in_the_West.pdf.

4. "Spain Train Bombing—Fast Facts. CNN, 4 November 2013 at http://edition.cnn.com/2013/11/04/world/europe/spain-train-bombings-fast-facts/. Accessed on 14 June 2014.

5. "Theo Van Gogh—Murdered by terrorist in Amsterdam—Filmmaker and Journalist Shot and Stabbed by Militant Islamist," Militant

Islam Monitor, 2 November 2004, http://www.militantislammonitor. org/article/id/309, accessed 15 June 2012.

6. Trevor Stanley, "Australian Anti-Terror Raids: A Serious Plot thwarted," *Terrorism Monitor,* volume 3, Issue 23, 16 December 2005 at http://www.jamestown.org/single/?no_cache=1&tx_ttnews%5Btt_news%5D=620#.U5_5wZR_v9U. Accessed 17 June 2014.

7. Isabel Teotonio, "The Toronto 18," *The Star,* at http://www3. thestar.com/static/toronto18/. Accessed on 17 June 2014.

8. "7/7 London Bombing," *History of London* at http://www.his tory.co.uk/study-topics/history-of-london/77-london-bombings . Accessed 17 June 2014.

9. "Times Square Suspect had Explosive Trainings Document Say," *CNN,* 5 May 2010 at http://edition.cnn.com/2010/CRIME/05/04/new.york.car.bomb/index.html. Accessed 17 June 2014.

10. Silber and Bhatt, p. 21.

11. "Journey of Belgian Suicide Bomber," *BBC,* 2 December 2005 at http://news.bbc.co.uk/2/hi/europe/4491334.stm. Accessed on 14 June 2014.

12. Silber and Bhatt, p. 21.

13. Ibid, pp. 24–25.

14. Andrea Elliott, Sabrina Tavernise and Anne Barnard, "For Times Sq. Suspect, Long Roots of Discontent," *The New York Times,* 15 May 2010, p. 1, http://www.nytimes.com/2010/05/16/nyregion/16suspect. html, accessed 4 June 2012.

15. Ibid.

16. Ibid.

17. Silber and Bhatt, p. 29.

18. "Profile: Jamal Ahmidan," *History Commons,* http://www.histo rycommons.org/entity.jsp?entity=jamal_ahmidan_1, accessed 4 June 2012.

19. "Jamal Zougam," *Global Jihad,* 14 March 2007, http://www.glo baljihad.net/view_page.asp?id=82, accessed 4 June 2012.

20. Silber and Bhatt, p. 26.

21. "Melbourne Cell Members," *Global Jihad,* 14 December 2007, http://www.globaljihad.net/view_page.asp?id=620, accessed 4 June 2012.

22. Silber and Bhatt, p. 27.

23. Ibid, p. 26.

24. Ibid.

25. Ibid.

26. Ibid.

27. Peter L. Bergen, *The Osama bin Laden I Know: An Oral History of al Qaeda's Leader,* New York: Free Press, 2006, p. 272.

28. Silber and Bhatt, p. 29.

29. "Muriel Degauque," *Global Jihad,* 29 February 2008, http://www.globaljihad.net/view_page.asp?id=751, accessed 4 June 2012.

30. Silber and Bhatt, p. 26.

31. "Willie Virgile Brigitte," *Global Jihad,* 18 November 2007, http://globaljihad.net/view_page.asp?id=557, accessed 4 June 2012.

32. "Who is Richard Reid?" *BBC News,* 28 December 2001, http://news.bbc.co.uk/2/hi/uk_news/1731568.stm, accessed 4 June 2012.

33. Silber and Bhatt, p. 25.

34. Ibid, p. 29.

35. American Foreign Policy Council, "Australia," *World Almanac of Islamism,* 14 July 2011, http://almanac.afpc.org/Australia, accessed 4 June 2012.

36. "David Hicks," *Global Jihad,* 16 November 2007, http://www.globaljihad.net/view_page.asp?id=550, accessed 4 June 2012.

37. Silber and Bhatt, p. 30.

38. Ibid.

39. Ibid.

40. Ibid.

41. Ibid.

42. Ibid, pp. 30–31.

43. Zachariah Amara, "The Tree!" 2001, http://forums.jolt.co.uk/archive/index.php/t-89886.html, cited in Silber and Bhatt, p. 35.

44. Trevor Stanley.

45. Silber and Bhatt, pp. 33–34.

46. Elliott, Tavernise, and Barnard, p. 1.

47. Shahzad's close relative, quoted in Elliott, Tavernise, and Barnard, p. 3.

48. Elliott, "Militant's Path From Pakistan to Times Square," *The New York Times,* 22 June 2010, http://www.nytimes.com/2010/06/23/world/23terror.html?pagewanted=all, accessed 4 June 2012.

49. Shahzad's close relative, quoted in Elliott, Tavernise, and Barnard, p. 3; Elliott, "Militant's Path."

50. Shahzad's classmate, in Elliott, Tavernise, and Barnard, p. 4.

51. Elliott, "Militant's Path."

52. Anonymous administration official, quoted in Elliott, "Militant's Path."

53. Elliott, Tavernise, and Barnard, p. 5.

54. Silber and Bhatt, pp. 36–38.

55. Ibid.

56. Originating also from Jamaica, Abu Faisal is currently serving a long-term prison sentence for radical activities.

57. Silber and Bhatt p. 36–39.

58. Elliott, Tavernise, and Barnard, p. 4.

59. Ibid.

60. Ibid. Taki al-Din Ibn Taymiyyah is a fourteenth-century Islamic Hanbali scholar, considered hard-line among Islamic scholars. Maududy was a chief architect of the Islamic revival and founder of Pakistan's largest Islamic political party, Jamaat-e-Islami.

61. Elliott, Tavernise, and Barnard, p. 4.

62. Elliott, Tavernise, and Barnard, p. 2.

63. Silber and Bhatt, pp. 43–46.

64. "Yemen Arrested 30 Militants," *Global Jihad*, 8 June 2010, http://globaljihad.net/view_news.asp?id=1496, accessed 4 June 2012.

65. Silber and Bhatt, pp. 46–53.

66. *United States of America vs. Faisal Shahzad* (S.D.N.Y. 29 September 2010), (10 Cr. 541 [MGC]), p. 9, http://www.nefafoundation.org/newsite/file/US_v_FaisalShahzad_sentmemo.pdf.

67. Ibid.

68. Ibid, p. 11.

69. Ibid.

70. Ibid, p. 12.

71. Ibid.

72. Ronald Sandee, "Dutch Fighters in Syria," *Kronos Advisory*, 23 October 2013 at http://www.kronosadvisory.com/Kronos_DUTCH.FIGHTERS.IN.SYRIA.pdf. Accessed on 17 June 2014.

73. "Jewish Convert to Islam Incarcerated for threatening Jewish Groups," *Ha'aretz*, 26 April 2014 at http://www.haaretz.com/jewish-world/jewish-world-news/1.587456. Accessed 17 June 2014,

74. The one exception is the 9/11 attacks as fifteen of the nineteen attackers were citizens and residents of Saudi Arabia who were used by al-Qaeda to infiltrate the United States. Yet, the profiles of the four pilots of the attack highlight the homegrown cell characteristic of the attack.

75. Letter addressed to "Abu Basir" (Nassir al-Wuhayshi, AQAP leader), Harmony Document SOCOM-2012-0000016, p. 4, http://www.ctc.usma.edu/wp-content/uploads/2012/05/SOCOM-2012-0000016-Trans.pdf.

76. Since the elimination of bin Laden three more leaders, mostly seniors, were killed. Atiya Abd al-Rahman the sort of al-Qaeda chief of

executives that actually ran the day-to-day activity of al-Qaeda and its close affiliates was eliminated in August 2011; al-Qaeda leader of the Religious Committee, Abu Yahiya Al Libi, was killed in June 2012. Al-Qaeda chief of operations in the Horn of Africa that led the operations against American and Israeli targets in the region was killed by Somali forces in June 2011.

77. SOCOM-2012-0000018-HT at http://www.ctc.usma.edu/wp-content/uploads/2012/05/SOCOM-2012-0000018-Trans.pdf .

78. SOCOM-2012-0000016 at http://www.ctc.usma.edu/wp-content/uploads/2012/05/SOCOM-2012-0000016-Trans.pdf, p. 3.

79. Ibid, pp 5–6.

80. For example, see http://azelin.files.wordpress.com/2012/05/dr-ayman-al-e1ba93awc481hirc4ab-22yemen-between-the-departing-agent-and-the-deputy-agent22-en.pdf and http://www.ynet.co.il/articles/0,7340,L-4237821,00.html.

81. The results of the presidential elections were very close and only 800,000 voices (out of 50,000,000 potential voters) separated the MB candidate Mohamed Morsi and Ahmad Shafiq from the old "Mubarak administration," especially taking into account the fact that about 1,000,000 "Blanco notes" were counted as well, and that the voting rate was only about 50 percent. See http://www.youtube.com/watch?v=Fea0vfhkwqE.

82. A low-budget, inappropriate, and foolish Internet film that portrayed Prophet Muhammad in an inappropriate manner was condemned by Western leaders.

83. The one exception is of course the 9/11 attack as fifteen attackers, citizens, and residents of Saudi Arabia were infiltrated by al-Qaeda inside the United States. Yet, non-homegrown cell characteristic of the 9/11 muscle hijackers highlight the homegrown cell characteristic of the four pilots of the attack.

84. SOCOM-2012-0000016-HT at http://www.ctc.usma.edu/wp-content/uploads/2012/05/SOCOM-2012-0000016-Trans.pdf, p. 3.

85. JTF-GTMO Detainee Assessment Muhammad Masud al-Jadid al-Uzaybi Abu Faraj al-Libi, 10 September 2008.

Index

About the Authors

Dr. Rohan Gunaratna is professor of security studies and head of the International Centre for Political Violence and Terrorism Research at Nanyang Technological University in Singapore. He is also a member of the Steering Committee of George Washington University's Homeland Security Policy Institute and serves on the Advisory Board of the International Centre for Counter-Terrorism, The Hague. He is the author and editor of fifteen books including *Inside Al Qaeda: Global Network of Terror*. Admiral William McRaven appointed him to the International Senior Advisory Panel of the U.S. Special Operations Command in 2013. For advancing international security cooperation, he received the Major General Ralph H. Van Deman Award in 2014.

Aviv Oreg, a veteran of the Israeli intelligence community, headed the al-Qaeda and Global Jihad desk in the Analysis and Research Division of the IDF Intelligence Branch. Following his discharge from the military, he founded CeifiT (Civil Effort in Fighting International Terrorism), which advises international—governmental, institutional and private—entities on issues relating to confronting Global Jihad and al-Qaeda threat. Oreg is a member of the Advisory Council of the terrorism and insurgency project of Imperial College Press in London and serves as a guest lecturer in academic and security institutions around the world. Oreg has published several publications in recent years, among them the memorandum "Al Qaeda Odyssey to Global Jihad" (coauthored with Yoram Schweitzer) that has been published by the Israeli Institution for National Security Studies (INSS) in January 2014.

CPSIA information can be obtained at www.ICGtesting.com
Printed in the USA
BVOW02*1857250615

405293BV00002B/2/P